The Promise
of
American History

Progress
and
Prospects

Stanley I. Kutler and Stanley N. Katz, Editors

The Johns Hopkins University Press
Baltimore, Maryland 21218

VOLUME 10 • NUMBER 4

REVIEWS IN AMERICAN HISTORY

DECEMBER
1982

Editor: *Stanley I. Kutler*, University of Wisconsin
Associate Editor: *Stanley N. Katz*, Princeton University
Assistant Editor: *Judith Kirkwood*

The Johns Hopkins University Press
Baltimore, Maryland 21218

Volume 10 • Number 4 • December 1982

Library of Congress Catalog Number 72-13938
ISSN: 0048-7511
ISBN: 0-8018-3031-1 (paperback)
ISBN: 0-8018-3032-X (hardcover)

Grateful acknowledgment is made for assistance from the
Department of History of the University of Wisconsin-Madison.

Please direct all subscription inquiries and business communications to the publisher:

Journals Department
THE JOHNS HOPKINS UNIVERSITY PRESS
Whitehead Hall, 34th & Charles Sts.
Baltimore, Maryland 21218

Frequency of publication: quarterly—March, June, September, December.
Subscription price: Individuals—$16 per year
                Institutions—$35 per year
                Students—$14 per year
Address all *editorial* correspondence to:

Stanley I. Kutler, Editor
REVIEWS IN AMERICAN HISTORY
Department of History, University of Wisconsin
435 North Park Street, Madison, Wisconsin 53706

Second-class postage paid at Baltimore, Maryland and at additional mailing offices.

Printed at Everybodys Press, Hanover, Pa., U.S.A.

Postmaster please send address changes to: The Johns Hopkins University Press, Journals Division, Baltimore, Maryland 21218.

VOLUME 10 • NUMBER 4 • DECEMBER 1982

REVIEWS IN AMERICAN HISTORY

The Promise of American History

Progress and Prospects

CONTENTS

PREFACE   vii

MICHAEL KAMMEN / Vanitas and the Historian's Vocation   1

DANIEL WALKER HOWE / European Sources of Political Ideas in
Jeffersonian America   28

SEAN WILENTZ / On Class and Politics in Jacksonian America   45

PETER KOLCHIN / Comparing American History   64

ERIC FONER / Reconstruction Revisited   82

HOWARD P. CHUDACOFF / Success and Security: The Meaning of
Social Mobility in America   101

DANIEL T. RODGERS / In Search of Progressivism   113

JON C. TEAFORD / Finis for Tweed and Steffens:
Rewriting the History of Urban Rule   133

NUMAN V. BARTLEY / In Search of the New South:
Southern Politics after Reconstruction   150

GAVIN WRIGHT / The Strange Career of the New Southern
Economic History   164

MARY P. RYAN / The Explosion of Family History   181

ESTELLE B. FREEDMAN / Sexuality in Nineteenth-Century America:
Behavior, Ideology, and Politics   196

ELAINE TYLER MAY / Expanding the Past: Recent Scholarship on
Women in Politics and Work   216

REGINALD HORSMAN / Well-Trodden Paths and Fresh Byways:
Recent Writing on Native American History   234

RONALD L. NUMBERS / The History of American Medicine:
A Field in Ferment   245

NATHAN REINGOLD / Clio as Physicist and Machinist   264

LAURENCE VEYSEY / The History of Education   281

JAMES WILLARD HURST / The State of Legal History   292

DAVID A. HOLLINGER / American Intellectual History:
Issues for the 1980s   306

THOMAS J. McCORMICK / Drift or Mastery? A Corporatist Synthesis for
American Diplomatic History   318

PREFACE

These essays were commissioned to celebrate the tenth anniversary of *Reviews in American History* and to summarize the astonishing quantity of new information and reinterpretation of American history produced in that decade. To some extent, the essays follow the traditional format of a historiographical piece, offering critical evaluations of recent and current writings in American history. Beyond that, our contributors have charted agendas to suggest or anticipate new paths for development.

It would be impossible to "cover" all areas, periods, and topics of American history in a volume of this size. We do not claim any logical or even chronological justification for the resulting product. In all honesty, the shape of the table of contents reflects the response to a large number of requests for essays we initiated nearly two years ago. We were gratified by the eagerness of those who offered to contribute; unfortunately, we were not able to use all the essays submitted. But we do believe that the contents reflect the vigor and diversity which characterize the current state of writing by professional historians of America.

Perhaps we should stress diversity, for it is both the hallmark and difficulty of the field of American history. The virtues of diversity are apparent. We study kinds of people who were relatively or absolutely neglected by earlier generations of Americans: women, minority groups, Indians, the poor and "inarticulate." We study activities which were previously insufficiently attended to, especially on the private side of American life: the family, ethnicity, gender, recreation, housing. Above all, we employ new techniques, especially those of the social sciences, and new languages, especially those of mathematics and the computer.

One of the risks of diversity, however, is that we have become specialized to an extraordinary and, perhaps, distressing degree. Some chronological fields, such as the colonial period, have become so dense and sophisticated as to be nearly incomprehensible to historians of the national era. Some methodological fields, such as parts of social and most of economic history, have become literally unreadable to the uninitiated. Certain other specialities have become so narrowly focused as to be precious, and possibly antiquarian. As professionals, many of us now identify ourselves with subfields, rather than with "American History." It is fair to guess that the newest edition of the Directory of American Scholars will reveal a continuing balkanization of our identification with subfields or with fields other than history —

demography, law, economics, geography, anthropology, architecture and the like.

This trend is inevitable in the short run, and it has had remarkable intellectual benefits for the study of American history. We surely understand the micro-process of change better than our predecessors. But the question is whether such efforts have been made at the expense of our interest in the larger scheme of American history. Is there no longer a role for the generalist? How do we relate specialized subfields to undergraduate education? How do we communicate with a general public which clearly retains its interest in American history? How do we influence the thinking of public policy makers? These are the problems which we must once again begin to ponder if we are to retain (or recover) our special position as interpreters of the American past to present Americans.

As always, we appreciate the willingness of colleagues to contribute to *Reviews in American History.* Throughout our years of publication we have found a remarkable professional commitment to writing for our format. It is the excellence of such efforts that has given the journal its special quality. For this particular volume, we also wish to acknowledge the efforts of the editorial board, past and present, who helped us critically evaluate the contributions. Judith Kirkwood, our assistant editor, offered her inestimable editorial skills. And, as always, Marie Hansen, of The Johns Hopkins University Press, enthusiastically supported our efforts.

Stanley I. Kutler
Stanley N. Katz

August 1982

VANITAS AND THE HISTORIAN'S VOCATION

Michael Kammen

Twenty-five years ago, when I started graduate study (with special concentration in early American history), to read the weighty works of Charles McLean Andrews was *de rigueur*. Before taking our general examinations, my fellow students and I staggered through the colossal *Colonial Period of American History* (1934–38: four volumes; 1,651 pages), *The Colonial Background of the American Revolution* (1924), and more—much more. Following my "generals," when I began to explore a dissertation topic concerning Anglo-American history on the eve of the Revolution, I became acquainted with Andrews's great *Guides* to manuscript materials for the history of the United States before 1783 (located in The British Library, The Public Record Office, and other English archives), published in three volumes (1908–14). Subsequently I read the *Festschrift* published in 1931 to honor Andrews, plus his posthumous "testament," entitled "On the Writing of Colonial History" (1944), and the fine biographical study by A. S. Eisenstadt (1956).

To a young and impressionable graduate student, lacking much confidence that he could ever complete a doctoral program, Charles McLean Andrews seemed legendary, an intellectual giant no longer living yet larger than life nonetheless—academic or otherwise. Merely to gaze at his photograph, published as the frontispiece in Eisenstadt's study, was rather daunting: a three-quarter view of Andrews's handsome face, with dark and deep-set eyes glowering imperiously upon my ignorance of the field he had charted. The picture summed up so much. Here, surely, was a self-assured historian, proud of his staggering achievements: the man himself every bit as magisterial as his work.

Imagine my intense fascination in late December 1981, when I found a letter from Andrews to Max Farrand among Farrand's papers at the Huntington Library in San Marino. The letter is dated November 4, 1915, and for several reasons I feel compelled to present a lengthy extract.

Dear Max:
    Of course I liked your letter. Who would not have liked to have something that made him feel that what he was trying to do was worth while. Expressions of interest in onesself or ones work are so rare in New Haven that I am almost tempted to have your letter framed. I get into the habit of wondering sometimes

0048-7511/82/0104-0001 $01.00
Copyright © 1982 by The Johns Hopkins University Press

PLATE 1. Pieter Claesz, "Vanitas" (1623), oil on wood. The Metropolitan Museum of Art, Rogers Fund, 1949 (49.107).

whether it is all worth the effort and the sacrifice and the drudgery. But I always come back to the one great solace that it is all to the good, and that whatever contributes to knowledge or to life is its own reward. Then I love it and that adds to my cares, lest I be doing that which is purely selfish because I am never happier than when I am at it. I am glad you liked the paper, and I am more glad that you told me you liked it.[1] I liked it myself, and felt that it opened a lot of possible interpretations that had not been in the past a part of our thought of colonial history. I sometimes in my climbing think that I am looking on a new world of colonial life, and that in the past we have been living like cave men instead of searchers for the truth and the light. I keep at it, but it [is] all so slow and there is so much to know. I wonder whether I shall live out the doing of what I want to do.

Andrews had left Bryn Mawr in 1907 to succeed his mentor, Herbert Baxter Adams, at Johns Hopkins. Three years later he accepted an appointment at Yale in order to be free from administrative responsibilities, "to throw off the character of general utility-man which I have had to assume here."[2] Yet at the age of 52, already a well-established scholar, and after five years at Yale, he nevertheless underwent a sustained crisis of confidence. He felt isolated and unappreciated. The letter that I have quoted may or may not supply some comfort to struggling Americanists today; but it does at least provide a parable for the rambling reflections that follow in this essay. Andrews's candor about his crisis of confidence is wonderfully refreshing. Haven't we all felt as he did? Haven't we all suffered self-doubt? And having achieved some goal—the arduous completion of a monograph, the presentation of a new course—haven't we wondered whether it was really worth the expenditure of time and psychic strength at the expense of some other activity? Were we adequately appreciated? Was the effort itself properly understood?

Although historians do not ordinarily address this aspect of their vocation, others have and do. The "vanitas" theme became very popular in western European art during the seventeenth century, especially in Calvinist cultures. Usually there is a skull, symbol of our mortality; and in addition an extinguished candle, a neglected book or two, an empty inkpot, a discarded quill pen whose nib is dulled, or perhaps an artist's palette on which the colors have dried and hardened (see Plate 1, "Vanitas" [1623] by the Dutch artist Pieter Claesz). Not surprisingly, this motif moved westward across the Atlantic, and we have a fine New England example from about 1690, Captain Thomas Smith's "Self-Portrait" (see Plate 2).[3] His hand rests upon a skull, which in turn is imposed upon a poem by Smith.

> Why why should I the World be minding
> therin a World of Evils Finding.
>> Then Farwell World: Farwell thy Jarres
>> thy Joies thy Toies thy Wiles thy Warrs
> Truth Sounds Retreat: I am not Sorye.
>> The Eternall Drawes to him my heart
>> By Faith (which can thy Force Subvert)
> To Crowne me (after Grace) with Glory.

It may have been easier in some respects for pious Puritans living in an age of faith to abjure good works and personal creativity as paths to immortality. For professional historians living in a more secular century, however, and especially for those inclined toward disbelief or doubt, the problem becomes more complex, sometimes even agonizing. Is there a more poignant pair of sentences in all of American historical writing during the past dozen years than these, composed by Richard Hofstadter while dying of cancer? Hofstadter refers to Jonathan Edwards's call to the presidency of the College of New Jersey (Princeton): "He accepted the invitation, but shortly after reaching Princeton he was inoculated against smallpox, took the inoculation badly, and died before he could take up his duties. At the end he was puzzled by the irrationality of it all—that God should have called him to this role and then left him no time to fill it."[4]

Hofstadter's example is unusually sad and admittedly not typical. Although he died prematurely, having sketched in merely the background of

PLATE 2. Thomas Smith, "Self Portrait" (c. 1690?), oil on canvas. Worcester
Art Museum.

a vast projected canvas, his work achieved recognition from the outset; he
was richly and justly honored throughout his career, and at the end he had
the satisfaction of knowing that his contribution and influence were enormous. What about those who had less cause for confidence? What about
those whose achievements were considerable, but who were not sanguine by
temperament?

■ Moses Coit Tyler wrote to his sister shortly before his death in 1900:
    "Much of the things I have toiled for in life now appear to me, as I
    approach the period of old age, to be mere froth and scum . . . ." [5]

■ William E. Dodd wrote to Erich Marcks, his former teacher in Leipzig, on April 27, 1915: "In the field of history-writing there is no fame any more . . . since Gibbon. To write a good book may win one the approval of a few good friends and some others, but in ten years the best book has to be rewritten." [6]

■ When J. Franklin Jameson discovered in 1927 that he would soon be put to pasture as Director of the Department of Historical Research at the Carnegie Institution, and that the whole apparatus he had labored to build would be allowed to lapse, he resigned and sent a bitter letter of explanation to friends on the Council of the American Historical Association and the editorial board of the *American Historical Review:* "Whereas I had supposed I could continue my present work as long as I was fit for it, it [is] the intention of President Merriam that I should be retired at the age of seventy (September 1929). It is evidently also his intention that no successor shall be appointed; that the present workers in the Department shall be allowed to finish their present tasks . . . but that no further work in United States history shall be undertaken." [7]

■ In 1959 Lewis Mumford wrote to Waldo Frank from Amenia, New York: "As for the difficult time you've been going through, dear Brother, I know many of the same symptoms, too: above all how important it is, no matter how self-rewarding one's work may be, to have some response from the world outside, from a public, however stupid, from editors, however grubbing. The difference between having it and not having it is like the difference between swimming in salt water or in fresh water; for in the latter one must work to keep one's head above water. And it's no consolation for either of us to remember that we have already made our mark and left a large opus: that may be true, but each day and year has its own demands and its own rewards; and there is a flavor in the last autumn fruits that is its own excuse for being and that one should be able to share with others." [8]

Clearly there is a *leitmotif* here, and such profoundly personal as well as touching observations warrant extended exegesis. One obstacle (among many) is that analysis or generalizations—whether psychobiographical or collective in nature—are exceedingly hazardous. To begin, not all historians are alike, obviously, or react in the same ways. Moreover, even those historians whom we believe we know well often turn out to be rather more complicated than anyone has hitherto imagined. Let me offer two illustrations pertaining to Frederick Jackson Turner, each one from correspondence previously unused (to the best of my knowledge) by those scholars engaged in the Turner canon and "industry."

First, let us consider the Turner who so admired social scientists and wanted historians to form intellectual alliances with them. In 1914 he wrote the following to George Lincoln Burr, the Cornell medievalist:

> I have never given so much thought to the underlying meaning and content of history as perhaps I ought. I know I haven't thought it out as you have, and if I come anywhere near what you approve of as the right conception of what history means in my own experiments, I shall be more than content, and you seem to honor me by saying that the thing to try to do is what is meant by the treatment of the *individual* element. . . . I merely have felt that history had a right to deal with large mass statistics, tendencies, etc., as well as [i.e., in addition to] the *event* and the individual psychology. I dislike to yield good territory to sociologists, political scientists, etc., on which the historian may raise good crops.[9]

Here Turner certainly does not disdain the methods of social science, but he clearly believed that history had something special to offer that the other social sciences could not. He anticipated Fernand Braudel's minimization of *l'histoire événementielle* as well as E. P. Thompson's insistence that ours is the "discipline of historical context."[10]

Second, there is the Turner who bears the double burden of environmental determinism *and* American "exceptionalism" as well. Once again, I find him not entirely guilty of the unsophisticated, chauvinistic naïvete with which he is commonly charged. Nevertheless—and this is why the matter is so pertinent to the theme of this essay—he was accused of intellectual parochialism near the end of his distinguished career by one of his oldest and dearest friends, Charles Homer Haskins. In 1925 Turner defended his views to Haskins:

> Just what you have in mind when you suggest that I look into French and German sectionalism because I would modify my "dogmatic negative" I don't know. On page 267 I point out that: "Unlike such countries as France and Germany the United States has the problem of the clash of economic interests closely associated with regional geography *on a huge scale.* Over areas equal to all France or to all Germany either the agricultural or the manufacturing types are here in decided ascendancy."
>
> I am hardly ignorant of the fact of sections in European countries, but unless I am mistaken they are not comparable in France or Germany with this large scale sectionalization of economic interests which make the American problem distinctive, areas equal or greater than a nation in Europe have preponderating economic interests of the same kind. This seems to me different from that *intra*-national sectionalization of interests in such a country as Germany; it is more like the subdivisions in a section such as New England or the South, or the North Central States.
>
> I should not bother you with this if I were not unwilling that you should think me dogmatic. Is it dogmatic to say that the United States is vastly larger in area than France? or that our sections affected by an economic interest are so large that they raise a special problem in the relation between sections and the contests of economic interest?[11]

What matters here is not whether Frederick Jackson Turner was substantively right or wrong. Rather, the significant issue involves that delicate relationship between the power to persuade and professional self-esteem. Turner and Haskins had been graduate students together at Johns Hopkins in the late 1880s and early 1890s. Subsequently they had been colleagues at the University of Wisconsin (where they even taught a seminar together), and later they were colleagues at Harvard.[12] Now, after more than thirty-five years of close contact and communication, Turner could not make Haskins comprehend and accept as valid a concept that dominated his professional work during the second half of his career. Surely that inability must have been a source of disappointment if not despair. At the age of sixty-four, Turner may be forgiven his frustration, his recognition of the fruits of vanitas in his chosen vocation.

Our understanding of mankind's quest for fame stretches as far back as our knowledge of public culture itself. Chancellor Robert R. Livingston of New York (1746–1813) called it "the culture of laurels," a phrase I cannot improve upon. Jacob Burckhardt compiled abundant evidence that such a culture flourished during the Italian Renaissance.[13] The iconography of that epoch demonstrates the point equally well, as we can see in Plate 3, the "Triumph of Fame," painted in the mid-fifteenth century by a Florentine known only as the Master of Fucecchio. Just as Burckhardt differentiated between the Renaissance sense of honor and the passion for fame, so we must acknowledge a fine distinction between vanitas and the passion for fame. (I rather suspect, by the way, that the sardonic Calvinist view of vanitas in the seventeenth century was, at least in part, a reaction against the semi-pagan, semi-Roman Catholic "culture of laurels" that had flourished during the fifteenth and sixteenth centuries.)

Be that as it may, the professionalization of historical scholarship in the United States brought with it, as a personal sort of epiphenomenon, the curiously contrapuntal relationship between a passion for fame and the acknowledgment of vanitas. Brooks Adams declared in 1915 that man's "greatest enemy is always his own vanity and self esteem," and in 1952 Felix Frankfurter reminded Mark Howe, the legal historian, of James B. Thayer's remark that "It is good for people to praise you, provided you don't inhale it."[14] Pari passu, however, we have Albert Bushnell Hart puffing to President A. Lawrence Lowell in 1922: "I hope it may be remembered for righteousness that next after Henry Adams and Henry Cabot Lodge, Channing and I have the honor of introducing on a considerable scale the study of special topics in American history."[15] One might proliferate such illustrations; but unfortunately they are all too familiar.

PLATE 3. The Master of Fucecchio, "Triumph of Fame." The birthplate of
Lorenzo de Medici (fifteenth-century Florentine). Courtesy of the New-York
Historical Society, New York City.

The memorable point, moreover, is not that historians boast of their
accomplishments; but rather that those accomplishments are, for the most
part, so swiftly forgotten by all but a handful of disciples. On the basis of my
(admittedly random) reading, it seems to me that perhaps three or four
"modern" historians may be said to have achieved widespread, enduring, and
therefore genuine fame in the United States: Edward Gibbon, Thomas Bab-
ington Macaulay, Francis Parkman, and Henry Adams. (Others may
undoubtedly be added; but even in the cases of Turner, Beard, and Becker,
for example, their reputations now seem as precarious as their influence once
was pervasive.) Historians of genius, such as William Hickling Prescott,
Henry Adams, and Charles Francis Adams, Jr., *idolized* Gibbon. The

enigmatic Henry said so in so many words in his *Education*. The more phlegmatic CFA, Jr., considered Gibbon "an orb of the first order," and his work "the most delightful of all books." Prescott cited Gibbon in his commonplace book early in 1822, once again as a cicerone in a letter of advice to his son written in 1843, and above all in 1857 when he explained to a friend how he had become a historian: "I had early conceived a strong passion for historical writing, to which perhaps the reading of Gibbon's *Autobiography* has contributed not a little. I proposed to make myself a historian in the best sense of the term, and hoped to produce something that Posterity would not willingly let die." Vanitas and the historian's vocation; but in Prescott's case, he had the rare qualities requisite to fulfill his aspiration.[16]

Macaulay served explicitly as a model for John Bach McMaster, James Ford Rhodes, Charles Francis Adams, Jr., and above all for Theodore Roosevelt and Henry Cabot Lodge. TR's feeling for Macaulay's work verged on adulation. Lodge tells us that in college "I read Macaulay and conceived for him an intense admiration; his force, his rhetoric, his sure confidence in his own judgment, his simplicity of thought, all strike a boy very vividly."[17] And finally, in 1889 TR sent Francis Parkman, then 66, a paean as remarkable for its forthrightness as for its comparisons.

> I have always had a special admiration for you as the only one—and I may very sincerely say, the greatest—of our two or three first class historians who devoted himself to American history; and made a classic work—not merely an excellent book of references like Bancroft or Hildreth.[18]

Some readers may protest that we have also had great historians in the twentieth century. I would not dispute that for a moment, but I *would* submit that all the evidence concerning them is not yet "in," and that some among the greatest have defied the injunctions of vanitas in a way that their more prudent predecessors did not. Allow me to cite a few attributes and attitudes to illustrate my point. Perry Miller, Samuel Eliot Morison, and Charles A. Beard all cultivated *personae* as "lone wolves." In the instances of Miller and Morison, their *personae* conveyed a massive arrogance that must inevitably dilute the measure of their human stature and enduring fame.[19]

At least Beard—whose influence was surely the broadest of the three, but whose work may prove to be least enduring in value—exuded a most refreshing unpretentiousness. I have seen a great many Beard letters scattered among diverse manuscript collections and am happy to concede that my admiration, indeed affection, for him increases apace. He did not correspond with one eye on Posterity. Half the time his letters are mildly irksome because undated; but he is *always* spontaneous, always the iconoclast, always free from cant. Here is a representative sample, written to August C. Krey, the medievalist, perhaps in 1944.

> What I fear most of all, AC, is becoming respectable. I love best the people who are not respectable, such as Francis of A, or Thomas à Kempis or Gene Debs or Marcus Aurelius. So if you hear that my stock is going up with the respectables, please jump on it, unload, sell it short, and call it a false alarm.[20]

Along with most of his contemporaries, however, Beard did participate in the highly questionable practice—intimately tied to the vanitas problem—of manipulative, indeed conspiratorial book reviewing. It was commonplace for authors to arrange to have their books reviewed by close friends in prominent newspapers or prestigious journals. In 1924, for example, when James M. Beck published *The Constitution of the United States: Yesterday, Today—And Tomorrow?*, he asked Charles Warren whether the *International Book Review* had requested a review. "I suggested your name for this purpose to the editor, and if you receive such an invitation I hope very much that you will review it." Beck then arranged for Warren to review his book in *The Washington Post*, and suggested to Warren that when he finished, "if you will send me a carbon copy of it, I will try to get it in some other newspaper or magazine."[21]

Yet another facet of the same phenomenon is the book review editor who prejudges a book, or simply wishes to savage another scholar, and consequently suggests to a reviewer an acceptable or desirable line of attack. Here is Samuel Eliot Morison inviting James Truslow Adams to review Charles K. Bolton's *The Real Founders of New England* for *The New England Quarterly*.

> I am sure that you will enjoy reviewing the book, which is a pretentious but a very silly one, making out that the fishermen and scattered settlers of the New England coast who didn't found anything were the "real" founders rather than the Plymouth and Massachusetts-Bay people. . . . The book deserves to be slashed thoroughly, and of course you can do it better than any of us here who have to live with Bolton and see him every few days.[22]

Bolton served as Librarian (i.e., director) of The Boston Athenaeum, and Adams obliged Morison with a hatchet job. The problem may have been, as Adams explained to Allan Nevins in 1924, that "I do not know what the professional ethics of such matters are . . . ." But I do not find that pitiful whimper persuasive: partly because the correspondence in which these requests appear is often marked "confidential," and partly because an implicit debate over the ethics of book reviewing had been underway *at least* since 1913, when J. Franklin Jameson made the following observation:

[Albert Bushnell] Hart's doctrine that no book should be severely reviewed in the *American Historical Review* if written by a man having an established historical reputation, or one of the best historical jobs, or relations of close friendship with the members of the Board of Editors, does not commend itself to me. If the *Review* had from the beginning been managed on those principles, its reviews would now be thought as worthless as, for instance, Hart's recommendations of his young men notoriously are.[23]

In 1909 Hart had declared, in his presidential address to the American Historical Association, that "critical historians are more or less cannibals: they live by destroying each others' conclusions . . . ." That has happened, on occasion, perhaps; but too often the criteria of critical reviewing have been blurry at best, mushy at the worst, and a "buddy system" continues to exist in certain quarters. I feel a certain affinity and affection for two sentences that James Parton wrote to George Bancroft back in 1867: "There is a time to forebear, and there is a time to hit out from the shoulder. As a general thing, we are too mild and forgiving. We are so afraid of being savage, that we are apt to be soft."[24]

I should like to make one last point about the quest for fame among American historians in the twentieth century, a point as simple as it is obvious: namely, that ambition may often result in a form of self-imprisonment, with psychological consequences that I cannot begin to fathom. In one sense, our chosen vocation makes us very privileged people. Bernard DeVoto observed in 1930 that "my profession requires me to read all the books that explain America to itself . . . ."[25] I empathize with that remark; more than that, I can identify with it. And attempting to fulfill it can be a highly pleasurable experience.

In yet another sense, however, our chosen vocation can become a compulsion, a form of entrapment. In 1948 Irving Brant asked Douglass Adair, "Did you notice Dumas Malone's conjecture in the Times Book section that the whole biography [of Jefferson] would run to six volumes? That would surely be a life sentence. He assumed, I suppose, that the remainder of it would be marked by the same detailed attention to political methods and events, which won't be the case."[26] Ha! Not only did Malone turn out to be prescient and Brant wrong, but obviously Brant could not foresee his own "life sentence": that he too would eventually devote six volumes and almost three decades to James Madison. The historian's vocation has its major and its minor ironies. This one strikes me as being particularly choice.

All of which brings us to a critical and unavoidable tension—sometimes creative, sometimes highly destructive—and that is the historian's vocation itself as a historical *problématique*. This tension, or issue, is profoundly important for many reasons; but I have space here to consider only two. The lesser (given the focus of this essay) concerns the confusion, hence the need for an explicit distinction, between history perceived as *what happened* in the past and History perceived as the artificial *product* of a particular vocation, calling, or craft. Even the most thoughtful Americans have tended to conflate the two. When John Adams wrote, in 1789, that "My experience has very much diminished my faith in the veracity of History," I *think* that he had the second definition in mind. When he asked Mercy Otis Warren rhetorically, in 1814, "What are we to think of history when, in less than forty years, such diversities appear in the memories of living persons, who were witnesses?" I *suspect* that he had the first definition in mind, but perhaps not exclusively.[27]

There is less ambiguity in a marvelous letter written by his great-grandson, Henry Adams, in 1908. "If you are in vein for an illustration of the law of growth from unity to multiplicity, do my favorite task! Read St. Augustine's Confessions, then read Rousseau's; then try to bring us together on one string. No Chinese puzzle is so amusing . . . history is one long muddle of eyes and fangs."[28] This wry remark seems resonant with the first definition (though I would not want to stake my reputation, such as it is, on that contention).

Why is this distinction even noteworthy in our context? Because we historians have a noble public obligation that might be described as "explaining a culture to itself" (more on that in the next section); because we take a fair amount of guff from shrewd gadflies who have at least one foot in the guild and one tongue in the cheek (quoth Henry Adams: "He knew no history; he knew only a few historians"[29]); *and* because we take even more guff, figuratively speaking, from smart men and women outside the guild who have certain expectations about what we can do, ought to do, and do do. My illustration, *toute seule,* is taken from Paul Freund's remarks at a dinner in honor of Justice Felix Frankfurter, held at the Somerset Club in Boston on June 14, 1956. Freund observed that the kinds of questions Frankfurter "puts to himself and to us cannot be answered by mere judges and lawyers alone":

> Whence come our notions of right and justice? Do they come from history? Do they come from historians—which is not the same thing, and by how much not the same thing? Do they come from ourselves distilling history through the filter of our own necessities, our own aspirations? Do they come from ourselves seeking perhaps to transcend history, to apprehend truths beyond and above history?[30]

Now then, what is the larger reason why the issue with which I began this section seems so important? Answer: A cluster of problems essentially internal to the profession—problems so hazardous that acknowledgment of them, more often than not, evokes shrill cynicism. In search of succinctness, I shall enumerate seven exemplars of the historian's vocation as historical *problématique*.

1. Historical scholarship is highly subject to trends and fads. Not so bad as some disciplines, such as literary criticism, to be sure; but bad enough. Garrett Mattingly said it all in 1959:

> In my more pessimistic moments I am sometimes inclined to imagine that the historical profession, instead of moving steadily forward through experience and self-criticism to deeper understanding and steadier, more penetrating vision, just swings aimlessly back and forth with the tides of fashion, like the ladies' garment industry. Even before the turn of the century, though history was emphatically still part politics, and international politics perhaps its most reputable branch, the deeper thinkers were in revolt against narrative, and exhorting their colleagues to break its drowsy spell. Already a growing faction of social and economic historians were telling each other that the occupants of the more famous and better paid chairs were incapable of seeing beneath the surface to the real currents of history. Before long, some of them already occupants of those coveted chairs, the vanguard were saying loudly that military and diplomatic history were idle and frivolous when they were not positively immoral, and that even political history was no better unless it exposed the molding of movements and institutions by the vast impersonal forces of social change. By the 1920's this fashion in history was everywhere triumphant, but already its champions could feel their heels being trodden on by hungry young men who despised materialism and positivism, Darwin and Dewey and Marx, and flaunted the *mystiques* of *élans vitals* and autonomously developing systems of ideas. Their turn came, and for the past fourteen years the dominant fashion has been some form of what we seem determined to call "intellectual history." . . . I have no guess as to how long the present phase may last or what will follow, but like women's fashions, fashions in history have only a limited number of ways to go. Perhaps military and diplomatic history may come back again, especially if the cold war ever thaws, and war and diplomacy cease to be such painful subjects.[31]

2. Even those historians capable of the highest methodological innovation and sophistication, somehow tend to ignore their own prescriptions when the time comes for them to put theory into practice. L. Pearce Williams provides a case in point in his essay review of two books by Thomas S. Kuhn, *The Essential Tension: Selected Studies in Scientific Tradition and Change* (1977) and *Black-body Theory and the Quantum Discontinuity, 1894–1912* (1978).

> There is some irony in the fact that *The essential tension* and the work on quantum theory have appeared in the same year. The essential tension in the work of Thomas Kuhn seems to be between his philosophical views which have created so much stir, and his actual practice as a historian. To follow his philosophy is to force historical evidence into a theoretical framework, which is about as unhistorical as one can get. On the other hand, to read Kuhn, the historian, is to see the philosophical structure vanish before one's eyes, like smoke.[32]

Similar criticisms have been leveled at Keith Thomas because of the discrepancy between his essays on anthropological history and his *Religion and the Decline of Magic* (1971), and at Quentin Skinner because of apparent discrepancies between his advocacy of new approaches to the history of ideas and the reality, however awesome, of his *The Foundations of Modern Political Thought: The Renaissance* and *The Age of Reformation* (1978), 2 volumes.

3. One hates to confess it publicly, but historians are quite capable of thinking and behaving unhistorically. In 1915, for example, John D. Bassett of Smith College wrote the following to Lyon G. Tyler of William and Mary:

> I am preparing a short account of the early Virginia historians and wish to ask if you will tell me how to get at all that has been said in behalf of Capt. John Smith . . . . There is no difficulty in finding things against him; but I have usually been on his side and I wish to find the evidence to support my intuitions.[33]

In October 1920 Worthington C. Ford read to the Massachusetts Historical Society a letter in which Charles Sumner "blackguarded his own divorced wife and the Hooper family in general." After the meeting James Ford Rhodes and Henry Cabot Lodge forced Ford to destroy the Sumner letter "in the interests of propriety."[34] In 1925 Lyon G. Tyler sent a polite inquiry to his old friend Philip A. Bruce, the most distinguished historian of Virginia, asking for evidence to support Bruce's claim that Pocahontas had died of smallpox. Bruce responded thus:

> As soon as I received a copy of my colonial history (vol. I Hist. of Virginia) from Lewis and Company, I gathered up all the notes of authorities on which the statements in that history were based; piled them up in the road back of my house; and set the whole mass off with a match. In asserting as I did that Pocahontas died of the smallpox, I am sure that I had some authority for it, but I cannot now say where this authority is to be found.[35]

Recent illustrations abound, most of them far more subtle and cerebral than mere acts of physical destruction; but the excessive length of this essay (not to mention the prohibitive cost of libel suits) prevents me . . . .

4. Historians have not been very successful in handling the problem posed by interpretations considered ideologically unpopular at any given moment. It is a great tribute to David M. Potter's subtlety as a scholar (and humanity as a person) that radicals did not revile him on account of his conservative political views. But consider the fates of Richard Hildreth in the mid-nineteenth century, or Hermann E. Von Holst in the late nineteenth century, or Charles A. Beard during the second quarter of the twentieth century. Let us recall, too, that John Adams's *Defence of the American Constitutions*

(1787–88) was used against him in fiercely partisan ways during the presidential election of 1796. According to Merrill Peterson, however, this did not bother Adams because "it caused the book to be read by more people during six months than would otherwise read it in a hundred years."[36]

5. Historians seem to be hopelessly split over the relative merits and handicaps of sociopolitical activism. Nor do I find the slightest correlation between engagement or detachment on the one hand and the quality of a historian's work on the other. Let J. H. Hexter speak for those superb historians—like Johan Huizinga, Dom David Knowles, Perry Miller, Carl Becker, and Richard Cobb—who were, or are, comparatively distanced from public affairs.

> For a small part of my day I live under a comfortable rule of bland intellectual irresponsibility vis-à-vis the Great Issues of the Contemporary World, a rule that permits me to go off half-cocked with only slight and occasional compunction. But during most of my day—that portion of it that I spend in dealing with the Great and Not-So-Great Issues of the World between 1450 and 1650—I live under an altogether different rule. The commandments of that rule are:
> 1. Do not go off half-cocked.
> 2. Get the story straight.
> 3. Keep prejudices about present-day issues out of this area.[37]

Now let Henry Glassie speak for other fine historians—like Pieter Geyl, Richard Hofstadter, Natalie Zemon Davis, Robert Jay Lifton, and Martin Duberman—who have been activists. "If you cannot enter passionately into the life of your own times, you cannot enter compassionately into the life of the past. If the past is used to escape the present, the past will escape you." It is important to note, moreover, that advocates of activism ordinarily do not differentiate between the historian's public vocation and his or her private obligations of conscience as a citizen. As Lifton has argued, "such things as ethical and political commitments are necessary rather than antithetical to scholarly work. Nowhere is this more true than in the study of psycho-history."[38]

6. The point is frequently made that historical writing in the United States has for quite some time proceeded along two separate channels: academic and popular. A few scholars, such as T. H. Von Laue, have pleaded that "history is, or ought to be, written not for the profession but for a public of educated, thoughtful, and intelligent citizens who turn to history for light amidst the baffling or frightening darknesses in their lives and times."[39] Despite such appeals, the process (or phenomenon) of professional specialization quickens, and scholars increasingly prefer the company of their "own kind" at well-focused subdisciplinary meetings. God help the well-meaning but unwitting amateur who poaches . . . because Clio doesn't seem likely to be sympathetic.[40]

Freelance historians, in their turn, have tended to be stridently anti-academic. As James Truslow Adams wrote to Allan Nevins in 1925:

> A university life is a life to a great extent apart from the main currents, particularly in a small place. Your contacts are with immature youth, with your fellow faculty members, and books. Yet in history you have to write of the active life, of all types of men. . . . One day up at Columbia, [Dixon Ryan] Fox and some others were talking . . . and the general opinion was that at present more and better historical writing was being done by men with no academic connection than by those who had such.[41]

I cannot say with assurance whether Fox and his friends may have been "putting Adams on," or whether Adams heard what he wanted to hear in the way that he wanted to hear it; but I do know that the rest of Adams's sentiments have been harshly re-echoed from his day to ours by Albert J. Beveridge, Kenneth Roberts, Walter D. Edmonds, Claude G. Bowers, James T. Flexner, Barbara Tuchman, and many others.

7. The final problem in this litany is multifaceted, and can best be introduced by paraphrasing the toughest question that Helen Vendler poses to, and about, poets: What sort of poem will you write when you are old and gray? Or, in her words: "What will this poet of plenty write when he becomes a poet of deprivation?" At the simplest level of analysis, the issue is not new; and the responses seem to be as varied as the temperaments of historians. When Gibbon finished his first three volumes, he seriously considered stopping. The fall of the Roman Empire in the West comprised a discrete unit; so for almost a year he diverted himself by reading classical texts. Then, however, he tells us that "in the luxury of freedom I began to wish for the daily task, the active pursuit, which gave a value to every book and an object to every inquiry." Gibbon then immersed himself in the age of Justinian. Three more volumes.[42]

There have not been many Gibbons, however, and the correspondence of American historians in the twentieth century reveals a plaintive refrain.

■ Max Farrand (1922): "You are quite right that it is high time I was publishing another book. . . . But with my many engagements I feel as if I should have to do as Turner threatened at one time, namely, to declare intellectual bankruptcy."[43]

■ Edward S. Corwin (1944): "Like yourself, I can't turn off as much work as once I could. . . . So I hesitate to swear on the Bible that I will do what you ask—finish off a systematic work on American constitutional development. My present inclination is toward a rather more limited assignment, a constitutional history of the Presidency."[44]

By contrast, however, we have a charming letter from Charles Beard in which he regrets that he never met Lord Acton, an *érudit* with an encyclopedic mind who published very little. "I believe that no man of my time *knew* more than Acton. He knew too much to write." Later, in the same letter, Beard added an observation that is richly self-revealing: "It is better to be wrong about something important than right about trivialities."[45] Beard himself, of course, remained prodigiously productive throughout his lifetime. Samuel Eliot Morison intensified his workload in his declining years. At the age of 76 he noted wistfully: "knowing that death will break my pen, I now work almost the year round, praying to be spared to write what is in me to write."[46] Vanitas and the historian's dogged determination.

A second aspect of this problem involves the knotty issue of intellectual generosity versus selfish careerism. I could recite an honor roll of talented historians who did not fulfill their own calling because they compulsively helped others to do so. Take the example of George Lincoln Burr. J. Franklin Jameson wrote this of Burr in 1926:

> I have always longed—all of us have always longed—that he should produce either or both of two great books, one on the history of witchcraft and one on the history of toleration, but I am pretty well convinced that he never will. He will always devote himself to doing the work of others, or work which others impose upon him. I rather resent his occupation with these matters of Henry C. Lea and President [Andrew Dickson] White, but if he were not doing them, he would be doing what the Tompkins County Historical Society or the Literary Club of McGrawville asked him to do, and if that is the case, he might as well be answering worthwhile questions for deserving historical scholars like you and me. The world does not contain a more unselfish man, but it is perhaps a pity for the world that the unselfishness and the wonderful learning have not been entrusted to two separate individuals.[47]

Stark contrasts are easily come by. In 1939, when Arthur O. Lovejoy asked Gilbert Chinard to serve as editor-in-chief of the newly founded *Journal of the History of Ideas,* Chinard replied that he "could not possibly assume the responsibility. For too long I have wasted my time reading other people's efforts. I have come to the point when I must make a choice: either give up my own work or concentrate more on it. The choice is made."[48] I do not mean to tarnish Chinard's well-deserved reputation; and perhaps his decision best served scholarship (as well as himself). But the contrast between Burr and Chinard is highly symptomatic. Everyone could supply his (or her) own surrogate examples.

A third facet of this problem involves the need—felt by some, but by no means all—for coming to terms with forebears and with followers. The former is much the easier task of the two, I believe, and has resulted in some distinguished contributions to scholarship. One thinks immediately of *The Progressive Historians* (1968) by Hofstadter, or John Hope Franklin's forthcoming biography of George Washington Williams, or the anticipated study of Arnold Toynbee by William H. McNeill. Coming to terms with successors is rather more difficult because Young Turks can be exceedingly cruel in torturing (if not actually killing) their fathers. During the 1940s and 50s, Big Bill Broonzy often discovered that younger blacks in his audience did not care for his music. "This ain't slavery no more," he was told, "so why don't you learn to play something else? . . . the way you play and sing about mules, cotton, corn, levee camps and gang songs. Them days, Big Bill, is gone for ever." [49] For intergenerational misunderstanding among historians in our own time, perhaps it will suffice to cite Jacques Barzun's *Clio and the Doctors: Psycho-History, Quanto-History & History* (1974) and the response it elicited. The problem with *epigoni* is that their work, however flawed, can make us feel very inadequate. They may do much for the vocation, but precious little for vanitas.

Now that we have peered through problems and frustrations at some length, perhaps we should direct our attention to matters of consolation and aspiration. Despite the obvious obstacles—methodological as well as philosophical—mine is not a counsel of despair. Jean Starobinski has taught us that History was gradually redefined, and came to be re-understood, during the third quarter of the eighteenth century. I suspect that the same may be true of the past twelve to fifteen years,[50] and of the decade ahead, with profound consequences for such questions as—why try? why continue? why write History at all in the face, not of our physical finitude (which after all is an old story), but in view of the ephemeral character of our labors, our audience, and the transitory nature of our profession?

Many people who heard Carl Becker deliver his presidential address, "Everyman His Own Historian," misunderstood his mood and his message. He spent the early months of 1932 trying to explain himself, as in this letter to Charles Homer Haskins.

> I gather from some things I have heard that there are people who had the impression that I was preaching the futility of historical research. Nothing could be farther from the truth, since the address is the outcome of a long process of muddled thinking, from many years back, in the effort to find a satisfactory answer to those who ask, "What is the good of history?" . . . The only condition in which I can conceive that historical research and writing would become futile is in [the] case, extremely unlikely, that the past of mankind should really be completely presented in "definitive contributions." If they were really definitive, there would seemingly be no further need of research. Some members of our guild seem to find the idea that each generation has to rewrite its history disillusioning. I confess I don't find it so at all.[51]

Nor do I, so I want to wind down by suggesting nine reasons why. What follows is less a creed, perhaps, than a gabby rationalization of what I have been doing for the past twenty-five years, and would like to be doing for the next twenty-five. If someone handed me a million dollars, with no strings attached, I would cheerfully accept; but I don't believe that it would alter my life in any significant way. I cannot conceive of myself in pursuit of any other vocation, nor can I imagine desisting from the only one I've ever had. Recall, for a moment, the fate of Diedrich Knickerbocker as described by Washington Irving:

> His history [of early New York] being published, he had no longer any business to occupy his thoughts, or any scheme to excite his hopes and anticipations. This, to a busy mind like his, was a truly deplorable situation . . . . There would have been great danger of his taking to politics, or drinking, —both which pernicious vices we daily see men driven to by mere spleen and idleness.[52]

Well then, what can historians realistically hope to do, and why should they?

1. First, humankind cannot begin to anticipate what sorts of knowledge may be found useful or interesting centuries hence. John Adams knew all about vanitas, but misperceived the value of maintaining a historical record of his own time. In 1802 he began his autobiography with these words:

> As the Lives of Phylosophers, Statesmen or Historians written by them selves have generally been suspected of Vanity, and therefore few People have been able to read them without disgust; there is no reason to expect that any Sketches I may leave of my own Times would be received by the Public with any favour, or read by individuals with much interest.[53]

To judge by the ecstatic responses of John F. Kennedy, Bernard Bailyn, and Edmund S. Morgan, Adams could not have been more wrong. Thank God for his perpetual motion pen, his historical perspective, and his vanitas.[54]

2. Moreover, we pay too little heed to a truism uttered by William A. Dunning way back in 1913; namely, that time and again a major "influence on the sequence of human affairs has been exercised, not by what really happened, but by what men erroneously believed to have happened." There is no more compelling argument for the serious study of historical myths, misperceptions, and misunderstandings.[55]

3. I am utterly persuaded by E. P. Thompson's argument that "the discipline of history is, above all, the discipline of context; each fact can be given meaning only within an ensemble of other meanings . . . ." Elsewhere he has insisted that "we cannot understand class unless we see it as a social and cultural formation, arising from processes which can only be studied as they work themselves out over a considerable historical period."[56] To fulfill these imperatives with absolute respect for the particularity of people and the specific integrity of varied social institutions and modes of thought requires the patience of a plodding historian. Rarely, very rarely, does the so-called

historical anthropologist or historical sociologist do the job as we do it. Nor should they be expected to. They have other goals in mind. But if we, whose vocation is the discipline of context, do not discover and amplify those contexts, it will never be done properly.

4. We all know that social memory is at least as fallible as individual memories, and pluralistic as well. Even more daunting, there is abundant evidence that historians' memories are just as imperfect as any other.[57] Nevertheless, historians *en bloc*—the historian's vocation acting collectively and interacting critically—can aspire to Leonard Krieger's maxim that "by its very nature, history is not the mere memory of humanity but the reformation of its memory." As Carl Becker put it in 1932, "critical history is simply the instinctive and necessary exercise of memory, but of memory tested and fortified by reliable sources."[58] There are additional complexities, and Becker goes on to discuss them; but I can live and work quite comfortably within the framework of his maxim.

5. It may well be that a chastened sense of vanitas and the historian's vocation has been at least partially responsible for a growing interest, during the past decade, in the history of failure. I have in mind diverse studies and different forms of failure. Bernard Bailyn's *The Ordeal of Thomas Hutchinson* (1974), for example, or Gerald H. Meaker's marvelous study of *The Revolutionary Left in Spain, 1914–1923* (1974), or Charles Gibson's subtle craftsmanship in his presidential address to the American Historical Association (1977).[59]

We also have books about the *sense* of failure, about shattered dreams and utopias, that have enriched immeasurably our understanding of individuals, communities, and what you might permit me to call coherent psychological moments in time. I am thinking of Pauline Maier's *The Old Revolutionaries: Political Lives in the Age of Samuel Adams* (1980), or Joseph J. Ellis, *After the Revolution: Profiles of Early American Culture* (1979), or William Dusinberre, *Henry Adams, The Myth of Failure* (1979). We can profit from an observation made by Denis Donoghue ten years ago that "we are likely to find that much American literature achieves its vitality by a conscientious labour to transform the mere state of failure into the artistic success of forms and pageants: it learns a style not from a despair but from an apparent failure." Donoghue concludes this provocative essay by asking, "Do we not feel that American literature thrives upon the conditions of failure and that it would lose its character, if not its soul, were it given the conditions of success?"[60] Wiser heads than mine will perceive some penetrating explanation; but I find it more than a minor puzzle that historical literature in the United States has, until quite recently, moved predominantly along a very different sort of channel than that of imaginative literature (novels, romances, short stories, poems, journals, etc.).

6. We do History—at least most of us ought to, and some of you actually do—to fulfill a sense of obligation to various sorts of communities. Burckhardt loved and admired the Florentine historians because "what they most desired was that their view of the course of events should have as wide and deep a practical effect as possible . . . . Like the ancients, they were citizens who wrote for citizens." [61] Burckhardt, we know, ceased at an early age to write very much so that he could devote himself fully to teaching and the responsibilities of citizenship in his beloved Basel. Such a pattern has never been common, either in the Old World or in the New. It constitutes a kind of ideal of which *some* are aware, and to which a very few, like George Lincoln Burr and William G. McLoughlin, are actively committed. [62]

7. Teaching plays a part in our vocation. Indeed for many historians it is the principal part. In the context of our vanitas theme, teaching has to be considered a mixed blessing. Haven't we all had students (even serious students) come to see us in order to discuss their inadequate performance on an exam. Often they show me their class notes, perhaps to affirm that they really were there when such-and-such a topic was presented; or to demonstrate that 'I really know it even though I couldn't quite get it all down on paper." More often than not, when I glance over their class notes I am horrified to discover the transmogrification of a point that I had made with stunning lucidity (I thought) into a garbled mess—what Eeyore might have called "a Confused Noise." We are fortunate to have Burckhardt's *Force and Freedom: Reflections on History* (1943), based upon his students' lecture notes. But I would much prefer that we had it first hand, that he had written it out himself. Heaven help me if my erstwhile students ever publish *my* classroom lectures; and I have been blessed with some very fine students! [63]

On the other hand, our students can be an immense source of pride, an extension of our very egos. And when that happens, our self-esteem is served most admirably. Henry Adams's impact as a teacher has been well documented. [64] In the papers of Edward S. Corwin, who taught American constitutional law and history at Princeton from 1911 until 1946, letters from former students testify to his enormous influence and to the satisfaction that he must have derived from following the careers of Thurman Arnold and others who became distinguished lawyers, judges, professors of law, and government officials. I cannot resist just one fine example, dated 1937.

A little more than a quarter of a century ago (what a long time a fraction of a century seems), I asked you a question at one of our weekly meetings when we were wading through Madison's Notes, item by item, the answer to which I have never forgotten. I asked you in substance this: "It must be a great bore to you to be going through this subject with me. What help can it be to your research to hear me asking stupid questions?" Your answer in substance was: "A specialist can easily get into an intellectual rut. You have a virgin mind, at work in a virgin field.

You are likely to "pop" me a question that will set my mind going. You wouldn't
be aware at the time that you had set up a chain of thought, but that can
happen." [65]

Herbert Levi Osgood of Columbia, dry-as-dust institutional historian though
he may have been, profoundly influenced Dwight Morrow. We could com-
pile a vast list, but the point is an elementary one: most teachers have no idea
how long a shadow they cast; but if they did, their euphoria might supply
enough psychic energy to warm their homes for weeks on end. True, we turn
our students off, too; but the less said about that the better. [66]

My final few points follow directly from this one, but are rather more personal in nature in the sense that they primarily concern what the pursuit of
History does for the historian rather than what it does for society, community, or individuals.

8. We do History, vanitas to the contrary notwithstanding, for pure
pleasure, for the excitement of the hunt, for satisfactions that are as palpably
sensuous as they are cerebral.

▪ Item: "I am simply one who loves the past and is diligent in
investigating it." [67]
▪ Item: "You ask if there were reasons of environment, education or
temperament which led me to write so much about the [American]
Revolution. I suppose there were. As near as I know them they were a
natural fondness from boyhood for history, a training in practising law
which compelled me to give authorities and evidence for every statement. I acquired a contempt for any one who wandered from the
record and had a contempt for myself whenever I did . . . . Then also
historical investigation, the hunt for facts and actualities is very much
like a rabbit or a quail hunt, of which I have done a good deal. Both are
full of surprises, disappointments, excitements, successes. If the history
was as invigorating as the quail hunt it would be a perfect sport." [68]
▪ Item: "In his analytic function he [the historian] is the rationalist,
perhaps even the scientist. In his empathic function he is the artist, and
it is research as art that redeems the drudgery of data-gathering.
    This form of art is as exigent as any other. It requires its practitioner
to enter into the past, to meet people who are very much alive yet different from him in ways that he can imperfectly apprehend, to view
them objectively for what they were, and then to portray them in all
their vitality. This is so large an assignment that his reach, he knows,
will exceed his grasp; and why should it not? Just as the subject matter
of research fascinates him because he will never be able to do it full
justice, so does the art of research. The requirements of that art are too

stringent for his comfort: they deny him the illusion that he has nothing more to learn, and keep him always reaching for what he cannot quite grasp. His own particular creativity is therefore at full stretch, and that is perhaps as near to pure joy as an academic can come." [69]

9. My final point is virtually banal, even though great glosses could be composed about it. We historians, as a guild, will almost always enjoy the last word. When the fancy-Dan journalists and instant-historians are done, when the jurists and novelists have kept faith with the imperatives of equity and imagination, we will second-guess them, and our predecessors, and even ourselves. The last word may indeed never be spoken; there can always be another. But with the passage of time, as history becomes History, the *latest* word will most likely be said (or written) by a historian. [70]

The rest is silence, save one sentence by William James in order to convey, perhaps, the sense of an ending: "I am finite once for all, and all the categories of my sympathy are knit up with the finite world *as such*, and with things that have a history." [71] I think he's playing my song.

1. This must refer to Andrews, "Anglo-French Commercial Rivalry, 1700–1750: The Western Phase," *American Historical Review* 20 (1915): 539–56, 761–80, the only paper he published in 1915.

2. Quoted in A. S. Eisenstadt, *Charles McLean Andrews: A Study in American Historical Writing* (New York: Columbia University Press, 1956), p. 145.

3. See Joseph Allard, "The Painted Sermon: the Self-Portrait of Thomas Smith," *Journal of American Studies* 10 (December 1976): 341–48.

4. Richard Hofstadter, *America at 1750: A Social Portrait* (New York: Alfred A. Knopf, 1971), p. 242.

5. Jessica Tyler Austen, ed., *Moses Coit Tyler, 1835–1900: Selections from His Letters and Diaries* (Garden City, N.Y.: Doubleday, Page, 1911), p. 325. See also James Ford Rhodes to John T. Morse, August 29, 1918, Morse Papers, The Massachusetts Historical Society, Boston.

6. Quoted in Robert Dallek, *Democrat and Diplomat: The Life of William E. Dodd* (New York: Oxford University Press, 1968), p. 79.

7. Jameson to Evarts B. Greene, November 9, 1927, Greene Papers, Butler Library, Columbia University. In 1980, when Marshall McLuhan retired at the age of 68, The University of Toronto dismantled his Center for Culture and Technology and refused to postpone his retirement. See *The New York Times,* June 22, 1980.

8. Mumford to Frank, August 29, 1959, Frank Papers, box 85, University of Pennsylvania Library, Philadelphia. See Paul Goldberger's excellent review of Mumford's *Sketches from Life: The Early Years* (New York: Dial Press, 1982), in *The New York Times Book Review,* May 16, 1982, pp. 13, 41.

9. Turner to Burr, September 5, 1914, from Darby, Montana, Burr Papers, box 11, Department of Manuscripts and University Archives, Cornell University Library, Ithaca, New York.

10. See E. P. Thompson, "Anthropology and the Discipline of Historical Context," *Midland History* 3 (1972): 41–55.

11. Turner to Haskins, May 6, 1925, Haskins Papers, The Seeley G. Mudd Manuscript Library, Princeton University, Princeton, New Jersey. This discussion concerns one of Turner's most famous essays, "The Significance of the Section in American History," published in *The Wisconsin Magazine of History* (March 1925), and reprinted in Turner, *The Significance of Sections in American History* (New York: Henry Holt, 1932), where the quotation appears on p. 36.

12. For details of their relationship, see Ray Allen Billington, *Frederick Jackson Turner: Historian, Scholar, Teacher* (New York: Oxford University Press, 1973), pp. 59, 66, 70–71, 95–96, 126, 180, 227, 243, 297, 310, 316, and 320.

13. See Jacob Burckhardt, *The Civilization of The Renaissance in Italy* (New York: Harper and Row, 1958), pp. 152, 404, 428.

14. Brooks Adams is quoted in Frederic Cople Jaher, "The Boston Brahmins in The Age of Industrial Capitalism," in Jaher, ed., *The Age of Industrialism in America: Essays in Social Structure and Cultural Values* (New York: The Free Press, 1968), p. 208; Frankfurter to Howe, November 4, 1952, Howe Papers, 2-10, The Harvard Law School Library, Langdell Hall, Cambridge, Mass.

15. Hart to Lowell, February 17, 1922, Hart Papers, Harvard University Archives, Pusey Library, Cambridge. For a striking example of a historian summarizing his entire lifetime's achievement, there is an extraordinary letter from Curtis P. Nettels (1898–1981) to Carl Bridenbaugh, May 6, 1980. I am indebted to Professor Bridenbaugh for sharing this letter with me.

16. Ernest Samuels, ed., *The Education of Henry Adams* (Boston: Houghton Mifflin, 1973), p. 386; Edward C. Kirkland, *Charles Francis Adams, Jr., 1835–1915: The Patrician at Bay* (Cambridge, Mass.: Harvard University Press, 1965), p. 137; C. Harvey Gardiner, ed., *The Papers of William Hickling Prescott* (Urbana: University of Illinois Press, 1964), pp. 41, 199, 379. For Gibbon's own views on vanitas and the historian's vocation, see his *Autobiography* (Boston: James R. Osgood, 1877), p. 230. See also James Ford Rhodes, "The Profession of Historian," in Rhodes, *Historical Essays* (New York: Macmillan, 1909), p. 56, as well as "Edward Gibbon," pp. 107–40.

17. See Eric F. Goldman, *John Bach McMaster: American Historian* (Philadelphia: University of Pennsylvania Press, 1943), pp. 13, 45, 48, 109, 119, 121, 124–27; Kirkland, *Adams*, pp. 201, 209; Roosevelt to James Ford Rhodes, November 29, 1904, in Elting E. Morison, ed., *The Letters of Theodore Roosevelt* vol. 4 (Cambridge, Mass.: Harvard University Press, 1951), p. 1049; Henry Cabot Lodge, *Early Memories* (New York: Charles Scribner's Sons, 1913), pp. 31, 234.

18. Roosevelt to Parkman, July 13, 1889, *Letters of Roosevelt* vol. 1, pp. 172–73. In 1923 the Canadian Historical Association created a Parkman Centennial Committee to plan a major public celebration in Montreal. See Lawrence J. Burpee to J. Franklin Jameson, June 27 and August 28, 1923, Jameson Papers, box 118, The Library of Congress, Washington, D.C.

19. See Perry Miller, "The Plight of the Lone Wolf," *The American Scholar* 25 (Autumn 1956): 445–51; Samuel Eliot Morison to Evarts B. Greene, December 16, 1929, Greene Papers, Columbia University; Bernard Bailyn, "Morison: An Appreciation," *Proceedings of The Massachusetts Historical Society* 89 (1977), esp. pp. 121–23.

20. Beard to Krey, March 31, [1944?], Krey Papers, folder #187, University Archives, University of Minnesota.

21. Beck to Warren, September 2, November 7 and 22, 1924, James M. Beck Papers, box 2, Seeley G. Mudd Manuscript Library, Princeton. See also Robert Seager, II, *Alfred Thayer Mahan: The Man and His Letters* (Annapolis: Naval Institute Press, 1977), p. 440; Philip A. Bruce to Worthington C. Ford, March 14, 1910, Ford Papers, box 7, New York Public Library (Annex), New York City; Charles A. Beard to Arthur M. Schlesinger, July 23, 1917, Schlesinger Papers, Pusey Library, Harvard University.

22. Morison to Adams, October 1, 1929, James Truslow Adams Papers, Butler Library, Columbia University. See also Morison to Adams, November 7, 1929, *ibid.*

23. Adams to Nevins, October 23, 1924, *ibid.*; Jameson to George Lincoln Burr, October 26, 1913, Burr Papers, box 11, Cornell University.

24. Albert Bushnell Hart, "Imagination in History," *American Historical Review* 15 (January 1910: 234–35; Parton to Bancroft, June 4, 1867, quoted in Milton E. Flower, *James Parton, The Father of Modern Biography* (Durham: Duke University Press, 1951), p. 201.

25. Bernard DeVoto, "The Centennial of Mormonism" (1930) in DeVoto, *Forays and Rebuttals* (Boston: Little, Brown, 1936), p. 81. In addition to Wallace Stegner's wonderful *The Uneasy Chair: A Biography of Bernard DeVoto* (Garden City, N.Y.: Doubleday, 1974), see Thomas Reed Powell's marvelous one-page sketch of DeVoto, dated November 15, 1936, Thomas Reed Powell Papers, A-2, Harvard Law School Library.

26. Brant to Adair, March 3, 1948, Brant Papers, box 16, Library of Congress.

27. Adams to Jeremy Belknap, July 24, 1789, in *Collections of the Massachusetts Historical Society*, 6th series, vol. 4 (Boston, 1891), p. 438; Adams to Mercy Otis Warren, February 2, 1814, *ibid.*, 5th series, vol. 4 (Boston, 1878), p. 505. For Herman Melville's cynical view of History, see *Billy Budd, Sailor (An Inside Narrative)* (Chicago: University of Chicago Press, 1962), pp. 130–31.

28. Adams to Worthington C. Ford, April 10, 1908, Ford Papers, New York Public Library (Annex). For memorable comments on the historian's vocation, however, see *The Education of Henry Adams*, pp. 36, 382, 395.

29. *Ibid.*, p. 293.

30. A copy of Freund's remarks may be found in the Mark Howe Papers, 2-12, Harvard Law School Library (the Freund-Howe folder). See also Felix Frankfurter's fascinating letter to Zechariah Chafee, Jr., July 9, 1954, Chafee Papers, 4-17, Harvard Law School Library. For a much more hostile view from someone entirely outside the guild, see Edward Albee, *Who's Afraid of Virginia Woolf? A Play* (New York: Atheneum, 1963), pp. 64, 68.

31. Garrett Mattingly, "Some Revisions of the Political History of the Renaissance," in *The Renaissance*, ed. Tinsley Helton (Madison: University of Wisconsin Press, 1961), p. 9.

32. L. Pearce Williams, "The Essential Thomas Kuhn," *History of Science* 18 (1980): 68–74. The quotation is from p. 74. See also K. R. Minogue, "Method in Intellectual History: Quentin Skinner's Foundations," *Philosophy* 56 (October 1981): 533–52.

33. Bassett to Tyler, January 5, 1915, Tyler Papers, group 5, box 4, Swem Library, College of William and Mary, Williamsburg, Va.

34. Robert Cruden, *James Ford Rhodes: The Man, the Historian, and His Work* (Cleveland: Western Reserve University Press, 1961), pp. 64–65.

35. Bruce to Tyler, July 15, 1925, Tyler Papers, group 5, box 4, Swem Library

36. Merrill Peterson, *Adams and Jefferson: A Revolutionary Dialogue* (Athens: University of Georgia Press, 1976), p. 63. For Beard, see his letters to Arthur M. Schlesinger, May 14 and July 23, 1917, Schlesinger Papers, Pusey Library; and Howard K. Beale, ed., *Charles A. Beard: An Appraisal* (Lexington: University of Kentucky Press, 1954), pp. 250–52. For the fascinating case of Karl Lamprecht in Germany, see Georg G. Iggers, *New Directions in European Historiography* (Middletown, Conn.: Wesleyan University Press, 1975), pp. 25, 28.

37. Hexter, "The Historian and His Day," in *Reappraisals in History: New Views on History and Society in Early Modern Europe* (New York: Harper and Row, 1963), pp. 7–8. For the fierce split within the Mississippi Valley Historical Association (1950–55) over the appropriateness of social reform activities within a professional association, see Ray Allen Billington, "From Association to Organization: The OAH in the Bad Old Days," *Journal of American History* 65 (June 1978): 75–84; and Thomas D. Clark, "Our Roots Flourished in the Valley," *ibid.*, esp. pp. 93–96.

38. Henry Glassie, "Meaningful Things and Appropriate Myths: The Artifact's Place in American Studies," *Prospects* 3 (1977): 29; Robert J. Lifton, *History and Human Survival: Essays on the Young and Old, Survivors and the Dead, Peace and War, and on Contemporary Psycho-history* (New York: Vintage Books, 1971), p. 16. Closely related to this issue is the whole question of writing "instant" or contemporary history. For an eloquent affirmation of its validity, see Arthur M. Schlesinger, Jr., "The Historian," *Proceedings of the Massachusetts Historical Society* 91 (1979): 86–97. For a strong statement in opposition, see Woodrow Wilson to Edward S. Corwin, August 30, 1918, Corwin Papers, Seeley G. Mudd Manuscript Library, Princeton University.

39. T. H. Von Laue, "Is There a Crisis in the Writing of History?" *Bucknell Review* 14 (December 1966): 1–15. See the very interesting praise for John Fiske in James M. Beck's letter to David Jayne Hill, September 3, 1924, Beck Papers, box 1, Seeley G. Mudd Manuscript Library, Princeton University.

40. For the genesis and development of this trend, see J. Franklin Jameson to Worthington C. Ford, April 20, 1910, Ford Papers, box 7, New York Public Library (Annex); Clarence W. Alvord's remarks in the *Annual Report of the American Historical Association for 1914*, vol. 1 (Washington, D.C., 1916), pp. 312–13; George Wilson Pierson to Mary Mapes, November 30, 1965, John Dos Passos Papers, 5950-ac, box 1, University of Virginia Library. Part of the prob-

lem lay in scholarly mistrust of what Becker, Corwin, and others of their generation called, always with pejorative implications, "fine writing." See Corwin's symptomatic review of Beveridge's *John Marshall*, vols. 1–2, in *The Mississippi Valley Historical Review* 4 (June 1917): 116–18.

41. Adams to Nevins, September 20, 1925, Adams Papers, Butler Library, Columbia University. See also James Ford Rhodes, "The Profession of Historian," p. 66.

42. Gibbon, *Autobiography*, p. 210.

43. Farrand to Ferris Greenslet, May 3, 1922, Greenslet Papers, Houghton Library, Harvard University.

44. Corwin to Oliver Peter Field, August 7, 1944, Corwin Papers, box 3, Princeton University. See also Philip Brown to Corwin, August 16, 1944, *ibid.*; Henry Steele Commager to Allan Nevins, December 13 [1966?], Nevins Papers, box 88, Butler Library, Columbia University.

45. Beard to August C. Krey, January 30 [1934?], Krey Papers, folder #103b, University of Minnesota. See also Gertrude Himmelfarb, *Victorian Minds* (New York: Alfred A. Knopf, 1968), pp. 168–69.

46. Quoted in Bailyn, "Morison: An Appreciation," pp. 120–21.

47. Jameson to Austin P. Evans, Aug. 10, 1926, Burr Papers, box 16, Cornell University.

48. Chinard to Lovejoy, February 19, 1939, Chinard Papers, Eisenhower Library, The Johns Hopkins University.

49. Quoted in Lawrence W. Levine, *Black Culture and Black Consciousness: Afro-American Folk Thought from Slavery to Freedom* (New York: Oxford University Press, 1977), p. 217.

50. See Jean Starobinski, "From the Decline of Erudition to the Decline of Nations: Gibbon's Response to French Thought," in *Edward Gibbon and the Decline and Fall of the Roman Empire*, eds. G. W. Bowersock et al. (Cambridge, Mass.: Harvard University Press, 1977), pp. 139–57, esp. pp. 139–41; Michael Kammen, ed., *The Past Before Us: Contemporary Historical Writing in the United States* (Ithaca, N.Y.: Cornell University Press, 1980); Bernard Bailyn, "The Challenge of Modern Historiography," *American Historical Review* 87 (February 1982): 1–24.

51. Becker to Haskins, February 19, 1932, Haskins Papers, Princeton University. I found this marvelous letter ten years after I believed that I had completed an exhaustive canvass in preparing and editing *"What Is the Good of History?" Selected Letters of Carl L. Becker, 1900–1945* (Ithaca, N.Y.: Cornell University Press, 1973). In some respects the patrician scholars who wrote two and three generations ago were intellectually less arrogant than their modern successors. On February 25, 1914, Charles Francis Adams, Jr., wrote to James Ford Rhodes that "in my opinion all history, including my own, needs to be rewritten once in ten years." Quoted in Kirkland, *Adams*, p. 208. See also James Ford Rhodes, "The Profession of Historian," p. 75.

52. Washington Irving, *Knickerbocker's History of New York* [1809], vol. 1 (New York: G. P. Putnam's Sons, 1894), pp. 18–19.

53. L. H. Butterfield, ed., *Diary and Autobiography of John Adams*, vol. 3 (Cambridge, Mass.: Harvard University Press, 1961), p. 253. See also Manton Marble to Worthington C. Ford, September 12, [1906?], Ford Papers, New York Public Library (Annex).

54. See Kennedy's review, *American Historical Review* 68 (January 1963): 478–80; Bailyn, "Butterfield's Adams: Notes for a Sketch," *William and Mary Quarterly* 19 (April 1962): 238–56; Morgan, "John Adams and the Puritan Tradition," *New England Quarterly* 34 (December 1961): 518–29.

55. Dunning, "Truth in History," *American Historical Review* 19 (January 1914): 217–29. See also Albert J. Beveridge to Edward S. Corwin, February 9, 1918: "The more I study history, the clearer it becomes to me that too little account is taken by historians of the human conditions under which men do things." Beveridge Papers, box 212, Library of Congress.

56. E. P. Thompson, "Anthropology and the Discipline of Historical Context," p. 45, and *The Making of the English Working Class* (New York: Vintage, 1963), p. 11.

57. See the wonderful speech by Neil McKendrick, "J. H. Plumb: A Valedictory Tribute," in McKendrick, ed., *Historical Perspectives: Studies in English Thought and Society in Honour of J. H. Plumb* (London: Europa, 1974), p. 8.

58. Leonard Krieger, "The Horizons of History," *American Historical Review* 63 (October 1957): 73; Becker to William E. Dodd, January 27, 1932, in Kammen, "*What Is the Good of History?*" p. 157.

59. Charles Gibson, "Conquest, Capitulation, and Indian Treaties," *American Historical Review* 83 (February 1978): 8. See also Alfred D. Chandler, Jr., "Industrial Revolutions and Institutional Arrangements," *Bulletin*, American Academy of Arts and Sciences, 33 (May 1980): 50.

60. Denis Donoghue, "The American Style of Failure," in *The Sovereign Ghost: Studies in Imagination* (Berkeley: University of California Press, 1976), pp. 104, 126.

61. Burckhardt, *The Civilization of the Renaissance in Italy*, pp. 250–51. Schlesinger quotes Theodor Mommsen's reflection upon his political entanglements: "In doing so I may have erred and made mistakes, but the worst mistake would have been to avoid my duties as a citizen, lest they interfere with my obligations as a scholar." "The Historian," *Proceedings of the Massachusetts Historical Society*, p. 93.

62. See Albert J. Beveridge to Edward S. Corwin, June 9, 1922, Corwin Papers, box 2, Princeton.

63. I have the following story from a year-long eyewitness and participant. Some time ago, one of the most distinguished historians of the United States (still quite active) would come into class carrying lecture notes that were visibly yellow-brown around the edges. After a few lacklustre performances, graduate students began to interrupt the professor with stimulating questions. His answers were invariably fresh, knowledgeable, and immensely interesting. As soon as he had answered one question, another came forth, and another, and another. I am also told that some of his finest lectures occurred just after the latest *Journal of Southern History* or the *Mississippi Valley Historical Review* had arrived, because fresh articles caused him to improvise and rethink his views on various topics.

Was the professor aware of his students' strategy? One never knows; but I suspect that he was. As between answering a question and puzzling out the hieroglyphics that one scratched twenty years earlier . . . it's really no contest.

64. See Stewart Mitchell, "Henry Adams and Some of His Students," *Proceedings of the Massachusetts Historical Society* 66 (1942): 294–310; Henry Adams to Charles W. Eliot, March 2, 1877, in *Henry Adams and His Friends: A Collection of His Unpublished Letters*, ed. Harold Dean Cater (Boston: Houghton, Mifflin, 1947), pp. 80–81.

65. Thompson Bradshaw to Corwin, March 2, 1937, Corwin Papers, box 2, Princeton University. See also Thurman Arnold to Corwin, March 27, 1932, and October 5, 1936, *ibid.*, box 1; William L. Underwood to Corwin, February 13 and April 2, 1936, *ibid.*, box 2; William B. Slade to Corwin, March 21, 1937, *ibid.*

66. Hence, in my view, all the more irony in that bizarre exchange of letters, called "The Relevance of History," between David H. Donald, Edward L. Keenan, and Blanche Wissen Cook, printed in the AHA *Newsletter* 15 (December 1977): 3–6.

67. *The Analects of Confucius*, quoted in Frances FitzGerald, *Fire in the Lake: The Vietnamese and the Americans in Vietnam* (New York: Vintage, 1973), p. 15.

68. Sydney George Fisher to Arthur M. Schlesinger, July 31, 1922, Schlesinger Papers, box 2, Pusey Library, Harvard University.

69. William B. Willcox, "The Psychiatrist, the Historian, and General Clinton: The Excitement of Historical Research" (1967), reprinted in Robin W. Winks, ed., *The Historian as Detective: Essays on Evidence* (New York: Harper and Row, 1969), p. 512.

70. For a marvelous analysis that is germane, see Carl Becker, *Everyman His Own Historian: Essays on History and Politics* (Chicago: Quadrangle, 1966), pp. 247–48.

71. William James, *A Pluralistic Universe: Hibbert Lectures on the Current Situation in Philosophy* [Oxford, 1909], (New York: Longmans Green, 1943), p. 48.

EUROPEAN SOURCES OF POLITICAL IDEAS
IN JEFFERSONIAN AMERICA

Daniel Walker Howe

Once upon a time, it seemed as if the sources of political ideology in the new American nation were few. In 1955, Professor Louis Hartz wrote a brilliant book, *The Liberal Tradition in America*, arguing that America was the prisoner of a bourgeois frame of political reference that had forestalled the development of either a strong radical or a strong conservative political tradition: "Lacking Robespierre [America] lacks Maistre, lacking Sydney it lacks Charles II." The only political theorist for Americans, Hartz insisted, was the quintessential bourgeois Englishman, John Locke. Rich in learning and powerfully argued, Hartz's book captured the imagination of a generation of students of American culture. The principal alternative point of view available at that time had been put forth by Daniel Boorstin in *The Lost World of Thomas Jefferson* (1948) and *The Genius of American Politics* (1953). Boorstin argued that no coherent ideology at all had been successfully transplanted from Europe to America. Instead of being confined in a Lockean straitjacket, Americans were free to be a pragmatic people, responding to and shaped by the environment of their rich continent. A generation ago, then, it seemed as if the young American republic had one political philosophy at most.[1]

During the 1960s and 1970s, the interpretations set forth by Hartz and Boorstin came under extensive challenge. In place of the single source that Hartz described, it now appears that Americans in the time of Jefferson derived their political ideas from a number of different sources. And far from being the isolationists and intellectual virgins portrayed by Boorstin, American revolutionaries and republicans seem to have been deeply aware of their membership in an Atlantic community and concerned with studying the example of Europeans while setting a good one themselves. This essay traces the recent changes in our understanding of the sources of political thought in Jeffersonian America, focusing on developments in the past decade.

Donald H. Meyer's *The Democratic Enlightenment* (1976) ably indicates the directions scholarship has been taking. "The intellectual life and the common life tended to merge" in Jeffersonian America, Meyer writes. "The [American] intellectual, far from being at the periphery of power, as was frequently the case abroad, was a part of his society and often a respected leader of it." Related to the democratic nature of the American Enlightenment was its practical quality. A newly settled society recently freed from foreign rule offered scope for putting new ideas into practice—for social "experiment." The fact that the eyes of Europe were on this experiment indicates a third characteristic of the American Enlightenment: it was a provincial part of a cosmopolitan whole. "Colonial America was what Louis Hartz calls a 'fragment culture', self-consciously a part of something larger than itself, namely European civilization." Lastly, Meyer turns his attention to "the Enlightenment as an American institution"—the process by which, during the first half-century of independence, the Enlightenment was permanently built into the structure of American life. The key to this process, he argues, was the adoption of many ideas from the Enlightenment in Scotland by the leaders of American political, educational, and religious institutions.[2]

Most of the historians who have worked on Jeffersonian politics during the past decade agree with Meyer that there is a close connection between political and intellectual history, especially during the early period of the republic's history when so many of our statesmen were themselves readers and thinkers. Then, if ever, ideas mattered to the course of public policy and debate. More than previous ones, this generation of historians has been concerned to place American developments within a larger North Atlantic context. The relevance of the Scottish Enlightenment to the American has been singled out repeatedly for particular notice. While overcoming the limitations of nationality, American historians were overcoming those of chronology as well, reaching farther and farther back in time to provide republicanism with an appropriate frame of reference. Indeed, they have discovered that many politically influential ideas in the young republic long antedated the Enlightenment. The Reformation and even the Italian Renaissance, we now realize, were still alive in the United States of Hamilton, Jefferson, and Madison. Because of this emphasis on the Renaissance, the Reformation, and the Scottish Enlightenment as sources of American political thought, there has been a continued tendency to diminish the prominence Hartz once accorded Locke.

A few months after Meyer's book, Henry F. May's *The Enlightenment in America* appeared. In this mature work, May was less interested in the political dimension of the Enlightenment than in its religious dimension. Unlike Meyer, he did not believe the Enlightenment had been a popular or "democratic" movement in America. Yet there were similarities in their treatments. May's title called attention to the fact that the Enlightenment in America was one country's version of an international phenomenon. Typically, he began by identifying a set of European ideas and then proceeded to describe their transplanting to America. May treated his subject under four headings: "The Moderate Enlightenment, 1688–1787," "The Skeptical Enlightenment, 1750–1789," "The Revolutionary Enlightenment, 1776–1800," and "The Didactic Enlightenment, 1800–1815." Of the four, it was the first that most fully engaged his sympathies. This was the Enlightenment that praised "the beauties of balance" and found its greatest expression in the Constitution of the United States. It was under the last heading, however, that May displayed the most originality. He identified the origins of the didactic enlightenment in the Scottish moral philosophy of Thomas Reid and Dugald Stewart, and he showed how it prepared the way for the nineteenth-century "Genteel Tradition." His terminal date of 1815 did not derive simply from the Battle of New Orleans but from the Unitarian Controversy of that year. "The Enlightenment was gracefully laid to rest and fully assimilated to nineteenth-century piety and reforming morality" in the life and works of the Unitarian patriarch William Ellery Channing. May had located the beginnings of the nineteenth-century American cultural synthesis whose disintegration he had described years before in *The End of American Innocence* (1959).[3]

In 1978 came two books dealing with the intellectual context of the Declaration of Independence: *Inventing America*, by Garry Wills, and *The Philosophy of the American Revolution*, by Morton White. The former attracted the more attention. Wills set out to supersede Carl Becker's classic, *The Declaration of Independence* (1922), by showing that Jefferson based the Declaration not on the ideas of John Locke but on those of the Scottish moral philosophers. With eloquence and forensic skill, Wills conveyed to the reader his own sense of excitement as, step by step, he revealed how much of Jefferson's store of knowledge and assumptions came from the Scottish Enlightenment. Both admirers and critics of Wills's book have emphasized its originality. Actually, his emphasis on Scottish origins represented not so much a new departure as one phase of a long historiographical development.[4]

Writings on the cultural relationship between Scotland and eighteenth-century America go all the way back to I. Woodbridge Riley's *American Philosophy* (1907). They include works by John Clive and Bernard Bailyn, Sydney Ahlstrom, Richard J. Petersen, and Caroline Robbins. In 1946, Herbert W. Schneider declared that "the Scottish Enlightenment was probably the most potent single tradition in the American Enlightenment."[5] Knowledge of the Scottish contribution to American moral philosophy — broadly defined to include most of what we today consider political and social science — was amplified by Wilson Smith in *Professors and Public Ethics* (1956) and Donald H. Meyer in *The Instructed Conscience* (1972). William Charvat's *Origins of American Critical Thought* (1936) recognized the Scottish philosophers' contribution to American literary history, as did

Terence Martin's *The Instructed Vision* (1961). Scottish philosophy has also been shown to have influenced American science, theology, education, and social thought. The trans-Atlantic Presbyterian network that Wills traced, connecting colonial colleges with intellectual centers in Scotland, had been identified by Douglas Sloan in *The Scottish Enlightenment and the American College Ideal* (1971). Adrienne Koch related Jefferson to the Scottish context in *The Philosophy of Thomas Jefferson* (1943). In the course of explaining Scottish moral philosophy and its importance to America, I commented briefly on its connection with the Declaration of Independence in *The Unitarian Conscience* (1970). When Elizabeth Flower and Murray Murphey published their *History of American Philosophy* (1977), the historiographical issue they addressed was not whether Scottish philosophy had influenced America, but whether it had done so for good or ill. What Wills achieved was to bring the issue to wider attention.[6]

At the time Wills's *Inventing America* and White's *Philosophy of the American Revolution* appeared, no one pointed out that they contradicted each other. Wills and White agreed that the Declaration embodied ideas from Scottish moral philosophy. But which ideas, from which thinkers? The philosophers of the Scottish Enlightenment were by no means in accord on the subject of ethics—or on metaphysics, religion, and politics, for that matter. Wills identified Jefferson's Declaration with the sentimentalist moral philosophy of Francis Hutcheson; White identified it with the rationalist position of Thomas Reid, Lord Kames, and Richard Price. Wills was a scintillating writer, whose narrative brilliantly evoked the personalities, circumstances, and moods of the delegates to the continental Congress. White, though tough-minded and even cantankerous, wrote on a more abstract plane. But if White's book was less eye-catching than Wills's, it possessed a significant merit: on the principal subject of disagreement between the two, White was right and Wills was wrong.

Francis Hutcheson (1694–1746), a minister in the church of Scotland, developed a theory that all human beings possessed a "moral sense." This moral sense distinguished good from evil by an immediate emotional reaction, without any rational calculation of advantage. Hutcheson considered the moral faculty a "sense" analogous to the five senses of sight, hearing, touch, taste, and smell—that is, it was an involuntary response to external stimulus. He likened the moral sense most closely, however, to our emotional response to beauty: moral sensitivity was akin to aesthetic feeling. Two other Scottish philosophers, Lord Kames (1696–1782) and Thomas Reid (1710–1796), used the term "moral sense" differently. They believed that the moral sense possessed by all people was not emotional but rational. They were using the word "sense" as we do in the expressions "good sense" or "common sense." According to them, human moral sense intuitively discerned moral axioms that provided the basis for conduct as quantitative axioms provided the basis for mathematics.

The heart of both White's book and that of Wills is their inquiry into what Jefferson meant by self-evident moral truths. White convincingly identifies Jefferson's use of the concept with the rational intuitionist position of Kames, who exerted a more direct influence on Jefferson than did Reid. His argument is more circuitous and repetitious than it needs to be, but he is essentially correct. Wills, on the other hand, identifies Jefferson with Hutcheson's sentimentalist thought. He mistakenly asserts that Hutcheson "established a meaning for 'moral sense' that dominated the whole Scottish Enlightenment," ignoring the rational intuitionist sense of the term. He tries to subordinate the influence of Kames to that of Hutcheson, although Kames's *Essays on the Principles of Morality and Religion* (1751), with Jefferson's annotations, is thought to be one of the few books to survive the burning of Jefferson's library in 1770. He draws his chief evidence for Jefferson's ethical sentimentalism not from the Declaration itself but from a letter Jefferson wrote to Peter Carr in 1787. This letter does suggest that in the years after 1776 Jefferson changed his views and became more of an ethical sentimentalist, but that would not affect the intellectual sources of the Declaration. Jefferson may well have been inconsistent, since although he was well read in moral philosophy he was not a professional moral philosopher (and, indeed, the thrust of his letter to Carr is that moral philosophers are often obscurantists). Wills sometimes uses evidence that Jefferson was a "sentimentalist" in the loose, everyday meaning of that word to imply that he was one in the technical sense of ethical theory, but this will not do. Many a philosopher who taught the rational intuitionist theory of ethics could still be moved by a sunset or a sonnet.[7]

A corollary disagreement between Wills and White relates to the influence of Locke on Jefferson's Declaration. Locke's ethical theory is an ambiguous one, which some interpreters have considered utilitarian and others as a form of rational intuitionism. Morton White, after wrestling with the problem at some length, concludes that Locke should be classified as a rational intuitionist, that is, with Kames and Reid. Consequently, White sees no reason to pluck Jefferson out of the Lockean tradition just because that tradition had been revised or restated by various thinkers—mostly but not entirely Scottish—in the interval between Locke's day and Jefferson's. Wills, on the other hand, having decided that Jefferson was an ethical sentimentalist, concludes that he must stand outside the Lockean tradition. But since Wills was mistaken in identifying the moral philosophy embodied in the Declaration, this attempt to demonstrate its un-Lockean nature fails. And here is the final weakness in Wills's argument: even if Jefferson had subscribed to Francis

Hutcheson's theory of morals, it would not have divorced him from the Lockean political tradition. Although Hutcheson did not follow Locke on the subject of ethics, he did follow him on the subject of political origins. When Hutcheson wrote about the nature of civil society, he did so in orthodox Lockean terms of social and political compacts. Carl Becker has not been refuted after all.

In 1975 a major book was published that pushed the intellectual origins of American republicanism back much earlier than the Enlightenment: J. G. A. Pocock's *The Machiavellian Moment*. Only about 10 percent of its 552 pages dealt with the American colonies or the United States, yet it was a landmark in American intellectual history. The book represented the culmination of what Robert E. Shalhope had termed "the emergence of an understanding of republicanism in American historiography." Pocock provided a comprehensive frame of reference for a number of outstanding earlier works. Caroline Robbins's seminal study, *The Eighteenth-Century Commonwealthman* (1959), had identified a strand of radical Whig-Dissenting thought that outlived the English Puritan experiment in republicanism and persisted down to the time of the American Revolution. Confirmation that the American rebels relied on this tradition had been supplied by Bernard Bailyn in his introduction to *Pamphlets of the American Revolution* and H. Trevor Colburn in *The Lamp of Experience*, both of which appeared in 1965. Gordon Wood's lengthy examination of the intellectual context surrounding *The Creation of the American Republic* (1969) had carried the story forward to the adoption of the Constitution.[8]

In *The Machiavellian Moment*, Pocock traces the origins of this political tradition back to the Renaissance city-state of Florence. Florentine civic humanists, the greatest of whom was Machiavelli, tried to understand the nature of republican government—what conditions made it possible, what circumstances caused it to flourish or decay. Pocock shows how the civic humanist ideal of a virtuous, independent citizenry came to be invoked after the Restoration in England by those who were trying to prevent the ministries from dominating Parliament through patronage and bribery. Opposition leaders affirming the value of members' independence called themselves the "country" party and the ministry the party of the "court." The country party was suspicious of a standing army and government involvement with the financial community (through a national debt and a central bank), which it perceived as forms of patronage that, like the use of "influence" on members of Parliament, tended to corrupt the commonwealth. Pocock believes the country party retained something of the old Spartan suspicion of prosperity as enervating and (as its name suggested) preferred the rural virtues to commercialism.

Eighteenth-century British writers on political economy by no means fall
neatly into the two classifications of "court" and "country," however, and
this is where Pocock's bipolar analysis needs further refinement. There were
really *two* country parties: one radical Whig and the other reactionary Tory.
The former is that delineated by Caroline Robbins; an intellectual portrait of
the latter is provided by Isaac Kramnick in *Bolingbroke and His Circle*
(1968).[9] Complicating the situation further, and even less well understood, is
the fact that there were also two court parties among political pamphleteers: a
Whig one including Daniel Defoe and a Tory one including Jonathan Swift
and David Hume. The most famous of all eighteenth-century British political
economists, the Scottish moral philosopher Adam Smith, cannot really be
classified at all in these terms. He approved of self-interest as conducive to the
common good (like the court writers), yet warned against the dangers of
government intervention in the economy (like the country writers).

The relevance of the commonwealth and country traditions to American
politics was originally discovered in connection with the Revolution. Did
Americans continue to draw on them after independence? Gordon Wood
argued that the ratification of the Constitution ended the classical conception
of politics—i.e., civic humanism—and ushered in a new era of political
thought based on popular sovereignty. Richard Buel, in *Securing the Revolution* (1973), analyzed the political debates between Federalists and
Republicans over whether the government of the new nation should be based
on a financial elite or on broad popular support. Buel confirmed the importance of ideological conflict to Jeffersonian politics but paid little attention to
identifying the sources of political ideas. He noticed in passing that the
Republicans sometimes invoked the same English radical Whig ideas that the
patriots of '76 had employed. Soon historians were to find the persistence of
country-party attitudes important in the early national period.[10]

Daniel Sisson, in *The American Revolution of 1800* (1974), undertook to
explain how and why Jefferson conceived of his election as a "revolution."
Jefferson, Sisson argued, shared the country party's fear of executive corruption and regarded Hamilton as a latter-day Sir Robert Walpole, betraying the
Whig cause into the hands of bankers. The historical profession had been
accustomed to interpreting the election of 1800 in different terms, and Sisson's
work was not accorded the recognition it deserved. Then Lance Banning, in
The Jeffersonian Persuasion (1978), elaborated the connection between the
new Republicans and the old country party. Meanwhile, studies of leading
Jeffersonian political theorists traced their ideas to the country party: C.
William Hill, *The Political Theory of John Taylor* (1977), Robert Dawidoff,
The Education of John Randolph (1979), and Robert E. Shalhope, *John
Taylor of Caroline* (1980). Forrest McDonald, in *The Presidency of Thomas*

Jefferson (1976), even attempted to substantiate the claim that "just about everything in Jeffersonian Republicanism was to be found in Bolingbroke." This is surely hyperbole. From more sober arguments, however, it began to appear that the emergence of the first party system in America did have much in common with the emergence of the first party system in Britain a century before.[11]

The parallel between the English court-country division and that of Federalists and Jeffersonians is pursued in John M. Murrin's brilliant sketch of political mimesis in *Three British Revolutions: 1641, 1688, 1776*, ed. J. G. A. Pocock (1980). In this synthesis of recent scholarship, Murrin not only connects a country ideology with Jefferson, but also a court ideology with Hamilton. He allocates to each a regional basis: the court party the North, the country party the South. He takes account of the dual composition of the country party and points out that the Jeffersonians too had their rural planter (Tory) and urban artisan (commonwealth) wings. The triumph of the Jeffersonian country party was so complete, he argues, that the court tradition withered and an American ideological consensus emerged.[12]

Some of the historians of the Jeffersonian country party have felt it enjoyed ideological hegemony from the start. Banning, for example, says the "court" identity of the Hamiltonians was less a function of their own self-definition than of Jeffersonian perceptions. Pocock, following Bailyn, asserts that in eighteenth-century America only the country party ideology existed, not the court. The country party monopoly on thought "accounts for the singular cultural and intellectual homogeneity of the Founding Fathers," he writes. "There was (it would almost appear) no alternative tradition in which to be schooled." In this view, the country party should be substituted for Locke as the source of American political ideology, but that ideology remains every bit as monochromatic and restrictive as it was for Hartz. Roland Berthoff sketched out a hypothesis in his essay in *Uprooted Americans: Essays to Honor Oscar Handlin* (1979) that country-party ideas continued to define the parameters of political discourse in the United States throughout the Jeffersonian period and beyond. Berthoff regards this prolonged domination of the American mind by an outmoded theory of politics as a great tragedy. Other recent scholarship on the period following American independence, however, indicates more ideological diversity and conflict than in colonial times. Taking the existence of a country party tradition in Jeffersonian America as having been reasonably well established, it seems worth investigating what other sources of political ideas were also available.[13]

One of the most fertile sources of political ideas in Jeffersonian America was David Hume. In politics a Tory and in metaphysics a skeptic, this great Scottish philosopher and historian can be identified in terms of political economy with the court party. Hume argued that an advance in commerce and industry was likely to promote progress in science, the arts, and social morality as well. Believing that men were governed by their passions, Hume saw nothing wrong with material self-interest as a motive. Hume's refutation of the country party's suspicion of luxury was readily taken up by Alexander Hamilton. Gerald Stourzh's splendid study, *Alexander Hamilton and the Idea of Republican Government* (1970), demonstrated the importance of Hume, Hobbes, and Blackstone as sources of Hamilton's political ideology. Stourzh also brought Locke and the English Whigs into his purview, but on such all-important issues as the legitimacy of self-interest, executive "influence" over the legislature, and the encouragement of commerce he found Hamilton siding with Hume against the country writers. Hamilton was willing to accept personal aggrandizement as a motive for patriotism in the belief that America had already passed the historical stage when citizen virtue could be an adequate foundation for the state. Stourzh judiciously concluded that Hamilton could best be classified as a "modern" Whig, that is, a Walpolean, as opposed to the "old" Whigs like the commonwealthmen. Forrest McDonald's biography of Hamilton (1979) confirmed Hume's influence and found that whatever use Hamilton made of country-party ideas before the Revolution, he rejected them soon thereafter.[14]

Another follower of Hume was James Madison. The parallels between Madison's famous *Federalist* number 10 and passages in Hume were discovered by Douglass Adair in his unpublished Yale doctoral dissertation of 1943. Two important books have recently appeared that develop the subject of Hume's influence on Madison further: Drew McCoy, *The Elusive Republic* (1980), and Garry Wills, *Explaining America* (1981).[15] McCoy's book provides the most comprehensive and reliable picture we yet have of political economy in Jeffersonian America and its relationship to party politics. McCoy describes a debate going on throughout the Western world over the morality of the commercial society that was taking shape. Bernard Mandeville represented the most unqualified acceptance and Jean-Jacques Rousseau the most extreme rejection of this new social order. Other thinkers took up intermediate positions along the spectrum of thought, he indicates, among them the Scottish philosophers and English commonwealthmen. In this way, McCoy is able to convey a fuller sense of the variety of Enlightenment political and economic thought than a simple court/country dichotomy does. McCoy shows how Madison used his wide knowledge of Hume and other moral philosophers to synthesize commercialism and agrarianism into a comprehensive system of political economy. Madison endorsed commerce and free trade because they would help farmers market their crops. Thanks to McCoy, we can now see that Madison had as integrated, sophisticated, and systematic a political program as did Hamilton, with social objectives just as clear. After reading McCoy's explanation of the two men's ideologies, one can understand better how Madison and Hamilton could collaborate on *The Federalist* and then diverge to become adversaries.

Explaining America is a sequel to *Inventing America.* It is written with less drama and flair but no less contentiousness. Here, Wills interprets *The Federalist Papers* in the light of their intellectual context, chiefly Scottish. Wills stresses the personal connections of Madison and Hamilton, as he did those of Jefferson, with the world of the Scottish Enlightenment. Hume is the central Scottish figure, as Hutcheson was in the earlier book, and this time Wills is on the right track. His most constructive service in *Explaining America* is to demonstrate that Madison's *Federalist* number 10 was not a statement of twentieth-century pluralism but of eighteenth-century moral philosophy. Madison still believed in an elite of the wise and virtuous, whose government would be best. He hoped that enlarging the size of the body politic by creating an effective national government over the states would help ensure that members of this elite would be elected as rulers. Enlarging the commonwealth would also, he hoped, so multiply selfish special interests and their political expression in "factions" that they would cancel each other out, leaving the wise and virtuous to govern in the interest of the community as a whole. It was not so much a philosophy of free competition as one of divide and rule.

The analysis of *The Federalist* in terms of moral philosophy can be carried further than Wills takes it. Madison explains that the danger of factions is "sown in the nature of man," in the different "faculties" making up that nature. Madison had been educated at Princeton by John Witherspoon, who introduced the Scottish moral philosophy of Thomas Reid. This philosophy envisioned the faculties of man as a hierarchy: conscience (moral sense) being the highest, followed by prudence. Below these two rational powers lay the baser animal powers, the emotions or "passions." Within the individual, conscience was weak and needed strengthening by other motives to virtue; the passions were strong and dangerous. Within the body politic existed an analogous problem. A "faction" was the collective form of "passion." It was vain to hope that unaided virtue could be strong enough to rule; "a nation of philosophers is as little to be expected as the philosophical race of kings wished for by Plato," wrote Madison in number 49. There were, unfortunately, only a few men who were habitually guided by conscience, but there were somewhat more who were guided by prudential reason. The rhetorical strategy of *The Federalist Papers* is to appeal, on behalf of virtue, to the enlightened self-interest of this group of prudent men against the danger of the mob, the factious and passionate. Thus is the rhetoric of Publius shaped by his faculty psychology. Wills, preoccupied with tracing the influence of Hume, neglects the faculty psychology. Concerned to show how *The Federalist* was an exercise in "explaining America," he misses the chance to show how it was also an exercise in "persuading America."

Besides Hume, other British Tories found a receptive audience in the new American republic. Linda Kerber's excellent cultural study of *Federalists in Dissent* (1970) shows how the defeated Federalists after 1800 turned to Tory Augustan satirists to express their feelings. Jonathan Swift, Alexander Pope, and Samuel Johnson couched their social criticism in terms of classical values that American Federalists found congenial. Kerber finds that the Federalists were more loyal to Augustan ideals than Jeffersonians were and that they tried to preserve the classical educational curriculum against the inroads of modern languages and practical subjects. Ralph Ketcham's forthcoming book, *Presidential Leadership in a New Republic*, argues that as the Americans turned from rebellion to constructive nation-building, the logic of their new situation caused them to turn from Whig writers concerned with the defense of liberty to Tory ones who wrote on the exercise of authority. Among the Tories he finds influencing American concepts of executive power are Dryden, Swift, Pope, and Bolingbroke. Ketcham's study will provide the best discussion available of the concept of presidential leadership that prevailed in America before the age of Jackson and the legitimation of two-party politics.[16]

Some of Jefferson's conservative opponents blended the country ideology with other elements. John R. Howe's *The Changing Political Thought of John Adams* (1966) convincingly linked its subject with moral philosophy, Scottish and English, including Locke, as well as with what came to be called the country party, a term Howe did not use. The book demonstrated (ironically, in view of its title) that amid changing circumstances and moods, Adams clung to his political ideas with dogged persistence. James M. Banner investigated the ideological origins of Massachusetts Federalism in *To the Hartford Convention* (1970). He found that both classical republicanism and the Puritan religion were important. They taught the same lessons: the warnings of cyclical political theorists that the life-span of republics could not be indefinitely prolonged were reinforced by the imprecations of Puritan jeremiads on the dangers of corrupt manners. The Federalists contrasted both their classical republicanism and their Puritanism with the radical social innovations of the French Revolution.[17]

Having established Puritanism as one source of Federalist political ideas, Banner was led to conclude that New England Federalists who left Calvinism for Unitarianism must have been less conservative in politics. However plausible, the conclusion does not seem to be confirmed by the evidence. My work on *The Unitarian Conscience,* published in the same year, found the intellectual leaders of New England Unitarianism staunchly Federalist and holding a conservative social outlook that could be termed Puritanism without Calvinism. The moral philosophers at Unitarian Harvard taught the organic rather than the contractual nature of society. (They could not, of course, deny the contractual nature of government in the United States, but thinkers ever since Locke had been distinguishing the origin of government from the origin of society.) The principal sources of their political theory, apart from Puritanism, were the Scottish moral philosophers and Edmund Burke. Burke, an apologist for the American Revolution and a critic of the French one, suited early nineteenth-century American conservatives perfectly and was more widely admired in this country than most historians realize. The presence of Burkean ideas illustrates how the range of conservative thought in Jeffersonian America extended beyond the categories of court and country.

Such is the considerable variety of conservative to moderate sources of political ideas that Americans in the time of Jefferson, Hamilton, and Madison knew and used. What about democratic and radical ideas? Staughton Lynd traced the *Intellectual Origins of American Radicalism* (1968) to Quakerism and other English radical dissent. He centered his attention on the concept of conscience, the "inner light" of the Quakers. Treating the Declaration of Independence as a radical document, he anticipated White's conclusion that it embodied the intuitionist doctrine of ethics. A central figure in Lynd's account was Richard Price (1723–93), a Scottish-educated English radical Dissenter who was also a leading moral philosopher of the rational intuitionist school and sympathizer with the American Revolution. Lynd sought to distinguish his Dissenters from the commonwealthmen, but upon close inspection the two groups merge: Price figured prominently in Robbins's book also. A conclusion to be drawn is that the commonwealthmen were more radical than we usually realize and should not be conflated with Tories like Bolingbroke.[18]

We still know little about the intellectual sources of popular radicalism in Jeffersonian America. Henry May identified the cities as centers of the Enlightenment in America, but he did not inquire into urban popular politics. Eric Foner's *Tom Paine and Revolutionary America* (1976), admittedly fragmentary, provides a stimulating preliminary look at an artisan version of the Enlightenment that synthesized commerce with democracy in a fashion unlike either the court or country parties. Isaac Kramnick's 1976 edition of Paine's *Common Sense* complements Foner's book well. Kramnick emphasizes that we cannot clearly differentiate, in preindustrial England and America, between working class and petit bourgeois radicalism. Richard

Twomey's unpublished dissertation on "Jacobins and Jeffersonians" (1974) examines the radicals who fled to America from England, Ireland, and Scotland during the repressions of the 1790s. These men—including Joseph Priestley, Thomas Cooper, and James Cheetham—illustrate as Paine does the trans-Atlantic quality of radicalism in this period. Twomey calls them the "left wing" of Jeffersonian republicanism. E. P. Thompson has argued that the British Tories were correct to fear eighteenth-century international radicalism; from Twomey's work, it seems that the corresponding fears of American Federalists also had some basis in reality.[19]

A plausible source for popular radicalism in the early republic would be evangelical religion. Alan Heimert presented the case for a native radical tradition stemming from evangelical Calvinism in *Religion and the American Mind* (1966), carrying his story as far as the election and revival of 1800. Although immensely learned, Heimert's argument suffered from heavy-handed special pleading and did not seem to square with the fact that many Calvinist revivalists in 1800 were arch-conservative Federalists. More persuasive in making connections between political and religious ideas are works focusing not on Calvinism but on the related topic of millennialism, such as Nathan O. Hatch's *The Sacred Cause of Liberty* (1977) and Ruth Bloch's *Visionary Republic* (forthcoming). However, much remains to be done to provide an appropriate trans-Atlantic dimension to the study of American religious history in the Jeffersonian period. May has supplied one for the religious rationalists of the "Moderate Enlightenment," but not for popular pietism and evangelicalism. (Scotland, it might be noted, was an important center of popular evangelical Calvinism as well as of the Enlightenment.) American deism and its political implications have also been little studied in recent years.[20]

The French Revolution involved Americans in a furious trans-Atlantic debate over the best design for republican government. Out of this debate emerged both John Adams's *Defense of the Constitutions of Government of the United States* in 1787/88, and in 1814 the long-delayed Jeffersonian rebuttal to it, John Taylor's *Inquiry into the Principles and Policy of the Government of the United States.* Essential for understanding the American implications of this debate are two articles by Joyce Appleby, published in 1973 and 1982. Appleby shows how Adams sided with the French *Anglomanes* who endorsed English country ideas of balanced government. Jefferson, she argues, broke with country party doctrine during this debate and espoused a more democratic form of political and economic liberalism. He supported the French *Americanistes* on behalf of simple majority rule. Appleby concludes that in the 1790s three ideological positions can be identified in the United States: the court party of Hamilton, the country party of Adams, and the

Enlightenment liberalism of the Jeffersonians, drawing upon Adam Smith and his French followers, the *physiocrates* and *ideologues.* Laissez-faire capitalism, she reminds us, could be a democratic creed in the time of Jefferson.[21]

It would be premature to predict how Appleby's challenge to Banning and the other historians who have interpreted Jefferson in terms of the country party will be resolved. It does appear, however, that instead of country ideology constituting a consensus within which all Jeffersonian political debate occurred, it was one intellectual option among several. These options ranged from Burkeanism and the court party on the right through the country party and Smithian liberalism to Christian and secular radicalisms on the left. All of these options made extensive use of Scottish ideas. The involvement of Americans in the political debates of the Atlantic world is well indicated in Robert Kelley, *The Cultural Pattern in American Politics* (1979). Kelley points out that the reception accorded different European currents of thought varied among different ethnic groups in the United States. Ethnic diversity, he reminds us, fostered intellectual diversity.[22]

An outstanding example of the way the history of Jeffersonian America should be written, indeed the finest work yet produced on the sources of political ideology in that period, is by David Brion Davis, *The Problem of Slavery in the Age of Revolution, 1770–1823* (1975). Resolutely trans-Atlantic in focus, the book treats both British and American slavery and antislavery, with comparative references to the French, Spanish, and Portuguese. In this volume and its predecessor, *The Problem of Slavery in Western Culture* (1966), Davis shows how Lockean liberalism, the moral sense of the Scottish philosophers, evangelical piety, Quaker benevolence, and even the primitivism of Rousseau (which has not attracted much attention lately from historians of American thought) all went into shaping the great assault upon slavery. Davis integrates his diverse material into a powerful interpretive structure. He links antislavery with the rise of industrial capitalism, but does so without discrediting its moral legitimacy. Davis sustains a magnificent sense of the complexity and ambiguity of history. Adam Smith receives his due as both a moral philosopher and a political economist; William Wilberforce, as both idealistic reformer and conservative politician; Thomas Paine, as Englishman, American, and honorary French citizen. Writing on the country party, Davis exposes its profoundly ambiguous implications for his subject: devoted to liberty and austere virtue but also jealous of local autonomy and property rights, the country party heritage could be and was invoked by both critics and defenders of slavery.[23]

What seems likely in the forseeable future is a continued interest in the European sources of Jeffersonian and Federalist political thought. There is little chance that we will return to the defensive assertion of American "exceptionalism" from European patterns of debate. With even more confidence one can predict that the conventional separation between colonial history and the history of the young republic will be broken down, to the benefit of the latter. More and more, it seems as if early American history possesses a certain continuity until the 1820s, when the coming of industrialization, population shifts, diplomatic isolation from Europe, the surfacing of the slavery question, and the break-up of the Republican party finally transformed the world of Jefferson.

Locke, it seems worth noticing, has not disappeared in Davis's account, despite all the attention devoted in the past two decades to identifying other sources of American political ideas. "The deemphasizing of Locke is for the present a tactical necessity," wrote Pocock in *The Machiavellian Moment*. "The historical context must be reconstructed without him before he can be fitted back into it." [24] I suggest that the time has now arrived for fitting Locke back in. The distinction between Locke and the commonwealthmen is not one that contemporaries drew. The same Earl of Shaftesbury who founded the country resistance to the court in England was also Locke's patron. Americans habitually invoked Locke along with other members of the country party as heralds of liberty: "Sydney, Harrington, and Locke"—the names cited might vary but Locke was usually among them. By the same token, the Scottish moral philosophers, whatever their differences with each other (and Hutcheson, Reid, Hume, and Smith disagreed over much), all admired Locke and interpreted their own work as carrying on his. We can now say that Louis Hartz was mistaken when he wrote that, "lacking Sydney," America "lacks Charles II" too. Algernon Sydney was a prominent commonwealthman beloved in America, and if King Charles II was no philosopher, the writings of other British Tories were admired in America. Still, Hartz has been supplemented rather than consigned to oblivion. American political culture has been more complex and varied than he once realized, but it still seems to have been, as he argued in *The Founding of New Societies* (1964) an overseas "fragment" of European culture. [25]

The intellectual history of the past generation has run counter to Daniel Boorstin's thesis that America was immune to European ideologies. Yet, if we now know that Americans in the age of Jefferson and Hamilton were more ideologically aware than Boorstin supposed, they still appear a practical people, as he insisted they were. Because they *were* innovative and creating a new nation, the Americans were willing to borrow ideas from a wide range of European sources. Different groups in America borrowed from different European thinkers, or interpreted the same ones differently, as Hamilton and Madison did Hume. In the process the Americans internalized, supplemented, synthesized, and adapted European ideas to their own purposes. Their practicality made these cantankerous republicans of America not isolationists but experimentalists. Americans in the time of Jefferson were eager to apply the ideas of the Old World to the experience of the New.

1. Louis Hartz, *The Liberal Tradition in America* (New York: Harcourt, Brace, 1955), p. 5; Daniel Boorstin, *The Lost World of Thomas Jefferson* (New York: H. H. Holt, 1948); and *The Genius of American Politics* (Chicago: University of Chicago Press, 1953).

2. Donald H. Meyer, *The Democratic Enlightenment* (New York: Putnam, 1976), pp. viii, 49–50.

3. Henry F. May, *The Enlightenment in America* (New York: Oxford University Press, 1976), p. 354; and *The End of American Innocence* (New York: Knopf, 1959).

4. Garry Wills, *Inventing America* (Garden City, N.Y.: Doubleday, 1978); Morton White, *The Philosophy of the American Revolution* (New York: Oxford University Press, 1978); Carl Becker, *The Declaration of Independence* (New York: Knopf, 1922).

5. I. Woodbridge Riley, *American Philosophy: The Early Schools* (New York: Dodd, Mead and Co., 1907); John Clive and Bernard Bailyn, "England's Cultural Provinces: Scotland and America," *William and Mary Quarterly* 11 (April 1954): 200–13; Caroline Robbins, "When It Is that Colonies May Turn Independent," *ibid.*, pp. 214–51; Sydney Ahlstrom, "Scottish Philosophy and American Theology," *Church History* 24 (September 1955): 257–72; Richard J. Petersen, "Scottish Common Sense in America, 1768–1850" (Ph.D. diss., American University, 1963); Herbert W. Schneider, *History of American Philosophy* (New York: Columbia University Press, 1947), p. 246.

6. Wilson Smith, *Professors and Public Ethics: Studies of the Northern Moral Philosophers* (Ithaca, N.Y.: Cornell University Press, 1956); Donald Meyer, *The Instructed Conscience: The Shaping of the American National Ethic* (Philadelphia: University of Pennsylvania Press, 1972); William Charvat, *Origins of American Critical Thought* (Philadelphia: University of Pennsylvania Press, 1936); Terence Martin, *The Instructed Vision: Scottish Common Sense Philosophy and the Origins of American Fiction* (Bloomington: Indiana University Press, 1961); Douglas Sloan, *The Scottish Enlightenment and the American College Ideal* (New York: Columbia Teachers College Press, 1971); Adrienne Koch, *The Philosophy of Thomas Jefferson* (New York: Columbia University Press, 1943); Daniel Walker Howe, *The Unitarian Conscience: Harvard Moral Philosophy, 1805–1861* (Cambridge, Mass.: Harvard University Press, 1970); Elizabeth Flower and Murray Murphy, *History of American Philosophy* (New York: Capricorn Books, 1977).

7. Wills, *Inventing America*, p. 194; Henry Home, Lord Kames, *Essays on the Principles of Morality and Religion* (Edinburgh: R. Fleming, 1751).

8. J.G.A. Pocock, *The Machiavellian Moment: Florentine Political Thought and the Atlantic Republican Tradition* (Princeton, N.J.: Princeton University Press, 1975); Robert E. Shalhope, "Toward a Republican Synthesis," *William and Mary Quarterly* 29 (January 1972): 49–80; Caroline Robbins, *The Eighteenth-Century Commonwealthman* (Cambridge, Mass.: Harvard University Press, 1959); Bernard Bailyn, "Introduction," in *Pamphlets of the American Revolution*, vol. 1 (Cambridge, Mass.: Harvard University Press, 1965); H. Trevor Colburn, *The Lamp of Experience: Whig History and the Intellectual Origins of the American Revolution* (Chapel Hill: University of North Carolina Press, 1965); Gordon Wood, *The Creation of the American Republic* (Chapel Hill: University of North Carolina Press, 1969).

9. Isaac Kramnick, *Bolingbroke and His Circle: The Politics of Nostalgia in the Age of Walpole* (Cambridge, Mass.: Harvard University Press, 1968).

10. Richard Buel, *Securing the Revolution* (Ithaca, N.Y.: Cornell University Press, 1973).

11. Daniel Sisson, *The American Revolution of 1800* (New York: Knopf, 1974); Lance Banning, *The Jeffersonian Persuasion* (Ithaca, N.Y.: Cornell University Press, 1978); C. William Hill, *The Political Theory of John Taylor* (Rutherford, N.J.: Farleigh Dickinson University Press, 1977); Robert Dawidoff, *The Education of John Randolph* (New York: Norton, 1979);

Robert E. Shalhope, *John Taylor of Caroline: Pastoral Republican* (Columbia: University of South Carolina Press, 1980); Forrest McDonald, *The Presidency of Thomas Jefferson* (Lawrence: University Press of Kansas, 1976), p. ix.

12. John M. Murrin, "The Great Inversion, or Court versus Country: A Comparison of the Revolution Settlements in England," in *Three British Revolutions: 1641, 1688, 1776*, ed. J.G.A. Pocock (Princeton, N.J.: Princeton University Press, 1980).

13. Pocock, *Machiavellian Moment*, p. 507; Roland Berthoff, "Independence and Attachment, Virtue and Interest: From Republican Citizen to Free Enterpriser, 1787–1837," in *Uprooted Americans: Essays to Honor Oscar Handlin*, eds. Richard Bushman et al. (Boston: Little, Brown, 1979).

14. Gerald Stourzh, *Alexander Hamilton and the Idea of Republican Government* (Stanford, Calif.: Stanford University Press, 1970); Forrest McDonald, *Alexander Hamilton* (New York: Norton, 1979).

15. Douglass Adair, "The Intellectual Origins of Jeffersonian Democracy," (Ph.D. diss., Yale University, 1943); Drew McCoy, *The Elusive Republic: Political Economy in Jeffersonian America* (Chapel Hill: University of North Carolina Press, 1980); Gary Wills, *Explaining America* (Garden City, N.Y.: Doubleday, 1981).

16. Linda Kerber, *Federalists in Dissent* (Ithaca, N.Y.: Cornell University Press, 1970); Ralph Ketcham, *Presidential Leadership in a New Republic* (Chapel Hill: University of North Carolina Press, forthcoming).

17. John R. Howe, *The Changing Political Thought of John Adams* (Princeton, N.J.: Princeton University Press, 1966); James M. Banner, *To the Hartford Convention* (New York: Knopf, 1970).

18. Staughton Lynd, *Intellectual Origins of American Radicalism* (New York: Pantheon Books, 1968).

19. Eric Foner, *Tom Paine and Revolutionary America* (New York: Oxford University Press, 1976); Thomas Paine, *Common Sense*, ed. Isaac Kramnick (Harmondsworth: Penguin, 1976); Richard Twomey, "Jacobins and Jeffersonians: Anglo-American Radicalism in the United States, 1790–1820," (Ph.D. diss., Northern Illinois University, 1974); E. P. Thompson, *The Making of the English Working Class* (London: Gollanez, 1963), esp. ch. 5.

20. Alan Heimert, *Religion and the American Mind* (Cambridge, Mass.: Harvard University Press, 1966); Nathan O. Hatch, *The Sacred Cause of Liberty* (New Haven, Conn.: Yale University Press, 1977); Ruth Bloch, *Visionary Republic: Millennial Themes in American Ideology* (forthcoming).

21. John Adams, *Defense of the Constitutions of Government of the United States* (London: J. Stockdale, 1794); John Taylor, *Inquiry into the Principles and Policy of the Government of the United States* (Fredricksburg, Va.: Green and Cudy, 1814); Joyce Appleby, "The New Republican Synthesis and the Changing Political Thought of John Adams," *American Quarterly* 25 (December 1973): 578–95; and "What Is Still American in the Political Philosophy of Thomas Jefferson?" *William and Mary Quarterly* 39 (April 1982): 287–304.

22. Robert Kelley, *The Cultural Pattern in American Politics: The First Century* (New York: Knopf, 1979).

23. David Brion Davis, *The Problem of Slavery in the Age of Revolution, 1770–1823* (Ithaca, N.Y.: Cornell University Press, 1975); and *The Problem of Slavery in Western Culture* (Ithaca, N.Y.: Cornell University Press, 1966).

24. Pocock, *Machiavellian Moment*, p. 424.

25. Louis Hartz, *The Founding of New Societies* (New York: Harcourt, Brace, and World, 1964).

ON CLASS AND POLITICS IN JACKSONIAN AMERICA

Sean Wilentz

"Our virtues are the virtues of merchants . . ."
> *The American Review; A Whig Journal of Politics.*
> *Literature, Art and Science* [New York], I (1845), p. 95.

Jacksonian political history, once a battleground of academic controversy, has been a quiet field of late (see Fig. 1). The recent shift in interest toward social history in part accounts for the calm, a point to which I will return later. Just as important, however, Jacksonian political historians more or less killed off interest in the subject themselves by failing to move beyond their advances of the 1960s and by obscuring the question that had originally stirred so many of them to action: What were the relationships between class and politics in the early nineteenth-century United States? Now that the weaknesses of the "new" Jacksonian political history have been pointed out, it is proper to reflect on its rise and decline—and on why the social historians failed to construct their own interpretation of class and politics. It is also time to build on the social historians' reconceptualizations of class and social relations in nineteenth-century America, and offer a different approach to the social history of politics in the 1830s and 1840s.

The great revision of Jacksonian politics began in earnest in the late 1940s, almost immediately after the publication of Arthur Schlesinger, Jr.'s celebratory, *The Age of Jackson*. Richard Hofstadter's savage and bitter discussion of Andrew Jackson's place in the genealogy of American liberal politics set the tone. Once Hofstadter had done in the prevailing Progressive and New Deal myths about The Man of the People, all of the old simplifications about class and politics began to fall. On close examination, the leading Jacksonians were shown to be not champions of deprived workers and small farmers, but cold-blooded political entrepreneurs, often men of great wealth or men eager to become wealthy, whose main purpose was to get power and keep it. Jackson himself, it turned out, was an inconsistent opportunist, a shady land speculator, a political fraud—and a strikebreaker to boot.[1]

It was left to Lee Benson to assault the Progressives' very concept of Jacksonian democracy, especially their ideas that the Whigs were a "conservative" business party and that party conflicts were the direct expressions of clashing

0048-7511/82/0104-0045 $01.00

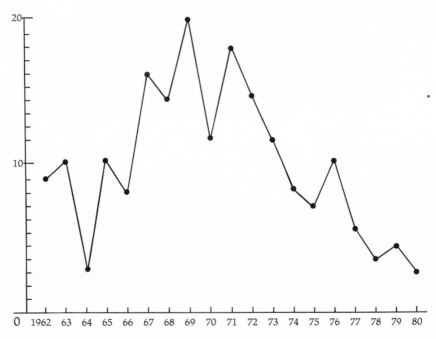

Figure 1. Number of journal articles on Jacksonian political history, 1962–1980, by year
Source: *Writings on American History: A Subject Bibliography*, Various editors
         (Washington, D.C., 1962–   ), 1962–79/80.

economic interests. Benson worded his major conclusion carefully: "[E]thnic
and religious differences tended to be *relatively* the most important sources of
political differences." His message, however, was clear, at least for New
York: wealthy men led both major parties; no significant relationship existed
between political affiliations and class; to the extent that ideology entered
into political struggles, it consisted of variants of liberalism and little more;
any appearance to the contrary, in the form of party rhetoric or "economic"
issues, was symbolic claptrap, which hid the essentially liberal motivations
and ethnoreligious discord that were most decisive in Jacksonian New York
politics.[2]

Because Benson's argument advanced on several fronts at once, it was a
formidable challenge. *The Concept of Jacksonian Democracy* raised a host of
questions about the complexity and character of American liberal political
culture that are only beginning to be debated and clarified;[3] even more, it
established the importance of what we now label the "social" issues—
temperance, comportment, morality—in any analysis of Jacksonian politics

in the North. Through the late 1970s, however, political historians working beside Benson or under his inspiration adhered most closely to a few counter-Progressive points. One exceptional study, Richard P. McCormick's state-by-state examination of party formation, criticized Benson on some matters, eschewed multivariate voting analysis, and concentrated on the parties and the politicians themselves—but appeared to clinch the argument that the "second party system" aimed to eliminate ideology and touchy issues from politics, not to agitate them.[4] More symptomatic was the rash of heavily quantitative studies on voting behavior and the social structure of party elites that refined and affirmed Benson's basic arguments about politics, culture, and class.[5]

When joined with similar work on the late nineteenth century, these "new," "scientific" political histories quickly hardened into an orthodoxy, a veritable ethnocultural school of American politics united by their belief that American political (and, by inference, social) divisions are explicable in terms of ethnicity and religion and not of class.[6] When joined with the work on Jacksonian party formation and professionalism, they so thoroughly marginalized class and economic change that class relations began to disappear from explanations of Jacksonian political history altogether. What had begun as an effective attack on Progressive economic determinism had turned into something different, a new interpretation of the key social determinants of American political consciousness and conflict. It all fit perfectly with that brand of consensus scholarship most closely identified with Richard Hofstadter—a view that allowed for conflict over "status" questions but that denied the centrality of class in a society unified by a "fiercely individualistic and capitalistic" political culture.[7]

In time, there were some demurrers and even some second thoughts. Studies of elite party affiliations and of evanescent third "parties" contended that class differences and conflicts were not entirely absent from the politics of the 1830s and 1840s.[8] Others pointed out that contrasting views on slavery—a matter of relatively little importance to the revisionists—tended to divide Democrats and Whigs, even though party chieftains tried to keep the question out of national politics.[9] At least one Jacksonian economic historian criticized the early revisionists' work from a Marxist perspective.[10] Some young political historians wondered if the ethnoculturalists imputed too much from the vote alone and if they threatened to replace one determinism with another.[11] Still, through the late 1970s, the revisionist paradigm continued to dominate the study of Jacksonian politics.[12] And that paradigm remained pretty much as it had been formulated by Samuel Hays in 1960: "Party differences in voting patterns were cultural, not economic."[13]

It is not surprising that so many of the social historians of the early nineteenth century in the late 1960s and 1970s read these revelations with varying degrees of boredom and hostility. Only the most thoroughgoing behavioralists and quantifiers had any real affinity for the political historians' work, and this was based as much on shared methodological obsessions as on shared concerns about political history. For most historians of slaves, free blacks, women, and the rest of the disfranchised majority, Jacksonian political history—Progressive or counter-Progressive—could not have been more irrelevant. Party systems and the vote were pertinent enough for historians of popular protest, radicalism, and reform, but had little to say directly about men and women of genuine moral passion and ideological commitment. Revisionist axioms about the paucity of any "meaningful" popular political consciousness ran counter to the entire enterprise of social history.[14] Above all, the revisionists' consensual approach and conclusions appeared dubious to historians who found little constancy or unity in Americans' attitudes toward capitalist development. As the ranks of the social historians grew, Jacksonian political history became a bothersome distraction, a subject to be crammed in for orals or for survey lectures but then quickly forgotten, an unimportant realm where the real conflicts did not take place.

By the mid-1970s, this instinctive distaste had sharpened into a critique of the limitations and biases of the revisionists' work.[15] The voting studies, some claimed, were marred by serious flaws—a tendency to argue from a few supposedly telling examples, an inability to overcome the limitations of available aggregate data on wealth, demography, and voting, an openness to misinterpretations of that data, a neglect of the interconnections between ethnicity, religion, and emerging class structure. In some cases, reassembly of the revisionists' voting data and use of more exact poll book records (when possible) yielded results at odds with the ethnocultural formula about politics and class.[16] Moreover, the critics reminded other historians that the voting studies, like all behavioral investigations, strictly speaking said nothing about consciousness and motivation (and hence about causality) apart from what they imputed from their analysis of the vote. They could help clear away some potent historical legends about the character of party politics and the direct correspondence of politics and economic interest. But beyond that (even if their correlations had been perfectly accurate), the voting studies did not prove why anyone—not one single voter, let alone an entire electorate— voted the way he did. Did, for example, an Irish hod carrier and his friends vote Democratic because they were poor, wage laborers, Irish, Catholic, or some combination of all four? The revisionists could not say.

It followed, the critics observed, that the revisionists had construed politics far too narrowly, and thereby distorted social relations, social consciousness, and the exercise of political power.[17] For the "new" political historians, politics virtually began and ended at the polling place and the party meeting hall. Other areas of life—religious life especially—occasionally entered in, but mainly as a way of working up categories and dichotomies with which to interpret the voting returns. All of the various social tensions and solidarities—of class, sex, and race—explored by the social historians were subordinated to the search for functionalist explanations of mass electoral behavior. Little allowance was made for how these tensions might have shaped the structure and conduct—the very social context—of party politics, and the use of power outside elections. By reconstructing political and social consciousness primarily on the basis of the vote the revisionists instead erected an odd double standard: believing they had shown the ethnocultural basis of voting behavior, they reasoned that other matters—especially economic or "class" questions—were either evanescent or symbolic, emblematic of the status and moral concerns at stake. What seemed to the social historians to be a matter of common sense—that early nineteenth-century campaigns, rhetoric, and statecraft reflected (in some way) changing economic and class relations—was consigned to the dustbin of erroneous progressivism.[18]

Lurking in all of these procedural criticisms were the social historians' fundamental objections to the revisionists' concepts of class and culture. For the "new" political historians following the dictates of empirical functionalist American sociology, the two were not unlike social institutions whose membership could be defined in purely statistical terms: class was some concatenation of wealth (usually) and occupation, which amounted to economic interest; "culture" was what church a voter belonged to, what accent he spoke with, where he (and, occasionally, his father) was born, which revealed a moral viewpoint or a status interest. To discover the relative impact of class and culture on politics, one lined up the voters (or, usually, a county, township, or ward) according to these indicators, ran innumerable operations through the voting data, and the ethnocultural models emerged.

Just as these models appeared, social historians were transforming their own concepts of class. To equate "class" politics with pure polarization of the parties along economic lines, it seemed, was only to reproduce the Progressives' strict economic determinism. More important, it was argued, little could be learned by analyzing class as an institution, as the sum of a series of static, "socioeconomic indicators" abstracted from their social and historical context. Class only had meaning as a dynamic social *relation*, a system of social domination determined largely by relations of production, not merely by wealth or occupation. Class relations assumed historical significance as people came to terms with that system, to define (often unselfconsciously) a common identity and a universalizing notion of rights and obligations, different from—and, at times, directly opposed to—those of other classes.[19] Moreover, the social historians pointed out, early nineteenth-century American history was marked by a range of interconnected, uneven processes of class *formation*, in which patriarchal, petty agrarian, and artisanal social relations gave way to new relations of wage labor (urban and rural), new market and credit relations, reordered sexual and family relations, and altered relations between producers and the state (primarily through banking and taxation). New perceptions and identities of interest took shape continually amidst these social transformations, in strikes and early trade unionism, in emerging middle class religion and reform, in rural disputes over land and property rights, in the law, in the meanest sides of everyday existence.[20] To understand the connections between class and politics required some understanding of how the structure and social relations of politics and the exercise of political power might have been related to these transitions—something unobtainable from behavioralist attempts to determine who voted for whom.

The social historians, moreover, considered culture not as something distinct from class, not as a series of affiliations or ideal types, but as the totality of perceptions, beliefs, practices, traditions, and innovations in which people express their relations with each other. All of those "values, attitudes, and beliefs" which the revisionists tied to ethnicity and religion and analyzed independent of class had no meaning unless the changing context of class relations in which they developed was taken into account. To take a well-studied example: to be an evangelical Protestant in the North in the 1830s and 1840s certainly signified adherence to a broad cultural outlook, a particular moral viewpoint. It also signified something about a person's social position or expected social position in an evolving class society; even more, that "culture," that moral viewpoint, was in part defined and reinforced by changing class relations, in which inherited religious ideals assumed new—and in this case, quintessentially bourgeois—meanings and forms. Working with such concepts, social historians like Herbert Gutman, Paul Johnson, and Mary Ryan found ways to explore the interactions of class formation and cultural expression without separating the two and without reducing culture to a mere byproduct of economic interest.[21] By contrast, the political historians, in trying to determine whether "class" or "culture" exerted greater independent influence on voting, fractured history beyond recognition.

These criticisms cleared the way for a fresh discussion of class and politics. For the revisionists, class relations would have been a significant factor in the politics of the age *if and only if* the "lower classes" (loosely defined) had gathered together and all (or mostly) voted for their own party, to counter the opposing party of property. Might there have been more subtle ways for class to have been a factor in politics—even the institutionalized politics of party—especially in an era of class formation? Might the ascendency of liberal, "middle class" politics have been due to something more than consensus among the politicians and the undeniable tensions of creed and ethnicity in the North and West? Might the very patterns of "ethnic" politics and elite party domination discussed by the revisionists have been associated with changing class relations?

Here, then, were some important questions that promised to reunite the study of society and politics. Unfortunately, by the time the questions began to be formulated, the social historians had all but forsaken the study of politics, especially party politics. They were interested in culture, not in the desiccated form served up by the political historians but in the form of lived experience, as social process, a process which seemed virtually unaffected by the empty machinations of the parties. Labor historians explored the taverns, debating clubs, churches, and other cultural milieux in which class was embedded; historians of slavery examined songs, jokes, and the oral tradition; historians of women and gender discovered "woman's sphere" and complex middle class and working class female worlds—and so on, with at best passing reference to Whigs and Democrats. Michael Rogin's provocative attempt to wed Freud and Marx to understand Jackson and America was something of an exception, but Rogin said little about party politics and nothing the "new" political historians would understand as such.[22] Otherwise, Andrew Jackson—indeed, politics—virtually disappeared from what had once been called the Age of Jackson.[23]

The salutary effects of this scholarly revolution are well-known. What is interesting was how, like all successful revolutionists just after the new regime is installed, the social historians looked at each others' work and grimaced. Early polemics pitted the behavioralist "new" social historians against their detractors; simultaneously, social historians of every description began to divide over the place of power, politics, and party in social history.[24] Could social historians, some asked, safely ignore parties and politics—the one area in which nineteenth-century America was profoundly different from the rest of the world? Could they possibly write about the exercise of social power—meant broadly as all systems of group and personal domination—without considering formal political power and institutions?

The more these questions appeared, the more troublesome they became, raising doubts about some of the most influential work on social history from the 1970s. How much, for example, could the paternalism of the plantation masters be considered the chief instrument of class rule in the slave South if this paternalism did not turn up in the discourse of southern state politics? [25] How truly separate was the "woman's sphere" of the emerging Jacksonian

middle class—and how separate from men's politics—given women's informal participation in politics and the early feminists' focus on winning the
vote? [26] Others responded, quite properly, that the study of some aspects of
social life would be distracted and diluted if forced to pay a great deal of
attention to party politics; above all, it was important not to subordinate the
study of social structures and relations to the study of political institutions, or
to pit the kind of political history the dissenting social historians had in mind
against other kinds of social history. [27] Still, the questions lingered for those
who wanted to keep their eye on the whole story, on the history of
nineteenth-century American society.

But how were the social historians to approach politics in ways sensitive to
their new conceptions of class and culture? The few attempts to link social
and political history in the early and mid-1970s inspired partial confidence at
best. Modernization theory promised to assemble all elements of society,
politics, and culture. In doing so, however, it also made a dangerous series of
ahistorical substitutions—functionalist teleology for historical process, static
and reified ideal types for complex social realities, temporal labels for social
categories—all while it eviscerated class relations and culture. Not only did
modernization theory (like certain strains of orthodox Marxism) transform
social life into an abstract struggle between intellectual inventions; it
hopelessly muddled the history of the Jacksonian parties, each of which contained elements of "tradition" and "modernity." [28]

Edward Pessen's important work on riches, class, and politics was of a different order; at least it presented some useful figures on growing inequality of
wealth in America's northern seaboard cities, showed that mercantile-
professional elites held municipal office through the 1840s, and offered some
fascinating glimpses of upper class urban social life. If nothing else, Pessen
forced historians to recognize that, in material terms, Jacksonian America (or
at least urban America) could hardly be described as egalitarian. But Pessen's
ripostes to Tocqueville (and by extension to the consensus historians and to
Benson) did not fully answer the social historians' questions. Pessen's conception of class remained much like that of earlier Progressives and their opponents, a social institution which could be outlined with figures on wealth,
social mobility, and inequality; changing social and economic *relations* of
class, and their relationships to the structure and meaning of party politics, all
but missed his gaze. More important, Pessen's evidence on inequality and the
cohesiveness of the urban elite did not refute Tocqueville's and Benson's main
point, that a widespread belief in democratic liberalism held sway over
American politics. Any number of sources—from Tocqueville's American
moral equivalent, James Fenimore Cooper, to the "uncommon" labor radicals
Pessen treated so well earlier—could have been cited to dispel any notions

that Americans believed they lived in a land of thoroughgoing social and material equality. The heart of Tocqueville's remarks on liberalism, egalitarianism, and American political beliefs, however, remained unshaken; indeed, given Pessen's figures, Tocqueville's interpretation of American politics appeared to be all the more compelling.[29]

So, into the early 1980s, the social historians were in a quandary. The labor historians made some admirable efforts to unite the culture of class and politics; unfortunately, their analyses remained beholden to ideal types, flattened out the necessarily dialectical process whereby these diverse types emerged, and said almost nothing about party politics.[30] Eric Foner's influential study of free labor ideology and politics in the North and West had been helpful in explaining some features of class, popular consciousness, and politics, and was a key work in restoring a more expansive concept of ideology—but Foner likewise slighted social process and conflict within the free states, ignored over one million northerners and westerners of the Old Democracy who saw things differently from Lincoln, Chase, Seward, & Co., and thus left little way of understanding how, in social terms, the free labor vision acquired political dominance outside the South.[31] David Montgomery's *Beyond Equality* was more help—but Montgomery (like Foner) had written about an age when politics truly were inflamed by moral passion, when the party system described by McCormick had broken down and was being reassembled along new lines.[32] On the South (too often excluded, at least since the 1940s, from "Jacksonian America") we had only begun to learn about the connections between politics and society.[33] And on the West, we still knew very little about changing social relations and perceptions.

It is not without irony, then, that some social historians, and some of the political historians they have influenced, are now returning with fresh eyes to the work of McCormick, Benson, and through them back to Hofstadter. Not that they are abandoning their concepts of class and culture and their criticisms about behavioralism—far from it. They are taking the revisionists' important insights—about the liberalism of party leaders, about the structure of party elites, and about the influence of religious impulses in the North— and placing them in a different frame of reference. More to the point, they are returning to the counter-Progressives' original problem: to explain the triumph of liberal democratic party politics just as the United States entered a revolution in market and class relations. Seen in this way, politics, and the social process whereby the legitimacy of a liberal party system was established and maintained *despite* the upheavals of class formation, becomes a central question for social historians interested in class and political power. With this social history of politics still in its infancy, any attempt at a new, overall synthesis on these matters would be premature. Enough has appeared, however, to offer some hypotheses and some fresh lines of inquiry—and to suggest the possible outlines of a new interpretation.

We may begin with the rich and important recent literature on political ideology, popular consciousness, and class. "Republicanism" has become the key concept here, but because it threatens to become a reified code word, it is important to be precise about its definition and significance. For Hofstadter and Benson (and nearly everyone else since World War II), American formal and informal political thought from at least the 1820s on was quintessentially liberal—materialistic, individualist, acquisitive, capitalist, post-Lockean, "middle class," liberal.[34] Recently, historians have come to see the nineteenth-century political universe rather differently. Jacksonian American individualism no longer seems to have been so closely bound up with a supposedly universal, Tocquevillean pursuit of self-interest; as Yehoshua Arieli suggested in 1964, Tocqueville and his later admirers had too readily construed American political libertarianism as a kind of American bourgeois egotism.[35] Even more, it now seems that early nineteenth-century politicians and party spokesmen thought primarily not in straightforward liberal terms but in classical republican terms leavened by egalitarian notions of natural political rights—of a polity of independent virtuous citizens, working to build and maintain a commonwealth of political equality.[36] Historians had been premature to claim that classical politics died in 1787.[37] Despite the Constitution, despite James Madison and Federalist #10, Americans continued to think (and, presumably, to act) in accordance with eighteenth-century republican ideals, ideals that stressed the primacy of politics in dictating social relations, ideals rooted in a social world of patriarchal, petty production and early commercial capitalism.[38]

What are we to make of this discovery? Classical republicanism was certainly not *necessarily* liberal or acquisitive; indeed, it contained, in its tension between virtue and commerce, between capitalist expansion and commonwealth, a tension that bordered on contradiction, one that led J. G. A. Pocock at one time to describe republicanism as "premodern" and "anticapitalist."[39] Does this mean that America's republican politicians of the early nineteenth century were not also liberals or becoming liberals—that American republicanism was so narrow and fixed a conception of politics and society that it could not be made to accommodate or fit liberal-capitalist principles? Of course not. If anything, the recent literature argues that politicians and lawmakers of all persuasions (including southern politicians, although in a manner that also accommodated plantation paternalism and Negro slavery) were becoming increasingly enamored of liberal concepts of property, the market, and (in the North) wage labor—although the timing, nature, and extent of these adaptations remains in dispute.[40] But does this in turn mean, as Hofstadter and the ethnoculturalists' work implies, that *all* Americans were liberal republicans, or liberal republicans in the Jeffersonian/Federalist, Jacksonian/Whig mold? Given all that we now know about class formation and popular ideology, clearly not. In any number of ways, capitalist social transformations led those who benefited least from—and those who were injured by—these transformations to interpret equality and the republican ideal to mean something very different from what liberal capitalist politicians had in mind. One finds these alternative definitions throughout the country, North and South, from as early as the 1790s through the 1850s, in rural conflicts, in the declarations of the first class-conscious trade unions, even (one historian discovers) in the views of southern slaves.[41]

What we have learned is this: Americans of all backgrounds (with the obvious exception of the American Indians) framed their political and social discourse in eighteenth-century republican terms. Between the Revolution and 1850 changing class and social relations led to recurring reinterpretations of republicanism and battles over what the republican legacy meant. During that period, some groups of Americans—preeminently, so far as we know, the nation's leading politicians and jurists but certainly many more—came increasingly to interpret the republican framework as one or another form of liberal capitalist polity and economy. They did not reject republicanism in favor of liberalism; they associated one with the other. Others—threatened or displaced small producers, laborers, journeymen in rapidly changing skilled trades—associated the revolution in market and class relations (and emerging liberal definitions of republicanism) with the decline of their own independence and "self-government," and therefore with the Republic's demise.

How, then, were these ideological developments and conflicts related to the reputedly intellectually inert politics of the 1830s and 1840s? Here we may turn to the literature on parties since McCormick. McCormick's depiction of party professionalism was certainly correct. Yet as Michael Wallace and (eventually) Hofstadter himself pointed out—and as Harry L. Watson has more recently demonstrated in his exemplary study of North Carolina—the creation of this antiideological party system was an act of profound social and ideological importance.[42] The leading proto-Jacksonians (above all those political pioneers, Martin Van Buren and the Albany Regency) held to all the familiar civic humanist rhetoric, but they also shattered resurgent eighteenth-century Commonwealth ideas on consensus and fear of faction and created a genuinely liberal party politics, a system based on competition for office by disciplined organizations of professional leaders and a loyal partisan rank-and-file. With this vision of politics and attacks on the "aristocratic," "privileged," "family" politics of their Adamsite opponents, the Jacksonians eventually consolidated power in vital states, elected their man to the presidency, and laid the foundations for a national Democratic party. Their adversaries, especially in the North, were horrified; they flailed away at the new system until (nudged by political entrepreneurs like Thurlow Weed), they learned the new party tactics and created the Whig party. Although a considerable number of Whig partisans remained unreconciled to the new system, their party gradually began to operate as a mirror image of the Jackson Democracy.

Put squarely, Jacksonian politics did not in themselves reflect either an all-pervasive, "middle class" liberalism or a challenge to capitalist values. Rather, the Jacksonian party system marked the advent of a specific conception of republican politics, one that combined republican rhetoric with a post-Madisonian liberalism, a politics in which republican virtue became what *The American Review* would call the virtues of merchants. In social terms, there is strong evidence that this political revolution brought a kind of *embourgeoisement* of party leadership in varying degrees in different parts of the country. Both the parties and local offices remained in the hands of the wealthy (as Benson and, in a different vein, Pessen had said) but both seem to have included far more men of recent wealth and standing, paragons of the Tocquevillean American.[43] In ideological terms, the new party professionals, although they proclaimed they followed principles and not men, in fact stood for the orderly pursuit of office, in which loyalty, merit, talent, and hard work for the party—not honor, reputation, and family connections, and certainly not the pursuit of larger ideological goals—brought preferment and power. As that conception of politics took hold in most of the nation, America's politicians and their closest allies either destroyed or dramatically transformed what remained of old-fashioned dynastic or "courthouse" parties, tried to cauterize political affairs from disturbing issues and ideas, and validated an ethos that might be described as the American republican equivalent of the European bourgeois liberalism of the 1830s and 1840s. Or, put simply, they took a critical step in the making of the American capitalist middle class.

But if liberal republicanism and middle class capitalist ideals were validated (and, in part, forged) in the creation of a professional party system, how did anything contrary to liberal republicanism play any role at all in politics? Here, we must remember that although the parties shared liberal values, they differed sharply about how to implement those values—differences that turned on related questions of party interest, political economy, and republican political morality. Had American political participation been wholly restricted to men of property, these differences might have been debated by legislators, with plenty of infighting among local notables and entrepreneurs and, in some areas no doubt, more than a few mobs. But by 1840, the states (with some important exceptions) had severed most of the important connections between property and citizenship; indeed, in certain key, well-studied states like New York, early battles between proto-Jacksonians and their opponents had brought about an expansion of the suffrage very much *against* the original designs of both emerging political groups. With the new professional party system falling into place in such a democratic setting, politicians had to be good, even enthusiastic democrats.[44]

It was in the manner that the parties and politicians approached the voters, at different times and in different areas of the country, that ideology, republicanism, class, and culture assumed such preeminent roles in politics. The timing here was obviously crucial: the quarter century in which the second party system emerged and flourished, roughly 1825–1850, also saw a rapid acceleration of American capitalist development and class formation.[45] In the process of defining their differences, liberal republican politicians, Democrat and Whig, laid the basis for political controversy, over banking, tariffs, moral reform, territorial expansion, and a host of local and regional issues. However, in translating these differences into party institutions, platforms, and rhetoric, the party leaders had to win the support of men who shared their entrepreneurial assumptions and those whom the social historians have shown did not. The rules of the American political system, as revised in 1787–88, eased some of the burden, by establishing important seats of power away from the most direct forms of popular control, and by allowing later politicians to make what McCormick has called the "presidential game" the central focus of popular participation in national affairs.[46] Beyond playing by the rules, meanwhile, politicians in both parties enlarged their institutional base and reached out for support and loyalty by turning local government into a fountain of patronage and by creating an ever-proliferating number of minor party posts and voluntary associations. Through these methods, and judicious reform, the parties deflected and coopted new social conflicts as they arose, keeping politics safe for the politicians and expanding their followings. Above all, the parties sealed their political identities by making their appeals not in liberal terms but with broader egalitarian republican language stressing the traditional republican assumption that social disorder stemmed from political corruption.

The first great example of this mass republican politicking was certainly Jackson's bank veto message, a document which, as Marvin Meyers noted, was clearly addressed to "a society divided into classes invidiously and profoundly antagonistic."[47] Jackson's genius lay in his language: by describing the Bank War in the broadest way as a struggle of virtuous farmers and mechanics against corrupt financier aristocrats, he provided a common ground on which entrepreneurs (seeking more banks or an end to legislative control over banking) could unite with wage-earners and small producers who sought to abolish banks or to remove bank control over the currency. Thereafter, Democrats and their opponents refined their republican appeals—to fight "purse-proud aristocrats" or "executive usurpers"—in ways that promoted their own political interests and liberal ideals but also yoked together, at least on election day, the support of a wide range of voters, across the lines of wealth and occupation.

The exact nature of these appeals varied at different times and in different places, stressing economic questions, "social" questions, and (at times) political personality. Through the thicket of popular politics, however, a general pattern can be discerned: while both Whigs and Democrats were liberal parties led by different members of new and existing elites, the Whigs *tended* to draw their *popular* support chiefly from men who believed that they (and the Republic) benefited from the ongoing transformations of American market and class relations. The Democrats *tended* to appeal to those who did not.[48]

How, then, can we move from hypothesis to writing a new social history of Jacksonian politics? Obviously, the economic and social history of the market revolution needs to be written in full, building on the still unsurpassed work of George Rogers Taylor and Paul Gates, but with an even greater emphasis on changing social relations and popular ideology.[49] While that project is being completed, a great deal can be learned about the character of the Jacksonian political system. How were the ideological tensions between republicanism and the market revolution handled by politicians and their allies at different times in all areas of the country? Given the recent work of Fred Siegel, J. Mills Thornton, and James Oakes, what was the character of southern political and economic liberalism in a slave society, in comparison with northern liberalism in a racist, free-labor society?[50] What *was* the political culture of the frontier—a question that despite Henry Nash Smith and Merle Curti has led as much to bald assertions about a universal "grasping materialism" as to informed investigations?[51] How did the parties turn popular perceptions to their own uses? How much did they reshape people's perceptions? What were the parties' popular institutions?[52] Who joined them, and how did they operate? What were the ideological and social issues at stake during the expansion of the suffrage in the first third of the century? How was policy—and the political economy of the emerging American state—related to class formation and party formation (a matter to take us back to the work of Louis Hartz and the Handlins)?[53] Did the sexual and family rearrangements so central to the rise of middle class evangelicalism in the North have any further impact on men's approach to politics—and if so, how? How common was "antipartyism" outside of politics and the Whig party? Who held such beliefs, and how were they expressed? Finally—the ultimate problem for Jacksonian historians—what were the social, ideological and political contradictions in the second party system, and especially in the Whig party, that led to the system's demise, and how did these contradictions arise?

Beyond raising these questions, meanwhile, we can also finally reorient the way we think about the place of the so-called Age of Jackson in American history. For too long, historians have seen the second quarter of the nineteenth century as a discrete epoch, with its own set of political and social institutions sealed off from what came before and from what followed. Instead, given the republican discourse of early nineteenth-century politics, given the social processes underway, it would make more sense to consider the era as a phase in the American experience of what Eric Hobsbawm has called the Age of Revolution, an age which began (to amend Hobsbawm slightly) with the democratic republican revolution of 1776, developed amidst the contradictions between the political legacy of the Revolution and the social consequences of the market revolution, and ended in the political chaos of 1848–1854.[54] Viewing the period this way, we may finally begin to bridge the distance between social and political history. And we may also begin to comprehend, as even Hofstadter did not, the supreme pathos of the triumphant American political tradition.

I would like to express my thanks to the members of the Davis Center seminar on political power and ideology and to the participants at the Symposium on Society and the Republic, Milan, Italy, June, 1982, sponsored by the Milan Group on Early United States History, for their demanding criticisms of an early draft of this article and for their supportive suggestions about revisions.

1. Richard Hofstadter, *The American Political Tradition and the Men Who Made It* (New York: Knopf, 1948), pp. 44–66. For a full bibliography on the Jackson controversy through the late 1960s, see Edward Pessen, *Jacksonian America: Society, Personality, and Politics* (Homewood, Ill.: Dorsey Press, 1969), pp. 384–93.

2. Lee Benson, *The Concept of Jacksonian Democracy: New York As a Test Case* (Princeton, N.J.: Princeton University Press, 1961), pp. 64–109, 123–207, 216–53, et passim.

3. See, for example, Daniel Walker Howe, *The Political Culture of the American Whigs* (Chicago: University of Chicago Press, 1979), which again confronts the problem of the Whigs' "morality" and party image, albeit very differently.

4. Richard P. McCormick, *The Second American Party System: Party Formation in the Jacksonian Era* (Chapel Hill: University of North Carolina Press, 1966).

5. Alexandra McCoy, "Political Affiliations of American Economic Elites: Wayne County, Michigan, 1844, 1860, As a Test Case" (Ph.D. diss., Wayne State University, 1965); Ronald P. Formisano, *The Birth of Mass Political Parties: Michigan, 1827–1861* (Princeton, N.J.: Princeton University Press, 1971); William G. Shade, *Banks Or No Banks: The Money Issue In Western Politics, 1832–1865* (Detroit: Wayne State University Press, 1972); William A. Gudelunas, Jr., and William G. Shade, *Before the Molly Maguires: The Emergence of the Ethno-Religious Factor in the Politics of the Lower Anthracite Region, 1844–1872* (New York: Amo Press, 1976). See also Michael F. Holt, *Forging A Majority: The Formation of the*

Republican Party, 1848–1860 (New Haven, Conn.: Yale University Press, 1969); Joel H. Silbey, *The Transformation of American Politics, 1840–1860* (Englewood Cliffs, N.J.: Prentice-Hall, 1967).

6. For a useful compilation and bibliography of this literature, see Joel H. Silbey and Samuel T. McSeveney, eds., *Voters, Parties, and Elections* (Lexington, Mass.: D. C. Heath, 1972). For a more detailed discussion and a discriminating critique, see Richard L. McCormick, "Ethno-Cultural Interpretations of Nineteenth-Century American Voting Behavior," *Political Science Quarterly* 89 (1974): 351–77.

7. Hofstadter, *American Political Tradition*, p. xxxix.

8. Frank Otto Gatell, "Money and Party in Jacksonian America: A Quantitative Look At New York's Men of Quality," *Political Science Quarterly* 82 (1967): 235–52; Edward Pessen, *Most Uncommon Jacksonians: Radical Leaders of the Early Labor Movement* (Albany, N.Y.: State University of New York Press, 1967).

9. Richard H. Brown, "The Missouri Crisis, Slavery, and the Politics of Jacksonianism," *South Atlantic Quarterly* 65 (1966): 55–72; John McFaul, "Expediency vs. Morality: Jacksonian Politics and Slavery," *Journal of American History* 62 (1975): 24–39.

10. Michael A. Lebowitz, "The Significance of Claptrap in American History," *Studies on the Left* 3 (1963), and "The Jacksonians: Paradox Lost?" in *Towards a New Past: Dissenting Essays in American History*, ed. Barton Bernstein (New York: Pantheon Books, 1968), pp. 65–89.

11. McCormick, "Ethno-Cultural Interpretations."

12. See, for example, Carl Degler, "Remaking American History," *Journal of American History* 67 (1980): 18.

13. Samuel P. Hays, "History As Human Behavior," *Iowa Journal of History* 58 (1960): 196.

14. Formisano, *Birth of Mass Political Parties*, p. 12; Philip E. Converse, "The Nature of Belief Systems in Mass Politics," in *Ideology and Discontent*, ed. David E. Apter (New York: Free Press, 1964), p. 245. Cf., Eric Foner, *Free Soil, Free Labor, Free Men: The Ideology of the Republican Party Before the Civil War* (New York: Oxford University Press, 1970), pp. 6–7.

15. In addition to the essays by Lebowitz in n. 10, see James R. Green, "Behavioralism and Class Analysis: A Methodological and Ideological Critique," *Labor History* 13 (1972): 89–106; James E. Wright, "The Ethno-Cultural Model of Voting: A Behavioral and Historical Critique," *American Behavioral Scientist* 16 (1973): 653–74; Richard P. Latner and Peter Levine, "Perspectives On Antebellum Pietistic Politics," *Reviews in American History* 4 (1976): 15–24; Michael Merrill, "Class and Polity: A Critique of the Ethno-Cultural Synthesis in American Political History," unpublished essay (1976). See also David Montgomery, "The New Urban History," *Reviews in American History* 2 (1974): 498–504; James A. Henretta, "The Study of Social Mobility: Ideological Assumptions and Conceptual Bias," *Labor History* 18 (1977): 165–78.

16. Lebowitz, "The Jacksonians," pp. 73–4, 86–7; Latner and Levine, "Pietistic Politics," pp. 19–23; Merrill, "Class and Polity," pp. 14–18. On the use of poll books, see Paul L. Bourke and Donald A. De Bats, "Identifiable Voting in Nineteenth-Century America: Toward a Comparison of Britain and the United States Before the Secret Ballot," *Perspectives in American History* 11 (1977–78): 257–88; and Formisano, *Birth of Mass Political Parties*, pp. 297–98, 318–23.

17. Eric Foner, *Politics and Ideology in the Age of the Civil War* (New York: Oxford University Press, 1980), pp. 17–19.

18. For a restatement of the revisionist equation of class analysis and economic determinism, see Ronald P. Formisano, "Toward a Reorientation of Jacksonian Politics: A Review of the Literature, 1959–1975," *Journal of American History* 63 (1976): 42–65.

19. The oft-misunderstood influence of E. P. Thompson and Herbert Gutman was here profound.

20. Christopher Clark, "The Household Economy, Market Exchange, and the Rise of Capitalism in the Connecticut Valley, 1800–1860," *Journal of Social History* 13 (1979): 169–90; Nancy Cott, *The Bonds of Womanhood: "Women's Sphere" in New England, 1780–1830* (New

Haven, Conn.: Yale University Press, 1975); David Brion Davis, *The Problem of Slavery in the Age of Revolution, 1770-1823* (Ithaca, N.Y.: Cornell University Press, 1975); Alan Dawley, *Class and Community: The Industrial Revolution in Lynn* (Cambridge, Mass.: Harvard University Press, 1976); Thomas Dublin, *Women At Work: The Transformation of Work and Community in Lowell, Massachusetts 1826-1869* (New York, 1979); Eugene Genovese, *Roll, Jordan, Roll: The World the Slaves Made* (New York: Pantheon Books, 1974); Herbert G. Gutman, *Work, Culture, and Society in Industrializing America* (New York: Knopf, 1975); Steven H. Hahn, "The Roots of Southern Populism: Yeoman Farmers and the Transformation of Georgia's Upper Piedmont, 1850-1890" (Ph.D. diss., Yale University, 1979); Morton Horwitz, *The Transformation of American Law, 1780-1860* (Cambridge, Mass.: Harvard University Press, 1977); Paul E. Johnson, *A Shopkeeper's Millennium: Society and Revivals in Rochester, New York, 1815-1837* (New York: Hill and Wang, 1978); Bruce Laurie, *Working People of Philadelphia, 1800-1850* (Philadelphia, Temple University Press, 1980); Carroll Smith-Rosenberg, "Beauty, the Beast, and the Militant Woman: A Case Study in Sex Roles and Social Stress in Jacksonian America," *American Quarterly* 23 (1971): 562-584.

21. Gutman, *Work, Culture and Society*; Johnson, *Shopkeeper's Millennium*; Mary P. Ryan, *Cradle of the Middle Class: The Family in Oneida County, New York, 1790-1865* (New York: Cambridge University Press, 1981).

22. Michael P. Rogin, *Fathers and Children: Andrew Jackson and the Subjugation of the American Indian* (New York: Knopf, 1975).

23. Among the exceptions were some noteworthy "traditional" works: Robert V. Remini, *Andrew Jackson and the Course of American Empire, 1767-1823* (New York: Harper and Row, 1977); Richard B. Latner, *The Presidency of Andrew Jackson: White House Politics, 1829-1837* (Athens, Ga.: University of Georgia Press, 1979).

24. Elizabeth Fox-Genovese and Eugene Genovese, "The Political Crisis of Social History: A Marxian Perspective," *Journal of Social History* 10 (1976): 205-20; Tony Judt, "A Clown in Regal Purple: Social History and the Historians," *History Workshop Journal* 7 (1979): 66-94.

25. Fred Siegel, "The Paternalist Thesis: Virginia As a Test Case," *Civil War History* 25 (1979): 246-61.

26. Ellen DuBois, "Politics and Culture in Women's History," *Feminist Studies* 6 (1980): 28-36. See also DuBois, *Feminism and Suffrage: The Emergence of an Independent Women's Movement in America* (Ithaca, N.Y.: Cornell University Press, 1978).

27. Carroll Smith-Rosenberg, "Politics and Culture in Women's History," *Feminist Studies* 6 (1980): 55-64.

28. Richard D. Brown, *Modernization: The Transformation of American Life, 1600-1865* (New York: Hill and Wang, 1976). More recent works influenced by modernization theory include Howe, *Political Culture of the American Whigs*; and, more decisively, James M. McPherson, *Ordeal By Fire: The Civil War and Reconstruction* (New York: Knopf, 1981). On the theory's shortcomings, see Dean C. Tipps, "Modernization Theory and the Comparative Study of Societies: A Critical Perspective," *Comparative Studies in Society and History* 15 (1967): 199-226.

29. Edward Pessen, *Riches, Class, and Power Before the Civil War* (Lexington, Mass.: D. C. Heath, 1973).

30. Alan Dawley and Paul Faler, "Working-Class Culture and Politics in the Industrial Revolution: Sources of Loyalism and Rebellion," *Journal of Social History* 9 (1976): 466-80.

31. Foner, *Free Soil, Free Labor, Free Men*.

32. David Montgomery, *Beyond Equality: Labor and the Radical Republicans, 1862-1872* (New York: Knopf, 1967).

33. Through the late 1970s, the most important works on society and politics in the South included Charles Grier Sellers, "Who Were the Southern Whigs?" *American Historical Review* 59 (1954): 335-46; William W. Freehling, *Prelude to Crisis: The Nullification Crisis in South Carolina, 1816-1836* (New York: Harper and Row, 1965); Lynn L. Marshall, "The Genesis of Grassroots Democracy in Kentucky," *Mid-America* 47 (1965): 269-87; McCormick, *Second Party System*; James R. Sharp, *The Jacksonians versus the Banks: Politics in the States After*

the Panic of 1837 (New York: Columbia University Press, 1970); Burton W. Folsom II, "Party Formation and Development in Jacksonian America: The Old South," Journal of American Studies 7 (1973): 217-29.

34. Hofstadter, American Political Tradition, p. xxxvii.

35. Yehoshua Arieli, Individualism and Nationalism in American Ideology (Cambridge, Mass.: Harvard University Press, 1964).

36. Linda K. Kerber, Federalists In Dissent: Ideology and Imagery in Jeffersonian America (Ithaca, N.Y.: Cornell University Press, 1970); Rush Welter, The Mind of America, 1830-1860 (New York, 1975), pp. 77-95; Lance Banning, The Jeffersonian Persuasion (Ithaca, N.Y., 1978); Robert L. Kelley, The Cultural Pattern in American Politics: The First Century (New York: Knopf, 1978)—although read with caution Kelley's interpretations of ethnicity and politics; Howe, The Political Culture of the American Whigs; Drew R. McCoy, The Elusive Republic: Political Economy in Jeffersonian America (Chapel Hill: University of North Carolina Press, 1980). For a synopsis, see Robert Shalhope, "Republicanism and Early American History," William and Mary Quarterly 3rd series, 39 (1982): 334-56.

37. Gordon Wood, The Creation of the American Republic, 1776-1787 (Chapel Hill: University of North Carolina Press, 1969), pp. 606-18.

38. Indeed, historians may have been too quick to see Madisonian "liberalism" and Federalist #10 as essentially pluralist. See Paul L. Bourke, "The Pluralist Reading of James Madison's Tenth Federalist," Perspectives in American History 9 (1975): 271-95.

39. J. G. A. Pocock, "Virtue and Commerce in the Eighteenth Century," Journal of Interdisciplinary History 3 (1972): 119-34, and The Machiavellian Moment: Florentine Political Thought and the Atlantic Republican Tradition (Princeton, N.J.: Princeton University Press, 1975), pp. 506-52.

40. See, for example, Joyce Appleby, "The Social Origins of American Revolutionary Ideology," Journal of American History 64 (1977): 935-58, and "What Is Still American in the Political Philosophy of Thomas Jefferson?," William and Mary Quarterly 3rd series, 38 (1982): 287-309; Siegel, "The Paternalist Thesis"; Horwitz, Transformation of American Law. For a dissenting view on the character and pervasiveness of liberalism in the North, see my Chants Democratic. New York City and the Rise of the American Working Class (New York: Oxford University Press, forthcoming). The great dissenter to the idea that liberalism took root throughout the United States is, of course, Eugene Genovese, The World the Slaveholders Made (New York: Pantheon Books, 1971), and Roll, Jordan, Roll.

41. David Szatmary, Shays' Rebellion: The Making of an Agrarian Insurrection (Amherst: University of Massachusetts Press, 1980); Clark, "Household Economy"; Hahn, "Roots of Southern Populism"; Dawley, Class and Community; Laurie, Working People; David Montgomery, "Labor and the Republic in Industrial America, 1860-1920," Le Mouvement Social 111 (1980): 201-15; Eugene Genovese, From Rebellion to Revolution: Afro-American Slave Revolts in the Making of the Modern World (Baton Rouge, La.: Louisiana State University Press, 1970).

42. Michael Wallace, "Changing Concepts of Party in the United States: New York, 1815-1828," American Historical Review 74 (1968): 453-91; Richard Hofstadter, The Idea of a Party System: The Rise of a Legitimate Opposition in the United States, 1780-1840 (Berkeley, Ca.: University of California Press, 1969); Harry L. Watson, Jacksonian Politics and Community Conflict: The Emergence of the Second Party System in Cumberland County, North Carolina (Chapel Hill: University of North Carolina Press, 1982).

43. For a summary, see Pessen, Jacksonian America, pp. 180-210.

44. See Watson, Jacksonian Politics, p. 151.

45. See George Rogers Taylor, The Transportation Revolution, 1815-1860 (New York: Holt, Rinehart, 1950). See also, on the pace of Northeastern industrialization, Thomas C. Cochran, Frontiers of Change: Early Industrialism in America (New York: Oxford University Press, 1981).

46. Richard P. McCormick, The Presidential Game: The Origins of American Presidential Politics (New York: Oxford University Press, 1982).

47. Marvin Meyers, *The Jacksonian Persuasion: Politics and Belief* (Stanford: Stanford University Press, 1957), p. 18.

48. A similar formulation—though elaborated in different terms—appears in Lynn Marshall, "The Strange Stillbirth of the Whig Party," *American Historical Review* 72 (1967): 445–68.

49. Taylor, *Transportation Revolution;* Paul W. Gates, *The Farmer's Age: Agriculture, 1815–1860* (New York: Holt, Rinehart, 1960).

50. Siegel, "Paternalist Thesis" and "The Virginia Ideology," *Reviews in American History* 7 (1979): 344–49; J. Mills Thornton III, *Politics and Power in a Slave Society: Alabama, 1800–1860* (Baton Rouge, La.: Louisiana State University Press, 1978); James Oakes, *The Ruling Race: A History of American Slaveholders* (New York: Knopf, 1982).

51. Henry Nash Smith, *Virgin Land: The American West As Symbol and Myth* (Cambridge, Mass.: Harvard University Press, 1950); Merle Curti, *The Making of an American Community* (Stanford: Stanford University Press, 1959).

52. A step toward answering these questions is taken by Anthony Boleslaw Gronowicz, "Revising the Concept of Jacksonian Democracy: A Comparison of New York City Democrats in 1844 and 1884" (Ph.D. diss., University of Pennsylvania, 1981). See also the important revision of Benson and others in Amy Bridges, *A City in the Republic: The Origins of Machine Politics in New York* (New York: Cambridge University Press, forthcoming).

53. Oscar and Mary Flug Handlin, *Commonwealth: A Study of the Role of Government in the American Economy: Massachusetts 1774–1861* (New York: New York University Press, 1947); Louis Hartz, *Economic Policy and Democratic Thought: Pennsylvania, 1776–1860* (Cambridge, Mass.: Harvard University Press, 1948).

54. Eric Hobsbawm, *The Age of Revolution, 1789–1848* (New York, 1964).

COMPARING AMERICAN HISTORY

Peter Kolchin

Comparative history is now in vogue. It provided the central theme for the 1978 annual convention of the American Historical Association, and for the October and December 1980 issues of the *American Historical Review*. Volumes surveying the state of the historical profession, such as Michael Kammen's recently published collection, *The Past Before Us*, regularly include a selection on comparative history. Specialists in both traditional and new fields of history routinely issue calls for new comparative efforts, while bemoaning their relative paucity to date. Indeed, as John Higham has noted, although actual comparative studies "are still sparse and scattered . . . a comparative consciousness has spread far and wide among historians in recent years."[1]

Whether everyone is actually doing comparative history or merely talking about it depends upon the meaning of the term, which is not, despite appearances, self-defining. Indeed, both practitioners and supporters of the discipline have widely differing conceptions of what it is, can be, and should be. In this essay I do not seek to produce a recipe for the "correct" practice of comparative history, much less to provide a comprehensive survey of the field. Rather, I intend to examine the practice and problems of comparing American history, using selected examples of studies on the frontier and slavery, two subjects that have attracted considerable comparative attention.

There are three broadly overlapping purposes or functions of comparative history. First and most basic, comparison can create an awareness of alternatives, showing developments to be significant that without a comparative perspective might not appear so. It is only in light of the failure of most other new world slave populations to reproduce themselves, for example, that the rapid natural growth of the American slave population—which approximately tripled during the half-century after the end of African imports in 1808—becomes significant. The historical insight here comes, at least initially, not from systematic comparison itself so much as from a comparative awareness leading to the posing of new questions.

The other two functions of comparison, which require more rigorous comparative analysis, involve the formulation and testing of hypotheses. In the first of these, scholars seek to explain historical differences or peculiarities, weighing and eventually isolating variables responsible for particular conditions. Comparison here serves as a primitive form of historical "experimentation," permitting the investigator to test the relative impact of various social, economic, demographic, political, or intellectual factors. In the second, historians seek to recognize common patterns and make historical generalizations; indeed, it is only through comparison that such generalizations can be made. Although it is sometimes suggested that there is a wide gulf separating these two kinds of comparison—that humanistically-oriented scholars will seek to describe and explain differences while scientifically-minded ones will aim to formulate generalizations—in fact, they are functionally the same: through comparison the historian can weigh the impact of different variables, distinguish the specific or incidental from the general or inherent, and test historical hypotheses.[2]

In this sense, the comparative historian does overtly what other historians do too, for virtually all historical statements are implicitly comparative. When we describe economic conditions as depressed, we mean in comparison to normal times; when we call the United States a "great power," we mean compared to most other countries in the world; when we say the American population is growing very slowly, we mean either in comparison to earlier or in comparison to elsewhere. Because most historical judgments are implicitly comparative, what we term comparative history constitutes the effort to do explicitly, rigorously, and thoroughly what most historians do most of the time. As Raymond Grew has argued, "[t]he question is not so much whether historians should make comparisons but whether the study of history benefits when those comparisons are made consciously and sometimes even systematically."[3]

An examination of efforts to deal in comparative fashion with the American frontier reveals some of the opportunities and difficulties inherent in explicit comparison. The impetus for most of these efforts was the controversial "frontier thesis" first propounded by Frederick Jackson Turner in 1893. Turner's hypothesis that "the existence of an area of free land, its continuous recession, and the advance of American settlement westward, explain American development"—in short, that the frontier was largely responsible for a number of unique American characteristics—was in itself an implicitly comparative judgment, as is any assertion of uniqueness. Indeed, it entailed a dual comparison: the frontier created a unique America, but within the United States the frontier also differentiated the relatively unpopulated West from the settled East. "The West, at bottom, is a form of society, rather than an area," Turner wrote; "[t]his 'West,' wherever found at different years, thought of itself and of the nation in different ways from those of the East."[4]

It is the first of these two comparisons—the United States with other countries—that has most intrigued historians. A number of countries other than the United States have had major frontier experiences, and scholars have been quick to see in their comparison with the American frontier a test of the Turner thesis. If the frontier created certain characteristics in the United States, its existence elsewhere presumably should have produced the same characteristics. "The principal failing of Turner, his followers, and most of his critics has been a neglect of comparative research," noted one scholar in 1960.[5] While admonitions to compare have been more numerous than actual comparisons, the 1950s and 1960s saw the publication of a number of works designed to test the Turner thesis by comparing the impact of the American frontier with that of Canadian, Australian, South African, Russian, and ancient Roman frontiers.

The results and conclusions of these efforts have been mixed. Several scholars have argued that other frontiers failed to have the same impact as America's frontier, either because they were basically different from the American frontier or because other factors impeded the development of individualism and democracy. Thus, Ray Allen Billington, probably Turner's most ardent modern defender, insisted that the American frontier experience was "virtually unique"; although other countries have had frontiers, "in no one of them was the physical environment conducive to exploitation by relatively propertyless individuals *and* the invading pioneers equipped by tradition to capitalize fully on that environment." A. L. Burt agreed that it was the particular character of the American frontier that was significant: "Nature made the heart of North America the largest and richest and solidest agricultural region in the world, but it made the heart of Australia a desert." Seymour Martin Lipset argued, by contrast, that the failure of other frontiers to replicate American character traits establishes "the role of core values in influencing the institutional structure of a nation . . . [and] suggest[s] that the egalitarian character of the American frontier was in some part determined by the values derived from the revolutionary political origins and the Calvinist work ethic."[6] The implication of these works was that the Turner thesis needed serious modification: it was not the frontier experience itself, but either the peculiar nature of the American frontier or the frontier in conjunction with a particular set of inherited cultural values that created the traits Turner attributed to the frontier.

Other historians, however, found evidence to support the Turner thesis. In the only major book comparing the impact of the frontier in America with that in another country, H. C. Allen concluded that "[t]he effects of the frontier in Australia are certainly such as to justify amply the essential Turner doctrine, the vital modifying effect of the open frontier." Like the American

frontier, the Australian promoted democracy, idealism, the rugged pioneering spirit, and national consolidation along lines strikingly different from
those of the British. True, there were some differences. The greater class consciousness and collectivism in Australia resulted from the relative harshness
of the frontier there, and confirmed Turner's opinion that it was "the
availability of *fertile* [my italics] free land on the American frontier which
made the difference." Still, Allen concluded, comparison of Australia with
the United States supported the essence of the Turner thesis.[7] Other
historians have seen at least some confirmation of Turner's ideas in the Canadian, Russian, and ancient Roman frontiers.[8]

Two major reasons, aside from the general contentiousness of historians,
suggest themselves for the continuing lack of consensus. With the exception
of Allen's book, virtually all of the frontier studies have been brief, suggestive
articles based on secondary sources, rather than detailed, systematic comparisons; their conclusions often seem to flow from their authors' predilections as much as from the evidence. Equally important is the vagueness of
Turner's thesis. Concepts such as "national character," "democracy," "individualism," and "frontier" itself are subject to numerous conflicting definitions, and Turner's critics have delighted in deploring his lack of precision.
Indeed, some historians have come to despair of any progress resulting from
comparative study of the Turner thesis. "Turner did not write a theory
capable of testing," declared John C. Hudson recently; "I see little to be
gained from making 'Turner-testing' the principal thrust of comparative frontier research."[9]

As a result, after flourishing briefly, comparative efforts to verify the
Turner thesis have languished during the past decade. Recent forays at international comparison of frontiers have tended to search for a new focus to
replace the Turner thesis. In the introduction to their just-published collection
of essays on the frontier in the United States and South Africa, for example,
Howard Lamar and Leonard Thompson view the frontier "not as a boundary
or line, but as a territory or zone of interpenetration between two previously
distinct societies. Usually, one of the societies is indigenous to the
region . . . : the other is intrusive."[10] There is much to be said for such an
approach: it enables historians to escape from the confines of Turner's definitions, eliminate the ethnocentrism implicit in his view of the frontier as a
line separating civilization from "free land," and turn to examine comparatively ethnic relations between indigenous and invading peoples. It also
risks eliminating, however, the unifying theme that one historian called "the
only theoretical basis for the whole endeavor."[11] Put most simply, without
the Turner thesis it is not always clear to what purpose frontiers are being
compared.

While such discouragement with "Turner-testing" is understandable, it appears excessive. First of all, the effort made to date has not been substantial enough to warrant judging it a failure. Not only does most of the existing work consist of suggestive articles rather than thorough studies, but many of these articles focus on one country in comparative perspective rather than being truly comparative. There have, for example, been two comparative collections of frontier studies published during the past five years; in the first collection, only three essays focus on two or more countries, while in the second, only the two introductory essays do, with the remaining essays "paired" between the United States and South Africa to allow the reader to draw his own comparative conclusions.[12] Second, the Turner thesis *does* yield a number of hypotheses that include the frontier's promotion of democracy, individualism, and a more homogeneous (in the case of the United States "American") population, as well as the overriding influence on society of the environment. Surely, that the frontier exerted some of the same influences in societies as different as tsarist Russia and nineteenth-century America suggests the fruitfulness of continued comparative investigation of the frontier's impact.[13]

A second approach to the subject, one implicit in Turner's assertion of the West's distinctiveness, has involved comparing frontier with nonfrontier areas within the United States. Although this kind of comparison has been less common, it is appealing because it permits one to study the frontier's impact on a people with a common history, thus eliminating the need to consider the influence of contrasting cultural "baggage" carried by peoples in different countries. An especially fruitful field for research, because of its high measurability, is the frontier's demographic impact. In a recent book, James E. Davis found relatively slight demographic differences between frontier and settled areas of early nineteenth-century America. Household size and structure were strikingly similar, although the frontier population was slightly younger and slightly more male than that of settled regions. (In frontier counties, 52 percent of the population was male, while in settled counties 50 percent was.) Davis's findings seemed to reinforce Julie Roy Jeffrey's conclusion that far from transforming women's roles or relationships with men, "the frontier experience served to reinforce many conventional familial and cultural ideals." In a more sophisticated demographic study, however, Richard A. Easterlin reached somewhat different conclusions. He divided 102 rural northern townships in 1860 into five categories, from old (most settled) to new (frontier), and found that as one went from old to new regions women married progressively earlier, continued childbearing longer, and consequently had more children—except in the newest, most frontier areas, where there was a significant reversal of these trends. He speculated that while "declining land availability in older areas created pressures for reduced fertility," in newer areas couples felt free to produce large families. (He ingeniously explained the apparently contradictory figures in the newest areas: "a disproportionately large number of those on the frontier built their families, not under frontier conditions, but in the more constraining environmental circumstances of their area of origin.")[14]

Thus, the verdict is still out on the Turner thesis, and is likely to remain so until we have the kind of systematic, detailed comparative works lacking so far. One further suggestion is in order: in their search for greater precision historians will probably have to distinguish among different frontiers within the same country. Although Turner and others spoke of "the frontier" as a single phenomenon, scholars are beginning to recognize that such a general concept can obscure as well as clarify. Daniel Blake Smith has pointed to "striking regional differences in mortality rates and population growth" between North and South in seventeenth-century America (virtually all of which was frontier), and James E. Davis saw the need to separate northern from southern frontier in his comparative volume. Jerome O. Steffen has recently made an equally interesting distinction between "insular frontiers" such as that of the early trans-Appalachian agricultural settlers, who kept relatively few links to the main body of American civilization, and the "cosmopolitan frontiers" experienced by fur traders, ranchers, and miners, who were much less isolated for prolonged periods of time from the parent culture. Not everyone will accept Steffen's suggestion that cosmopolitan frontiers experienced a "lack of fundamental economic, political, and social change," but the kind of distinction he makes among frontiers will surely be necessary as historians develop more sophisticated ways of comparing frontier experiences.[15]

Like comparative studies of the frontier, those of slavery and race relations have centered on the testing of a hypothesis, that of Frank Tannenbaum and Stanley Elkins concerning the contrast between Latin America and the United States. In a little book titled *Slave and Citizen* published in 1946, Tannenbaum put forth the thesis that the Iberian cultural tradition proved much more conducive than the English to accepting Negroes as human beings regardless of color. Tannenbaum suggested that slavery in Latin America, softened by "Spanish law, custom, and tradition" as well as by the Catholic Church, was more benign than in the United States, but his emphasis was on the ease of manumission and the ready social acceptance of former slaves in Latin America, in contrast to the racial exclusivity practiced by the English and their descendents. "If the Latin American environment was favorable to freedom," he wrote, "the British and American were hostile." This thesis drew support from Stanley Elkins's *Slavery*, first published in 1959. While Tannenbaum had stressed race relations, Elkins shifted his focus to the nature of the slave systems themselves, elaborating on his mentor's contention that North American slavery was a much harsher variant of the institution than South American. In Iberian America, Church and Crown intervened to ameliorate the worst features of slavery, protecting the sanctity of slave marriages and limiting the ability of masters to punish their slaves; in the United States, however, where "the dynamics of unopposed capitalism" reigned supreme, no institutions came between master and slave. The former's powers were unlimited and the latter's rights nonexistent; North American slavery, unlike Latin American, "operated as a 'closed' system" that stripped its victims of their very personalities and left them childlike Samboes.[16]

In the 1960s and early 1970s, a host of scholars sought to put the Tannenbaum-Elkins thesis to the test. Their work was in general based on far more substantive and detailed research than the largely speculative pieces on frontiers and produced more of a consensus as well. Perhaps this was in part because slavery is a less nebulous concept than the frontier, and hence is more easily subjected to comparative test, but it was also because historians of slavery consciously strove to bring precision to their comparative efforts. In an important essay published in 1969, Eugene D. Genovese pointed out that "treatment" of slaves encompassed three distinct subjects: the slaves' material conditions, their quality of life, and their access to freedom.[17] As research continued, it quickly became clear that the Tannenbaum-Elkins thesis actually consisted of two interrelated but separable hypotheses: one, emphasized by Tannenbaum, concerning race relations and access to freedom, and the other, stressed by Elkins, concerning the nature of slavery itself. While both of these have prompted considerable historical research, it has been Elkins's reformulation of the Tannenbaum thesis, with the notion of a harsh versus a lenient slavery, that most attracted historians' attention.

Although an early book by Herbert Klein comparing slavery in Cuba and Virginia seemed to provide evidence to support Elkins, comparative analysis has since produced a broad consensus refuting the notion of a mild Latin American and harsh North American slavery. If Spanish and Portuguese law ostensibly provided slaves with greater protection than English and American, nowhere was law automatically translated into fact, and actual slave treatment depended far more on concrete socioeconomic conditions than on legal or religious tradition. In general, for example, slaves were driven far more relentlessly during boom times than during periods of economic stagnation; had Klein examined nineteenth- instead of eighteenth-century Cuba he would have found a brutal, exploitative labor system that contrasted unfavorably with Virginian slavery, for under the impact of a major sugar boom the character of Cuban slavery was totally transformed during the half-century after 1763. In short, as David Brion Davis concluded, "differences between slavery in Latin America and the United States were no greater than regional or temporal differences within the countries themselves"; despite these differences, "Negro bondage was a single phenomenon whose variations were less significant than underlying patterns of unity." [18]

Other historians pushed the refutation of Elkins considerably further. In a major comparative study of slavery and race relations, Carl Degler argued that "the physical treatment of slaves in Brazil may well have been harsher than in the United States." The notion that in at least some respects American slavery was milder, not harsher, than Latin American received further support from Eugene D. Genovese, who contrasted the "seigneurial" slave system that prevailed in the United States and parts of Brazil with the "capitalistic" regime of the Caribbean; nowhere else, Genovese suggested, did slaveholders develop such a "patriarchal and paternalistic ethos" as in the antebellum South.[19] While not all historians accepted Genovese's concept of planter paternalism, widespread agreement has emerged that on a purely physical and material level the treatment of southern slaves improved markedly during the century prior to emancipation, and compared favorably with that of most Latin American slaves.

Comparison has thus revealed that slavery in the United States was indeed unique, although in a way very different from that postulated by Tannenbaum and Elkins. The causes seemed to be less those of national, religious, or cultural influences than of economics and demography, for slavery in the United States differed not only from that in Spanish, Portuguese, and French America, but also from that in the English colonies of the Caribbean. The most basic of all contrasts was a telling one: only in the United States did the slave population grow through natural reproduction; elsewhere its growth was dependent on continued imports from Africa. There were several contributing reasons for this contrast, the relative importance of which are still debated, but differences in material standards of living, disease systems, and sex ratios are clearly among the most important. All of these, however, tend to suggest a harsher slavery elsewhere than in the United States; where males outnumbered females by almost two to one, for example, as they did in Cuba in the early nineteenth century, normal family life was unattainable for many no matter what the law might stipulate.[20] Even when there was little difference in sex ratios, however, American slaves were unique in their rate of reproduction. Richard Dunn, comparing two large plantations, Mount Airy in Virginia and Mesopotamia in Jamaica, found that although the latter had a slightly higher proportion of females, its birth rate was less than half that of the former (18.39 per 1,000 vs. 39.83), while its mortality rate was substantially higher (35.49 vs. 20.64); as a result, Mount Airy had a net population increase of 1.9 percent per year over a two-decade period in the early nineteenth century, while Mesopotamia had a net decrease of 1.7 percent. Dunn suggested that differences in diet and female workload were primary causes of the contrast, but concluded that it was easier to document than to explain it.[21]

Other demographic differences contributed significantly to the contrasting treatment of slaves in the United States and other countries. American slaves constituted a smaller proportion of the population than those in the Caribbean, and generally lived with resident masters on far smaller holdings than those in Jamaica, St. Domingue, or much of Brazil, where absentee ownership was prevalent. In addition, the cutting off of the African slave trade encouraged American slaveowners to treat their slaves carefully if for none other than pecuniary reasons, while the continuation of African imports in Cuba and Brazil until mid-century helped preserve the notion that slave life was cheap.

Comparison has thus pointed to the need to distinguish sharply between the nature of slavery and the nature of race relations, for if scholars have demolished the notion that American slavery was uniquely harsh, they have rarely quarreled with Tannenbaum's observation that American race relations were unusually rigid. Not only was manumission more difficult and acceptance of freed slaves and their descendents into society more grudging than elsewhere, but Americans generally adopted a "two-color" system of categorizing people—one was either totally white or totally black, with the tiniest admixture of black "blood" making one black—rather than the three or multicolor system prevalent elsewhere. In short, a "mild" version of slavery did not necessarily produce a correspondingly "mild" version of race relations.

Here too, scholars have tended to find the key in economic and demographic—not national or cultural—variables. Carl Degler argued that "the most important reason for the large amount of miscegenation in Brazil was the shortage of Portuguese or white women," while in the United States, "[t]hanks to the rough balance between the sexes among whites, there was little demographic pressure for black-white matings." George Fredrickson made a very similar argument in his comparison of race relations in the United States and South Africa. Others, such as Marvin Harris, Harry Hoetink, and Laura Foner, have suggested that a three-tiered racial system emerged where small white populations, needing a buffer between themselves and their more numerous slaves, created a privileged group of free mulattoes to serve essential economic, social, or military functions, while America's two-tier system was the product of a large, secure white population, only a minority of whom were slaveowners.[22]

A smaller number of historians have been impressed with *similarities* of racial attitudes held by the dominant class across a broad range of slaveholding societies. In a fascinating recent article, William McKee Evans showed that the curse of Ham, used by the defenders of southern slavery to justify the enslavement of the black ("Hamitic") race, had previously been used elsewhere to legitimize the subjugation of numerous non-African peoples; he concluded that "patterns of both race relations and prejudice are determined by power relationships," not "pre-existing prejudices of whites." Similarly, I found that Russian defenders of serfdom used "racial" arguments close to those employed by American slaveowners, even though no somatic difference separated nobleman and serf. But these interpretations shared with the majority the underlying assumption that racial views and behavior were largely functions of socioeconomic rather than cultural or religious conditions.[23]

Indeed, perhaps the most striking trait common to the majority of comparative studies of slavery and race relations is their underlying materialism. Concrete material conditions, rather than cultural tradition, religion, law, or innate sentiment are seen as shaping the nature of both slavery and white racial attitudes. Nowhere is the triumph of this materialism more evident than in George M. Fredrickson's pathbreaking book *White Supremacy*, a work that impresses for its insights as well as its extension of the comparative focus. Like other recent historians Fredrickson—previously best known for his careful delineation and analysis of ideas—attributed the rigid American approach to race-mixing largely to the even sex ratio that prevailed among the seventeenth-century colonists; in South Africa, by contrast, early white settlers were mostly unmarried males "dependent on nonwhite women for sexual comradeship." Although I find myself in basic agreement with this approach, I wonder if recent scholars have not gone too far in playing down cultural and intellectual forces. One wonders, for example, why there was so little intermarriage between English settlers and Indian women in early seventeenth-century Virginia, where a great sexual imbalance existed, or why early Dutch settlers in South Africa shunned the indigenous Khoikoi, who appeared "so outlandish that there was some doubt at the beginning as to whether they were fully human."[24] Both of these attitudes seem to suggest the necessity of recognizing a greater role for the cultural baggage of the dominant group, as does the existence of important exceptions to the restrictive American racial ethic in southern Louisiana and coastal South Carolina—both regions settled by distinctive groups of Europeans.[25]

The Tannenbaum-Elkins thesis, like the Turner thesis, has had both a unifying and a limiting impact on the writing of comparative history. Because comparative historians of slavery concentrated so heavily on testing the validity of the Tannenbaum-Elkins thesis, they focused their attention almost exclusively on white racial ideology and treatment of slaves, all but ignoring the central topic explored in recent years by noncomparative historians of American slavery: the communal life and culture of the slaves themselves. Equally serious, the dismantling of the Tannenbaum-Elkins thesis removed what appeared to be the *raison d'etre* of examining slavery comparatively. It is no accident, then, that the flurry of comparative slavery studies peaked in the late 1960s and very early 1970s, and all but died down during the remainder of the 1970s.

During the past four years the comparative study of slavery appears for the first time to be breaking out of its previous boundaries. Two new thrusts are evident. One consists of attention to previously ignored subjects, such as slave resistance and emancipation. Equally significant is the widening of the comparative focus beyond the western hemisphere, to include South African and eastern European systems of forced labor. Although it is too early fully to evaluate these new trends, it seems as if comparative slavery may be entering upon a period of renaissance, building upon but freed from the restraints of earlier work in the field.[26]

What, then, can be said about the nature, problems, and prospects of comparative history? To begin with, one must confront the question of what comprises comparative history. In a recent essay, George Fredrickson argued that the term should be reserved for "a relatively small but significant body of scholarship that has *as its main objective* the systematic comparison of some process or institution in two or more societies that are not usually conjoined within one of the traditional geographical areas of historical specialization."[27] This definition contains two essential statements, one concerning the appropriate units of comparison, which he suggested must be between two separate countries (or at least "societies"), and the other concerning the desirability of systematic as opposed to casual comparison. The second of these statements contains more merit, I believe, than the first.

Although comparative history is often assumed to require comparison across national or societal boundaries, there is a valid basis for comparison of three basic types *within* given countries. The first of these is geographic, between or among regions or localities, as in the comparison of frontier and settled areas discussed above. Take, for example, the extensive work that has been done comparing the antebellum North and South. Questions such as the economic (or for that matter noneconomic) impact of slavery on southern society imply a sectional comparison, a comparison that numerous works have made explicitly, although often while focusing on the South itself.[28] Equally useful is comparison over time within a particular society. Of course history is by definition concerned with change over time, and hence implicitly involves temporal comparison, but there can often be advantages to making this sort of comparison explicit, as in the contrast between eighteenth- and nineteenth-century Cuban slavery. In a fine recent article combining both temporal and geographical comparison, Ira Berlin examined the differing evolution of slavery in three regions of the British mainland American colonies—North, upper South, and lower South—and emphasized "the importance of time and place in the study of American slavery."[29] Finally, one can compare the experience of different groups within the same country; as several historians have recently noted, for example, a comparison of immigrant groups in the United States can help reveal the impact of distinct cultural and ethnic values.[30]

That system or rigor is desirable in comparison is an assumption that is easier to defend, although the range of what is commonly meant by comparative history is so great that one is tempted to agree with Raymond Grew that "there is no comparative method in history," that "[t]o call for comparison is to call for a kind of attitude—open, questioning, searching—and to suggest some practices that may nourish it."[31] At one end of the spectrum lie works that exhibit a comparative consciousness but do not actually compare two or more cases, and comparative collections that juxtapose essays that are not themselves comparative, leaving to the reader the actual comparison.[32] Similar are works that focus exclusively on single cases, but seek to plug them into broader patterns or apply to them general social science theories; such an approach, evident in several of the frontier studies discussed above, has been especially prevalent in works dealing with modernization or socioeconomic development.[33] Scholarship of a more systematic comparative nature may be divided into intensive historical examinations of two or more cases, and generalizing works propounding universal theories, of a Marxian or non-Marxian variety, of societal development.[34]

The utility and appeal of these approaches to comparison vary considerably. The attempt to set forth general theories of human development, although attracting a small but devoted band of "social science" historians, has involved mainly economists, sociologists, and political scientists, while arousing widespread skepticism among most historians. This is not so much because historians oppose making generalizations—although some do—as because they are leery of making generalizations on such a grand scale, involving so many variables that no individual could hope to master them all. It is no accident that with the partial exception of Marx, the major practitioners of this kind of generalizing history have relied more on selected secondary works than on intensive examination of primary sources, more on theory and taxonomy than on direct historical evidence. Take, for example, the disagreement among scholars over the nature of "modernization." Samuel

P. Huntington defined political modernization as entailing "rationalization of authority," specialization of function, and broad popular political participation, and posited three differing patterns of modernization—continental, British, and American. Lee Benson proposed "establishment of a standard classification system having six categories (stages) of national political development" ranging from low "government demand" coupled with low-to-moderate "public compliance" (stage 1) to "high demand" and "moderate to high compliance" (stage 6). Richard D. Brown distinguished traditional from modern societies on the basis of "patterns of thought, behavior, and organization," while C. E. Black defined modernization as "the dynamic form that age-old process of innovation has assumed as a result of the explosive proliferation of knowledge in recent centuries," and outlined six patterns of political modernization. W. W. Rostow saw world modernization going through five stages of economic development, from traditional to "high mass consumption," while Barrington Moore, Jr. distinguished three routes to modernization—bourgeois, capitalist-reactionary or "Prussian," and communist—by which he meant "the transformation from agrarian societies . . . to modern industrial ones." Moore argued that "the ways in which the landed upper classes and the peasants related to the challenge of commercial agriculture were decisive factors" in determining which of these political routes would be followed. The best of these works—such as Moore's—are extremely thought-provoking, but they must be regarded more as speculations on history than as rigorous works of comparative history.[35]

At the other extreme, single case studies, undertaken with a broader perspective, constitute a major advance toward the reduction of historical parochialism and the testing of general theories. By focusing on post-Civil War Alabama, for example, Jonathan M. Wiener was able to apply Barrington Moore's theory of modernization on a historically manageable scale; Wiener argued that Alabama, and by extension the whole South, followed the Prussian rather than the bourgeois path to modernization.[36] Valuable as they are, however, such case studies do not strictly speaking constitute comparative history so much as the first step in its direction, based on the common-sense proposition that nothing should be studied in a vacuum.

It is at the middle level, then, between propounding cosmic theories and conducting detailed case studies, that true comparative history is most feasible. Comparison of common or similar institutions, processes, and events across space and time holds the prospect of revealing much both about these institutions, processes, and events, and about the environments in which they existed. Because there is some confusion on this matter, it is worth emphasizing that although the items being compared must be similar to each other—it would not make much sense to compare frontiers with civil wars—their respective environments need not be, and often should not be. Indeed, since one of the central functions of comparison is to distinguish between characteristics inherent in the items being compared and those resulting from given environmental conditions, the existence of significant differences between environments being compared is essential. Those frontier historians who argue, for example, that Latin American and Russian history are too different from American history to make comparison of their frontiers meaningful miss the mark. Obviously, similar frontiers in virtually identical environments will have similar results; the true test of the frontier thesis is whether the frontier produces similar effects in widely varying environments.[37]

A vast array of "middle-range" topics would benefit from systematic comparison. One thinks immediately of the family, the position of women, revolutions, wars, civil conflicts, labor relations, social structure, mobility, and political behavior. In some of these, historians have reached the stage of comparative consciousness (and even of occasional, sporadic comparison) without having embarked yet on a full-scale comparative effort. Authors of community studies, for example, regularly discuss, at least in passing, the typicality of their cases, without, however, actually comparing them with others. Similarly, labor historians ask why the labor radicalism of western Europe has been largely absent in the United States, and scholars debate whether the American Revolution was a "real" revolution—a comparative question that presupposes a model for revolution—or merely a war for independence. In all these, an awareness of alternatives is a necessary first step toward actual comparison.[38]

If a comparative consciousness is now widespread among American historians, a number of concrete problems confront the discipline of comparative history and have limited the proliferation of truly comparative works. These include an absence of methodological training and the difficulty of acquiring expertise in two or more areas, but probably the most serious problems are associated with the actual writing of comparative history. Not only is the discipline by nature analytical and problem-oriented, and therefore not conducive to the narrative style favored by most historians; it also requires coming to grips with the thorny organizational problem of how to present in detail two or more cases at the same time. Although the most successful resolution of this problem involves interweaving brief examinations of individual cases with comparison, too often scholars have chosen to take the easy way out, presenting first one case and then another and finally summing up similarities and differences in a brief conclusion, thus largely substituting juxtaposition for true comparison. Like some other new branches of history, in short, comparative history demands special attention to the fusion of artistry with analytical writing.

Despite these problems, George Fredrickson's conclusion that "the dominant impression that is bound to arise from any survey of recent comparative work by American historians is not how much has been done but rather how little" strikes me as an overly pessimistic evaluation, stemming in part from an excessively narrow definition of comparative history.[39] The comparative consciousness that now exists is in itself a major sign of progress, and explicit comparison has yielded positive results in a number of areas. While slavery is the most obvious example of a subject that has benefited from international comparison, a much larger number of topics has seen significant comparative work done over space and time *within* the United States. Prospects for the future appear far from bleak, for comparative history is part of a broad trend toward breaking out of the geographical and methodological parochialism that so long plagued the practice of history; in this sense comparison lies squarely in the mainstream of the "new" history. This is true in another sense as well, since comparative history involves doing explicitly what historians do implicitly all the time. The function of comparative judgment is to increase the accuracy of our knowledge of the past, and that, after all, is what history is all about.

1. See George M. Fredrickson, "Comparative History," in *The Past Before Us: Contemporary Historical Writings in the United States*, ed. Michael Kammen (Ithaca: Cornell University Press, 1980), pp. 457–73; W. Turrentine Jackson, "A Brief Message for the Young and/or Ambitious: Comparative Frontiers as a Field for Investigation," *Western Historical Quarterly* 9 (January 1978): 5–18; Robert P. Swierenga, "Computers and Comparative History," *Journal of Interdisciplinary History* 5 (Autumn 1974): 269; John Higham, review of *The Past Before Us*, ed. Kammen, in *American Historical Review*, 86 (October 1981): 808.

2. For differing perspectives on the nature and goals of comparative history, see, in addition to works cited above, William H. Sewell, Jr., "Marc Bloch and the Logic of Comparative History," *History and Theory* 6, 2 (1967): 208–18; C. Vann Woodward, "The Comparability of American History" and "The Test of Comparison," in *The Comparative Approach to American History*, ed. Woodward (New York: Basic Books, 1968), pp. 3–17, 346–57; Robert F. Berkhofer, Jr., *A Behavioral Approach to Historical Analysis* (New York: The Free Press, 1969), pp. 250–69; J. Rogers Hollingsworth, "American History in Comparative Perspective," in *Nation and State Building in America: Comparative Historical Perspectives*, (Boston: Little, Brown, 1971), pp. 1–6; Richard P. McCormick, "The Comparative Method: Its Application to American History," *Mid-America* 56 (October 1974): 231–47; Raymond Grew, "The Case for Comparing Histories," *American Historical Review* 85 (October 1980): 763–78.

3. Grew, "The Case for Comparing Histories," p. 769.

4. Quotations are from Turner, "The Significance of the Frontier in American History" (1893), "The Problem of the West" (1896), and "The Significance of the Section in American History" (1925), all reprinted in *Frontier and Section: Selected Essays of Frederick Jackson Turner* (Englewood Cliffs, N.J.: Prentice-Hall, 1961), pp. 37, 63, 116.

5. Marvin W. Mikesell, "Comparative Studies in Frontier History" (1960), reprinted in *Turner and the Sociology of the Frontier*, eds. Richard Hofstadter and Seymour Martin Lipset (New York: Basic Books, 1968), p. 152.

6. Ray Allen Billington, "Frontiers," in *The Comparative Approach to American History,* ed. Woodward, p. 77; A. L. Burt, "If Turner Had Looked at Canada, Australia, and New Zealand When He Wrote About the West," in *The Frontier in Perspective,* eds. Walker D. Wyman and Clifton B. Kroeber (Madison: University of Wisconsin Press, 1957), p. 75; Seymour Martin Lipset, "The Turner Thesis in Comparative Perspective: An Introduction," in *Turner and the Sociology of the Frontier,* eds. Hofstadter and Lipset, p. 12.

7. H. C. Allen, *Bush and Backwoods: A Comparison of the Frontier in Australia and the United States* (Sydney: Augus & Robertson, 1959), pp. 111, 100, 111.

8. See Burt, "If Turner Had Looked at Canada, Australia, and New Zealand," pp. 60–61; A. Lobanov-Rostovsky, "Russian Expansion in the Far East in the Light of the Turner Hypothesis," in *The Frontier in Perspective,* eds. Wyman and Kroeber, pp. 79–94; Donald W. Treadgold, "Russian Expansion in the Light of Turner's Study of the American Frontier," *Agricultural History* 26 (October 1952): 147–52; Paul L. Mackendish, "Roman Colonization and the Frontier Hypothesis," in *The Frontier in Perspective,* eds. Wyman and Kroeber, pp. 3–19.

9. John C. Hudson, "Theory and Methodology in Comparative Frontier Studies," in *The Frontier: Comparative Studies,* eds. David Harry Miller and Jerome O. Steffen (Norman: University of Oklahoma Press, 1977), p. 12. For a similar view, see Dietrich Gerhard, "The Frontier in Comparative View," *Comparative Studies in Society and History* 1 (March 1959): 228–29.

10. Leonard Thompson and Howard Lamar, "Comparative Frontier History," in *The Frontier in History: North America and Southern Africa Compared,* eds. Thompson and Lamar (New Haven: Yale University Press, 1981), p. 7.

11. Hudson, "Theory and Methodology in Comparative Frontier Studies," p. 12.

12. Miller and Steffen, eds., *The Frontier: Comparative Studies;* Lamar and Thompson, eds., *The Frontier in History.*

13. See Lobanov-Rostovsky, "Russian Expansion in the Far East"; Treadgold, "Russian Expansion in the Light of Turner's Study of the American Frontier."

14. James E. Davis, *Frontier America, 1800–1840: A Comparative Demographic Analysis of the Frontier Process* (Glendale, Calif.: Arthur H. Clark, 1977); Julie Roy Jeffrey, *Frontier Women: The Trans-Mississippi West, 1840–1880* (New York: Hill and Wang, 1979), p. 106; Richard A. Easterlin, "Factors in the Decline of Farm Fertility in the United States: Some Preliminary Research Results," *Journal of American History* 63 (December 1976): 600–14, quotation, p. 612.

15. Daniel Blake Smith, "The Study of the Family in Early America: Trends, Problems, and Prospects," *William and Mary Quarterly* 3rd. ser., 39 (January 1982): 10; Davis, *Frontier America, 1800–1840;* Jerome O. Steffen, "Insular V. Cosmopolitan Frontiers: A Proposal for Comparative American Frontier Study," in *The American West: New Perspectives, New Directions,* ed. Steffen (Norman: University of Oklahoma Press, 1979), pp. 94–123; and *Comparative Frontiers: A Proposal for Studying the American West* (Norman: University of Oklahoma Press, 1980), quotation, p. xiii.

16. Frank Tannenbaum, *Slave and Citizen: The Negro in the Americas* (New York: Alfred A. Knopf, 1946), pp. 52, 65; Stanley M. Elkins, *Slavery: A Problem in American Institutional and Intellectual Life,* 3rd ed. (Chicago: University of Chicago Press, 1976), pp. 37, 81.

17. Eugene D. Genovese, "The Treatment of Slaves in Different Countries: Problems in the Application of the Comparative Method," in *Slavery in the New World: A Reader in Comparative History,* eds. Laura Foner and Genovese (Englewood Cliffs, N.J.: Prentice-Hall, 1969), pp. 202–03.

18. Herbert Klein, *Slavery in the Americas: A Comparative Study of Virginia and Cuba* (Chicago: University of Chicago Press, 1967). See Franklin W. Knight, *Slave Society in Cuba During the Nineteenth Century* (Madison: University of Wisconsin Press, 1970); Marvin Harris, *Patterns of Race in the Americas* (New York: Walker & Company, 1964), esp. ch. 6; the essays in Foner and Genovese, eds., *Slavery in the Americas.* David Brion Davis, *The Problem of Slavery in Western Culture* (Ithaca: Cornell University Press, 1967), ch. 8, quotation p. 229.

19. Carl N. Degler, *Neither Black nor White: Slavery and Race Relations in Brazil and the United States* (New York: Macmillan, 1971), ch. 2, quotation, p. 67; Eugene D. Genovese, *The World the Slaveholders Made: Two Essays in Interpretation* (New York: Pantheon Books, 1969), pt. I, quotation, p. 96.

20. C. Vann Woodward, "Southern Slaves in the World of Thomas Malthus," in *American Counterpoint: Slavery and Racism in the North-South Dialogue,* ed. Woodward (Boston: Little, Brown, 1971), pp. 78-106; Genovese, *The World the Slaveholders Made,* pt. I, *passim;* Degler, *Neither Black nor White,* pp. 52-67. For information on the number of slaves imported to the various regions of the Americas, see Philip D. Curtin, *The Atlantic Slave Trade: A Census* (Madison: University of Wisconsin Press, 1969), and the slightly revised figures in James A. Rawley, *The Trans-Atlantic Slave Trade: A History* (New York: W. W. Norton, 1981).

21. Richard S. Dunn, "A Tale of Two Plantations: Slave Life at Mesopotamia in Jamaica and Mount Airy in Virginia, 1799 to 1828," *William and Mary Quarterly* 3rd ser., 34 (January 1977): 40-64.

22. Degler, *Neither Black nor White,* pp. 227, 239; George M. Fredrickson, *White Supremacy: A Comparative Study in American and South African History* (New York: Oxford University Press, 1981), pp. 94-135; Harris, *Patterns of Race in the Americas,* ch. 7; Harry Hoetink, *Slavery and Race Relations in the Americas: An Inquiry into their Nature and Nexus* (New York: Harper & Row, 1973), pp. 36-37; Laura Foner, "The Free People of Color in Louisiana and St. Domingue: A Comparative Portrait of Two Three-Caste Slave Societies," *Journal of Social History* 3 (Summer 1970): 415.

23. William McKee Evans, "From the Land of Canaan to the Land of Guinea: The Strange Odyssey of the Sons of Ham," *American Historical Review* 85 (February 1980): 15-43, quotation p. 43; Peter Kolchin, "In Defense of Servitude: American Proslavery and Russian Proserfdom Arguments, 1760-1860," *ibid.* (October 1980): 810-12.

24. Fredrickson, *White Supremacy,* pp. 126, 39.

25. For the suggestion that the French cultural background in southern Louisana was a major factor in that region's development of a three-tiered color system, see Foner, "The Free People of Color in Louisiana and St. Domingue."

26. See Eugene D. Genovese, *From Rebellion to Revolution: Afro-American Slave Revolts in the Making of the New World* (Baton Rouge: Louisiana State University Press, 1979); Fredrickson, *White Supremacy;* and "After Emancipation: A Comparative Study of White Responses to the New Order of Race Relations in the American South, Jamaica, & the Cape Colony of South Africa," in *What Was Freedom's Price?* ed. David G. Sansing (Jackson: University of Mississippi Press, 1978), pp. 71-92; C. Vann Woodward, "The Price of Freedom," *ibid.,* pp. 93-113; Evans, "From the Land of Canaan to the Land of Guinea"; Ira Berlin, "Time, Space, and the Evolution of Afro-American Society in British Mainland North America," *American Historical Review* 85 (February 1980): 44-78; Peter Kolchin, "The Process of Confrontation: Patterns of Resistance to Bondage in Nineteenth-Century Russia and the United States," *Journal of Social History* 11, 4 (1978): 457-90; and "In Defense of Servitude"; Shearer Davis Bowman, "Antebellum Planters and *Vormärz* Junkers in Comparative Perspective," *American Historical Review* 85 (October 1980): 779-809; Robert M. Berdahl, "Paternalism, Serfdom, and Emancipation in Prussia," in *Oceans Apart? Comparing Germany and the United States: Studies in Commemoration of the 150th Anniversary of the Birth of Carl Schurz,* eds. Erich Angermann and Marie-Luise Frings (Stuttgart: Klett-Cotta, 1981), pp. 29-44.

27. Fredrickson, "Comparative History," p. 458.

28. There is a vast literature on both the economic and general comparison between North and South. For two recent treatments of the former, see Robert William Fogel and Stanley L. Engerman, *Time on the Cross: The Economics of American Negro Slavery* (Boston: Little, Brown, 1974), pp. 247-57; Fred Bateman and Thomas Weiss, *A Deplorable Scarcity: The Failure of Industrialization in the Slave Economy* (Chapel Hill: University of North Carolina Press, 1981). For a recent treatment of the latter, see Edward Pessen, "How Different from Each Other Were the Antebellum North and South?," *American Historical Review* 85 (December

1980): 1119–49. For the argument that comparison need not cross national lines, see Grew, "The Case for Comparing Histories," p. 767.

29. Berlin, "Time, Space, and the Evolution of Afro-American Society," p. 77.

30. See Laurence A. Glasco, "The Life Cycle and Household Structure of American Ethnic Groups: Irish, Germans, and Native-Born Whites in Buffalo, New York, 1855," *Journal of Urban History* 1 (May 1975); 339–64; Myfanwy Morgan and Hilda H. Golden, "Immigrant Families in an Industrial City: A Study of Households in Holyoke, 1880," *Journal of Family History* 4 (Spring 1979); 59–68; Elizabeth H. Pleck, "A Mother's Wages: Income Earning among Married Italian and Black Women, 1896–1911," in *The Amerian Family in Social-Historical Perspective*, 2nd. ed., ed. Michael Gordon (New York: St. Martin's Press, 1978), pp. 490–510. Numerous other works deal, in passing, with differences among ethnic groups: see, e.g., Stephan Thernstrom, *Poverty and Progress: Social Mobility in a Nineteenth Century City* (Cambridge: Harvard University Press, 1964), pp. 99–102, 109–11, 155–57, 200–01, 237–38.

31. Grew, "The Case for Comparing Histories," p. 776.

32. In most "comparative" collections, only a small minority of selections are themselves comparative: see e.g., Lamar and Thompson, eds. *The Frontier in History;* Foner and Genovese, eds., *Slavery in the New World.*

33. For examples of works that apply broad developmental theories to case studies, see Richard D. Brown, *Modernization: The Transformation of American Life, 1600–1865* (New York: Hill and Wang, 1976); Jonathan M. Wiener, *Social Origins of the New South: Alabama, 1860–1885* (Baton Rouge: Louisiana State University Press, 1978).

34. See, in addition to works cited below in note 35, Karl Marx, *Capital: A Critique of Political Economy* 3 vols., trans. Samuel Moore (New York: International Publishers, 1967); Seymour Martin Lipset, *The First New Nation: The United States in Historical and Comparative Perspective* (New York: Basic Books, 1963); Louis Hartz, *The Founding of New Societies: Studies in the History of the United States, Latin America, South Africa, Canada, and Australia* (New York: Harcourt, Brace & World, 1964).

35. Samuel P. Huntington, "Political Modernization: America Vs. Europe," (1966), reprinted in *Nation and State Building in America*, ed. Hollingsworth, pp. 27–62; Lee Benson, "The Empirical and Statistical Basis for Comparative Analysis of Historical Change," in Benson, *Toward the Scientific Study of History: Selected Essays* (Philadelphia: J. B. Lippincott, 1972), pp. 168–69; Brown, *Modernization,* p. 9; C. E. Black, *The Dynamics of Modernization: A Study in Comparative History* (New York: Harper & Row, 1966), p. 7; W. W. Rostow, *The Stages of Economic Growth: A Non-Communist Manifesto* (Cambridge, England: Cambridge University Press, 1960), p. 50; Barrington Moore, Jr., *Social Origins of Dictatorship and Democracy: Lord and Peasant in the Making of the Modern World* (Boston: Beacon Press, 1966), pp. xi, xvii.

36. Wiener, *Social Origins of the New South.*

37. For the assertion that frontiers should only be compared from countries with similar histories, see Mikesell, "Comparative Studies in Frontier History," pp. 152–56.

38. For comparative work on some of these topics, see R. R. Palmer, *The Age of the Democratic Revolution: A Political History of Europe and America, 1760–1800 — The Challenge* (Princeton: Princeton University Press, 1959); Stuart M. Blumin, "Rip Van Winkle's Grandchildren: Family and Household in the Hudson Valley, 1800–1860," *Journal of Urban History* 1 (May 1975): 293–315; Daniel J. Walkowitz, *Worker City, Company Town: Iron and Cotton-Worker Protest in Troy and Cohoes, New York, 1855–84* (Urbana: University of Illinois Press, 1978); Michael Stephen Hindus, *Prison and Plantation: Crime, Justice, and Authority in Massachusetts and South Carolina, 1767–1878* (Chapel Hill: University of North Carolina Press, 1980); Roger Thompson, *Women in Stuart England and America: A Comparative Study* (Boston: Routledge, 1974); Leila Rupp, *Mobilizing Women for War: German and American Propaganda, 1939–1945* (Princeton: Princeton University Press, 1978).

39. Fredrickson, "Comparative History," p. 472.

RECONSTRUCTION REVISITED

Eric Foner

In the past twenty years, few periods of American history have been the subject of so thoroughgoing a reevaluation as Reconstruction. Inspired in large measure by the rise and fall of the "Second Reconstruction"—the revolution in race relations of the 1960s—historians have produced a flood of works reexamining the political, social, and economic experiences of black and white Americans in the aftermath of the Civil War. Yet one prominent historian recently declared that the study of Reconstruction today confronts a "crisis of the most serious proportions," [1] for historians have failed to produce a coherent modern portrait of Reconstruction either as a specific time period or as the effort of American society to come to terms with the results of the Civil War and the consequences of emancipation.

For much of this century, Reconstruction historiography was dominated by a "traditional" interpretation that portrayed the years following the Civil War as ones of unrelieved sordidness in political and social life. [2] In this view, vindictive Radical Republicans fastened black supremacy upon the defeated South, unleashing an orgy of corruption presided over by unscrupulous carpetbaggers, traitorous scalawags, and ignorant freedmen. Eventually, the white community of the South overthrew this misgovernment and restored Home Rule (a euphemism for white supremacy). The heroes of the story were President Andrew Jackson, whose lenient Reconstruction plans were foiled by the Radicals, and the self-styled "Redeemers," who restored honest government. Originating in anti-Reconstruction propaganda of southern Democrats during the 1870s, this viewpoint achieved scholarly legitimacy in the work of the Dunning school early in this century and reached a mass public through Claude Bowers's best-selling work of fiction masquerading as history, *The Tragic Era.*

Except for the criticisms of a handful of surviving Reconstruction participants, this traditional interpretation received its first sustained critique in the 1920s and 1930s. Howard K. Beale, influenced by the Beardian contention that the Civil War era witnessed the consolidation of national economic and political power in the hands of northeastern capitalists, shunned the previously dominant race issue in favor of an economic interpretation of the politics of the Johnson administration. Beale did not challenge the tradi-

0048-7511/82/0104-0082 $01.00
Copyright © 1982 by The Johns Hopkins University Press

tionalists' characterization of radical Reconstruction as a tragic era; simultaneously, however, a more sympathetic appraisal appeared in the works of the black historians A. A. Taylor and W.E.B. DuBois, and white scholars Francis Simkins and Robert Woody.[3] But not until the 1960s, under the impact of the Second Reconstruction, was the full force of this Reconstruction "revisionism" felt. Modern revisionism radically reinterpreted national Reconstruction politics, and placed the activities and aspirations of blacks at the center stage of the drama in the South. President Johnson was now portrayed as a stubborn, racist politician, whereas his abolitionist and Radical opponents, acquitted of vindictive motives, emerged as idealists in the best nineteenth-century reform tradition. As for the freedmen, the pioneering work of Joel Williamson depicted Reconstruction in South Carolina as a time of extraordinary progress for blacks in political, economic, and social life. Revisionism also directed attention to the positive accomplishments of Reconstruction—the establishment of public school systems in the South and the expansion of national citizenship to include the freedmen, for example—while tending to understate the more unsavory aspects of the period, such as pervasive corruption.

By the end of the 1960s, the old interpretation had been completely reversed. Southern freedmen were the heroes, Redeemers the villains, and if the era was "tragic," it was because change did not go far enough. Reconstruction appeared as both a time of real progress, and a golden opportunity lost for the South and the nation.[4] Yet, as is so often the case with historical revisionism, the end result was essentially a series of negative judgments.[5] The Reconstruction governments were not as bad as they had been portrayed; "black supremacy" was a myth; the Radicals were neither cynical manipulators of the freedmen nor agents of northern capitalism. If it was no longer possible to characterize Reconstruction as "the blackout of honest government," no alternative version of the quality of political and social life in these years emerged to replace the now discredited traditional view.

Even in the mid-1960s, moreover, the more optimistic assumptions of many revisionist writers were challenged by those who took a skeptical view of the entire Reconstruction enterprise. C. Vann Woodward contended that, from the outset, racial prejudice severely compromised northern efforts to assist the freedmen. August Meier argued that, in contrast to the Second Reconstruction, the first was fundamentally "superficial."[6] During the 1970s, this mode of thought was extended to virtually every aspect of the period by what may be called a "postrevisionist" generation of historians. Instead of seeing the Civil War and its aftermath as a second American Revolution (as Charles Beard and his disciples did), a regression into barbarism (Bowers and the traditionalists), or a revolutionary impulse thwarted (the revisionists), postrevisionist writers questioned whether much of importance had happened at all. Recent studies of politics, social structure, and ideology have been united by a single theme—continuity between the Old and New South. Summing up the past decade's writing, Woodward observed that historians now understood "how essentially nonrevolutionary and conservative Reconstruction really was."[7]

Building upon the findings of the revisionists, recent writers have reached conclusions rather different in emphasis. Eric McKitrick, John and LaWanda Cox, and other revisionists had challenged the traditional notion that Radicals dominated the post-Civil War Congresses, emphasizing instead the guiding hand of moderate Republicans in drafting Reconstruction legislation. They did not doubt, however, that these laws marked a major departure in American politics and race relations. In the 1970s, Michael Les Benedict used the prominence of moderate Republicans to challenge the idea of Radical Reconstruction itself, emphasizing instead how federal policy was guided by the goal of "preserving the Constitution" and minimizing changes in federal-state relations. Similarly, Michael Perman argued that northern Reconstruction strategy eschewed radical departures in favor of seeking the cooperation of southern whites, and was therefore extremely vulnerable to southern obstructionism. A similar emphasis informed the massive study of the Grant administration's Reconstruction policy by William Gillette, which suggested that the North's commitment to the freedmen had never been particularly strong. The final collapse of Reconstruction in 1877, Gillette demonstrated, merely formalized a steady retreat throughout the 1870s.[8]

Thus, postrevisionist writers insisted the impact of the Civil War upon American life was less pervasive than had once been believed. Important studies of the postwar polity by Harold Hyman and Morton Keller argued that the initial broadening of the powers of postwar national and state governments proved extremely short-lived, as localism, individualism and racism—persistent themes of nineteenth-century American life—quickly reasserted themselves.[9] Studies of the previously neglected northern Democrats have portrayed a group clinging to its traditional ideology even in the face of what its National Chairman, August Belmont, called "the most disastrous epoch in the annals of the party." As for northern Republicans, James Mohr did discern a parallel between Radical Reconstruction and the policies adopted by New York Republicans between 1865 and 1867 on such issues as state regulation of the police, fire, and health affairs of New York City and the enfranchisement of the state's blacks. But few studies of other northern states found much evidence of internal radicalism. In most, the pattern seemed to follow that outlined by Felice Bonadio for Ohio: the emergence of a breed of party politician little affected by political radicalism (or any ideology, for that matter), and interested exclusively in the preservation and success of the party itself.[10]

A similar stress on continuity rather than change, and on the moderate character of Republican policies, has defined recent studies of the South during Reconstruction. Challenging the contention that the Civil War signaled the eclipse of the old planter class and the rise to power of a new entrepreneurial elite, social histories of localities scattered across the South demonstrated that planters survived the war with their landholdings and social prestige more or less intact. (The areas investigated, it should be noted, were ones which largely escaped wartime military action.)[11] Long-standing intrastate sectionalism—the tension, for example, between western and eastern North Carolina—was shown to have strongly influenced Reconstruction political alignments.[12] And the three major state studies which appeared during the 1970s on Reconstruction in Louisiana, Florida, and Mississippi offered little reason to believe that Reconstruction had significantly improved the lot of the freedmen.[13]

Nor did historians of the 1970s find much to praise in federal policy toward the emancipated blacks. The Freedmen's Bureau, criticized in traditional accounts for excessive radicalism and regarded by revisionists as a sincere effort to ameliorate the legal, educational, and economic plight of the freedmen, emerged in William McFeely's influential study as a practitioner of racial paternalism, working hand in glove with the planters to force emancipated blacks back to work on the plantations. McFeely's findings were reinforced by Louis Gerteis's examination of wartime Army policies toward blacks. In the 1960s Willie Lee Rose, in a landmark of revisionist writing, had portrayed the Sea Island experiment (a typically American amalgam of humanitarianism and pursuit of economic profit) as a rehearsal for Reconstruction which, despite limitations, allowed blacks to achieve a real measure of control over their lives. Gerteis argued that the experience of blacks in Civil War Louisiana, where General Nathaniel P. Banks established a labor system that critics charged resembled slavery, shaped Reconstruction far more powerfully than events on the Sea Islands. More recent studies of the Bureau's efforts at medical care for blacks and its legal work conclude that federal policy failed to meet the pressing needs of the freedmen. Leon Litwack's *Been in the Storm So Long*, a culmination of two decades of writings on the black experience during and after the Civil War, fully reflects these postrevisionist conclusions. Utilizing a remarkable array of sources, Litwack eschewed generalization in favor of portraying a kaleidoscope of black responses to emancipation. But regarding whites, one theme stood out: federal, Army, and state authorities were equally indifferent to the freedmen's aspirations.[14]

Even previously unchallenged achievements of the Reconstruction era were now subjected to searching criticism. The establishment of schools for blacks by federal authorities and northern missionary associations and the creation of state-supported common school systems in the South were once hailed as the finest legacy of Reconstruction. Now a series of studies indicted northern teachers for seeking to stabilize the plantation order and inculcate "middle-class" northern values like thrift, self-discipline, temperance, and respect for authority. If the critique struck a familiar note, it was because it represented an extension southward of the "social control" theory of education so prominent in recent discussions of northern educational reform. Like northern common schools, black education in the South was increasingly seen as a form of cultural imperialism, an effort to create a disciplined and docile labor force.[15]

If any assumption united traditionalists like Dunning and revisionists ranging from DuBois to Williamson, it was the essential radicalism of Reconstruction. Postrevisionism thus represents a fundamental departure from previous interpretations. The great advantage of its stress on continuity lies in emphasizing that Reconstruction was, in fact, an integral part of southern and national history, rather than some kind of bizarre aberration, as has often been portrayed. Yet, like their revisionist predecessors, the postrevisionist writers have failed to produce a modern synthesis. The denial of change does not in itself provide a compelling interpretation of a turbulent era.[16]

Whether a convincing overall portrait of Reconstruction based on postrevisionist premises can be constructed is, indeed, open to question. LaWanda Cox has chided recent writers for "presentism"—that is, using today's standards to judge the attitudes and accomplishments of the past. The reevaluation of freedmen's education, to take one example, seemed often to view the 1860s through the lens of the 1960s. One study criticized northern educators for lacking a commitment to "black power and pride"—rallying cries of the Second Reconstruction but not necessarily major concerns of the first.[17]

Central to postrevisionist literature is the failure of land reform which, it has been argued, both exemplified the absence of a genuine northern commitment to the freedmen, and ensured that the political gains achieved by blacks would be fragile and transitory. Without denigrating the importance of the land question, it may be suggested that the failure to provide blacks with "forty acres and a mule" has loomed so large in recent literature that politics and social life, and even the realm of labor, have been largely written off as arenas of conflict and accomplishment. Moreoover, the precise relationship between the freedmen's subordinate economic status and the ultimate failure of Reconstruction has not been fully worked out. Economic intimidation was, it is true, employed against black voters, but far more important in the overthrow of Reconstruction was violence, precisely because other pressures proved ineffective. The idea that political equality is meaningless without economic independence paradoxically leaves its advocates occupying much the same stance with regard to the black condition as Booker T. Washington.[18]

Ironically, the entire postrevisionist reevaluation of federal policy on labor, education, and other matters, which arose from the laudable desire to reinterpret history from the black point of view, ended up by returning blacks to their traditional status as passive victims of white manipulation. But if the Freedmen's Bureau served only the interests of the planters, why did blacks so vociferously demand that it remain in the South? If education served simply to promote social control, why did the black community thirst after literacy and esteem those who could read and write? Little consideration has been given to the uses the freedmen may have made of the education provided them, including the much maligned virtues of self-discipline, temperance, and thrift. Only when a better appreciation is achieved of how the desire for education was related to blacks' overall conception of the meaning of freedom and of how black beliefs affected Republican policy can the role of education in Reconstruction be fully understood. The point is that the postemancipation outcome was shaped by blacks as well as whites, in ways historians have only begun to investigate.

Rather than simply emphasizing conservatism and continuity, a coherent portrait of Reconstruction must take into account the subtle dialectic of continuity and change in economic, social, and political relations as the nation adjusted to emancipation. For blacks, one might begin with an observation made over forty years ago by the historian Francis Simkins. While Reconstruction, Simkins wrote, was conventionally seen by white southerners as an attempt to "Africanize" the South, the exact opposite appeared to be true: "Reconstruction can be interpreted as a definite step . . . in the Americanization of the blacks." Recent work on the black experience makes it possible today to point to the crucial changes in black society wrought by emancipation, and in each instance the truth of Simkins's remark is apparent, if by "Americanization" we understand a narrowing of the chasm separating black life from that of the larger white society. Reconstruction witnessed the demise of the quasi-communal slave quarter and its replacement by small tenant farms, with individual families occupying distinct parcels of land. It was the time of the emergence of the black church— previously the "invisible institution"—along with a host of black fraternal, benevolent, and self-improvement organizations. Reconstruction saw the reconstitution of black family life with the withdrawal (temporary, as it turned out) of black women from field labor, and the institutionalization, with the suffrage, of a distinction between the public world of men and the private sphere of women. In these and other ways, Reconstruction gave birth to the modern black community, whose roots lay deep in slavery, but whose structure reflected the consequences of emancipation.[19]

Nowhere, however, was the transformation in black life more profound and the "Americanization" of the black experience more striking than in politics.[20] The 1970s witnessed a broad reassessment of black political leadership during Reconstruction, largely undertaken by a new generation of black scholars. The signal contribution of this literature was to reject the idea that Reconstruction was simply a matter of black and white. Divisions among whites have long been known to have shaped the course of Reconstruction; attention, it is now clear, must also be directed to conflicts within the black community. The "representative colored men," as Nell Painter termed national black leaders, were upbraided for being cut off from the black masses and therefore failing to provide effective political leadership. Thomas Holt's *Black Over White*, the most influential recent study of Reconstruction black politics, reversed Williamson's pioneering conclusions about South Carolina. For Williamson, the fatal flaw of Reconstruction politics was that Republican leaders were concerned only with their own constituents and incapable of reaching out to hostile whites. For Holt, black leaders, largely deriving from the free mulatto class of Charleston, were concerned too little, not too much, with the needs of the black community. Primarily interested in civil rights legislation and "basically bourgeois in their origins and orientation . . . [they] failed to act in the interests of black peasants," especially on the all-important questions of land and labor. Holt's conclusion, paralleled in David Rankin's study of New Orleans black leadership, was, in a way, a culmination to the persistent demand that blacks be placed at the center of the Reconstruction story. If indeed they were active agents rather than passive victims, then blacks could not be absolved of blame for the failure of Reconstruction.[21]

In its emphasis on the persistence from slavery of divisions between free and slave, black and brown, this new literature reflected the increasing concern with continuity and conservatism in Reconstruction; and, like other postrevisionist works, it is vulnerable to charges of exaggerating the victimization of ordinary blacks, and ignoring historical changes that did occur. That the free colored elite was more fully integrated into the culture of Victorian America than the newly freed slaves is clear. Yet the political salience of this fact is not. The vast majority of blacks lived not in cities like Charleston and New Orleans but in the black belt, where there were few free blacks before the war. We now know a good deal about black congressmen and state legislators, but the arduous task of analyzing the local leadership of black Reconstruction has barely begun. Twelve counties in Mississippi, for example, elected black sheriffs during Reconstruction but, except for Blanche K. Bruce and John R. Lynch, who went on to achieve national reputations, we know virtually nothing about these men, or how their presence affected the daily lives of blacks and whites in the Mississippi Delta. Those few studies which do exist, however, indicate that local leaders, even those who had been free before the Civil War, often championed the social and economic aspirations of their constituents and sometimes made a real difference in their day to day lives.[22]

More importantly, the use of static categories like free and freed, black and brown, ignores the historical process by which new patterns of leadership emerged during Reconstruction. The remarkable political mobilization of the black community is one of the most striking features of the period, and so too is the emergence, with the right to vote and the creation of Union Leagues and the Republican party, of a new black political class. In early Reconstruction, blacks turned to ministers, ex-soldiers, free blacks, and men who had, for one reason or another, achieved prominence as slaves, to represent them politically. During Congressional Reconstruction, new men came to the fore, most prominently black artisans, who possessed the skill, independence, and often, literacy that marked them as leaders, but who were still deeply embedded in the life of the freedmen's community. Such individuals were uniquely suited to serve as a bridge between the black world and the public political sphere dominated by whites.[23]

Even in South Carolina and Louisiana, the recent characterization of black leaders as "bourgeois" may be open to question. The black elite of Charleston and New Orleans lacked captial and economic autonomy. William Hine shows that Charleston's black leaders were unable to raise the funds to build a streetcar line after receiving a charter from the state legislature. The few really wealthy blacks, Hine contends, avoided politics—their economic standing was too dependent on close ties with wealthy whites to oppose them politically.[24]

If the danger exists of exaggerating the dichotomy between black political leaders and their constituency, another set of false polar opposites dominates analysis of the content of black politics. Integration vs. segregation, civil rights vs. economic legislation, nationalism vs. assimilation: these dualisms have shaped writing on black thought. Only a few works, like Wilson Moses's *The Golden Age of Black Nationalism,* explore the common assumptions shared by nationalists and assimilationists, by moving from a consideration of specific issues to the language of politics itself, the underlying paradigms of political thought.[25] There is an interesting historiographical point here. The past fifteen years have demonstrated the value, indeed the indispensability, of bringing to bear on the study of the American past the insights derived from black history. But by the same token, the insights of students of other aspects of American life can illuminate in new ways the black experience.

Particularly relevant in this regard are the studies of political language and culture by J.G.A. Pocock and others, which have done so much to recover the history of republican thought.[26] Pocock's approach suggests that black politics in Reconstruction should be analyzed not as a set of discrete issues or demands, but as the attempt to forge from diverse elements in the black and American experiences a coherent political response to the unprecedented situation of emancipation. These elements included both values emanating from slavery and traditional American ideals, although often with a specifically black interpretation, such as the dignity of labor, messianic religion, and, especially, the quest for full incorporation as citizens of the republic. Perhaps black leaders can best be understood as those most capable of appropriating the available political language of American society and forging from it an expression of the aspirations of the freedmen.

The work of J. Mills Thornton, Michael Holt, and Harry Watson demonstrates the vitality of republicanism as one paradigm of antebellum southern political thought.[27] It should occasion no surprise that free blacks learned this language. The extent to which slaves absorbed it is difficult to assess but during Reconstruction, republican ideas about the nature of citizenship suffused black political culture. Like northern Radical Republicans, blacks found in the Constitution's guarantee clause, a provision, as William Wiecek writes, "almost Delphic" in its ambiguity, a reservoir of federal power over the states, imposing a duty upon Congress to eliminate caste and class legislation as incompatible with republican government.[28]

An emphasis on republican citizenship as a key organizing theme of Reconstruction black politics underscores the pitfalls involved in treating civil rights and land reform as if they were somehow mutually exclusive. Republicanism was, after all, simultaneously a model of polity and society. The republican tradition, with its emphasis on ownership of productive property as the guarantor of personal and political independence, helped blacks legitimize both the demand for equality before the law and the pervasive desire for land. Attention to the quest for republican citizenship also reveals the limited utility of the integration-segregation dichotomy for understanding the black experience.[29] If black economic and social life was marked by a struggle for autonomy, reflected in the demand for land and the withdrawal from religious and social institutions controlled by whites (a process misinterpreted by some historians as "acceptance" of legalized segregation)—black politics was fully absorbed into the American republican heritage.[30]

The Civil War transformed the black response to American nationality. Appeals to the ideals of American political culture had been commonplace in that strand of antebellum black protest dubbed "The Great Tradition" by Vincent Harding. But this affirmation of Americanism had always been tempered by an understandable alienation born of slavery and racial injustice. As the conflict reshaped the attitude of American intellectuals to their society, submerging, at least temporarily, an earlier alienation within a renewed commitment to the nation-state, so black spokesmen sacrificed an edge of criticism of American institutions in the quest for equal citizenship. Nathan Huggins has demonstrated this convincingly in the case of Frederick Douglass. The same Douglass who so brilliantly articulated the ambiguity of the black condition in his eloquent prewar address on the meaning of the Fourth of July to the slave could now support the Grant administration's scheme to swallow up Santo Domingo in the name of bringing the blessings of Anglo-Saxon civilization to the natives there.[31]

Republican citizenship, moreover, was what made the postemancipation experience of the United States unique. The history of other societies which underwent the transition from slavery to freedom casts serious doubt on the current idea that American Reconstruction was "conservative." In a comparative context, Reconstruction stands as a unique and dramatic experiment, the only instance when blacks, within a few years of emancipation, achieved universal manhood suffrage and exercised a real measure of political power. The comparative analysis of postemancipation societies, indeed, may provide ways of overcoming some of the problems which now afflict the study of Reconstruction. Certainly, contemporaries sensed that the examples of other societies shed light on the complex situation Americans confronted in the aftermath of their own Civil War. Thaddeus Stevens examined the emancipation of the Russian serfs; white southerners debated the lessons of Haitian and British Caribbean abolition. But few American historians have followed their example.[32]

There are, of course, dangers inherent in the comparative method, most notably the temptation to slight the distinctiveness of particular historical experiences in the quest for overarching generalizations.[33] Nonetheless, a comparative analysis permits us to develop a more sophisticated understanding of the problem of emancipation and its aftermath. Everywhere, the end of slavery was succeeded by a struggle for the scarce resources of plantation economies, paramount among which was the labor of the former slaves themselves. The desire among freedmen to own their own land and in other ways establish their autonomy seems to have been all but universal, and so too was the effort of planters to force blacks back to work as a dependent plantation labor force.[34]

From this perspective, the aftermath of emancipation emerges as a struggle over class formation and transformation, in which the rights, privileges, and social role of a new class, the freedmen, were defined. The degree of economic and social autonomy achieved by the former slaves depended upon an elaborate series of power relationships, including the connection of the former slave society to the larger world economy and to outside, usually colonial, political authorities, the relative scarcity of land, and the degree to which, despite abolition, the planter class retained its local political hegemony. The results ranged from the total collapse of the plantation regime in Haiti to the coexistence of "reconstituted peasantries" with surviving plantations employing immigrant indentured labor in Trinidad and British Guiana, to the virtually unchanged plantation system of Barbados. In every postemancipation society, politics and economics were thoroughly intertwined. What makes the United States unique is that, for a time, black suffrage made the polity itself a battleground between former master and former slave.

Viewing Reconstruction as a unique episode in a prolonged process of adjustment to emancipation may shed new light on a number of continuing debates about the period. A considerable literature was produced in the 1970s on the reasons for the economic retardation of the postbellum South, and the dire poverty of southerners, particularly blacks. One school of thought, applying neoclassical economic theory to southern development, solved the problem by concluding that there was no problem. In a competitive marketplace in which rational, calculating self-interest determined the behavior of blacks and whites alike, the market produced the optimal possible result, given the economic resources of the South. By assuming what ought to be the subject of investigation—how men and women did in fact respond to an expanding market—these writers portrayed sharecropping as a rational choice serving the interests of both tenants and landlords, freely entered into by individuals from both groups, rather than the outcome of changing relationships of class and social power.[35] A somewhat different approach was that of Roger Ransom and Richard Sutch, who also employed a neoclassical model but concluded that because of local merchants' monopoly of credit the market failed to function properly and the South became locked into a cycle of cotton overproduction and worsening impoverishment. All these works, however, assumed that the free market, when functioning properly, serves the interests of all social classes. The idea that, especially in a colonial economy, the market itself may produce poverty and inequality, was not considered.[36]

Most strikingly, this literature, by examining economics but not political economy, overlooked the extent to which the plantation's survival and continued dominance had little to do with superior economic efficiency. Instead, in most postemancipation societies, it depended upon planters monopoly of rural economic resources and political power. Only a few writers have treated the postemancipation outcome within the context of class relations and political economy, most notably Jonathan Wiener, who described the competition of freedom, planters, and merchants in post-Civil War Alabama. Wiener showed how planters, after the overthrow of Reconstruction, were able to use the state to bolster their own interests at the expense of other groups. His study concluded that sharecropping emerged not simply as a matter of individual choice, but as a compromise resulting from the conflict between planters' need for a disciplined labor force and the freedmen's demand for autonomy. Ronald L. F. Davis went even further, contending that sharecropping was less a compromise than an unwilling concession forced upon reluctant planters by blacks' refusal to labor for wages under direct supervision.[37] In time sharecropping, in association with the crop lien, became a byword for semipeonage. But during Reconstruction it offered blacks a degree of control over their time, labor, and family arrangements inconceivable under slavery.[38]

Changes in class relations in the aftermath of emancipation may also provide the key to unlocking the experience of that shadowy presence, the nonslaveholding yeomanry. No irony in the study of the South is more profound than the distortion caused by historians' disregard of this unstudied majority. And no synthesis is possible until the nineteenth-century South is understood as more than a story of the blacks and their masters. We now know that the Civil War unleashed forces which swept the previously subsistence-oriented white upcountry into the cotton kingdom, a transformation which, as Steven Hahn explains, involved profound changes in economic, social, and political institutions among white farmers.[39] The economic dislocations spawned by the spread of cotton production and agricultural tenancy among whites may in time add a new dimension to the traditional debate over southern white Republicanism as well as the largely neglected post-Reconstruction Independent movements in several southern states. It is now clear that scalawags, as their opponents called them, were predominantly small farmers, whose loyalty to the Republican party rested on a combination of prewar hostility to the planter regime, persistent intrastate sectionalism, and wartime Unionism. But the changing class relations in the white upcountry also underscore the importance of such political concerns of Reconstruction as homestead exemptions and debtor relief, which, for a time, attracted many whites to the Republican party in states like North Carolina and Georgia.[40]

Like black suffrage, the size and political significance of the white yeomanry sets the American postemancipation experience apart from that of other countries. But Hahn's work also reemphasizes how, as in other societies, the law was employed in an attempt to redefine class relations in the aftermath of slavery. In recent years, there has been an increase of interest in the law's relationship to economic change and the impact of the judicial system on property rights and class relations. Morton Horwitz, for example, demonstrated how legal changes in the antebellum North redefined private property in the interests of corporations while restricting the traditional property rights of small-scale owners. Some work along these lines has already been done for the postwar South, particularly studies of the coercive labor legislation enacted during Presidential Reconstruction, repealed during Republican rule, and then reenacted, with modifications, upon Redemption. Laws punishing vagrancy, barring the "enticement" of laborers, regulating agricultural liens, and making breaches of contract punishable under the criminal law, all reflected an effort to use the power of the state to solidify the plantation's control over its labor force. Attention to these and less studied issues such as the changing incidence of taxation, the use of convict labor, and the regulation of hunting and fishing rights, reveals a vastly different picture of Republican Reconstruction than the conservative interlude portrayed in much recent literature. Reconstruction stands as a unique moment between two periods when the law was molded with one idea in mind—to maintain the plantation economy. If Reconstruction did not destroy the planter class, it did prevent the putting into place of a comprehensive legal code meant to shape the political economy of emancipation in the planters' interests. Even the refusal of Republican governments to enact labor control measures was itself a significant departure from the pattern in other postemancipation societies.[41]

To take full account of issues like these it will be necessary to reopen that strangely neglected question, the role of economic motives and influences in shaping Reconstruction politics. In reaction to inherited Beardian views of Reconstruction political alignments as little more than a conflict between industry and agriculture, revisionist writers like Irwin Unger, Robert Sharkey, and Stanley Coben insisted that there was no simple economic explanation for Reconstruction politics and no unified Radical economic policy or interest. But, as Lawrence Powell points out, these scholars "proved only that there were many economic interests during the period, not that there were none." Yet recent writings continue to avoid discussion of economic interests within both the national and southern Republican party, and the impact of profound changes in American economic enterprise— including the completion of the national railroad network, the rapid expansion of factory production, and the opening of the mining frontier—on the evolution of the party's southern policy.[42] The best recent work on the South, however, reminds us that the shape of the southern economy and the future role of blacks within it, were central points of political conflict during Reconstruction. What Mark Summers calls the "gospel of prosperity"—the idea of a New South developing along lines marked out by the urbanizing, industrializing North—animated southern Republican politics, inspiring both the extensive railroad schemes whose details have so often baffled historians, and the vision of a society freed from the dominance of the plantation, in which social advancement would be open to all on the basis of individual merit, not inherited caste distinctions.[43]

Here, of course, was a vision which was not to be. Yet it arose from a society in which all forms of social relations were in turmoil, in which the foundations of the social and political order were, for a time, open for discussion, in which seemingly trivial encounters between black and white became tests of racial and class power. Petty incidents—the failure of a freedman to yield the sidewalk or to address a former employer with the proper deference—sparked seemingly irrational acts of violence. Indeed, the very pervasiveness of violence in the post-Civil War South may be considered an indication of how high were the stakes being fought over.[44] Reconstruction's promise certainly exceeded its accomplishments. Yet so long as Reconstruction survived, so too did the possibility of further change, a prospect only foreclosed with Redemption and, later, the final implementation of segregation and disfranchisement. If, in retrospect, the outcome of the postemancipation struggle appears all but inevitable, it is equally certain that Reconstruction transformed the lives of southern blacks in ways unmeasurable by statistics and in areas unreachable by law. It raised blacks' expectations and aspirations, redefined their status in relation to the larger society, and allowed space for the creation of institutions that enabled them to survive the repression that followed. Its legacy deserves to survive as an inspiration to those Americans, black and white alike, who insist that the nation live up to the professed ideals of its political culture.

    1. August Meier, "An Epitaph for the Writing of Reconstruction History?" *Reviews in American History* 9 (March 1981): 87.
    2. Surveys of the Reconstruction literature include Bernard A. Weisberger, "The Dark and Bloody Ground of Reconstruction Historiograpy," *Journal of Southern History* 25 (November 1959): 427–47; and Richard O. Curry, "The Civil War and Reconstruction, 1861–1877: A Critical Overview of Recent Trends and Interpretations," *Civil War History* 20 (September 1974): 215–28.
    3. John R. Lynch, "Some Historical Errors of James Ford Rhodes," *Journal of Negro History* 2 (October 1917): 345–68; Howard K. Beale, *The Critical Year?* (New York: Harcourt Brace, 1930); Alrutheus A. Taylor, *The Negro in South Carolina During the Reconstruction* (Washington: The Association for the Study of Negro Life and History, 1924); W.E.B. DuBois, *Black Reconstruction in America* (New York: S. A. Russell, 1935); Francis B. Simkins and

Robert H. Woody, *South Carolina During Reconstruction* (Chapel Hill: University of North Carolina Press, 1932).

4. Major works of revisionism include Eric L. McKitrick, *Andrew Johnson and Reconstruction* (Chicago: University of Chicago Press, 1960); LaWanda Cox and John H. Cox, *Politics, Principle, and Prejudice 1865-1866* (Glencoe, Ill.: The Free Press, 1963); W. R. Brock, *An American Crisis* (London: St. Martin's, 1963); James M. McPherson, *The Struggle for Equality* (Princeton, N.J.: Princeton University Press, 1964); Joel Williamson, *After Slavery* (Chapel Hill: University of North Carolina Press, 1965); Hans L. Trefousse, *The Radical Republicans* (New York: Knopf, 1969). Kenneth M. Stampp, *The Era of Reconstruction* (New York: Knopf, 1965) summarized revisionism at its high point of influence.

5. This point is made effectively in Willie Lee Rose, *Slavery and Freedom* (New York: Oxford University Press, 1982), pp. 100–01.

6. C. Vann Woodward, "Seeds of Failure in Radical Race Policy," *American Philosophical Society Proceedings* 110 (1966): 1–9; August Meier, "Negroes in the First and Second Reconstructions of the South," *Civil War History* 13 (June 1967): 114–30.

7. C. Vann Woodward, review of *The Confederate Nation, New Republic,* March 17, 1979, p. 26.

8. Michael Les Benedict, *A Compromise of Principle* (New York: Norton, 1974), "Preserving the Constitution: The Conservative Basis of Radical Reconstruction," *Journal of American History* 61 (June 1974): 65–90, and "Preserving Federalism: Reconstruction and the Waite Court," *Supreme Court Review* (1978): 39–79; Michael Perman, *Reunion Without Compromise* (New York: Cambridge University Press, 1973); William Gillette, *Retreat from Reconstruction 1869-1879* (Baton Rouge: Louisiana State University Press, 1979).

9. Harold M. Hyman, *A More Perfect Union* (Boston: Houghton, Mifflin, 1975); Morton Keller, *Affairs of State* (Cambridge, Mass.: Harvard University Press, 1977). A similar argument was made in Philip S. Paludan, *A Covenant With Death* (Urbana: University of Illinois Press, 1975).

10. Joel H. Silbey, *A Respectable Minority* (New York: Norton, 1977); Edward L. Gambill, *Conservative Ordeal* (Ames: Iowa State University Press, 1981); Jerome Mushkat, *The Reconstruction of the New York Democracy, 1861-1874* (Rutherford, N.J.: Fairleigh Dickinson University Press, 1981). Lawrence Grossman did discern (and perhaps exaggerated) a new departure in Democratic racial attitudes during the 1870s in *The Democratic Party and the Negro* (Urbana: University of Illinois Press, 1976). On the North, see James C. Mohr, *The Radical Republicans and Reform in New York During Reconstruction* (Ithaca, N.Y.: Cornell University Press, 1973); Mohr, ed., *Radical Republicans in the North* (Baltimore: Johns Hopkins University Press, 1976); Eugene H. Berwanger, *The West and Reconstruction* (Urbana: University of Illinois Press, 1981); Felice A. Bonadio, *North of Reconstruction* (New York: New York University Press, 1970). Two indispensable works that shed light on the general decline of radicalism are David Montgomery, *Beyond Equality* (New York: Knopf, 1967); and Ellen DuBois, *Feminism and Suffrage* (Ithaca, N.Y.: Cornell University Press, 1978).

11. C. Vann Woodward, *Origins of the New South* (Baton Rouge: Louisiana State University Press, 1951). Critics of Woodward include Jonathan Wiener, *Social Origins of the New South 1860-1885* (Baton Rouge: Louisiana State University Press, 1978); Dwight B. Billings, Jr., *Planters and the Making of a 'New South'* (Chapel Hill: University of North Carolina Press, 1979); and James T. Moore, "Redeemers Reconsidered: Change and Continuity in the Democratic South, 1870-1900," *Journal of Southern History* 44 (August 1978): 357–78. Among studies of "planter persistence" are Lee W. Formwalt, "Antebellum Planter Persistence: Southwest Georgia—A Case Study," *Plantation Society in the Americas* 1 (October 1981): 410–29; and A. Jane Townes, "The Effect of Emancipation in Large Landholdings, Nelson and Goochland Counties, Virginia," *Journal of Southern History* 45 (August 1979): 403–12. James Roark's *Masters without Slaves* (New York: Norton, 1977) argues that the planter class declined in power and prestige after the Civil War.

12. William T. Auman and David D. Scarboro, "The Heroes of America in Civil War North Carolina," *North Carolina Historical Review* 58 (Autumn 1981): 327–63.

13. Joe Gray Taylor, *Louisiana Reconstructed, 1863-1877* (Baton Rouge: Louisiana State University Press, 1974); Jerrell H. Shofner, *Nor Is It Over Yet* (Gainesville: University Presses of Florida, 1974); William C. Harris, *The Day of the Carpetbagger* (Baton Rouge: Louisiana State University Press, 1979). Harris sympathized more fully with Mississippi's conservative Republican Governor James L. Alcorn than with his radical successor Adelbert Ames. This was partly because he inexplicably failed to consult the Ames Papers at Smith College, in which numerous letters from local black officials detail the devastating impact of Alcorn's conciliatory policy toward Mississippi Democrats on the Republican party and its black constituency. There are still no modern and comprehensive histories of Reconstruction in Alabama, Arkansas, Georgia, Tennessee, Texas, and, most strikingly, South Carolina.

14. William S. McFeely, *Yankee Stepfather* (New Haven, Conn.: Yale University Press, 1968); Louis S. Gerteis, *From Contraband to Freedom* (Westport, Conn.: Greenwood Press, 1973); Willie Lee Rose, *Rehearsal for Reconstruction* (Indianapolis: Bobbs-Merrill, 1964); Donald G. Nieman, *To Set the Law in Motion* (Millwood, N.Y.: Kraus International, 1979); Todd L. Savitt, "Politics in Medicine: The Georgia Freedmen's Bureau and the Organization of Health Care," *Civil War History*, 28 (March 1982): 45-64; Leon F. Litwack, *Been in the Storm So Long* (New York: Knopf, 1979). More favorable views of the Banks labor system appeared in Peyton McCrary, *Abraham Lincoln and Reconstruction* (Princeton, N.J.: Princeton University Press, 1978); and LaWanda Cox, *Lincoln and Black Freedom* (Columbia: University of South Carolina Press, 1981).

15. Important recent works on black education in Reconstruction include Robert C. Morris, *Reading, 'Riting, and Reconstruction* (Chicago: University of Chicago Press, 1981); Jacqueline Jones, *Soldiers of Light and Love* (Chapel Hill: University of North Carolina Press, 1980); Ronald E. Butchart, *Northern Schools, Southern Blacks and Reconstruction* (Westport, Conn.: Greenwood Press, 1980); Kenneth B. White, "The Alabama Freedmen's Bureau and Black Education: The Myth of Opportunity," *Alabama Review* 34 (April 1981): 107-24. For a critique of northern education, see Michael B. Katz, *The Irony of Early School Reform* (Cambridge, Mass.: Harvard University Press, 1968); Stanley K. Schultz, Samuel Bowles, and Herbert Gintis, *Schooling in Capitalist America* (New York: Basic Books, 1976).

16. The recent collection of essays edited by Otto H. Olsen, *Reconstruction and Redemption in the South* (Baton Rouge: Louisiana State University Press, 1980), does not even attempt to sum up the conclusions of the individual case studies or draw out common themes or patterns. The essays all, however, reflect an emphasis on the timidity of southern Republicans and the moderation of Reconstruction as a whole.

17. Cox, *Lincoln and Black Freedom*, pp. 142-84; Butchart, *Northern Schools*, p. 113.

18. On the land issue, see Claude F. Oubre, *Forty Acres and a Mule* (Baton Rouge: Louisiana State University Press, 1978); and Eric Foner, *Politics and Ideology in the Age of the Civil War* (New York: Oxford University Press, 1980), pp. 128-49. In a number of works, Herman L. Belz has stressed the importance of equality before the law for blacks, criticizing neorevisionist premises: see "The New Orthodoxy in Reconstruction Historiography," *Reviews in American History* 1 (March 1973): 106-13, *A New Birth of Freedom* (Westport, Conn.: Greenwood Press, 1976), and *Emancipation and Equal Rights* (New York: Norton, 1978). Problems of blacks who did obtain land are detailed in Elizabeth Bethel, *Promiseland* (Philadelphia: Temple University Press, 1981).

19. Francis B. Simkins, "New Viewpoints of Southern Reconstruction," *Journal of Southern History* 5 (February 1939): 49-61. Changes in black social and cultural life after emancipation are treated in Arnold H. Taylor, *Travail and Triumph* (Westport, Conn.: Greenwood Press, 1976); and Lawrence W. Levine, *Black Culture and Consciousness* (New York: Oxford University Press, 1976). On the black church, see Clarence G. Walker, *A Rock in a Weary Land* (Baton Rouge: Louisiana State University Press, 1982); and for fraternal organizations, Armstead L. Robinson, "Plans dat Comed from God: Institution Building and the Emergence of Black Leadership in Reconstruction Memphis," in *Towards a New South?*, eds. Orville V. Burton and Robert C. McMath Jr. (Westport, Conn.: Greenwood Press, 1982), pp. 71-102. On family structure, Herbert G. Gutman's *The Black Family in Slavery and Freedom, 1750-1925* (New York: Pantheon, 1976) tends to stress continuity of family structure rather than the

impact of emancipation and the suffrage on the roles of men and women within the black family. Our understanding of the impact of emancipation on blacks will be greatly advanced by the forthcoming appearance of the outstanding multivolume collection, *Freedom: A Documentary History of Emancipation,* edited by Ira Berlin, Joseph P. Reidy and Leslie S. Rowland.

20. For example, see these recent biographies of black political leaders: Okon E. Uya, *From Slavery to Public Service: Robert Smalls 1839-1915* (New York: Oxford University Press, 1971); Victor Ullman, *Martin Delany* (Boston: 1971); Peggy Lamson, *The Glorious Failure: Black Congressman Robert Brown Elliott and Reconstruction in South Carolina* (New York: Norton, 1973); Peter D. Klingman, *Josiah Walls* (Gainesville: University Presses of Florida, 1976); Loren Schweninger, *James T. Rapier and Reconstruction* (Chicago: University of Chicago Press, 1978).

21. Nell I. Painter, *Exodusters* (New York: Knopf, 1976); Thomas Holt, *Black Over White* (Urbana: University of Illinois Press, 1977). Among younger black scholars, conflicts among blacks were emphasized in Armstead L. Robinson, "Beyond the Realm of Social Consensus: New Meanings for Reconstruction for American History," *Journal of American History* 68 (September 1981): 276-97; whereas Charles Vincent, in *Black Legislators in Louisiana During Reconstruction* (Baton Rouge: Louisiana State University Press, 1976), took a rather more positive view of black legislators. On New Orleans, see David C. Rankin, "The Origins of Black Leadership in New Orleans During Reconstruction," *Journal of Southern History* 40 (August 1974): 417-40.

22. See Vernon Burton, "Race and Reconstruction: Edgefield County, South Carolina," *Journal of Social History* 11 (Fall 1978): 31-56; Edward Magdol, *A Right to the Land* (Westport, Conn.: Greenwood Press, 1977); Barry A. Crouch, "Self-Determination and Local Black Leaders in Texas," *Phylon* 39 (December 1978): 344-55; Walter J. Fraser, Jr., "Black Reconstructionists in Tennessee," *Tennessee Historical Quarterly* 34 (Winter 1975): 362-82. James W. Leslie's "Ferd Harris: Jefferson County's Black Republican Leader," *Arkansas Historical Quarterly* 37 (Autumn 1978): 240-51, exemplifies what needs to be done in terms of local black leadership.

23. John T. O'Brien's "Reconstruction in Richmond: White Reconstruction and Black Protest, April-June 1865," *Virginia Magazine of History and Biography* 89 (July 1981): 259-81, reveals the swift emergence of black political organization. Peter Kolchin, in *First Freedom* (Westport, Conn.: Greenwood Press, 1972), stresses the changes in political leadership and the prominent role of artisans. Robinson, in "Plans dat Comed from God," finds artisans played a prominent part in black political leadership in Memphis, while taking little role in the religious/benevolent institutions of the black community.

24. William C. Hine, "Charleston and Reconstruction: Black Political Leadership and the Republican Party, 1865-1877" (Ph.D. diss., Kent State University, 1978).

25. Wilson J. Moses, *The Golden Age of Black Nationalism, 1850-1924* (Hamden, Conn.: Shoe String Press, 1978). Another work transcending traditional dichotomies is David A. Gerber's *Black Ohio and the Color Line 1860-1915* (Urbana: University of Illinois Press, 1976), probably the outstanding study of blacks in a single state published in the past decade.

26. See J.G.A. Pocock, *The Machiavellian Moment* (Princeton, N.J.: Princeton University Press, 1975); and Gordon S. Wood, *The Creation of the American Republic 1776-1787* (Chapel Hill: University of North Carolina Press, 1969), among numerous other works on republicanism.

27. J. Mills Thornton, III, *Politics and Power in a Slave Society* (Baton Rouge: Louisiana State University Press, 1978); Michael F. Holt, *The Political Crisis of the 1850s* (New York: Wiley, 1978); Harry L. Watson, *Jacksonian Politics and Community Conflict* (Baton Rouge: Louisiana State University Press, 1981).

28. Article IV, Section 4: "The United States shall guarantee to every State in this Union a Republican Form of Government." See William M. Wiecek, *The Guarantee Clause of the U.S. Constitution* (Ithaca, N.Y.: Cornell University Press, 1972).

29. Howard N. Rabinowitz's *Race Relations in the Urban South 1865-1890* (New York: Oxford University Press, 1978) added a third element, "exclusion," arguing that segregation was perceived by blacks as a step forward from being excluded altogether from public facilities.

30. This combination of social separation and political inclusion parallels the experience of many immigrant groups, suggesting that that old chestnut, the black-immigrant comparison, still possesses some vitality, so long as it is not employed simply to identify the "cultural failings" which supposedly account for blacks' slower rate of advancement, as in Thomas Sowell, *Ethnic America* (New York: 1981).

31. Vincent Harding, *There Is a River* (New York: Harcourt, Brace, Jovanovich, 1981); George M. Fredrickson, *The Inner Civil War* (New York: Harper and Row, 1965); Nathan I. Huggins, *Slave and Citizen* (Boston: Little, Brown, 1980).

32. For an assessment of recent work in "comparative history" and various definitions of the genre, see George M. Fredrickson, "Comparative History," in *The Past Before Us*, ed. Michael Kammen (Ithaca, N.Y.: Cornell University Press, 1980), pp. 457–73. Fredrickson's *White Supremacy* (New York: 1981) is an exemplary comparative study of the evolution of systems of racial domination in the United States and South Africa. Cf. C. Vann Woodward, "The Price of Freedom," in *What Was Freedom's Price?*, ed. David L. Sansing (Jackson: University of Mississippi Press, 1978), pp. 93–113; Stanley L. Engerman, "Economic Aspects of the Adjustments to Emancipation in the United States and the British West Indies," *Journal of Interdisciplinary History* (forthcoming); Stanley Greenberg, *Race and State in Capitalist Development: Comparative Perspectives* (New Haven, Conn.: Yale University Press, 1980); Eric Foner, *"Nothing But Freedom": The Aftermath of Emancipation* (Baton Rouge: Louisiana State University Press, 1983), ch. 1.

33. For example, Jay R. Mandle, *The Roots of Black Poverty* (Durham, N.C.: Duke University Press, 1978), transposing the model of "plantation society" from the Caribbean to the American South, treats the period 1865–1919 as an undifferentiated unit, and derives economic structure, social relations, and black and white thought (including an "ideology of subservience" supposedly prevalent among the freedmen) from the overall model, rather than investigating them empirically.

34. Among the works on the aftermath of emancipation in other societies most valuable for students of the American South are Sidney W. Mintz, *Caribbean Transformations* (Chicago: University of Chicago Press, 1974) and "Slavery and the Rise of Peasantries," *Historical Reflections* 6 (Summer 1979): 213–42; Thomas C. Holt, " 'An Empire over the Mind': Emancipation, Race and Ideology in the British West Indies and the American South," in *Region, Race and Reconstruction*, eds., J. Morgan Kousser and James M. McPherson (New York: Oxford University Press, 1982), pp. 283–313; William A. Green, *British Slave Emancipation* (Oxford: Oxford University Press, 1976); Alan H. Adamson, *Sugar Without Slaves* (New Haven, Conn.: Yale University Press, 1972); Rebecca J. Scott, "Postemancipation Adaptations in Cuba, 1880–1899" (American Historical Association annual meeting, Los Angeles, 1981); Frederick Cooper, *From Slaves to Squatters* (New Haven, Conn.: Yale University Press, 1980).

35. Stephen J. DeCanio, *Agriculture in the Postbellum South* (Cambridge, Mass.: Harvard University Press, 1974); Robert Higgs, *Competition and Coercion* (New York: Cambridge University Press, 1977); Joseph D. Reid, "Sharecropping as an Understandable Market Response—the Post-Bellum South," *Journal of Economic History* 33 (March 1973): 106–30; Harold D. Woodman, "Sequel to Slavery: The New History Views the Postbellum South," *Journal of Southern History* 44 (November 1977): 523–54.

36. Roger L. Ransom and Richard Sutch, *One Kind of Freedom* (New York: Cambridge University Press, 1977). For several articles relating to this work, see *Explorations in Economic History* 16 (January and April 1979), especially the introductory remarks to the January issue, by William N. Parker.

37. Wiener, *Social Origins of the New South*, and "Class Structure and Economic Development in the American South, 1865–1955," *American Historical Review* 84 (October 1979): 970–92; Ronald L. F. Davis, "Labor Dependency Among Freedmen, 1865–1880," in *From Old South to New: Essays on the Transitional South*, eds. Walter J. Fraser and Winfred B. Moore (Westport, Conn.: Greenwood Press, 1981), pp. 155–65. Davis also cast doubt on the view that the Army's wartime wage labor experiment on Mississippi Valley plantations shaped Reconstruction policies, contending that the experience helped convince blacks to reject wage labor altogether.

38. Unfortunately, virtually the entire debate has thus far focused on the cotton South,

where sharecropping replaced slave labor. Little work has been done on rural class formation in sugar, where wage-labor plantations succeeded slavery, on rice, where a black peasantry not unlike that of the Caribbean came into existence, or on the Upper South, which experienced a complex process of economic diversification after the end of slavery. But see J. Carlyle Sitterson, *Sugar Country* (Lexington: University of Kentucky Press, 1953); and Joseph P. Reidy, "Sugar and Freedom: Emancipation in Louisiana's Sugar Parishes" (American Historical Association annual meeting, Washington, D.C., 1980); James M. Clifton, "Twilight Comes to the Rice Kingdom: Postbellum Rice Culture on the South Atlantic Coast," *Georgia Historical Quarterly* 62 (Summer 1978): 146–52; and Thomas F. Armstrong, "From Task Labor to Free Labor: The Transition Along Georgia's Rice Coast, 1820–1880," *Georgia Historical Quarterly* 64 (Winter 1980): 432–47; Foner, "Nothing But Freedom," ch. 3; Barbara J. Fields, "The Maryland Way from Slavery to Freedom" (Ph.D. diss., Yale University, 1978); Crandall A. Shifflett, *Shadowed Thresholds* (Knoxville: University of Tennessee Press, 1982).

39. Steven H. Hahn, "The Roots of Southern Populism: Yeoman Farmers and the Transformation of Georgia's Upper Piedmont, 1850–1890" (Ph.D. diss., Yale University, 1979). Cf. Forrest McDonald and Grady McWhiney, "The South from Self-Sufficiency to Peonage: An Interpretation," *American Historical Review* 85 (December 1980): 1095–1118.

40. On the scalawags, the classic article by David Donald, "The Scalawag in Mississippi Reconstruction, " *Journal of Southern History* 10 (November 1944): 447–60, stressed the role of the Whig planters among southern Republicans. Works stressing the role of upcountry small farmers include Gordon B. McKinney, *Southern Mountain Republicans 1865–1900* (Chapel Hill: University of North Carolina Press, 1978); Allen W. Trelease, "Who Were the Scalawags?" *Journal of Southern History* 29 (November 1963): 445–68. William T. Blain, "Banner Unionism in Mississippi, Choctaw County 1861–1869," *Mississippi Quarterly* 29 (September 1976): 207–20, is an outstanding study of the links between Unionism and white Republicanism in one Mississippi hill county.

41. Morton J. Horwitz, *The Transformation of American Law, 1780–1860* (Cambridge, Mass.: Harvard University Press, 1977); Harry N. Scheiber, "Regulation, Property Rights, and Definition of 'The Market': Law and the American Economy," *Journal of Economic History* 41 (March 1981): 103–09. On coercive labor legislation, see Daniel A. Novak, *The Wheel of Servitude* (Lexington: University of Kentucky Press, 1978); Pete Daniel, "The Metamorphosis of Slavery, 1865–1900," *Journal of American History* 66 (June 1979): 88–99; William Cohen, "Negro Involuntary Servitude in the South, 1865–1940: A Preliminary Analysis," *Journal of Southern History* 42 (February 1976): 31–60; and Harold D. Woodman, "Post-Civil War Southern Agriculture and the Law," *Agricultural History* 53 (January 1979): 319–37. Disputes over fencing and hunting rights are treated by Steven Hahn in "Common Rights and Commonwealth: The Stock-Law Struggle and the Roots of Southern Populism," in Kousser and McPherson, eds., *Region, Race and Reconstruction,* pp. 51–88, and "Hunting, Fishing, and Foraging: The Transformation of Property Rights in the Postbellum South," *Radical History Review* (forthcoming); and by J. Crawford King in "The Closing of the Southern Range: An Exploratory Study," *Journal of Southern History* 48 (February 1982): 53–70. These issues are also discussed in Foner, "Nothing But Freedom", ch. 2.

42. Irwin Unger, *The Greenback Era* (Princeton, N.J.: Princeton University Press, 1964); Robert P. Sharkey, *Money, Class, and Party* (Baltimore: Johns Hopkins University Press, 1959); Stanley Coben, "Northeastern Business and Radical Reconstruction: A Re-Examination," *Mississippi Valley Historical Review* 46 (June 1959): 67–90; Lawrence N. Powell, "The American Land Company and Agency: John A. Andrew and the Northernization of the South," *Civil War History* 21 (December 1975): 293–308. On economic change, see Alfred D. Chandler, Jr., *The Visible Hand* (Cambridge, Mass.: Harvard University Press, 1977).

43. Mark W. Summers, "Radical Reconstruction and the Gospel of Prosperity" (Ph.D. diss., University of California, Berkeley, 1980).

44. Allen W. Trelease's *White Terror* (New York: Harper and Row, 1971) remains the sole comprehensive study of the problem of Reconstruction violence, a subject whose profound impact on political, economic, and social relations remains to be fully explored.

SUCCESS AND SECURITY:
THE MEANING OF SOCIAL MOBILITY IN AMERICA

Howard P. Chudacoff

Russell Conwell, the Baptist minister and self-appointed spokesman for the Gospel of Success, preached the same message night after night to countless millions in late nineteenth-century America. In his famous sermon, "Acres of Diamonds," which he delivered over six thousand times, Conwell declared, "I say to you . . . that there was never a time in your history . . . when the opportunity for a poor man to make money . . . is so clearly apparent as it is at this very hour. . . . You have no right to be poor. It is your duty to be rich."[1] According to this message, success in the United States not only was possible; it was a moral obligation.

For years this belief nurtured the hopes of those trying to succeed and salved the consciences of those who had attained material success. Moreover, the availability and ease of success through social mobility supposedly distinguished the New World from the Old. A half century before Conwell wrote "Acres of Diamonds," Alexis de Tocqueville observed that, unlike Europe, America had few huge inherited fortunes and that its wealthy men typically were self-made. "In America," he noted, "most of the rich men were formerly poor."[2] Poverty was not a barrier to success. In fact, to some, such as Horatio Alger and Andrew Carnegie, poverty was a prerequisite, a quality that gave a person the incentive to achieve success.

In the twentieth century, sociologists, beginning with Pitrim Sorokin, and later, historians, beginning with Stephan Thernstrom, undertook wide-ranging efforts to assess the nature and extent of social mobility in American society.[3] Their studies have disclosed that the meaning and effects of social mobility are very complex. Although the patterns that have been identified seem to support the contention that mobility has been a basic fact of American culture, they also include subtleties that have eluded interpretation.[4]

As several scholars have indicated, the concept of social mobility is deceptively simple.[5] Most analysts would probably accept a definition that includes the movement, upward and downward, by an individual or group between higher and lower social positions. But just what constitutes social position, how to specify a hierarchy of positions, and how to define movement among

0048-7511/82/0104-0101 $01.00

positions have prompted considerable debate. Moreover, the criteria for hierarchies and rates of movement are subject to regional, cultural, and chronological variations. Different groups of people living at different time periods may have different values about the possible determinants of social standing, which include income, family, residence, religion, associational networks, and other variables.

Lacking elaborate survey data and the ability to interact with their subjects, historians have used basically three indicators to define social position and to gauge movement between positions: occupation, property, and residence. Occupation has been the most useful index chiefly because it is the most available one. With its scales of income, prestige, and influence, occupation offers the analyst opportunities to assess upward and downward movement; moreover, the extant historical data on individuals, such as censuses and city directories, are more likely to include occupational information than any other socioeconomic variable. But although it is the most commonly used index, occupation may be less important in understanding the extent and meaning of social mobility in American history than other factors—as I shall try to indicate later in this essay.

Wealth, represented by property holding and defined simply by dollar value, offers a more singularly ordinal scale for determining rank and mobility. Information about such holdings, however, is often scarce, especially after 1870 when the federal census no longer recorded property values for urban dwellers. In addition, large numbers of people either did not own property to have its value recorded or were able to divide and obscure their holdings so that tax records and other listings did not accurately represent individual or family wealth.

Residence has implied both wealth and prestige; more importantly, change of residence—geographical mobility—has implied movement on the social scale. But this movement has provoked debate over its interpretation. Traditionally, observers believed that geographical mobility was tied to social betterment. Thernstrom and others, however, have asserted that there is little reason to believe that the people who left a community benefited from upward mobility, given the circumstances under which they left.[6] Furthermore, most historians who have addressed the issue of geographical mobility have linked an individual's persistence in a community to upward social mobility, particularly acquisition of property.

Although time and space constraints preclude a detailed summary of the patterns of mobility that historical studies have identified in American cities, an overview of these findings can establish a context for discussion and speculation. Most historical studies written in the past decade or so support Thernstrom's initial conclusion that large numbers of people experienced small increments of occupational mobility and that in almost all places the amount of upward movement outweighed the downward. In new, fast-growing cities like Atlanta, Los Angeles, and Omaha, about one in five manual workers rose to white collar positions in ten years, provided that they stayed in the city for that long. In older, northeastern cities such as Boston, Poughkeepsie, and Newburyport, upward mobility averaged closer to one in six in ten years.[7] Roughly 40 percent of the men traced in most communities attained occupational levels that were higher than those of their fathers, while incidences of shifts downward from father's rank hovered around 20 percent.[8] Findings concerning property mobility are harder to compare because different communities had varied real estate markets that created different opportunities for property acquisition. It seems, however, that small improvements in wealth were common, though in larger, denser cities like New York property acquisition was more difficult than it was in smaller communities like Warren, Pennsylvania.[9]

In spite of these general frequencies, many people faced persistent barriers to mobility while others benefited from advantages. Men with working class backgrounds normally were not able to rise into white collar occupations, and sons of businessmen and professionals attained and retained white collar status with relative ease. Family connections and assistance gave advantages to some men, especially those entering into business.[10] Ethnicity and race considerably affected one's chances for success. In almost all instances blacks suffered from stifled opportunities.[11] Foreign born men also encountered more obstacles than native born did, though in certain trades and businesses, and especially in the attainment of small retail establishments, immigrant entry into white collar ranks outpaced that of natives.[12] Thus although there was, and still is, fluidity in the American social system, privilege often prevailed.

Although the empirical evidence has contradicted observations such as the one by Tocqueville and has disproved the so-called rags-to-riches myth, historians have drawn meaningful generalizations from the actual patterns of mobility. For example, many have posited social mobility as a mechanism used by immigrants in adapting to urban-industrial America. In spite of limited opportunities and differences between ethnic groups, some improvement in occupational rank and property holding was real for most groups—if not for an individual, then for his or her children and neighbors. Such reality reinforced immigrants' reasons for coming to the United States.[13] In addition, scholars have viewed the modest but extensive incidences of mobility as a mitigating factor in community politics and the workplace. According to this interpretation, upward mobility and acceptance of the success myth helped to blunt class-based protest which the displacements of industrialization may otherwise have exacerbated.[14]

A few historians have focused their analysis more finely in an attempt to perceive how the process of mobility did or did not work in discrete situations. Clyde and Sally Griffen discovered that immigrants generally chose upward paths that led from manual labor into small proprietorships while natives either bettered themselves by moving into expanding, lucrative construction trades or climbing into managerial and proprietary positions in larger, more stable establishments. Moreover, within the manual ranks, certain trades like cabinetmaking and shoemaking were being deskilled by mass production and offered little prospect, while carriagemaking involved skills that allowed craftsmen to enhance opportunities for self-employment.[15] Others have reinforced this view, pointing out that a city's particular social structure influenced the pattern of social mobility and that the work setting itself, especially its size, was a factor in determining a person's opportunities and security.[16]

Michael Katz has reminded us, however, that social mobility can occur only in a society where distributions of status and resources are unequal and where therefore there are chances for people to gain or lose. Though the point may appear obvious, Katz's identification of inequality and transiency as the major themes of nineteenth-century urban history in North America is significant because it sets the context in which social mobility could occur. In turn, the existence or opportunities for mobility enabled people to accept the capitalistic system despite its perpetuation of privilege and poverty. Katz, Doucet, and Stern say that industrial capitalism created two distinct classes: a working class, including a huge army of immigrants, who sold their labor; and a business class, also containing migrants, which controlled resources and bought labor. Although people changed occupations and acquired property over time, says Katz, the shifts occurred chiefly within these two rigidifying structural divisions, with the new effect being that the same socioeconomic position was passed from one generation to another. People moved upward and downward but seldom far. Thus the inequality of a capitalistic class system persisted in a seemingly fluid society.[17]

The study of mobility, then, has identified important and generally consistent patterns of social structure in American cities. But the data and speculations of these studies have elicited questions that point in new directions. While most historians have tried to interpret the mobility process in terms of its effects on society and its meaning for individuals trying to fulfill goals of success, only a few have placed their analyses within a broad context of people's attempts to adapt to their environment. I would submit that the mobility studies have shown that movement up and down scales of occupational status and wealth represent only a few of the alternatives available in a society where decisions operated in a continuum of security and risk.

As John Modell has indicated, the industrial transformation of America in the nineteenth century created a society characterized by "widespread externally-imposed uncertainty." Dangers such as death, sickness, and food shortage, which had plagued preindustrial society, combined with employment instability, housing shortages, industrial accidents, and other threats to individual and family security, causing people to assume what Modell labels a "defensive mode" of adaptation. Such a strategy involved use of kinship, voluntary associations, formal agencies (such as insurance), and especially cooperation within the nuclear family (such as which and how many family members would enter the work force) to minimize uncertainty.[18] Individual and group efforts to defend against uncertainty are not unique to nineteenth-century America, but the concepts of risk and security involved in Modell's interpretation have important implications for understanding various patterns of mobility and alternatives to them.

In part, these implications derive from the problems of measuring what constitutes significant upward or downward mobility. I already have mentioned that historians have used occupation as the most available index of social position, but many of them have admitted that occupation is an imperfect and even deceptive standard to employ. Most have adopted the hierarchical schemes developed by Thernstrom or by Katz, Blumin, Griffen, and Hershberg.[19] Strong justification can be made that these scales do represent relative rankings of probable earnings and other status-related factors. Nevertheless, even some of those who fashioned the rankings find serious fault with them. First, the occupational titles reported in the census manuscripts which most mobility historians use are often ambiguous and misleading, and they must be clarified by combination with other information such as presence of servants in the household or designations of self-employment indicated in city directories.[20] In addition, scholars analyzing wage data in censuses of manufacturing have uncovered so much variation in wages paid to skilled workers as well as between skilled and unskilled workers that they have questioned the validity of such categories for indexes of social mobility.[21]

Broadly defined occupational divisions of manual and nonmanual ranks, blue collar and white collar, have been used to gauge "significant" mobility; that is, the most meaningful social-structural moves have been said to entail upward and downward shifts between these two categories.[22] This analytical technique, which has facilitated hypothesis testing and comparisons between communities, has several pitfalls. First, the two categories are so large and diverse that they can mask the importance of shifts within them. Second, recent studies have presented information that challenges the assumption that a move from blue collar to white collar really represented upward mobility. Many nonmanual clerical workers received lower wages than manual laborers did. Moreover, movement into nonmanual proprietary ranks was an extremely risky venture. The failure rates of small businesses in the nineteenth-century city were remarkably high: in some places a firm had only a one in three chance of surviving for three years.[23] Thus movement into white collar status could augur downward mobility as well as upward.

More importantly, given the risks involved in climbing the mobility ladder and in the general nature of life, individuals made choices that were influenced by their cultural values and by the availability, or unavailability, of alternatives. Thernstrom noted that rags-to-respectability, rather than rags-to-riches, was the path that Americans sought most.[24] But recent studies of the American working class have shown that respectability comprised a part of a larger goal: security. In a world where almost capricious swings of the business cycle and employers' quests for profits buffeted workers among the uncertainties of wage cuts and layoffs, a secure job—and the steady income it would bring—could have more relevance in terms of success than attainment of a higher social status.[25] The search for security did not necessarily mean that workers were a beaten class struggling to survive in an oppressive industrial order. Their efforts often were driven by a sense of dignity and ideals of equal rights, and their unions and protests did achieve some success. Eventually, it is true, they were mostly coopted by capitalist culture, but this process occurred gradually, sometimes not until the twentieth century. In the nineteenth century and early twentieth, manual workers sought their own brand of security, one which included a life of comfort and dignity where they had control over their labor and the fruits of their toil.[26]

The role of alternatives is probably the most important but least explored factor in the mobility process. This factor first received attention in David Crews's study of mobility in a German industrial town, Bochum, in the Ruhr.[27] Although his samples were small and statistically inconclusive, Crews suggested that the structure of work influenced the mobility choices available to manual laborers. Bochum factory workers, when they moved upward occupationally, tended to remain within manual ranks; they learned enough skills to tend a machine or undertook apprenticeships and became craftsmen. Miners, on the other hand, rose into nonmanual ranks by becoming proprietors of small businesses. This contrasting pattern derived from differences in available alternatives. Within factory work—in Bochum and, by implication, in other industrial cities—there was a hierarchy through which a man could rise, each step promising more security as well as higher wages. This path was one of familiarity and safety. The mining industry, however, lacked a multigraded job hierarchy, and virtually the only upward escape was a route leading to shopkeeping and nonmanual status. Upwardly mobile miners had to take the risk of opening a business; upwardly mobile factory workers did not.[28]

Clyde and Sally Griffen have taken a similar perspective on the American city of Poughkeepsie, New York, concluding that the type of occupation one started in influenced that person's opportunities and choices. For example, as mass production made the custom work of cabinetworkers and shoemakers less necessary, artisans who remained in these trades faced choices of either taking the risks of becoming retailers or accepting lower incomes of repair work or factory labor. Like Bochum's miners, their choices were limited. On the other hand, expanding trades such as machinists and moulders offered more opportunities for stability and attracted newcomers who had no previous experience. Moreover, the Griffens found that immigrants, because they lacked the skills, familiarity, and family connections that were needed in the job market, concentrated in employment where deskilling and mass production created low wages and poor working conditions. Those who were upwardly mobile took the path to self-employment (with impressive frequencies), especially in marginal neighborhood shops where they sold food, drink, and clothing to fellow immigrants. Natives, by contrast, had advantages and safer opportunities. Born more often into stable nonmanual statuses, which they tended to retain, or predominating in the more secure construction and industrial trades, natives had different alternatives. The Griffens conclude that the process of mobility involved "individual choices, however much the choices seemed to be shaped by circumstances and prevailing attitudes."[29]

A further affirmation of the quest for security comes from John Bodnar in his study of Steelton, Pennsylvania, 1870–1940. By analyzing the various subcommunities of this steel-mill town—native whites, native blacks, northern Europeans (mostly German and Irish), and eastern and southern Europeans (Croatians, Serbs, Slovenes, Slavs, and Italians)—Bodnar concludes that the adjustments and new class alignments necessitated by industrialization caused "individuals . . . to be less interested in mobility than in security."[30] As deskilling and prejudice reduced the mobility opportunities for new immigrants from southern and eastern Europe, these groups sought to adapt by choosing alternative paths to security such as the formation of ethnic group associations inside and outside the workplace and, later, the organization of unions. Blacks, lacking ethnic networks that could provide an associational social life and aid in the securing of jobs, took the option of moving somewhere else in search of steady work. Thus again, the mix of individual choice with a community's particular social structure determined the meaning of mobility.

Bodnar and others have suggested that immigrants and other groups took different views of the American success ethic. These historians have recognized the importance of cultural values pertaining to family, religion, social organization, and other aspects of group life as providing contexts in which people could strive for success when occupational or other economic avenues

were closed.[31] Although some immigrants may have compared unfavorably
with natives when measured on scales of economic status, their achievements
in terms of other values may have been significant. As the Griffens perceptively observe, the "settling by wageearners into niches with a protected
social life need not imply lack of ambition nor lack of awareness of how outsiders saw them and their jobs. . . . It does suggest that many of them much
of the time did not look at their own working lives from the perspective of the
American success ethic, even its more modest versions."[32]

Finally, the concept of security as a goal in an uncertain world provides a
broader setting for assessing the meaning of geographical mobility. As I mentioned earlier, the tendency by mobility historians has been to interpret persistence rates (whether and for how long people remained in one community)
by equating stability with success. According to this view, those who seemed
to improve by rising on the occupational ladder and/or increasing their property holdings were the ones who had persisted in the community, while the
propertyless and occupationally immobile were the ones who left. Yet few
have sufficiently considered geographical mobility—lack of persistence—as a
strategy to maximize opportunity and overcome uncertainty. Low rates of
persistence could signal that a community suffered from declining opportunites and that people involved in outmigration were making calculated
choices to improve their lives. Thus, for example, the considerable outmigration that Thernstrom found in Newburyport may represent people sensibly
fleeing a stagnant city rather than a "floating proleteriat" of men who rarely
won economic gains.[33]

In sum, then, mobility, geographical as well as social, can be seen within
cultural and economical contexts where values and alternatives varied. For
vast numbers of people, American cities were—and for some, still are—
places of uncertainty. If Michael Katz and others are correct in concluding
that the industrial capitalism emerging in the nineteenth century created
structures of inequality within which movement occurred, but never enough
to refashion the social order, then the concepts of security and success would
seem to have more trenchant relevance for interpreting people's behavior and
motivations than mere rising and skidding on scales of occupation and
wealth.

American historians have been examining social mobility for nearly two
decades. From Thernstrom on, their work has been enlightening and provocative. But obviously old questions remain unanswered, and continued
research has unearthed new questions. Many of these questions prevail
because historians have avoided using sophisticated analytical tools. Most
analyses have tried merely to explain social or geographical mobility in terms

of "influencing" variables considered separately in disjointed chapters; that is, the joint and cumulative effects on mobility of race, ethnicity, skill, father's occupation, and other such determining characteristics have not been measured. For example, early studies identified a positive relationship between persistence and high occupational rank, but as yet only Katz, Doucet, and Stern have tried to identify the relative influences of occupation along with age, nativity, wealth, family size, and other factors considered together. Except for Katz, Doucet, and Stern, historians have not attempted multivariate techniques such as multiple classification analysis or analysis of variance to refine their interpretations.[34] Nor have they expanded their explanatory framework to include ecological variables (such as job markets, transportation, and housing) with the individual-level variables (such as age, ethnicity, and property) that they commonly use.[35] Such advanced techniques and conceptualization are necessary for a more comprehensive assessment of mobility as historians and sociologists have defined it.

But also, as I have tried to suggest, historians ought to broaden the scope of their analysis to include a larger definition of mobility and its alternatives. Hierarchical scales of occupation and wealth existed in a society where the perceptions and expectations that guided decisions were not uniform from one individual or group to another. Moreover, the nature of work and community profoundly influenced the extent of opportunity. A few mobility historians and labor historians have begun to address these issues.[36] But as yet no study of an American community has sufficiently assessed mobility by considering the questions of availability, alternatives, and security that David Crews raised for a German community.

Furthermore, only one study, that of Poughkeepsie by Clyde and Sally Griffen, has examined in an extensive way the meaning of mobility for women.[37] Yet for women, as well as for men, social and geographical mobility constituted important components in the search for security. Many women, from the Lowell millworkers to twentieth-century factory and clerical workers, used jobs as a means of improving their lives, though for some female laborers work was so exploitive that they yearned for the security and flexibility of domestic life.[38] Women also attained higher social status through marriage—as did men. Yet little research has been done on the opportunites and alternatives available to women and the risks and perceptions involved in their decisions.

Perspectives could be broadened in other ways as well. The field of mobility studies could benefit from more comparative analyses, especially comparisons between urban and rural communities such as the unique work done by Gordon W. Kirk.[39] Also, more research needs to be done on the newly opened routes to mobility in the nineteenth century such as sports and politics. By sports, I mean not just professional athletics but also the associational life and leisure activities that expanded and provided a broadened set of choices beyond the world of work.[40] Very little is known about interrelationships between mobility, persistence, and political participation in American cities. In a review of Thernstrom's *The Other Bostonians*, for example, Sam Bass Warner, Jr. observed that Thernstrom's data suggested that "the persistent community is the political community."[41] Yet only one study has attempted to link voting lists and registrations with mobility records, and the results of that linkage seem to contradict Warner's speculation by suggesting that the people who moved most frequently had a higher probability of political participation than those who were more stable.[42]

I have not intended the foregoing essay to be a comprehensive review of all American works on social mobility. I know there are many studies that I have not cited and that valuable work currently is in progress. Rather, I have attempted to identify the strengths and weaknesses of existing analyses and to suggest ways that the interpretative context has been and can be expanded. During the mid-1970s, after publication of Thernstrom's *The Other Bostonians* with its sweeping scope and excellent synthesis of other studies, there was for a time some feeling that mobility studies had reached their apex. Recently published works, however, should dissolve that feeling and provoke new research that will enable mobility history to blend with and enhance the fields of urban and social history even more than it has in the past.

1. Russell H. Conwell, "Acres of Diamonds" in *Modern Eloquence, Volume Eight: Famous Lectures,* ed. Ashley H. Thorndike (New York: Modern Eloquence Corporation, 1923), pp. 145, 150.

2. Alexis de Tocqueville, *Democracy in America,* vol. 2, ed. Phillip Bradley (New York: Vintage Books, 1945), p. 54.

3. Pitrim Sorokin, *Social Mobility* (New York: Harper & Bros., 1927); Stephan Thernstrom, *Poverty and Progress: Social Mobility in a Nineteenth Century City* (Cambridge, Mass.: Harvard University Press, 1964).

4. A number of these subtleties, including the ideological biases of mobility historians, have been perceptively outlined in James A. Henretta, "The Study of Social Mobility: Ideological Assumptions and Conceptual Bias," *Labor History* 18 (Spring 1977): 164–78.

5. See, for example, Edward Pessen, ed., *Three Centuries of Social Mobility in America* (New York: D.C. Heath, 1974).

6. Thernstrom first developed this point in *Poverty and Progress* and elaborated it in *The Other Bostonians: Poverty and Progress in the American Metropolis, 1880–1970* (Cambridge, Mass.: Harvard University Press, 1973). See also Peter R. Knights, *The Plain People of Boston: A Study in City Growth* (New York: Oxford University Press, 1971).

7. See Thernstrom, *The Other Bostonians,* Table 9.4, p. 234 for a compilation of rates for these cities.

8. Thernstrom, *The Other Bostonians,* pp. 241–50.

9. Thomas Kessner, *The Golden Door: Italian and Jewish Immigrant Mobility in New York City, 1800–1915* (New York: Oxford University Press, 1977); Michael P. Weber, *Social*

Change in an Industrial Town: Patterns of Progress in Warren, Pennsylvania from the Civil War to World War I (University Park: Pennsylvania State University Press, 1976).

10. Clyde Griffen and Sally Griffen, *Natives and Newcomers: The Ordering of Opportunity in Mid-Nineteenth Century Poughkeepsie* (Cambridge, Mass.: Harvard University Press, 1978); Peter R. Decker, *Fortunes and Families: White Collar Mobility in Nineteenth Century San Francisco* (Cambridge, Mass.: Harvard University Press, 1978).

11. See, for example, Richard J. Hopkins, "Occupational and Geographical Mobility in Atlanta, 1870–1896," *Journal of Southern History* 34 (May 1968): 200–13; Griffen and Griffen, *Natives and Newcomers*, pp. 77–78, 214–15; Thernstrom, *The Other Bostonians*, ch. 8.

12. See, for example, Kessner, *The Golden Door*, ch. 5; Griffen and Griffen, *Natives and Newcomers*, ch. 8; Dean Esslinger, *Immigrants and the City: Ethnicity and Mobility in a Nineteenth Century Midwestern Community* (Port Washington, N.Y.: Kennikat, 1975); Howard P. Chudacoff, *Mobile Americans: Residential and Social Mobility in Omaha, 1880–1920* (New York: Oxford University Press, 1972), ch. 5.

13. Josef Barton, *Peasants and Strangers: Italians, Rumanians, and Slovaks in an American City, 1890–1950* (Cambridge, Mass.: Harvard University Press, 1975); Humbert S. Nelli, *The Italians in Chicago, 1860–1920: A Study in Ethnic Mobility* (New York: Oxford University Press, 1970); Kessner, *The Golden Door*; Griffen and Griffen, *Natives and Newcomers*; Esslinger, *Immigrants and the City.*

14. This point is best developed in Thernstrom, *Poverty and Progress* and *The Other Bostonians*, and in Daniel J. Walkowitz, *Worker City, Company Town: Iron and Cotton-Worker Protest in Troy and Cohoes, New York, 1855–1884* (Urbana: University of Illinois Press, 1978), though it is challenged in Alan Dawley, *Class and Community: The Industrial Revolution in Lynn* (Cambridge, Mass.: Harvard University Press, 1976).

15. Griffen and Griffen, *Natives and Newcomers*, chs. 6–8.

16. John Bodnar, *Immigration and Industrialization: Ethnicity in an American Mill Town* (Pittsburgh: University of Pittsburgh Press, 1977); Bruce Laurie, Theodore Hershberg, and George Alter, "Immigrants and Industry: The Philadelphia Experience, 1850–1880," *Journal of Social History* 9 (Winter 1975): 219–48.

17. Michael B. Katz, *The People of Hamilton, Canada West: Family and Class in a Mid-Nineteenth Century City* (Cambridge, Mass.: Harvard University Press, 1975); Michael B. Katz, Michael J. Doucet, and Mark J. Stern, *The Social Organization of Early Industrial Organization* (Cambridge, Mass.: Harvard University Press, 1982).

18. John Modell, "Changing Risks, Changing Adaptations: American Families in the Nineteenth and Twentieth Centuries," in *Kin and Communities: Families in America*, eds. Allan Lichtman and Joan R. Callinor (Washington, D.C.: Smithsonian Institute Press, 1979), pp. 119–20. This point is substantiated in Tamara K. Hareven, *Family Time and Industrial Time: The Relationships Between Family and Work in a New England Industrial Community* (Cambridge, Mass.: Harvard University Press, 1982).

19. See Thernstrom, *The Other Bostonians*, appendix B; Katz, *The People of Hamilton, Canada West*, appendix 2.

20. Michael B. Katz, "Occupational Classification in History," *Journal of Interdisciplinary History* 3 (Summer 1972): 63–68; Clyde Griffen, "The Study of Occupational Mobility in Nineteenth Century America: Problems and Possibilities," *Journal of Social History* 5 (Spring 1972): 310–30.

21. Laurie, Hershberg, and Alter, "Immigrants and Industry." See also Stuart Blumin, "The Historical Study of Vertical Mobility," *Historical Methods Newsletter* 1 (September 1968): 1–13.

22. Again, Thernstrom's pioneering efforts in *Poverty and Progress* and *The Other Bostonians* set the precedents for this interpretation.

23. Griffen and Griffen, *Natives and Newcomers*, ch. 5; Katz, *The People of Hamilton, Canada West*, ch. 5; Decker, *Fortunes and Families.*

24. Thernstrom, *The Other Bostonians.*

25. This point emerges most clearly in Bodnar, *Immigration and Industrialization* and in Walkowitz, *Worker City, Company Town*.

26. See Dawley, *Class and Community;* Herbert G. Gutman, *Work, Culture, and Society in Industrializing America: Essays in American Working-Class and Social History* (New York: Knopf, 1976).

27. David Crews, "Definitions of Modernity: Social Mobility in a German Town, 1880-1901," *Journal of Social History* 7 (Fall 1973): 51-74.

28. Crews, "Definitions of Modernity," pp. 55-57. Crews notes that miners could expand their alternatives by shifting to factory work but that few did so because their age and social prejudice against them made it hard for them to make such shifts successfully.

29. Griffen and Griffen, *Natives and Newcomers*, chs. 7-8, quotation, p. 261.

30. Bodnar, *Immigrants and Industrialization*, p. xv.

31. See, for example, Barton, *Peasants and Strangers*, chs. 5-6; Griffen and Griffen, *Natives and Newcomers*, ch. 2. Henretta, "Study of Social Mobility," pp. 170 ff., has made this same point, asserting that "Any valid analysis of historical experience must consider the expectations and goals of the actors themselves; to do otherwise is to interpret their lives in terms of an alien conceptual framework."

32. Griffen and Griffen, *Natives and Newcomers*, p. 49.

33. Thernstrom, *Poverty and Progress*, pp. 84-90, and *The Other Bostonians*, p. 42.

34. Katz, Doucet, and Stern, *The Social Organization of Early Industrial Capitalism*, chs. 3-5.

35. A forceful argument for this point can be found in Theodore Hershberg, ed., *Philadelphia: Work, Space, Family, and Group Experience in the Nineteenth Century* (New York: Oxford University Press, 1981), p. 124.

36. See. particularly, Griffen and Griffen, *Natives and Newcomers;* Bodnar, *Immigration and Industrialization;* Walkowitz, *Worker City, Company Town;* Dawley, *Class and Community;* Hareven, *Family Time and Industrial Time*.

37. Griffen and Griffen, *Natives and Newcomers*, ch. 11.

38. See, for example, Thomas Dublin, *Women and Work: The Transformation of Work and Community in Lowell, Massachusetts, 1826-1860* (New York: Columbia University Press, 1979); Susan Estabrook Kennedy, *If All We Did Was to Weep at Home: A History of White Working-Class Women in America* (Bloomington: Indiana University Press, 1979); Leslie Woodcock Tentler, *Wage-Earning Women: Industrial Work and Family Life in the United States, 1900-1930* (New York: Oxford University Press, 1979); Hareven, *Family Time and Industrial Time*, ch. 10.

39. Gordon W. Kirk, *The Promise of American Life: Social Mobility in a Nineteenth Century Immigrant Community, Holland, Michigan, 1847-1894* (Philadelphia: American Philosophical Society, 1978).

40. See Steven A. Reiss, "Sport and the American Dream: A Review Essay," *Journal of Social History* 14 (Winter 1980): 295-303.

41. Sam Bass Warner, Jr., review of *The Other Bostonians* by Stephen Thernstrom, *Political Science Quarterly* 89 (June 1974): 413.

42. Chudacoff, *Mobile Americans*, ch. 8.

IN SEARCH OF PROGRESSIVISM

Daniel T. Rodgers

No one needs to be told that the concept of "progressivism" fell into trouble in the 1970s. For decades the notion that the political and intellectual ferment of the Roosevelt and Wilson years cohered into an entity called progressivism was one of the central organizing principles of American history.[1] How that coherence should be defined was a matter of starkly divided opinion; but the term itself was as crucial a part of the historiographical scaffolding as "republicanism" or "Jacksonian democracy." The search for progressivism — undertaken with implicit confidence that the expedition would reveal some typical progressive profile, coherent political agenda, or, at least, definable ethos — helped attract more historical talent to the first two decades of the twentieth century than to any other period of modern America. Yet the 1970s had barely begun when Peter Filene attacked the whole notion of a coherent progressive movement as a semantic and conceptual muddle, and declared it dead and buried.[2]

Those who shared Filene's doubts did not win the easy victory Filene had envisioned. Progressivism shuffled through the 1970s as a corpse that would not lie down. Few historians seriously tried to get along without the term "progressivism" or "progressive movement." For every historian who, like Jack Kirby, declared outright that the covering term "progressivism" "cannot withstand rigorous definition," there were others ready to try their hand at the task.[3] But it was impossible to miss the mounting undertone of apology behind the efforts at definition, the increasingly elaborate qualifications attached to lists of shared "progressive" goals and values, the occasional candid admission that the conflicting interpretations of progressivism could not be made to add up, and the suggestions that the traditional questions had been played out, if not in some way misconceived.

The nervous tick was particularly conspicuous in that litmus test of historiographical moods: the undergraduate survey text. By the mid 1970s, many undergraduates were being warned at the outset that they would find the Progressive era "confusing." "The concept of progressivism turns out to be curiously elusive," they were cautioned. The movement "may never be fully understood," they were told, before being shuttled off to the obligatory chapters on Roosevelt and Wilson and the unenviable task of demonstrating

0048-7511/82/0104-0113 $01.00
Copyright © 1982 by The Johns Hopkins University Press

their triumph over professional disagreement and confusion on their final exams.[4] But there was nothing in these candid asides that professional historians did not know full well. The "babble of disagreement" over the meaning of progressivism, as David Kennedy put it in 1975, was acute and troubling.[5]

Yet by the end of the decade there were signs that beneath the definitional wrangling historians had been striking out in significantly new directions — away from the debate over the essence of progressivism, so brilliantly started by Richard Hofstadter's generation, and toward questions of context. Much of the best writing of the 1970s inquired less about the progressives themselves than about their surroundings; less about the internal coherence of the progressive "movement" than about the structures of politics, power, and ideas within which the era's welter of tongues and efforts and "reforms" took place. The answers were important and wide-ranging: some pointed to critical changes in the rules of the political game; some emphasized revolutions in power and organization; others hinted at new ways of comprehending the era's rhetoric and social thought. Set beside these gains, the 1970s failure to agree on the characteristics of progressivism may turn out not really to matter.[6]

Of these developments, one of the most significant has been the emergence of a pluralistic reading of progressive politics, in which the fundamental fact of the era is not reform in any traditional sense of the term, but the explosion of scores of aggressive, politically active pressure groups into the space left by the recession of traditional political loyalties. The first intimations of this account of the period came in Filene's "obituary" of 1970 and a companion essay by John D. Buenker in 1969.[7] Both historians began by insisting that the progressive movement was not, in the strict sense of the term, a "movement" at all. Those whom historians had labeled progressives shared no common party or organization. They were rent by deep disagreements over anti-trust policy, women's suffrage, direct democracy, and any number of other specific issues. Finally, Buenker argued, the Procrustean exercise of trying to stretch those who called themselves progressives over a single ideological frame, far from revealing a common ethos, had either produced a list of ideas "so general as to be held by practically everyone or so ambiguous, and even contradictory, as to foreclose the possibility that members of the same movement could hold them simultaneously."[8] Only by discarding the mistaken assumption of a coherent reform movement could one see the progressives' world for what it really was: an era of shifting, ideologically fluid, issue-focused coalitions, all competing for the reshaping of American society.

The more devastating the attack, the fiercer the resistance, and the unconvinced were quick to point out that no one had really claimed that progressivism was a "movement" in the narrow sense of the term that Filene and Buenker employed. That progressive politics was coalition politics, prone to internal fissures, was a commonplace.[9] For a good many historians, in fact, the progressives had made most sense when divided in two. By the end of the 1970s one could take one's pick of nearly a dozen dichotomies: "social" reformers vs. "structural" reformers (Holli), western democratic Bryanites vs. eastern elitist Rooseveltians (Hackney), "social justice" progressives vs. "social order" progressives (Church and Sedlak), consumer conscious "insurgents" vs. job conscious "modernizers" (Thelen), or in Buenker's case, heedless of his own theoretical advice, new-stock, urban liberals vs. old-stock, patrician reformers.[10]

If Buenker and Filene meant to imply, however, that the rage for bifurcation had not really helped resolve the problem of coherence, they were surely right. Though the ideological checklists looked considerably less muddled when sliced in two, that clarity was purchased at the cost of finding any sizable number of self-professed progressives who did not draw their ideas from both sides of all such divisions. The post facto dichotomies touched deep moral nerves in the historians who employed them. But what usually amounted to routing the false progressive ideas out of genuine "progressivism" did not succeed in making it clear why a "democratic" progressive like Charles Beard should have cozied up so closely to the "structural reformers" of the Bureau of Municipal Research; why an "insurgent" like Robert La Follette should have thrown in his lot with a social gospeler turned efficiency expert like John R. Commons; why an archetypical "social justice" progressive like Jane Addams and an archetypical "corporate liberal" like George W. Perkins should have landed in the same political camp in 1912; or why, in short, the air was so full of what Robert Wiebe shrewdly described as "strange theoretical combinations."[11] What Buenker and Filene proposed was to accept these apparent anomalies as characteristic: to split the progressive movement not in two but into dozens of pieces, bound only by the rules of competitive, pluralistic politics.

But why then did so many issue-oriented groups demanding so many novel changes burst on the scene at once? That, clearly, was the critical question, and Buenker could only appeal to the big, driving forces of industrialization, urbanization, and immigration, all of which had been around for an embarrassingly long time before the turn-of-the-century explosion of pressure groups they were said to have triggered. It was here that the political scientists entered the argument, and the key book was Walter Dean Burnham's *Critical Elections and the Mainsprings of American Politics* (1970). What impressed Burnham about the Progressive era was that it coincided with what appeared to be a seismic shift in American electoral behavior: not a party realignment of the sort familiar to the nineteenth century, but a critical weakening of all party loyalties and a massive decline in voting itself.[12] Why, given the heated political atmosphere of the Progressive years, Americans chose that moment to begin their long twentieth-century slide toward political inactivity has now become a matter of intense debate among political scientists and political historians. Some of the withdrawal from politics was, of course, deliberately contrived in the form of tighter registration laws and, in the South, outright disfranchisement of black and many poor white voters. But the rest now seems closely related to the failure of the political parties to bring their partisans to the polls in the numbers characteristic of the late nineteenth century. Whether the parties weakened because of new ballot laws which made ticket splitting easier, because the party realignment of the 1890s left more and more states without meaningful electoral contests, the direct primary system shattered the power base of the old-style party managers, new mass circulation newspapers eclipsed the old party sheets as primary information sources, or because the issues of the Progressive era simply did not touch deep popular nerves—no one really knows.[13] But as party loyalties eroded, the parties could no longer sustain their former role as the single most important channel through which Americans tried to affect the policies of governments.

The result was to spring open the political arena to extra-party pressure groups of all sorts: manufacturers' organizations, labor lobbies, civic leagues, trade associations, women's clubs, professional associations, and issue-oriented lobbies, all trying directly to shape policy. This was the context within which maverick politicians could vault into office and "reform" (and "antireform") coalitions of all sorts could blossom. Progressive politics—fragmented, fluid, and issue-focused—was, in short, part of a major, lasting shift in the rules of the political game.

Such a scheme is easier to sketch in broad strokes than to work out in detail, but its promise is already apparent in Richard L. McCormick's fine study of New York politics, *From Realignment to Reform* (1981).[14] By looking most closely not at the reformers but at the old-time bosses, McCormick demonstrates how their hold was shaken by the assaults of mugwump, anti-party crusaders, by muckracking, and by the unsettling rise of new zero-sum issues not resolvable by the parties' traditional method of distributing favors all around—how, in sum, one form of politics gave way to another. What happened in New York is not likely to be precisely duplicated elsewhere.[15] Neither McCormick nor anyone else has yet described how the new extra-party techniques of lobbying and coalition building exactly worked, how quickly or how thoroughly they supplanted the old party channels, or how and by whom the new-style legislative contests were most often won. The causes of party disaffection remain, even in McCormick's hands, dauntingly complex and interdependent, and no one has yet tried to write a historical sociology of party disengagement. But at the least the discernment that the voters drawn to progressive issues formed a slimmed-down electorate of highly specific loyalties, always in flux, promises a major gain over the old wrangle about the identity of the "typical" progressive.[16]

The recovery of the particular political fluidity of the Progressive years also promises to reopen the question David Thelen raised at the beginning of the 1970s as to how the reform coalitions came together: how techniques and grievances were passed from one issue group to another, how channels of communication were established and supported, how new methods of mobilizing public opinion were invented and employed—muckracking, the celebrity picket line, the forcing of an official witness-calling investigation, the launching of a referendum campaign, or the puffing of fads like city planning or commission government.[17] To insist that reform efforts come in clusters precisely because of this sort of interlocking of techniques and activists is not to deflate the progressives' moral fervor. Like all reformers, those of the Progressive era were made piece by piece, as unease and anger were channeled into vocabularies and techniques that were always in motion.

What is at hand, however, is not simply a new set of questions. In the work of McCormick, Burnham, and Buenker one senses the beginning of a major new synthesis which will situate the progressives in the context of a much bigger phenomenon: the rise of modern, weak-party, issue-focused politics.

For other historians writing in the 1970s the central fact of the Progressive era was not its political fluidity at all; rather it was its unprecedentedly tight organization of social and economic power. Thus Filene had barely proclaimed the death of any simple understanding of the era when Louis Galambos swept the period's fragments together into what seemed to him and to others a fundamental revolution in social organization: the eclipse of the local, informal group as the basic frame of American life, and its replacement by vastly bigger, bureaucratically structured formal organizations, among them the big business corporation and its putative adversary, the active, regulatory, progressive state.[18]

Galambos's essay was in large part a gloss on Robert Wiebe's immensely influential *The Search for Order* (1967), in which Wiebe had laid particular stress on the connections between "progressivism" and the surrounding organizational (or, as he called it, bureaucratic) revolution. In a nation rushing pell-mell out of its crisis-ridden villages toward new bureaucratic organizations and social values, none ran faster or worked harder than the progressives to rationalize and organize what they saw as their chaotic surroundings. Scratch the moralistic veneer off progressivism, Wiebe argued, particularly after 1910, and what you found was a movement of organization men caught up in dreams of social efficiency, systematization, and scientifically adjusted harmony. Progressivism was not "the complaint of the unorganized against the consequences of organization," as Hofstadter had had it. It was, in Wiebe's telling, precisely the reverse.[19]

If Wiebe's analysis gained its effect by deliberately simplifying the progressives' ideas, he did brilliantly illustrate the parallel between one of the strains in progressive social thought and one of the central social transformations of the twentieth century. When it came to asking how the values of social efficiency burst into political life, however, the answers of the "organizational" historians tended to lead toward a series of knots and tangles. Wiebe himself had posited a "new middle class" as the prime carriers of the novel bureaucratic values, a somewhat formless group organized, it appeared, around a core of professionally conscious doctors, lawyers, social workers, educators, and engineers, all in the throes of professional organization at the turn of the century. The study of their professionalization turned into one of the boom enterprises of the 1970s, and some of the results seemed to confirm Wiebe's hunch that the drive to rationalize the professions and the progressives' drive to rationalize society were part and parcel of the same process. Professional architects and engineers remapped cities in the Progressive years; professionally conscious educators revamped education; doctors reached out to put chaotic systems of sewage and water supply in order.[20]

But professional goals and bureaucratic *social* visions, historians also found, were by no means identical. If the "professions" had any trait in common, it seemed not to be a political ethos but a common desire for job control. Professionally conscious lawyers, for example, if Jerold Auerbach is right, worked far harder to drive the "disrespectable," night school educated elements out of their ranks than to straighten out legislation. Doctors, only a fraction of whom entered the field of public medicine, found the progressive state most useful as a guarantor of their private monopoly. Professionalization and the search for a rationalized social order it now seems clear, was no tightly organized expedition.[21]

Other historians who tried to pin down the source of the new bureaucratic values turned to more abstract and more impersonal schemes. The most sophisticated and wide-ranging of all the "organizational" syntheses came from Samuel P. Hays. As Hays described it, the context of progressive politics began with a massive growth in "technical systems" (large-scale organizations dependent on mastery of large inputs of data: payrolls, oil reserves, truancy records, whatever); in occupational specialization, and in communications networks and "functional organizations" binding those specialists together; and in the scientific and bureaucratic values suited to the new organizational systems. Together these processes hastened the growth of "cosmopolitan" forces as opposed to "local" ones. And that, in turn, generated the essential dynamic of progressive politics, the flow of decision making upward, from ward bosses to city managers, townships to counties, school teachers to superintendents.[22]

To describe Hays's scheme in this way is to simplify it drastically, but it is not to parody its peculiar bloodlessness. In a famous essay in 1964 on the origins of urban "reform," Hays wrote of the capture of urban politics by a self-conscious, upper class elite.[23] Returning to that question ten years later, he described something resembling the workings of a giant accordion: an urban system opening up in the nineteenth century, as physical expansion produced a dispersal of power into urban wards and brought middling class men into political office; and then squeezing closed again after 1900, as new forms of communication recentralized the city, as functional relations multiplied, and the "cosmopolitans" were swept back in. The second scheme, being vaster, may also be truer than the first. But like most big functionalist theories, in which everything is linked to everything else, it is all but impossible to imagine what a definitive scheme of proof might look like. Moreover, for those who persisted in asking what human intentions drove the great social engine, other than those bound up in the fashionable incantation "modernization," Hays's answers, still more than Wiebe's, seemed vexingly obscure.[24]

This causal impasse may explain why the most widely read "organizational" histories in the 1970s came not from students of Hays or Wiebe but from scholars on the Left. The explanatory engine closest at hand, after all, was the big business corporation. No other "technical systems" approached the size or complexity of the new corporate entities being put together at the turn of the century. Nowhere else were the concepts of efficiency, rationality, and predictability being more carefully worked out or embedded more quickly in organizational forms—certainly not in the universities, with their load of archaic customs, or in such entrepreneurial strongholds as the law or medicine.[25] If organization and organizational values were what the Progressive era was all about, here was surely a good place to look.

The most influential book on the Left in this regard was James Weinstein's *The Corporate Ideal in the Liberal State* (1968), though it took some time for it to emerge from Gabriel Kolko's shadow. Weinstein's concern was much bigger and subtler than Kolko's preoccupation with the federal regulatory process.[26] It was how, in the face of a major crisis of legitimacy, the leaders of corporate capitalism had managed to capture dissent itself. What others called "progressivism," and Weinstein called "corporate liberalism," was at bottom, he argued, a series of measures designed to draw the teeth of rank-

and-file militancy and middle class resentment—an abandonment of the cut-throat ethics of entrepreneurial capitalism for new ideals of social harmony and new schemes of business-government cooperation which would insure a social order safe for the new corporate phase of capitalism. Insofar as progressives dreamed of social efficiency, Weinstein suggested, they attested to a brilliantly successful capture of ideas and policies by the most powerful organizations around.[27]

This welding of the rationalizing side of progressive ideas and actions to a precise economic base had a very strong appeal in the 1970s. Certainly historians looking for the business-public policy connections characteristic of the corporate liberal state did not have far to look. They were evident in some measure or another in the framing of virtually all industrial and economic legislation as business leaders exchanged the tactics of resistance for the tactics of cooptation. From new strongholds in the philanthropic foundations and public policy groups, corporation-tied figures played a prominent role in the redesign of medicine, the restructuring of cities, and the investigation and interpretation of industrial unrest.[28] The best books in this vein focused on education, and there, as David Tyack, David F. Noble, Joel Spring, and others demonstrated, the influence of businessmen, although not unopposed, was massive.[29]

All of these studies were hotly debated in the 1970s, but it would be a mistake to dismiss them as merely reflections of the political crosscurrents of the decade.[30] That businessmen in crucial parts of the economy did shift from an ideology of competition to one of stability and (where their vital interests were not at stake) cooperation is unmistakable. That they tried hard on every level to rationalize their economic environment—by internal administrative reforms, by efforts to stabilize markets, and attempts to seize control of their regulators—is just as clear.[31] So is the fact that businessmen tried to impose the organizational model of the corporation on everything from schools to timberlands, an effort to which those who called themselves progressives often gave enthusiastic support.[32] And finally, given the work of a new generation of labor historians, there is no doubt that all this was done, not in Hofstadter's relatively genial period of "sustained and general prosperity," but against a backdrop of acute labor crisis.[33]

But how much of the game did the corporations win? More than enough to keep them going as the dominant force in economic life but, as other historians working in the 1970s showed, not enough to amount to an unqualified victory. The record of workmen's compensation legislation, one of the central social issues of the Progressive era, now reveals a tangle of competing interests and varied compromises.[34] The same is true of business regulation. In a crucial progressive state like Wisconsin, for example, the railroads succeeded in regulating the commission designed to govern them, but they were unable to stave off a corporate income tax which, if Elliot Brownlee is right, soaked the corporations for the benefit of Wisconsin's farmers.[35] As Robert Cuff has shown, the wartime linchpin of the business-progressive complex, the War Industries Board, likewise fell considerably short of the hopes the corporate liberals had for it.[36] The balance sheet for the Progressive era as a whole, however, is still only roughly drawn. The period remains ripe for more enterprises like Carl V. Harris's fine study of Birmingham, Alabama, which—holding in abeyance preconceived notions of victors and losers—tries to ask which social and economic groups won precisely what from the era's politics.[37]

Equally needed is a far less schematic understanding of the relations between progressive social thought and the ideas flowing out of the corporation boardrooms and industrial laboratories in the Progressive years. One of the reasons for the rising appeal to the concept of cultural "hegemony" by historians on the Left is a recognition that far too much of the case for the corporations' capture of progressive social ideals rests simply on a functionalist sense of the "fit" between progressive policies and what seem in hindsight to have been the needs of corporate capitalism. Yet virtually all cultural systems, even starkly divided ones, "function" in hindsight. Until the tissue of connections between the corporations, the bureaus, the professional schools and universities, and the progressive publicists has been much more fully explored, "hegemony" promises to mystify quite as thoroughly as the term "modernization."[38]

Still, were the organizational historians to adopt less schematic notions of ideas and social outcomes, there seems no reason why the 1970s concern with organizational structures, the big business corporation, and with pluralistic politics could not be brought together to the advantage of them all. In the newly fluid, issue-focused political contests of the Progressive era, the better organized players—the professional lobbies, the well-disciplined interest groups, and, above all, the corporations—held massive advantages. The ideological commitments at stake for pluralists, functionalists, and Marxists alike may not bode well for such a commonsensical view of the era, but by the end of the 1970s the evidence for it was everywhere at hand.

Where in this contested terrain, however, was "progressivism" to be found? What ideational glue allowed some of the coalition builders to recognize each other in the new sea of competing interest groups—as they clearly did—and to adopt, somewhat late in the day, in late 1910 and early 1911, the common label "progressive"?

If progressivism qualifies as an "ism" at all, surely it is as a system of shared ideas; yet nowhere in the 1970s was the historiographical discord greater than when it came to describing progressive social thought. Progressives could be found who admired the efficiency of the big corporation and who detested the trusts, who lauded the "people" and who yearned for an electorate confined to white and educated voters, who spoke the language of social engineering and the language of moralistic uplift, or (to make matters worse) did all these things at once. The enterprise of extracting a stable list of core progressive values from the welter of things progressives said and wrote contined through the 1970s.[39] But as the lists grew longer and more convoluted without growing any more coherent, at least one careful historian was driven to conclude that what characterized the progressive mind was its "muddle-minded" jumble of oppositions.[40]

The obstacles in the way of getting progressive social thought straight have little to do with insufficient evidence; progressives shared an inordinate faith in the word, as Otis Graham pointed out long ago, and they preached and wrote with consuming zeal.[41] One of the results, however, was a rhetoric thick with straw men and partisan exaggerations which can be safely read only with a sense of context and contest as strong as the progressives' own. "Social justice" is a case in point—a powerful Rooseveltian slogan in 1912 which, in the absence of anyone willing to defend "social injustice," worked its magic in large part through its half-buried innuendoes and its expansive indistinctness. The progressives' appeal to "the people" is a more complicated example of the phenomenon; but one of the reasons for the triumph of that particularly elastic phrase (as opposed to the term "democracy," for example) was that it allowed those who sincerely believed in a government serving the needs of "the people" to camouflage from voters the acute distrust many of those same persons harbored of political egalitarianism.[42] Above all, when the progressives exaggerated, they were prone to exaggerate their triumph over what they belittled as the drift and pessimism of their predecessors, counting on their audiences not to inquire too closely into the relationship between the frenetically active, progress-imbued nineteenth century and the progressives' deliberate caricature of it.[43] Yet in the lists of the characteristic ideological ingredients of progressivism compiled in the 1970s one could still find the terms optimism, activism, democracy, and social justice—too often with only a thin sense of the traps surrounding each of them. Like all partisans, the progressive publicists used words less to clarify a political philosophy than to build a political constituency. What their slogans meant lay not only in what they said but in what these slogans were designed to accomplish.

The trouble with comprehending "progressivism" as a list of beliefs is a deeper one, however, than the presence of some misleading or exaggerated elements on many such lists. The deeper problem stems from the attempt to capture the progressives within a static ideological frame. If the contradictory lists prove anything it is that those who called themselves progressives did not share a common creed or a string of common values, however ingeniously or vaguely defined. Rather what they seem to have possessed was an ability to draw on three distinct clusters of ideas—three distinct social languages—to articulate their discontents and their social visions. To put rough but serviceable labels on those three languages of discontent, the first was the rhetoric of antimonopolism, the second was an emphasis on social bonds and the social nature of human beings, and the third was the language of social efficiency.

These three did not add up to a coherent ideology we can call "progressivism." All three tended to focus that discontent on arbitrary, unregulated individual power—enough so to make the trust, the political boss, and the sweatshop terms of enormous bearing. But on a deeper level the three languages—full of mutual contradictions—did not add up at all. They had distinctly different historical roots, and they rose into currency and fell into disuse at distinctly different times. We can best imagine those who called themselves progressives as drawing from each of them—some more from one, some more from another—without undue concern for philosophical consistency. Together they formed not an ideology but the surroundings of available rhetoric and ideas—akin to the surrounding structures of politics and power—within which progressives launched their crusades, recruited their partisans, and did their work.

Of these languages, antimonopolism was the oldest, the most peculiarly American, and, through the first decade of the century, the strongest of the three. When Tom Johnson took on the streetcar franchises, when Frederic Howe plumped for municipal ownership of natural monopolies, when the muckrakers flayed the trusts, there was nothing essentially new in the grievances they dramatized or the language they employed. The disproportionately large number of single taxers in the early progressive crusades was clue enough that this line of attack on "privilege" and "unnatural" concentration of wealth ran back through the Populists, through Henry George, and on at least to Andrew Jackson. But this understanding of economics and politics in terms of graft, monopoly, privilege, and invisible government had almost always before been the property of outsiders: workers, farmers, Democrats, Populists.[44] What was new in the Progressive years was that the language of antimonopolism suddenly gained the acceptance of insiders: the readers of slick magazines and respectable journals, middle class family men, and reasonably proper Republicans. William A. White caught the point in 1905. "It is funny how we have all found the octopus," he mused, when less than a decade earlier, backed up against the wall by Populism, his like had denied that animal's very existence.[45]

The reasons for that middle class discovery of the octopus have not yet all been sorted out. One of them surely goes back to the fact that there was almost nothing in the reigning conceptions of political economy to prepare middle class Americans for the sudden, turn-of-the-century ascendancy of finance capitalism, except to decry the agglomerations of the financiers as "unnatural" and conspiratorial. Still closer to home, another part of the answer may be the expansion of private streetcar, gas, and electric networks which, by the end of the century, had begun to give urban dwellers the experience of vulnerability to monopoly that had once been the peculiar possession of the railroad-captive farmers.[46] Yet another thread, of the sort most recently worked by Jackson Lears, may lead back to a kind of fin de siècle ennui and a rapidly rising need for the sort of sensation that the muckrakers provided.[47] All these strands, as Richard L. McCormick has reemphasized, were powerfully concentrated in the exposures of 1905–1908 and in the anti-railroad and anticorruption campaigns those investigations let loose.[48] A decade later the antimonopoly cry had devolved on outsiders once more, leaving the muckrakers suspended without an outlet. But one of the characteristics of the Progressive years was that, for a moment, the language of antimonopolism was able to focus and impel the energies of a broader cross-section of Americans than had felt its force for generations.

The second cluster of ideas from which the progressives drew—the language of social bonds—was more specific to the Progressive years, and at the same time much less peculiarly American. To call it, in Thomas Haskell's terms, the discovery of "interdependence" runs a risk of misunderstanding. That human beings live in a web of social relations has never been open to doubt. Much of the thrust of academic social thought in the nineteenth century had, in fact, consisted of a finer and finer elaboration of what the term "society" meant. Still the most common explanations most Americans gave to political, economic, and social questions at the end of the century were couched in terms of largely autonomous individuals: poverty and success were said to hinge on character; the economy was essentially a straight sum of individual calculations; governance was a matter of good men and official honesty. Part of what occurred in the Progressive era was a concerted assault on all these assumptions, and, in some measure, an assault on the idea of individualism itself. That was what the era's "revolt against formalism" was all about: not a revolt against formal categories of thought, for progressive intellectuals were full of them, but against a particular set of formal fictions traceable to Smith, Locke, and Mill—the autonomous economic man, the autonomous possessor of property rights, the autonomous man of character. In its place, many of the progressives seized on a rhetoric of social cohesion.[49]

Like the language of antimonopolism, the language of social bonds focused its users' anger on the irresponsible, antisocial act; but it directed its users' longings not to honesty but to a consciously contrived harmony. The yearning to purge society of what now seemed its individualistic excesses took several forms. In social terms it took the form of a new interest in the social and physical environment, the discovery of new forms of social sinning and corresponding new measures of social control, and a vivid, nervous concern with social cohesion. In economic terms it took the form of a newly intense sympathy with what now seemed the innocent casualties of industrialism (women and child workers, the victims of industrial accidents, the involuntarily unemployed), and a keen desire for industrial peace and cooperation. In educational terms it took the form of schooling in teamwork, cooperation, and vocational responsibilities. In political terms it took the form of talk of the social organism and the common good. In philosophical terms it took the form of a virtual dissolution of the boundaries between self and society. Men were but "plastic lumps of human dough" to be pressed into shape on the great "social kneadingboard," E. A. Ross maintained. John Dewey's one-time student, Charles H. Cooley put the point still more insistently: "the notion of a separate and independent ego is an illusion." [50]

Statements of this sort pushed the concern with social bonds to the extreme, and disguised a critical disagreement over how "society" ought to be conceived. At the one extreme were those like Croly and Roosevelt for whom the lines of social connection always ran toward the nation, the state, and the social whole. At the other extreme were those who, like Jane Addams, talked habitually of the bonds of family, community, and neighborhood. That unresolved debate helped make the state the object of so many of the progressives' hopes and at the same time the focus of so much of their uneasiness. But it would be a mistake to assume that all the concern with social cohesion lay on the Rooseveltian side of the campaign-exaggerated division between the advocates of New Nationalism and New Freedom. When Wilson himself, his 1912 speeches splayed between the need to bring out Democratic voters through traditional Democratic and antimonopoly appeals and the political theories Wilson had tried to inculcate in Princeton students, came to confess the "image of liberty" he had in mind, it was that of "a great engine," its elements "so assembled and united and accommodated that there is no friction, but a united power in all the parts." [51]

Where did such an acute consciousness of society come from? Some of it, perhaps, derived from the memories of persons who had made the trek from tightly-knit villages to anomic cities. [52] Some of it, certainly, came from the 1890s' brutal demonstration of what unmediated interdependence was really all about in the world of industrial capitalism. [53] But the language of social bonds was an international language, not fully explainable by experiences endemic to the United States.[54] Perhaps the most significant clue to its origin is that, of the three social languages on which the progressives drew, this was the one most tightly attached to the churches and the university lecture halls. Its roots stretched toward Germany and, still more importantly, toward the social gospel. When progressives talked of society and solidarity the rhetoric they drew upon was, above all, the rhetoric of a socialized Protestantism, though how that transatlantic reconstruction of Protestantism took place remains at the moment a very large and very open question.[55]

The last of the three clusters of ideas to arrive—so very different in outward form from the other two—was the one we associate with efficiency, rationalization, and social engineering. Some of the progressives never stomached the new bureaucratic language of budgets, human costs, and system, nor felt comfortable translating social sins into the new-fangled language of social waste. For others, however, the language of social efficiency offered a way of putting the progressives' common sense of social disorder into words and remedies free of the embarrassing pieties and philosophical conundrums that hovered around the competing language of social bonds. Like Charles Beard or John R. Commons they were ready to put their Ruskins and their Christian Sociology on the shelf in exchange for the stripped down language of social science—and for the new occupational niches available for social scientific experts.

Like the rhetoric of social bonds, the rhetoric of social efficiency was a transatlantic language. Large pieces of it could be picked up in the scientific laboratories through which a good number of the progressives moved.[56] Other pieces, as Neil Harris has argued, were embedded in the increasingly specialized and technical ways in which people everywhere went about acquiring their everyday knowledge.[57] But clearly it was the merger of the prestige of science with the prestige of the well-organized business firm and factory that gave the metaphor of system its tremendous twentieth-century potency—and it was presumably for this reason that that metaphor flourished more exuberantly in the United States, along with industrial capitalism itself, than anywhere else.[58]

It is not yet clear through what channels the language of social efficiency worked its way out of the laboratories and factories and into political discourse—there to make it possible for many self-professed progressives to slide back and forth between criticism of business-made chaos and schemes to reorganize government on business lines. Nor is it clear how fast the process proceeded. But the dates most often pointed to cluster right in the middle of the Progressive era: 1910, the year scientific management went public; 1908, the year Arthur Bentley's *The Process of Government* swept all grand theorizing about politics aside as obsolete; or 1909, the first big year of the city commission boom. Similarly, in the small but critical realm of formal academic thought the crucial intellectual transition takes place not at either end of the period but within it. As late as 1905, the "state," society grandly conceived, and philosophical idealism held preeminent place. By 1915 they were all being brushed into the corners by a new concern with governmental technique and political behavior, by the precise behavioristic curiosities of a new breed of sociologist, and by antiphilosophical scientism. If these hints are correct, the language of efficiency was clearly no more typically "progressive" than the other two social languages upon which progressives drew. It came late on the scene, and it endured long after the Progressive era itself was over.[59]

What made progressive social thought distinct and volatile, if this reading is correct, was not its intellectual coherence but the presence of all three of these languages at once. If we imagine the progressives, like most of the rest of us, largely as users rather than shapers of ideas, this was the constellation of live, accessible ways of looking at society within which they worked, from which they drew their energies and their sense of social ills, and within which they found their solutions. It did not give those who called themselves progressives an intellectual system, but it gave them a set of tools which worked well enough to have a powerful impact on their times. To think of progressive social thought in this way is to emphasize the active, dynamic aspect of ideas. It is also to admit, finally, that progressivism as an ideology is nowhere to be found.

Whether historians in the 1980s will call off the search for that great, overarching thing called "progressivism" is hard to predict. Certainly historians working in the 1970s manifestly failed to find it. In recompense they found out a vast amount about the world in which the progressives lived and the structures of social and political power shifting so rapidly around them. To acknowledge that these are the questions that matter and to abandon the hunt for the *essence* of the noise and tumult of that era may not be, as Filene's first critics feared, to lose the whole enterprise of historical comprehension. It may be to find it.

1. A historical sketch of the term "progressivism" has yet to be written. The label "progressive," which Woodrow Wilson was still explaining as a "new term" in January 1911, came into vogue during the 1910 electoral campaigns. The phrase "progressive movement" was a product of 1912. But the modern label "progressivism," launched in 1912 as an antonym to toryism and socialism, was never a common term of self-identification, and did not come into widespread use until picked up, sometime after the fact, by journalists and historians.

2. Peter G. Filene, "An Obituary for 'The Progressive Movement'," *American Quarterly* 22 (1970): 20–34.

3. Jack T. Kirby, *Darkness at the Dawning: Race and Reform in the Progressive South* (Philadelphia: J. B. Lippincott, 1972), p. 3.

4. Melvyn Dubofsky, Athan Theoharis, and Daniel M. Smith, *The United States in the Twentieth Century* (Englewood Cliffs, N.J.: Prentice-Hall, 1978), p. 104; Irwin Unger and Debi Unger, *The Vulnerable Years: The United States, 1896–1917* (Hinsdale, Ill.: Dryden Press, 1977), p. 97; Richard L. Watson, Jr., *The Development of National Power: The United States, 1900–1919* (Boston: Houghton Mifflin, 1976), p. 84. There were other textbooks, of course, which strode into the subject with far more outward confidence. For example, see Richard M. Abrams, *The Burdens of Progress, 1900–1929* (Glenview, Ill.: Scott, Foresman, 1978); John W. Chambers II, *The Tyranny of Change: America in the Progressive Era, 1900–1917* (New York: St Martin's Press, 1980).

5. David M. Kennedy, "Overview: The Progressive Era," *Historian* 37 (1975): 453.

6. The discussion that follows does not pretend to be a full inventory of the Progressive era scholarship of the 1970s. For a comprehensive list of titles, see John D. Buenker and Nicholas C. Burckel, eds., *Progressive Reform: A Guide to Information Sources* (Detroit: Gale Research, 1980); and, on the South, Dewey W. Grantham, "The Contours of Southern Progressivism," *American Historical Review* 86 (1981): 1035–59.

7. Filene, "Obituary for 'The Progressive Movement'"; John D. Buenker, "The Progressive Era: A Search for a Synthesis," *Mid-America* 51 (1969): 175–93.

8. John D. Buenker, John C. Burnham, and Robert M. Crunden, *Progressivism* (Cambridge, Mass.: Schenkman, 1977), p. 33.

9. See, for example, Arthur S. Link, "What Happened to the Progressive Movement in the 1920s?" *American Historical Review* 64 (1959): 833–51.

10. Melvin G. Holli, *Reform in Detroit: Hazen S. Pingree and Urban Politics* (New York: Oxford University Press, 1969), pp. 157–81; Sheldon Hackney, *Populism to Progressivism in Alabama* (Princeton, N.J.: Princeton University Press, 1969), p. xiii; Robert L. Church and Michael W. Sedlak, *Education in the United States: An Interpretive History* (New York: Free Press, 1976), pp. 255–60; William L. O'Neill, *The Progressive Years: America Comes of Age* (New York: Dodd, Mead, 1975), p. 155; David P. Thelen, *Robert M. La Follette and the Insurgent Spirit* (Boston: Little, Brown, 1976), pp. 98–111; John D. Buenker, *Urban Liberalism and Progressive Reform* (New York: Scribner's, 1973). For a more complicated scheme, see David P. Thelen, "Urban Politics: Beyond Bosses and Reformers," *Reviews in American History* 7 (1979): 411–12.

11. Robert H. Wiebe, *The Search for Order, 1877–1920* (New York: Hill and Wang, 1967), p. 153.

12. Walter Dean Burnham, *Critical Elections and the Mainsprings of American Politics* (New York: W. W. Norton, 1970), chs. 4–5.

13. J. Morgan Kousser, *The Shaping of Southern Politics: Suffrage Restriction and the Establishment of the One-Party South, 1880–1910* (New Haven, Conn.: Yale University Press, 1974); Jerrold G. Rusk, "The Effect of the Australian Ballot Reform on Split Ticket Voting, 1876–1908," *American Political Science Review* 64 (1970): 1220–38; Walter Dean Burnham, "Theory and Voting Research," *ibid.* 68 (1974): 1002–23.

14. Richard L. McCormick, *From Realignment to Reform: Political Change in New York State, 1893–1910* (Ithaca, N.Y.: Cornell University Press, 1981). This should be read in conjunction with two important essays: "The Party Period and Public Policy: An Exploratory Hypothesis," *Journal of American History* 66 (1979): 279–98; and "The Discovery that Business Corrupts Politics: A Reappraisal of the Origins of Progressivism," *American Historical Review* 86 (1981): 247–74.

15. See, for example, Robert W. Cherny, *Populism, Progressivism, and the Transformation of Nebraska Politics, 1885–1915* (Lincoln: University of Nebraska Press, 1981).

16. For beginnings in this direction, see Michael P. Rogin and John L. Shover, *Political Change in California: Critical Elections and Social Movements, 1890–1966* (Westport, Conn.: Greenwood Press, 1970), chs. 2–3; and Roger E. Wyman, "Middle-Class Voters and Progressive Reform: The Conflict of Class and Culture," *American Political Science Review* 68 (1974): 488–504.

17. David P. Thelen, *The New Citizenship: Origins of Progressivism in Wisconsin,*

1885-1900 (Columbia, Mo.: University of Missouri Press, 1972). Parts of the reform nexus are sketched in Clarke A. Chambers, *Paul U. Kellogg and the Survey* (Minneapolis: University of Minnesota Press, 1971); and Steven J. Diner, *A City and Its Universities: Public Policy in Chicago, 1892-1919* (Chapel Hill: University of North Carolina Press, 1980). On the spread of new fads and techniques, see Bradley R. Rice, *Progressive Cities: The Commission Government Movement in America, 1901-1920* (Austin: University of Texas Press, 1977); and Lloyd Sponholtz, "The Initiative and Referendum: Direct Democracy in Perspective, 1898-1920," *American Studies* 14 (1973): 43-64.

18. Louis Galambos, "The Emerging Organizational Synthesis in Modern American History," *Business History Review* 44 (1970): 279-90.

19. Richard Hofstadter, *The Age of Reform* (New York: Knopf, 1955), p. 214; Wiebe, *Search for Order*, chs. 6-7.

20. Judd Kahn, *Imperial San Francisco: Politics and Planning in an American City, 1897-1906* (Lincoln: University of Nebraska Press, 1979); David Tyack and Elisabeth Hansot, *Managers of Virtue: Public School Leadership in America, 1820-1980* (New York: Basic Books, 1982); Stuart Galishoff, *Safeguarding the Public Health: Newark, 1895-1918* (Westport, Conn.: Greenwood Press, 1975); Jerry Israel, ed., *Building the Organizational Society: Essays on Associational Activity in Modern America* (New York: Free Press, 1972).

21. Jerold S. Auerbach, *Unequal Justice: Lawyers and Social Change in Modern America* (New York: Oxford University Press, 1976); James G. Burrow, *Organized Medicine in the Progressive Era: The Move toward Monopoly* (Baltimore: Johns Hopkins University Press, 1977). See also David J. Rothman, *Conscience and Convenience: The Asylum and Its Alternatives in Progressive America* (Boston: Little, Brown, 1980); Edwin T. Layton, Jr., *The Revolt of the Engineers: Social Responsibility and the American Engineering Profession* (Cleveland: Press of Case Western Reserve University, 1971); and, more generally, Wayne K. Hobson, "Professionals, Progressives and Bureaucratization: A Reassessment," *Historian* 39 (1977): 639-58.

22. Samuel P. Hays, "The New Organizational Society," in *American Political History as Social Analysis* (Knoxville: University of Tennessee Press, 1980).

23. Samuel P. Hays, "The Politics of Reform in Municipal Government in the Progressive Era," *Pacific Northwest Quarterly* 55 (1964): 157-69. The lasting impact of this initial formulation of the urban reform question is manifest in the essays in Michael H. Ebner and Eugene M. Tobin, eds., *The Age of Urban Reform: New Perspectives on the Progressive Era* (Port Washington, N.Y.: Kennikat, 1977).

24. Samuel P. Hays, "The Changing Political Structure of the City in Industrial America," in Hays, *American Political History*. Wiebe's understanding of the period moved in much the same direction: Robert H. Wiebe, "The Progressive Years, 1900-1917," in *The Reinterpretation of American History and Culture*, eds. William H. Cartwright and Richard L. Watson (Washington, D.C.: National Council for the Social Studies, 1973).

25. Daniel Nelson, *Managers and Workers: Origins of the New Factory System in the United States, 1880-1920* (Madison: University of Wisconsin Press, 1975); Alfred D. Chandler, *The Visible Hand: The Managerial Revolution in American Business* (Cambridge, Mass.: Harvard University Press, 1977).

26. Gabriel Kolko, *The Triumph of Conservatism: A Reinterpretation of American History, 1900-1916* (New York: Free Press, 1963).

27. James Weinstein, *The Corporate Ideal in the Liberal State, 1900-1918* (Boston: Beacon Press, 1968). Ellis Hawley has tried to claim the term "corporate liberalism" for a social-political order in which the key public policy decisions are made by private, voluntary business associations. The *structure* Hawley describes may, indeed, flow from the *ideology* of "corporate liberalism." But the proper name for what Hawley describes is a liberal form of "corporatism," and the invitation to confusion seems gratuitous. Ellis W. Hawley, "The Discovery and Study of a 'Corporate Liberalism'," *Business History Review* 52 (1978): 309-20.

28. Ronald Radosh and Murray N. Rothbard, eds. *A New History of Leviathan: Essays on the Rise of the American Corporate State* (New York: Dutton, 1972); E. Richard Brown, *Rockefeller Medicine Men: Medicine and Capitalism in America* (Berkeley: University of

California Press, 1979); David W. Eakins, "The Origins of Corporate Liberal Policy Research, 1916–1922: The Political-Economic Expert and the Decline of Public Debate," in Israel, ed., *Building the Organizational Society.*

29. David B. Tyack, *The One Best System: A History of American Urban Education* (Cambridge, Mass.: Harvard University Press, 1974); David F. Noble, *America by Design: Science, Technology, and the Rise of Corporate Capitalism* (New York: Knopf, 1977); Joel Spring, *Education and the Rise of the Corporate State* (Boston: Beacon Press, 1972). See also Samuel Bowles and Herbert Gintis, *Schooling in Capitalist America: Educational Reform and the Contradictions of Economic Life* (New York: Basic Books, 1976); Clarence J. Karier, Paul C. Violas, and Joel Spring, *Roots of Crisis: American Education in the Twentieth Century* (Chicago: Rand McNally, 1973); Paul C. Violas, *The Training of the Urban Working Class: A History of Twentieth Century American Education* (Chicago: Rand McNally, 1978); Harvey Kantor and David B. Tyack, eds. *Work, Youth, and Schooling: Historical Perspectives on Vocationalism in American Education* (Stanford: Stanford University Press, 1982).

30. See, for example, Diane Ravitch, *The Revisionists Revised: A Critique of the Radical Attack on the Schools* (New York: Basic Books, 1978).

31. Stuart D. Brandes, *American Welfare Capitalism, 1880–1940* (Chicago: University of Chicago Press, 1976); Mansel G. Blackford, *The Politics of Business in California, 1890–1920* (Columbus: Ohio State University Press, 1977).

32. Martin J. Schiesl, *The Politics of Efficiency: Municipal Administration and Reform in America, 1880–1920* (Berkeley: University of California Press, 1977); James Gilbert, *Designing the Industrial State: The Intellectual Pursuit of Collectivism in America, 1880–1940* (Chicago: Quadrangle, 1972).

33. David Montgomery, *Workers' Control in America: Studies in the History of Work, Technology, and Labor Struggles* (Cambridge, England: Cambridge University Press, 1979); Bruno Ramirez, *When Workers Fight: The Politics of Industrial Relations in the Progressive Era, 1898–1916* (Westport, Conn.: Greenwood Press, 1978); Richard Edwards, *Contested Terrain: The Transformation of the Workplace in the Twentieth Century* (New York: Basic Books, 1979).

34. Robert Asher, "Radicalism and Reform: State Insurance of Workmen's Compensation in Minnesota, 1910–1933," *Labor History* 14 (1973): 19–41; Joseph F. Tripp, "An Instance of Labor and Business Cooperation: Workmen's Compensation in Washington State (1911)," *ibid.* 17 (1976): 530–50; Robert F. Wesser, "Conflict and Compromise: The Workmen's Compensation Movement in New York, 1890s–1913," *ibid.* 12 (1971): 345–72.

35. Stanley P. Caine, *The Myth of a Progressive Reform: Railroad Regulation in Wisconsin, 1903–1910* (Madison: State Historical Society of Wisconsin, 1970); W. Elliot Brownlee, Jr., *Progressivism and Economic Growth: The Wisconsin Income Tax, 1911–1929* (Port Washington, N.Y.: Kennikat, 1974). See also William Graebner, *Coal-Mining Safety in the Progressive Period: The Political Economy of Reform* (Lexington: University Press of Kentucky, 1976); Thomas K. McCraw, "Regulation in America: A Review Article," *Business History Review* 49 (1975): 159–83.

36. Robert D. Cuff, *The War Industries Board: Business-Government Relations during World War I* (Baltimore: Johns Hopkins University Press, 1973).

37. Carl V. Harris, *Political Power in Birmingham, 1871–1921* (Knoxville: University of Tennessee Press, 1977).

38. Compare Herman and Julia R. Schwendinger's ambitious and schematic *The Sociologists of the Chair: A Radical Analysis of the Formative Years of North American Sociology (1883–1922)* (New York: Basic Books, 1974); and the comments by Joseph Featherstone, David K. Cohen, and Bella H. Rosenberg in "Symposium: Schooling in Capitalist America," *History of Education Quarterly* 17 (1977): 111–68.

39. See, for example, Grantham, "Contours of Southern Progressivism," pp. 1044–46; John A. Gable, *The Bull Moose Years: Theodore Roosevelt and the Progressive Party* (Port Washington, N.Y.: Kennikat, 1978), pp. 86–93; George B. Tindall, *The Persistent Tradition in*

New South Politics (Baton Rouge: Louisiana State University Press, 1975), p. 57; G. Edward White, "The Social Values of the Progressives: Some New Perspectives," *South Atlantic Quarterly* 70 (1971): 62–76; John C. Burnham's contribution to Buenker et al., *Progressivism.*

40. Don S. Kirschner, "The Ambiguous Legacy: Social Justice and Social Control in the Progressive Era," *Historical Reflections* 2 (1975): 88.

41. Otis L. Graham, Jr., *An Encore for Reform: The Old Progressives and the New Deal* (New York: Oxford University Press, 1967), pp. 11–12.

42. That tension, particularly acute in the South, is elaborated in Kirby, *Darkness at the Dawning;* Bruce Clayton, *The Savage Ideal: Intolerance and Intellectual Leadership in the South, 1890–1914* (Baltimore: Johns Hopkins University Press, 1972); and John Dittmer, *Black Georgia in the Progressive Era, 1900–1920* (Urbana: University of Illinois Press, 1977).

43. Herbert Croly and Walter Lippmann were by no means unique among the progressives in working the theme of a late nineteenth-century America held in thrall by Herbert Spencer and the creed of laissez-faire. For the limits of the caricature, see Robert C. Bannister, *Social Darwinism: Science and Myth in Anglo-American Social Thought* (Philadelphia: Temple University Press, 1979); and Morton Keller, *Affairs of State: Public Life in Late Nineteenth Century America* (Cambridge, Mass.: Harvard University Press, 1977).

44. Robert Kelley, "Ideology and Political Culture from Jefferson to Nixon," *American Historical Review* 82 (1977): 531–62.

45. Quoted in Gene Clanton, "Populism, Progressivism, and Equality: The Kansas Paradigm," *Agricultural History* 51 (1977): 579.

46. Thelen, *New Citizenship,* chs. 11–12.

47. T. J. Jackson Lears, *No Place of Grace: Antimodernism and the Transformation of American Culture, 1880–1920* (New York: Pantheon, 1981).

48. McCormick, "Discovery That Business Corrupts Politics."

49. Thomas L. Haskell, *The Emergence of Professional Social Science: The American Social Science Association and the Nineteenth-Century Crisis of Authority* (Urbana: University of Illinois Press, 1977); Mary O. Furner, *Advocacy and Objectivity: A Crisis in the Professionalization of American Social Science, 1865–1905* (Lexington, Ky.: University Press of Kentucky, 1975); Morton White, *Social Thought in America: The Revolt against Formalism* (New York: Viking Press, 1949).

50. Quoted in Paul C. Violas, "Progressive Social Philosophy: Charles Horton Cooley and Edward Alsworth Ross," in Karier et al., *Roots of Crisis,* pp. 63, 44. See also David E. Price, "Community and Control: Critical Democratic Theory in the Progressive Period," *American Political Science Review* 68 (1974): 1663–78; Paul Boyer, *Urban Masses and Moral Order in America, 1820–1920* (Cambridge, Mass.: Harvard University Press, 1978).

51. John W. Davidson, ed., *A Crossroads of Freedom: The 1912 Campaign Speeches of Woodrow Wilson* (New Haven, Conn.: Yale University Press, 1956), p. 520.

52. Jean B. Quandt, *From the Small Town to the Great Community: The Social Thought of Progressive Intellectuals* (New Brunswick: Rutgers University Press, 1970).

53. Thelen, *New Citizenship.*

54. Kenneth O. Morgan, "The Future at Work: Anglo-American Progressivism 1890–1917," in *Contrast and Connection: Bicentennial Essays in Anglo-American History,* eds. H. C. Allen and Roger Thompson (London: Betts, 1976); Morton Keller, "Anglo-American Politics, 1900–1930, in Anglo-American Perspective: A Case Study in Comparative History," *Comparative Studies in Society and History* 22 (1980): 458–77.

55. The Protestant social gospel strain is emphasized by Robert M. Crunden in Buenker et al., *Progressivism;* Joseph F. Kett, *Rites of Passage: Adolescence in America, 1790 to the Present* (New York: Basic Books, 1977); Clyde Griffen, "The Progressive Ethos," in *The Development of an American Culture,* eds. Stanley Coben and Lorman Ratner (Englewood Cliffs, N.J.: Prentice-Hall, 1970); and John Higham, "Hanging Together: Divergent Unities in American History," *Journal of American History* 61 (1974): 24–25.

56. Tyack and Hansot, *Managers of Virtue,* pp. 114–28.

57. Neil Harris, "The Lamp of Learning: Popular Lights and Shadows," in *The Organization of Knowledge in Modern America, 1860–1920,* eds. Alexandra Oleson and John Voss (Baltimore: Johns Hopkins University Press, 1979).

58. For an effort to document the rising prestige of business in the Progressive years, despite the outcry against the trusts and the railroads, see Louis Galambos, *The Public Image of Big Business in America, 1880–1940: A Quantitative Study in Social Change* (Baltimore: Johns Hopkins University Press, 1975).

59. Wiebe made most of these same points in a series of qualifications which were all but swamped in the inquiries his work precipitated: *The Search for Order,* ch. 6.

FINIS FOR TWEED AND STEFFENS:
REWRITING THE HISTORY OF URBAN RULE

Jon C. Teaford

Since the mid-nineteenth century urban government has suffered the dubious distinction of ranking among the major problem areas in American life. As early as the 1840s a New York City newspaper described the board of aldermen as "a miscellaneous body, who are half bewildered by the superintendence of these vast institutions of a vast population."[1] During the 1850s the exploits of those bribed aldermen known as the Forty Thieves and the audacity of Mayor Fernando Wood further tarnished the image of municipal rule. The peculations of Boss Tweed brought new opprobrium during the late 1860s and early 1870s, and throughout the last two decades of the century scandals in other municipalities added to the earlier testimony of corruption and supposed incompetence. In the late 1880s the distinguished British observer James Bryce could claim that "the government of cities is the one most conspicuous failure of the United States."[2] Conscientious middle class citizens throughout the land nodded their assent to Bryce's words, and the failure of American urban rule became an axiomatic truth in the minds of many.

College texts in American government conveyed Bryce's views to new generations of educated citizens, and muckraking exposés by Lincoln Steffens and his fellow journalists lambasted urban rule as the shame of the cities. Meanwhile, among the academic professionals in the nascent field of political science the problems and shortcomings of city government became a favorite topic of investigation and thought. These academics, together with reform-minded amateurs, industriously penned scores of articles and monographs on municipal structure, urging efficiency, professionalism, centralization, civil service, the short ballot, the commission plan, the city manager plan, and a variety of other panaceas for curing those ills which wracked urban government. Occasionally during the early twentieth century an optimist such as Charles Zueblin wrote on municipal progress and the achievements of revitalized and reformed city administrations.[3] But the behavior of Chicago's notorious Mayor "Big Bill" Thompson in the 1920s and the investigations into the corrupt administration of New York City's Mayor Jimmy Walker in the early 1930s deflated any high hopes that might have earlier lifted the spirits of

0048-7511/82/0104-0133 $01.00

students of municipal rule. In the 1930s, as in the 1880s, very few political scientists, historians, or educated Americans in general regarded city government as a source of national pride.

Instead, the prevailing portrait of big-city politics and government sketched by journalists and academics alike was one of scandal, corruption, and dictatorial rule by self-seeking party machines which exploited the political system for the profit of partisan leaders. "Boss rule" supposedly represented the norm in America's major cities, and dedicated, civic-minded reformers only occasionally and momentarily freed their cities from the grasp of the much criticized bosses. Prior to World War II opinionmakers in the newspapers and in the classroom conceived of the history of big-city government in the United States as a conflict between the forces of dark and light, with the dark generally having the upper hand. When Americans wished to express their frustrations with governmental authority, they repeated the aphorism, "You can't fight city hall." For city hall rather than Washington or Albany was the symbol for irresponsible rule and the failure of democracy.

The 1960s marked the beginning of a new era in the study of big-city politics and government. During this decade concern about the so-called urban crisis spawned the subfield of urban history. Scores of historians from university campuses throughout the country began to dissect the urban past with an enthusiasm typical of converts to a new faith. Many concentrated on the residential and social mobility of city and town dwellers, and by the 1970s case studies replete with statistical data and methodological appendixes dominated the study of America's urban past. Some, however, turned from those anonymous residents rising and falling and moving to and fro each decennial census and examined instead the politics and government of the city. Such academic historians as Alexander Callow, Zane Miller, Melvin Holli, and Lyle Dorsett all authored works on the subject, offering sophisticated accounts that went beyond the muckracking exposés and reform pieties of the past.[4] Yet each continued to depict American urban government primarily as a duel between bossism and reform set against a general tableau of incompetence and debacle. The motives and machinations of the boss and the reformer in a world of urban disorder and crisis remained the focus of attention.

There were, of course, some changes in interpretation. As early as 1949 the sociologist Robert Merton had identified the latent functions of the political machine, relieving the party organization of some of its traditional opprobrium. During the following decade Richard Hofstadter began stripping reformers of their noble rhetoric in order to discover their ulterior motives. And in the 1960s Samuel Hays added his imprimatur to the search for the social and cultural biases of reformers.[5] Others carried on this initiative, and the result was an unusually rosy image of bossism, while the reform impulse appeared less glowing. Party bosses became necessary and useful components of urban rule, uniting the decentralized structure of government, catering to the needs of jobless newcomers, and speaking for the alternative morality of the Germans, the Irish, the Italians, and the Poles. They may have profited from their power, but they also made the system work for those in the immigrant neighborhoods. In the literature of the 1960s and 1970s municipal reformers, in contrast, appeared less as paragons of public virtue and more as proponents of middle class social control. They spoke for the mores of the established native Americans and sought to ensure that the "better elements" of society ruled. By the 1960s and 1970s the morally charged rhetoric of the turn of the century had yielded to scholarly prose informed by sociological insight. Thus the former good guys and bad guys of the urban drama no longer bore their traditional moral labels as academic historians attributed some good to those who had formerly appeared to be all bad and unearthed some bad in those who had previously been monuments of civic righteousness. In the process that former king of corruption Boss Tweed shifted from scoundrel to social necessity.

Yet the duel between reform and bossism persisted as the dominant theme in the history of big-city rule. Even some who were willing to depart from traditional methodology and apply quantitative techniques remained safely in the established boss-reform groove. John Allswang computed Pearson's r correlations in order to discover the sociocultural basis for bossism. And Martin Shefter painstakingly calculated the regression coefficients for ethnicity, social class, and Tammany's vote during the 1880s and 1890s.[6] Whether the approach was quantitative or traditional, urban government of the period 1850 to 1940 was seen as a clash between upper middle class reformers seeking centralized, efficient, moral rule and the political machines dedicated to rewarding party loyalists and securing the mass of immigrant votes through favors and service. This was the dichotomy that seemed to typify urban rule during the last half of the nineteenth century and the first decades of the twentieth century, and this has been the framework of the leading historical accounts of municipal government in America.

After two decades of vigorous historical digging into the urban past, a reevaluation of this framework seems appropriate. Is this scenario an adequate one to describe the complexity of municipal development in the United States or has it, in fact, ignored vital elements in the story of urban rule? Has the rhetoric of this long-heralded clash diverted the historian too long from other actors in municipal government and other problems vital to urban politics? Such questions need to be asked if the historian's understanding of municipal rule is to advance. Otherwise discussion of the subject will atrophy with a few well-worn scholars debating the latent functions of the boss and the overt prejudices of the reformer. In 1979 David Thelen complained that historians had not moved beyond the boss-reformer synthesis, a complaint echoed by others tired of the standard bromides.[7] During the 1980s it seems possible to rewrite the history of urban politics and government along new lines that do not neglect the diversity of decisionmakers nor the significance of such areas of public policy as sanitation, recreation, public safety, and public works.

If historians are to recognize the diversity of decisionmakers and calculate the varied forces determining policy, they must first identify to what degree the boss actually bossed. The failure to define the clout of party leaders has been a major weakness of the traditional accounts. Most have classed all so-called bosses together and have assumed that they pulled the strings of city government. But is the term "boss" appropriate, and can historians neatly lump various party leaders in a category so labeled without distorting historical reality? For example, were Tammany's Boss Croker and St. Louis's Boss Butler in the same class? It seems doubtful. Croker headed a citywide, long-established organization; Butler was a freelance operator who made the most of his local base in two wards and bartered for power, sometimes winning and sometimes losing. A typology of political leaders is necessary to determine whether a so-called boss was merely a party wheeler-dealer making the most of his limited clout, or whether he was one of a clique of party leaders who could fix the course of the party's municipal conventions, or whether he was, in fact, the supreme nabob who decided both party nominations and public policy. In his recent study of San Francisco's Boss Buckley, William Bullough writes of Buckley as if he were the boss of the city, and yet he admits that Buckley-backed members of the municipal board of supervisors did not concur on policy questions and did not conform to a single course of action.[8] Was, then, Buckley only a party boss who decided which aspirants won nominations and received jobs but who could not dictate city policy? Were even the supposedly all-powerful bosses, the Coxes, the Pendergasts, and the Crokers, primarily dispensers of patronage? And what appointments could the party leaders dictate? Did they hand the mayor a list of worthy heelers deserving of such jobs as dog catcher or deputy clerk? Or did they foist upon the executive a full slate of party workers to fill the higher policymaking posts as well as the lower menial offices.

These are significant questions that need to be answered. Historians have dissected the reform cause classifying some as structural reformers and some as social reformers, but they have been less analytical in their treatment of the boss. Certainly the professional leaders of party organizations played a vital role in city government of the late nineteenth and early twentieth centuries.

But what was that role? Traditional myths of dictatorial sway based on reform-inspired apocrypha are no longer adequate. Further work is necessary to distinguish the impact of the boss not simply on the voter and the immigrant but also on the city council, the mayor, the municipal departments, and the state legislature.

Having defined the party leader's sphere of influence, the historian can then proceed to study those most obvious but often neglected participants in urban government, the public officials. The boss-reform synthesis has so dominated the study of urban politics and government that the actual holders of official power have receded into the shadows yielding the pages of history to party leaders and reform crusaders. Accounts of New York City's political and governmental history move from Tweed to Kelly, to Croker, to Murphy. None of these Tammany bosses held the highest policymaking offices in the city, and elsewhere party leaders likewise often held no official post. But party leaders dominate the urban history texts. Formal officeholders are rarely mentioned, for descriptions of the supposedly omnipotent boss seem sufficient.

It is time that scholars examined more closely municipal officialdom. Mayors, for example, have been significant figures, and in most cities they were not mere puppets masking the active hand of a party potentate. Some mayors, such as Detroit's Hazen Pingree, New York's Fiorello LaGuardia, and New Orleans's DeLesseps Morrison are the subjects of scholarly studies, but chiefly because of their importance as reform leaders.[9] The office of mayor as such has seemed of little interest. Recently Melvin Holli and Peter d'A. Jones, codirectors of the Project for the Study of American Mayors, have edited a biographical dictionary of the mayors of fifteen major cities, providing background data on scores of previously faceless urban executives.[10] Such information is valuable for an understanding of the formal leaders of municipal government, and the Project promises further rewarding publications. Historians need to examine seriously those who served as municipal executives, what power they exercised, and what were the political limitations on their clout. Standard assumptions about the power structure should not suffice.

Other municipal officials also wielded real power and helped determine the policies and programs of city government. Municipal comptrollers generally drafted the budgets and oversaw finances, winning recognition among knowing observers as second only to the mayor in authority. Yet amid all the stories of bosses and reformers these figures who actually supervised the distribution of public monies receive at best a footnote citation. City engineers likewise fail to win notice in most accounts of municipal rule. The vast waterworks and sewerage systems of metropolitan America were their handiwork and reflect their predilections and professional judgments. Only in the late 1970s, however, have the first books and articles appeared tracing the work of these public officials. Municipal attorneys also rank among the chief functionaries of city government, but they too win little attention.

And the whole staff of professional bureaucrats filling the offices of every major city hall in the twentieth century merit much more study than historians have granted them. These career officials survive in office for decades through one political administration after another, and they play a significant role in implementing the policy of the municipality. They are the technical experts vital to day-to-day operations. But they are also the intransigent bureaucrats who seem to have more loyalty to their departments than to their city and who tend to view urban residents more as statistical data than as human beings. American urban history abounds with examples of formidable civil servants who left as much of an imprint as any mayor or political leader and who ruled their particular realm of municipal service as unchallenged czar. For example, San Francisco's "Uncle John" McLaren reigned as that city's park superintendent from the late 1880s until his death in 1943 at the age of ninety-six. Though they determined the destiny of urban services, the McLarens of the American city remain largely unknown.

Comptrollers, engineers, park superintendents, and civil servants generally make dry copy when compared with audacious bosses renowned for dubious exploits. Everyone loves a scoundrel, and the tales of Boss Tweed will certainly sell better than the saga of Tweed's contemporary, Alfred W. Craven, who administered New York City's Croton Aqueduct system for two decades and influenced water supply technology throughout the nation. But the history of city government is not simply a story of flamboyant political chieftains and juicy scandals. It is a story that must include the formal occupants of public office. Who were they? What did they do, and what were the consequences in terms of municipal policy? Urban historians know less about the highest officials of the city than they do about those previously anonymous masses huddled in the immigrant wards who have been the subject of so many recent dissertations and monographs.

Also missing from the pages of most urban histories are the professional consultants who offer their services for a fee to cities throughout the nation. Since the late nineteenth century, when landscape architects such as Frederick Law Olmsted and sanitary engineers like Rudolph Hering sold their expertise to municipalities, these figures have proved a significant component in the history of city government. In the twentieth century urban planning firms have proliferated, advising and educating mayors and council members from Massachusetts to California. Mel Scott has written an official, laudatory history of the urban planning profession, but historians have generally failed to examine critically the impact of these paid consultants who strongly influence the public policy of communities to which they have no personal commitment.[11] Serving cities in all sections of the country, they may well have realized a homogenization of municipal policy, a uniformity based on professional precepts. In any case, these "expert" participants in the governing process merit further examination.

Officials and consultants comprise the formal structure of rule; but also of importance are the informal, extralegal actors in municipal government. The fire insurance underwriters demanding improved fire protection, the neighborhood associations petitioning for better services, the labor unions speaking for municipal employees, the real estate developers lobbying for zoning ordinances—all are among those who have determined municipal policy and who warrant a place in urban histories. Moreover, historians cannot categorically assign these groups either to the side of bossism or to that of reform. Though fire insurance interests took a "reform" stance in supporting an efficient, nonpartisan fire department, they severely criticized reform Mayor Seth Low's treatment of the department and defended Chief Edward Croker, the nephew of Tammany Boss Richard Croker. Scholars have traditionally seen public utilities as the bosom friends of bossism, yet Tammany Mayor Hugh Grant battled the electric light companies over the issue of overhead wires. City government was not a neat two-sided affair with the parties rigidly aligned. The private lobbyists played all parts of the political spectrum, winning whatever they could from whomever was in power. By recognizing the multitude of particular bodies demanding a voice in municipal policymaking, historians can better sketch the complex picture of urban government. It is a picture encompassing party regulars, reform factions, and private groups dedicated to neither the partisan machine nor the reform clique but to some particular cause, whether fire protection or higher wages.

While the traditional focus on bosses and reformers has diverted historians from many of the significant actors in city government, it has also distracted them from consideration of the vital services at the heart of urban rule. Urban government encompasses more than election campaigns and civic crusades. Waterworks, sewers, parks, libraries, schools, fire brigades, and police departments have been basic to municipal rule, and an understanding of the evolution of city government requires an understanding of these essential services. Until the late 1960s, academic historians had virtually ignored this aspect of urban administration. The rough-and-tumble of politics attracted the scholar's attention; questions of public policy did not. Even into the 1980s some areas of municipal service are unknown territory for the historian.

The past decade has, however, witnessed a rash of studies on city police and city schools. For amid the urban tumult of the late 1960s the police and public schools seemed particularly culpable, and both were most definitely in need of examination. Ghetto schools and brutal cops, in fact, seemed symbolic of all that was wrong with the city. Consequently, these municipal services first suffered the scrutiny of historians seeking the source of contemporary ills.

By the early 1980s the list of police studies had grown especially long. Roger Lane initiated the stream of scholarship, describing the nineteenth-century origins of Boston's police force. James Richardson soon followed suit examining in his first book the political and administrative history of New York City's police force and then in a second work expanding his coverage to the nation as a whole. During the late 1970s Samuel Walker and Robert Fogelson likewise contributed monographs describing twentieth-century reform of law enforcement agencies and the professionalization of American city police. Meanwhile, Wilbur Miller attempted a different approach in his comparative history of the early police forces in New York City and London, a work that illuminates the distinctive characteristics of the American police tradition. More recently Eric Monkkonen has added to the literature on police history with a statistical study based on official records.[12] Together these works constitute a formidable achievement. Overall the focus has been on professionalization and the gradual transition from the politicized, patronage squads of the nineteenth century to the nonpartisan bureaucracy of the mid-twentieth century.

The histories of urban schooling likewise focused on the development of a professional bureaucracy, though historians proved less sympathetic to public school reforms of the nineteenth and early twentieth centuries than to reforms in police work. In fact, the accounts of schooling in the city have been notable for their hostility to the educational bureaucrat. The creators and administrators of city school systems have appeared in the pages of recent educational histories as agents of social control, molding young minds to fit middle class values. Both Carl Kaestle's history of public schooling in New York City between 1750 and 1850 and Stanley Schultz's account of Boston public education from 1789 to 1860 have emphasized the school reformers' desire to secure social order amid the mounting disorder of the city. Michael Katz, David Tyack, and Marvin Lazerson have also commented critically on the rise of urban school systems and the emergence of an educational bureaucracy. Leading the challenge to these revisionists has been Diane Ravitch, who believes that school reformers were responding to the inadequacies of the educational system rather than conspiring to impose stifling regimentation.[13] But generally the school superintendents of the past have suffered a number of hard knocks during the late 1960s and the 1970s.

Other areas of municipal service have suffered more from neglect than abuse. A rash of literature appeared in the 1970s on Frederick Law Olmsted and the origin of urban parks. Laura Roper's biography of Olmsted and Albert Fein's study of Olmsted's role in the origins of urban planning both paid homage to the ideas and achievements of the great landscape architect, and he certainly survived the 1970s with far more laurels intact than did his benighted counterparts in the realm of public schooling.[14] Yet beyond this literature on Olmsted there has been little work on the history of urban parks. The work of other landscape architects such as Horace Cleveland and Charles Eliot deserves further consideration. And historians need to look beyond the design stage dominated by the landscape architect and examine the administration and maintenance of the urban parklands. What happened to the great municipal preserves of the nineteenth century? How did areas designed as scenic refuges from urban mayhem win a reputation for muggings and violence? What factors have nurtured the decay of these municipal parks? Is it a question of inadequate funding, changing tastes in recreation, neighborhood deterioration, or governmental incompetence? Twentieth-century park development, in fact, suffers virtually total neglect. The impact of the automobile on inner city parks and the evolution of metropolitan park systems along the suburban fringe are both subjects meriting attention.

Public health efforts in urban America have likewise received some consideration but deserve further work. John Duffy's two-volume chronicle of public health efforts in New York City offers a straightforward account of epidemics and reforms over a three-century period. Stuart Galishoff's study of the public health department of Newark, New Jersey, in contrast, restricts itself to the period from 1895 to 1918 and describes the impact of advances in bacteriology. Yet neither fully exploits the relationship of public health policy to the changing political and social order of the city. In recent case studies of Milwaukee, New York City, and Cincinnati, Judith Walzer Leavitt, Daniel M. Fox, and Alan I. Marcus have examined the politics of public health.[15] But more work is needed along these lines. Traditional histories of public health have too often resembled paeans to the triumphs of the medical profession. No one can deny that cities today are healthier than 100 or 150 years ago. Yet historians are warranted to have a certain skepticism about the medical profession, public health practitioners, and the medical school faculties who so often dominated the municipal hospitals and operated them as teaching clinics.

Public health departments were, however, a minor element in the city budgets as compared with another much neglected subject, municipal public works. During the three centuries of city government in America, municipalities have paved and lighted millions of miles of streets, have constructed mammoth water and sewer systems, and have erected monumental bridges. Yet until the past few years the historical literature on this aspect of city government was almost nonexistent. Historians obsessed with tales of bossism and analyses of reform paid little attention to the actual purpose of municipal government, the provision of public services.

In the past decade some historians have begun to remedy this oversight. David McCullough has presented a detailed and highly readable account of the creation of the Brooklyn Bridge, the most famous municipal project of the nineteenth century. Louis Cain has traced the changing public policy with regard to sewerage in Chicago, and Robert Caro has written a massive 1,200-page biography of the master of public works in twentieth-century New York City, Robert Moses.[16] Caro's work probably reveals more about urban government in twentieth-century America than any other volume. He recognizes both the social and political costs of the gigantic public works of the past half century and the motives and maneuvers that underlie their creation. Expressways and bridges are not simply expressions of technological triumph; they are products of a governmental system that Caro exposes to the scrutiny of his reader. Though perhaps too harsh and one-sided in his condemnation of Moses, Caro's work is a model that others could imitate.

Less awesome volumes on municipal public works have also enlightened the student of urban history in recent years. In recognition of the growing interest in the subject, the *Journal of Urban History* devoted its entire issue for May 1979 to articles on street paving, waterworks, and drainage. The guest editor for this special issue was Joel Tarr, who has served as mentor for many concerned with the engineering achievements of city government. Stanley Schultz and Clay McShane have coauthored a significant article which also emphasizes the role of the municipal engineer and the construction of public works in late nineteenth-century urban development.[17] Moreover, the Public Works Historical Society has sponsored a series of pamphlets on the history of public engineering, most of them dealing with urban improvements. Among these essays in public works history are accounts of the development of water supply systems in such cities as Chicago, Fresno, and Wilmington, Delaware, as well as short studies on major municipal engineers like George Waring, John Jervis, and George W. Fuller. This same society has also embarked on an oral history project, publishing interviews with some of the leading municipal engineers of the twentieth century.

Thus during the 1970s, historians began to make headway in the area of municipal public works. But as yet the scholarship consists largely of articles and pamphlets and a few narrowly defined monographs. A broader synthesis is needed, one that will attempt to examine the relationship of municipal engineering to the social and political currents in the city and not simply describe the technological advances and triumphs of the engineering corps. What has been the relationship between the municipality's technical staff and its political leadership? To what extent have the public works policies of engineering professionals reflected the middle class assumptions and biases of these experts? Who has promoted the grand public works projects and who have been the chief beneficiaries? To what extent have municipal engineers served the will of the urban citizenry and to what extent have they been guided by the precepts of their profession regardless of the views of the citizenry? These and other questions should be answered if historians are to understand urban government and the development of the city in general.

Still other areas of municipal endeavor demand similar consideration. For example, the history of municipal fire protection has been virtually ignored. Students of city government have generally regarded the fire department as one of the most successful agencies of municipal rule, especially in comparison with the more politicized police department. A comparative study of the history of police and fire protection might well prove useful in illuminating the distinctive factors determining their development. Only recently have historians begun the study of municipal refuse services and the city's battle against pollution. *Pollution and Reform in American Cities*, edited by Martin V. Melosi, offers a collection of seminal essays dealing with this problem and the municipal response.[18] The origins and implementation of such policies is a subject of significance, well deserving the attention of Melosi and his colleagues.

Basic to all municipal policies, however, is the question of finance, and this topic is one of the most neglected. Around the turn of the century students of public finance published a series of monographs on the history of municipal finance in such cities as New York, Baltimore, Cleveland, Providence, and Boston.[19] And in 1977 Alan Anderson presented a theoretical model based on municipal financing that supposedly explained the history of city government in the late nineteenth and early twentieth centuries.[20] Unfortunately, Anderson's stimulating work rested on suppositions rather than fact. Other than Anderson, however, few since the Progressive era have delved into the history of municipal expenditures, taxation, and debt.[21] Historians have written blithely about waste, incompetence, and inefficiency in city government without ever testing these generalizations against the municipal ledgers. Likewise, they have characterized bosses as generous in their distribution of funds for public works and patronage jobs, while reformers have assumed the appearance of tight-fisted accountants careful to avoid expense. Yet again there has been no analysis of expenditures to support this view. Moreover, no one has systematically examined the incidence of local taxation and the effect taxing policy has had on urban development. Who has disproportionately shouldered the burden of local government expenditures, and how has the incidence of taxation shifted over the past one hundred years? In an age replete with local tax abatements for corporations willing to construct downtown headquarters, it seems worthwhile to consider the consequences of past business-boosting fiscal policies. And no one has sufficiently recognized the significance of the national money market on public policy and the creation of public works. Whether reformers or party operatives presided at city hall may have been unimportant in influencing the construction of public works. Tight money and high interest rates may have been much more decisive in determining whether sewers were built and waterworks expanded.

Such questions have assumed new significance in the wake of recent financial crises in New York City and Cleveland. Municipalities have never enjoyed unlimited resources, and both bankers and state legislators have had a major voice in how much city governments could spend. The changing pattern of municipal taxation, spending, and borrowing needs to be charted if historians are ever to fathom the development of urban rule.

Increasingly important for local finances in recent years has been federal government policy. Big-city mayors of the 1970s and 1980s have looked longingly at the federal purse to bail out their beleaguered municipalities, and the developing relation between the federal government and the locality certainly merits the attention of historians. During the past fifteen years some volumes have appeared focusing on the origins of federal involvement in the cities. The traditional emphasis on bosses and reformers has naturally led historians to consider the impact of federal aid on urban party lords. Thus Bruce Stave has examined the effect of New Deal urban programs on the political machines of Pittsburgh, while Lyle Dorsett has attempted a broader study of Franklin D. Roosevelt and the city bosses. The emerging consensus has been that the New Deal did not mark the last hurrah of bossism.[22]

Others have examined federal-city relations without focusing primarily on the political machine. For example, Charles Trout has examined the New Deal as applied to Boston, considering the effect of federal programs not only on the local party chiefs but also on the community's business, labor, and religious leaders. Mark Gelfand approached the origins of federal urban programs from another direction, focusing more on policymaking in Washington and less on the local impact. His work offers a detailed account of the framing of federal programs and the maneuverings in the nation's capital that resulted in a federal commitment to the cities. Philip J. Funigiello has described federal-city relations during World War II, like Gelfand focusing primarily on policymaking at the national level.[23]

Though adding greatly to the literature on urban government these monographs leave many questions unanswered. Still needed is an examination of the implementation of vital postwar urban renewal programs and further study of Cold War military spending and its effect on local government agencies. What was the reaction of the local community to federal schemes? And what was the impact of this new largesse on the local governing structure? Also, what was the relation between Washington and the cities? Municipal officials have complained bitterly of Washington red tape and interference. Did federal agencies wield an iron hand? To what extent have the cities been victims of an uncompromising federal government, an unrealistic planning profession, and incompetent local housing and renewal authorities?

All of these questions are especially pertinent for Americans in the early 1980s. Federal urban programs have been under attack, and President Reagan's chief domestic policy advisor, Martin Anderson, won his national reputation as a vigorous critic of the urban renewal program.[24] The federal government has now played a significant role in city government for half a century. It is time for historians to apply their hindsight, evaluate how federal programs have operated, and consider their impact.

Another development of the past half century also warrants increased investigation. From the 1920s through the 1960s the rate of suburbanization accelerated, with millions of Americans moving from the central cities to the fringes of suburbia. By the 1970s the United States was a suburban nation, yet few historians have dealt with the adaptation of government structures, practices, and policies to the suburban trend. Some studies appeared in the 1970s which dealt with the governmental fragmentation of the metropolis and past proposals for metropolitan reform.[25] In the early 1980s Carl Abbott's study of sunbelt cities presented new and valuable information on the emerging conflict between central city and suburbs in the booming metropolitan areas of the South and West. And Zane Miller has recently suggested a periodization based on changing perceptions of the suburban community and its government.[26] But there is a need for further work. How have governmental institutions and patterns of political behavior adapted to the move to suburbia? Is there a distinctive historical pattern for suburban government? Despite much talk about a back-to-the-city movement, the center of metropolitan life is continuing to shift from the old urban core to the outlying regions. Corporate headquarters have joined residents and retailers in abandoning the central city. It is time for historians to recognize this massive migration by focusing more attention on suburbia and its government.

Suburbanization has clearly complicated the pattern of government as lawmakers have applied new layers of local agencies overlapping the traditional municipalities. Thus special-function districts have proliferated, yet little is known of their historical evolution and how they have operated.

Metropolitan park, water, and transit authorities all provide vital services to millions of Americans, most of whom do not know who is in charge of these agencies or how special-district officials are chosen. Historians need to consider what these authorities have achieved and the social, economic, and political costs of their achievements. Has the anonymity of manifold autonomous special-function districts resulted in government irresponsible to the public? Decades of experience with such agencies as the New York Port Authority and the Metropolitan Water District of Southern California should provide some significant answers about the government of twentieth-century America.

One traditional government unit that has assumed new importance in suburban America is the county. County governments perform a wide range of functions traditionally associated with municipalities and for millions of suburban residents living in unincorporated areas the county is the primary agent of local authority. Today the supervisor of St. Louis County is responsible for governing more than twice as many people as the mayor and council members of the city of St. Louis. Likewise, the executive of Baltimore County presides over nearly as many residents as the mayor of Baltimore. Throughout the nation suburban counties are rivaling the central cities in importance as governmental units, and county government seems likely to assume even greater significance in the future.

Yet the historical development of the suburban county is uncharted territory. Historians need to examine the factors that led to the expansion of county functions and why suburbanites often seem to prefer county rule to traditional municipal government. What have been the advantages and disadvantages of the new county governments of suburban America? Moreover, how has the expansion of county government affected the political and social development of suburbia? These are questions scholars should confront in order to better comprehend the recent past.

Since the birth of urban history as a subdiscipline in the 1960s, historians have penned many volumes on city government and politics. Yet their neglect is as noteworthy as their achievement. The "new urban history" with its emphasis on patterns of social change and its aversion to institutional history has drawn attention away from the formal structures and services that shaped urban life. Historians have expended many words on the merits of the manuscript census as a source but have wasted few on water, sewerage, fire protection, and park development—all subjects vital to the development of the city and the social environment of its inhabitants. When historians have examined urban government and politics they have rarely been able to break out of the straight jacket of boss versus reformer. Party operatives and self-styled reformers were among the lead players in the drama of urban rule. But others were in the cast as well.

Historians are now beginning to recognize these neglected actors. The mayor's project directed by Melvin Holli and Peter d'A. Jones is evidence of a new concern for the most obvious but often ignored participants in urban government. Joel Tarr's efforts to stimulate research in public works history likewise is producing significant scholarship on the urban past. And the appearance of a growing number of articles and books on the public policy of the city bodes well for a broader understanding of municipal rule. Old-fashioned tales of scandal and corruption do not adequately describe city government and politics, nor do new-fashioned analyses of the sociocultural foundations of bossism and reform. Such accounts provide valuable insights into the politics of the period. But urban government is not simply an ethnocultural feud between clashing social factions. It is a struggle to provide vital services for millions of Americans demanding unprecedented levels of comfort and convenience. It is a story of technological achievement and sophisticated financing, a story of greater breadth and complexity than has yet been recorded.

1. *Evening Post*, May 11, 1847, as quoted in Edward K. Spann, *The New Metropolis: New York City, 1840-1857* (New York: Columbia University Press, 1981), p. 60.

2. James Bryce, *The American Commonwealth*, vol. 1 (Chicago: Charles H. Sergel & Co., 1891 ed.), p. 608.

3. Charles Zueblin, *A Decade of Civic Development* (Chicago: University of Chicago Press, 1905); and *American Municipal Progress* (New York: Macmillan Company, 1916).

4. Alexander Callow, *The Tweed Ring* (New York: Oxford University Press, 1966); Zane Miller, *Boss Cox's Cincinnati: Urban Politics in the Progressive Era* (New York: Oxford University Press, 1968); Melvin G. Holli, *Reform in Detroit: Hazen S. Pingree and Urban Politics* (New York: Oxford University Press, 1969); Lyle W. Dorsett, *The Pendergast Machine* (New York: Oxford University Press, 1968).

5. Robert K. Merton, *Social Theory and Social Structure* (Glencoe, Ill.: Free Press, 1949); Richard Hofstadter, *The Age of Reform: From Bryan to F.D.R.* (New York: Knopf, 1955); Samuel P. Hays, "The Politics of Reform in Municipal Government in the Progressive Era," *Pacific Northwest Quarterly* 55 (October 1964): 157-69.

6. John M. Allswang, *Bosses, Machines, and Urban Voters: An American Symbiosis* (Port Washington, N.Y.: Kennikat Press, 1977); Martin Shefter, "The Electoral Foundations of the Political Machine: New York City, 1884-1897," in *The History of American Electoral Behavior*, eds. Joel H. Silbey et al. (Princeton: Princeton University Press, 1978), pp. 263-98.

7. David P. Thelen, "Urban Politics: Beyond Bosses and Reforms," *Reviews in American History* 7 (September 1979): 406-12. Lyle Dorsett has also attacked the boss-reformer dichotomy in "The City Boss and the Reformer: A Reappraisal," *Pacific Northwest Quarterly* 63 (October 1972): 150-54.

8. William A. Bullough, *The Blind Boss and His City* (Berkeley: University of California Press, 1979), see pp. 136-37.

9. Arthur Mann, *LaGuardia Comes to Power, 1933* (Philadelphia: Lippincott, 1965); Charles Garrett, *The La Guardia Years: Machine and Reform Politics in New York City* (New Brunswick, N.J.: Rutgers University Press, 1961); Holli, *Reform in Detroit*; Edward F. Haas, *DeLesseps S. Morrison and the Image of Reform: New Orleans Politics, 1946-1961* (Baton Rouge: Louisiana State University Press, 1974).

10. Melvin G. Holli and Peter d'A. Jones, eds., *Biographical Dictionary of American Mayors, 1820-1980* (Westport, Conn.: Greenwood Press, 1981). See also Eugene J. Watts, *The*

Social Bases of City Politics: Atlanta, 1865–1903 (Westport, Conn.: Greenwood Press, 1978) for an examination of the social backgrounds of officeholders in one southern city.

11. Mel Scott, *American City Planning Since 1890: A History Commemorating the Fiftieth Anniversary of the American Institute of Planners* (Berkeley: University of California, 1969).

12. Roger Lane, *Policing the City: Boston, 1822–1885* (Cambridge: Harvard University Press, 1967); James F. Richardson, *The New York Police: Colonial Times to 1901* (New York: Oxford University Press, 1970); and *Urban Police in the United States* (Port Washington, N.Y.: Kennikat Press, 1974); Samuel Walker, *A Critical History of Police Reform: The Emergence of Professionalism* (Lexington, Mass.: Lexington Books, 1977); Robert M. Fogelson, *Big-City Police* (Cambridge: Harvard University Press, 1977); Wilbur R. Miller, *Cops and Bobbies: Police Authority in New York and London, 1830–1870* (Chicago: University of Chicago Press, 1977); Eric H. Monkkonen, *Police in Urban America, 1860–1920* (Cambridge, U.K.: Cambridge University Press, 1981). See also Gene E. Carte and Elaine H. Carte, *Police Reform in the United States: The Era of August Vollmer, 1905–1932* (Berkeley: University of California Press, 1975); William J. Bopp, *"O. W." O. W. Wilson and the Search for a Police Profession* (Port Washington, N.Y.: Kennikat Press, 1977).

13. Carl F. Kaestle, *The Evolution of an Urban School System: New York City, 1750–1850* (Cambridge: Harvard University Press, 1973); Stanley K. Schultz, *The Culture Factory: Boston Public Schools, 1789–1860* (New York: Oxford University Press, 1973); David B. Tyack, *The One Best System: A History of American Urban Education* (Cambridge: Harvard University Press, 1974); Marvin Lazerson, *Origins of the Urban School; Public Education in Massachusetts, 1870–1915* (Cambridge: Harvard University Press, 1971); Michael B. Katz, "The Emergence of Bureaucracy in Urban Education: The Boston Case, 1850–1884," *History of Education Quarterly* 8 (Summer-Fall 1968): 155–88, 319–57; Diane Ravitch, *The Revisionists Revised: A Critique of the Radical Attack on the Schools* (New York: Basic Books, 1978); and *The Great School Wars, New York City, 1805–1973: A History of the Public Schools as Battlefield of Social Change* (New York: Basic Books, 1974).

14. Laura Wood Roper, *FLO: A Biography of Frederick Law Olmsted* (Baltimore: Johns Hopkins University Press, 1973); Albert Fein, *Frederick Law Olmsted and the American Environmental Tradition* (New York: G. Braziller, 1972); Geoffrey Blodgett, "Frederick Law Olmsted: Landscape Architecture as Conservative Reform," *Journal of American History* 62 (March 1976): 869–89. For an earlier work tracing the origins of a city park system, see William H. Wilson, *The City Beautiful Movement in Kansas City* (Columbia: University of Missouri Press, 1964).

15. John Duffy, *A History of Public Health in New York City, 1625–1866* (New York: Russell Sage Foundation, 1968); and *A History of Public Health in New York City, 1866–1966* (New York: Russell Sage Foundation, 1974); Stuart Galishoff, *Safeguarding the Public Health: Newark, 1895–1918* (Westport, Conn.: Greenwood Press, 1975); Judith Walzer Leavitt, "Politics and Public Health: Smallpox in Milwaukee, 1894–1895," *Bulletin of the History of Medicine* 50 (Winter 1976): 553–68; and *The Healthiest City: Milwaukee and the Politics of Health Reform* (Princeton: Princeton University Press, 1982); Daniel M. Fox, "Social Policy and City Politics: Tuberculosis Reporting in New York 1889–1900," *Bulletin of the History of Medicine* 49 (Summer 1975): 169–95; Alan I. Marcus, "Professional Revolution and Reform in the Progressive Era: Cincinnati Physicians and the City Elections of 1897 and 1900," *Journal of Urban History* 5 (February 1979): 183–207.

16. David G. McCullough, *The Great Bridge* (New York: Simon and Schuster, 1972); Louis P. Cain, *Sanitation Strategy for a Lakefront Metropolis: The Case of Chicago* (DeKalb, Ill.: Northern Illinois University Press, 1978); Robert A. Caro, *The Power Broker: Robert Moses and The Fall of New York* (New York: Knopf, 1974).

17. *Journal of Urban History* 5 (May 1979); Stanley K. Schultz and Clay McShane, "To Engineer the Metropolis: Sewers, Sanitation, and City Planning in Late-Nineteenth-Century America," *Journal of American History* 65 (September 1978): 389–411.

18. Martin V. Melosi, ed., *Pollution and Reform in American Cities, 1870–1930* (Austin: University of Texas Press, 1980). See also, Melosi, *Garbage in the Cities: Refuse, Reform, and the Environment, 1880–1980* (College Station: Texas A & M University Press, 1981).

19. Edward Dana Durand, *The Finances of New York City* (New York: Macmillan Company, 1898); Jacob H. Hollander, *The Financial History of Baltimore* (Baltimore: Johns Hopkins University Press, 1899); Charles C. Williamson, *The Finances of Cleveland* (New York: Columbia University Press, 1907); Howard Kemble Stokes, *The Finances and Administration of Providence* (Baltimore: Johns Hopkins University Press, 1903); Charles Phillips Huse, *The Financial History of Boston* (Cambridge: Harvard University Press, 1916).

20. Alan D. Anderson, *The Origin and Resolution of an Urban Crisis: Baltimore, 1890–1930* (Baltimore: Johns Hopkins University Press, 1977). Clifton K. Yearly, *The Money Machines: The Breakdown and Reform of Governmental and Party Finance in the North 1860–1920* (Albany: State University of New York Press, 1970) also has some material on municipal finances.

21. A notable exception to the pattern of neglect is Carl V. Harris's *Political Power in Birmingham 1871–1921* (Knoxville: University of Tennessee Press, 1977), which offers two chapters on the subject of municipal revenues. J. Rogers and Ellen Hollingsworth deal with the expenditures of smaller cities in *Dimensions in Urban History* (Madison: University of Wisconsin Press, 1979).

22. Bruce M. Stave, *The New Deal and the Last Hurrah: Pittsburgh Machine Politics* (Pittsburgh: University of Pittsburgh Press, 1970); Lyle W. Dorsett, *Franklin D. Roosevelt and the City Bosses* (Port Washington, N.Y.: Kennikat Press, 1977).

23. Charles H. Trout, *Boston, the Great Depression, and the New Deal* (New York: Oxford University Press, 1977); Mark I. Gelfand, *A Nation of Cities: The Federal Government and Urban America, 1933–1965* (New York: Oxford University Press, 1975); Philip J. Funigiello, *The Challenge to Urban Liberalism: Federal-City Relations During World War II* (Knoxville: University of Tennessee Press, 1978).

24. See Martin Anderson, *The Federal Bulldozer: A Critical Analysis of Urban Renewal, 1949–1962* (Cambridge: M.I.T. Press, 1964).

25. Kenneth T. Jackson, "Metropolitan Government Versus Political Autonomy: Politics and the Crabgrass Frontier" in *Cities in American History*, eds. Kenneth T. Jackson and Stanley T. Schultz (New York: Knopf, 1972), pp. 442–62; Jon C. Teaford, *City and Suburb: The Political Fragmentation of Metropolitan America, 1850–1970* (Baltimore: Johns Hopkins University Press, 1979).

26. Carl Abbott, *The New Urban America: Growth and Politics in Sunbelt Cities* (Chapel Hill: University of North Carolina Press, 1981), see pp. 167–210; Zane Miller, *Suburb: Neighborhood and Community in Forest Park, Ohio, 1935–1976* (Knoxville: University of Tennessee Press, 1981).

IN SEARCH OF THE NEW SOUTH:
SOUTHERN POLITICS AFTER RECONSTRUCTION

Numan V. Bartley

Only recently has the study of southern politics begun to emerge from the shadows cast by C. Vann Woodward's *Origins of the New South* and V. O. Key's *Southern Politics in State and Nation*.[1] These two brilliant and intimidating volumes appeared at mid-century—*Origins* in 1951 and *Southern Politics* in 1949—and for a generation have largely dominated the writing of post-Reconstruction southern political history. New works continued to be published, and a considerable number of them were quite good; but rarely did they stray much beyond the parameters established by Woodward and Key.

The main features of the Woodward–Key synthesis are well-known. Although the two authors differed in emphasis and conflicted on specific points, they both advanced Beardian interpretations that emphasized economic conflict between the haves and have-nots of southern society. Both regarded race as something of an "artificial" issue that disrupted the "natural" alliance of have-nots across color lines. In Woodward's analysis, the Civil War and Emancipation broke planter domination of southern politics and transferred power to modernizing bourgeois elites composed of merchants, businessmen, and industrialists. The Populist movement was an assault by agrarian have-nots on the exploitive Redeemer policies at home and the short-sighted Redeemer Right Fork alliance with northeastern capitalism nationally. With the failure of the Populist revolt, town and business oriented middle class Progressives led the South back into national politics, albeit not before shackling the region with disfranchisement, the one-party system, and de jure segregation. Key's study focused on the debilitating results of these institutions. For more than half a century they stunted southern political development and undermined the formation of a biracial New Deal coalition of have-nots.

A Woodward–Key synthesis structured the teaching and writing of New South politics for three decades. Much of this analysis remains valid today, of course—indeed, Key's *Southern Politics* is still largely unchallenged—but in recent years vague outlines of a different synthesis have begun to emerge. Comparative history, especially comparative studies of slavery, has par-

0048-7511/82/0104-0150 $01.00

ticularly influenced the new literature. The experiences of other plantation societies have suggested new approaches to the study of southern history, and, following a decade of lavish attention to slavery and the antebellum South, researchers have extended their interests into the post-Reconstruction era. As with the study of slavery and the Old South, class, labor, and race relations and their ideological manifestations have been central points of concern. Generally, recent literature has tended to stress the distinctiveness of southern society rather than its similarity with the states to the north, and in varying degrees has emphasized continuity from the Old South to the New rather than change. The trend seems clearly away from "psychological" explanations for southern political behavior—mythology, romanticism, separate and nationally unique historical experiences, individual and psychological racism, and the like.[2] Instead recent studies, which have often been Marxist or quasi-Marxist in orientation, have tended to link the attitudes and ideologies of social groups to the labor system, social structure, economic organization, and class relationships in the region.

Doubtless, Eugene D. Genovese is the scholar most responsible for laying the foundations for new directions in southern historiography, although Barrington Moore and William A. Williams have been important sources of theory.[3] Genovese has emphasized the "special social, economic, political, ideological, and psychological content" of antebellum southern society. Although a part of the world capitalist economy, the South, according to Genovese, "did not have an essentially market society" and consequently was basically different from the increasingly laissez-faire society of northern states. The prebourgeois southern planter class espoused an ideology of paternalism that bore little resemblance to the free labor ideology popular among northern elites and especially those who joined the Republican party.[4] Such differences ultimately produced civil war.

The Civil War and Emancipation broke the national power of the southern planters, but the extent to which "their way of life and its attendant ideology went down also" has become the central question of contemporary scholarship.[5] If the Old South was an established and prosperous society with its own economic, social, and ideological foundations, why would such a society so quickly collapse in the wake of Appomattox and the Thirteenth Amendment, particularly since the Radical Republican attempt to reconstruct that society ended in failure? The answer to this question remains debatable, but at least for the moment the initiative has plainly passed to the proponents of continuity.

Only the boldest scholars have suggested that nothing very important happened during the 1860s; yet a variety of studies have documented important elements of continuity that survived the transition. Economic historians continue to disagree about the causes of southern postwar poverty, but they are largely in agreement that the South remained economically distinct from the rest of the nation long after the end of Reconstruction.[6] Some works, such as Jay R. Mandle's *The Roots of Black Poverty*, have focused on the plantation as the central institution in southern life and have insisted that plantation agriculture continued to dominate southern development through the first third of the twentieth century.[7] Other recent studies have revived the once popular theory that the Civil War consolidated the South's position as a dependent colonial appendage to the North. Even if the South was in Joseph Persky's apt term a "favored colony," its peripheral position as an internal colony was, as Woodward argued in *Origins of the New South*, a central element in shaping its political relations with the northern core.[8]

Urban historians have tended in recent years to study southern urbanization within a regional context and to suggest that southern cities, rather than being the aggressive vanguards of the New South, were economically, culturally, racially, and in a variety of other ways strongly influenced if not substantially shaped by the surrounding countryside. As David R. Goldfield has argued, ruralism, race, and colonialism molded nationally distinctive southern urban communities within a nationally distinctive region.[9] Howard N. Rabinowitz has demonstrated that race relations changed less dramatically during the post-Civil War era than had previously been assumed. Not only did segregation become the normal form of race relations soon after Emancipation but it was largely preceded by exclusion of blacks altogether rather than integration.[10] These and other works have suggested new directions in southern political research.

The two books that have contributed most directly to a reinterpretation of New South politics are Jonathan M. Wiener's *Social Origins of the New South* and Dwight B. Billings's *Planters and the Making of a "New South."* Both works are controversial, and they are on some questions more provocative than convincing. At the same time they have stimulated a rethinking of political and social development in the New South, and they, perhaps more than any other studies of post-Reconstruction politics, have managed to incorporate much of the recent literature on the South into logically coherent interpretations. Borrowing from Barrington Moore, both Billings and Wiener find the New South following the "Prussian Road" to modernization.

Of the two works, Billings's study of North Carolina stresses continuity with a vengeance. He finds basic links in North Carolina "between the world the slaveholders built and the world they rebuilt after their nationalist failure." The precapitalist planter class promoted industrial self-sufficiency prior to the Civil War, and, following that unpleasantness, elements of "North Carolina's landed upper class provided postwar leadership in textile manufacturing, banking, insurance, railroad building, and other large business enterprises." In so doing they transferred agrarian social relations and planter ideology into industry, especially in the important case of the mill village. Since only the upper echelon of more prosperous planters possessed the excess capital to participate in these ventures, the lesser landholders, themselves intensely conservative and traditionalist, organized the Populist party. After the demise of the Populists and the disfranchisement of blacks, "the landed upper class could begin to use state government as an instrument for modernization." Thus Billings offers a relatively straightforward account of "a revolution from above" that produced "conservative modernization" in North Carolina.[11]

Jonathan Wiener's analysis of developments in Alabama is more complex. As in North Carolina, a "dominant nonbourgeois planter class" guided Alabama's social and economic development along the Prussian Road "that preserves and intensifies the authoritarian and repressive elements of traditional social relations." This path was by no means a smooth one. Planters encountered a series of challenges from newly freed blacks, merchants, and industrialists. These conflicts forced planters to compromise, but they did not overturn landlord leadership. The blacks compelled planters to abandon the gang system of plantation labor, but the resulting system of tenancy, along with debt peonage and northern corporate imperialism, were crucial factors in limiting the extent of Alabama's economic development. The planters successfully routed the merchants and checked the expansion of commercial values in the plantation counties, but the merchants did become established in nonplantation counties. When industrialists and their New South bourgeois spokesmen vied for ideological hegemony with the New South creed, planters and their allies struck back with the Myth of the Lost Cause. Finally, with the "threat from below" by "the Populist tenant farmers," the previously antagonistic planters and industrialists joined together in a Prussian Road alliance.[12]

A concept so encompassing as the Prussian Road to capitalism raises almost as many questions as it answers. The theory includes a number of assumptions regarding the solidarity within a dominant class, the nature of class conflict, and the reality of ruling class "hegemony," the latter being defined as the ability of a ruling class to convert the rest of society to its ideology, that are not altogether self-evident, especially to non-Marxist scholars. The very nature of this approach to the study of southern history may well tend to exaggerate the extent of continuity between the Old South and the New. Yet the studies by Billings and Wiener have focused attention on fundamental social and political questions. It is true that coercive forms of labor control remained common in the region long after the demise of slavery, and it is surely arguable that the South moved toward industrialization without establishing a bourgeois "political and social democracy." At any rate conventional wisdom no longer assumes that the Redeemers "were of middle-class origin, having but nominal connections with the old planter regime and with primarily an industrial, capitalist outlook." [13]

A number of state studies published over the past dozen or so years have suggested that Redeemer economic policies were less oriented toward business and industrial development than had been generally assumed. Governing a poverty-stricken region, Bourbon governments could hardly fail to favor economic progress. Five states gave tax concessions to new industry, several continued at least for a time the Reconstruction policy of providing state aid for railroad construction, and none showed a noticeable interest in conserving public lands. Yet, nine of the eleven southern states adopted new constitutions during the 1870s and 1880s, and they consistently denied state monetary support to private endeavors and in other ways circumscribed expenditures for the internal improvements that would have been necessary to promote rapid industrial growth. The Bourbon preoccupation with social stability, low taxes, and limited government does not necessarily suggest a governing elite preoccupied with economic development. James Tice Moore, after surveying the literature on the Bourbon period, concluded: "Recent state studies for the most part suggest that traditionalist, agriculturally oriented elites grasped the New South as firmly as they had the Old." [14]

These trends in southern scholarship are apt to spur renewed interest in the spokesmen for the New South. The standard study of the subject remains Paul M. Gaston's *The New South Creed.* Largely developing points suggested by Woodward's interpretation, Gaston argued that the New South idea was a program for a new departure that flourished in the political atmosphere provided by the commercial and industrial orientation of the capitalist Redeemer governments. Its goal was sectional reconciliation, racial peace, and "a new economic and social order based on industry and scientific, diversified agriculture . . . ." Although there was for a time conflict between the defenders of the cult of the Lost Cause and the advocates of a New South, the latter soon incorporated "the romantic, idealized legend of the Old South" into their New South vision. At approximately the same time, the New South creed underwent another "metamorphosis and soon came to be a description not of what ought to be, but of what already was." [15] Thus, according to Gaston's analysis, Henry W. Grady and his ideological kinsmen adopted during the early 1880s a romanticized Old South and increasingly insisted that the New South was an accomplished fact, despite the region's laggard economic growth.

In a perceptive chapter in *Social Origins of the New South,* Wiener offers a new and in many ways a more intrinsically satisfying explanation for the evolution of the New South creed. Like Gaston, Wiener views New South spokesmen as propagandists for bourgeois values, but thereafter the two interpretations increasingly diverge. "The ideologists of the New South," Wiener states, "were attempting to cast off the cultural domination of the planter class . . . ." The planters responded with a glorification of the Old South, and "the New South ideologists embraced the Old South myth because they were not strong enough to attack it, even though it posed a sharp critique of their own program." Thwarted in their drive for ideological hegemony, the spokesmen for the New South professed allegiance to the Old South in "a strategic attempt at accommodation with an opponent they were unable to defeat," moderated their program, and accepted the status quo as the fulfillment of their goals.[16]

Other writers have offered alternative interpretations of the New South movement. Dwight Billings found no conflict between the cult of the Old South and the idea of the New South, since the powerholders in the Old South also dominated the New South.[17] In a recent survey of southern history, I. A. Newby suggests that the New South creed was in part "a formula for colonializing the southern economy and inveigling the southern people to accommodate themselves to the needs of the colonializers."[18] Although Newby does not fully develop the point, it does perhaps merit consideration. As the New South movement progressed, it increasingly envisioned southern industrial development through the importation of northern capital. By basing the industrial future of the region on the propitiation of dominant economic interests in the North, New South advocates clearly limited the scope of their movement and thus may not have been quite the hard-driving modernizers that they have often been depicted as.

However the debates over the principal features of the Redeemer era are resolved, the most fundamental challenge to the established order was the Populist revolt. For a time the embattled Populists were under attack from a variety of scholarly sources. Richard Hofstadter's assault from a consensus perspective on populism's reform credentials in *The Age of Reform* is well known, and that book led to a general decline in Populist prestige in academic circles. The most significant attempt to apply Hofstadter's assumptions to the study of southern populism was Sheldon Hackney's *Populism to Progressivism in Alabama*. Hackney found Alabama Populists to be motivated by "feelings of powerlessness," by "emotions such as hatred or resentment," and by an addiction to "conspiracy theories." More interested in power than policy, Hackney's Populists "lacked an ideology" and "were, patently, not reformers."[19] Roger L. Hart, in his study of *Redeemers, Bourbons, and Populists* in Tennessee, came to somewhat similar if less devastating conclusions regarding the origins of the Peoples Party.[20]

Robert H. Wiebe's influential *The Search for Order,* which rested upon a modernization theoretical framework, found the Populists to be "narrowly local" defenders of island community values at a time when leadership was passing to national elites. On the Left, William A. Williams dismissed the Populists as petty bourgeois defenders of a declining stage of capitalist economic development.[21] More recently both Billings and Wiener, their emphasis directed toward the struggle for "hegemony" among dominant elites, have dealt with populism in a relatively cursory manner.

Despite all of this, southern Populists have survived with their radical credentials relatively intact. Woodward, in *Origins of the New South* and elsewhere, treated the Populists with great sympathy, and his interpretation remained more or less standard in historical surveys of the South and in state histories. Quite recently, it has been enthusiastically reaffirmed in Lawrence Goodwyn's *Democratic Promise.*[22] Although the Populists were authentic local reformers, the central thrust of their movement, according to Goodwyn, was an attack on northeastern finance capitalism. Woodward labeled the chapter in *Origins of the New South* that deals with the maturing of populism "The Revolt Against the East," a title that would summarize Goodwyn's interpretation. *Democratic Promise* assumes that the Redeemer opponents of populism were bourgeois businessmen, but, if the studies cited earlier in this essay are correct in arguing that agricultural interests remained dominant in the New South, there is little in Goodwyn's analysis that would fail to support the theory that populism in the South was a small farmer revolt from colonial dependency and a plantation oriented leadership that accepted northeastern corporate domination in exchange for "home rule."

Goodwyn stresses economic motivations in accounting for the origins of populism and he vigorously rejects interpretations that find Populists driven by status anxieties, narrow provincialism, or reactionary values. Although less encompassing in its interpretation, Robert C. McMath's study of the Southern Farmers' Alliance, while more sensitive than Goodwyn's work to the complexities and even contradictions within the movement, also stresses its seriousness of purpose and the rationality of its solutions to the crushing problems of southern agriculture. McMath dwells on the cultural and religious factors that both strengthened Alliance solidarity and complicated its transformation into a third party, but his "community of true believers" seems not to differ in any basic way from the "movement culture" described by Goodwyn.[23] A more recent examination of southern Populist thought by Bruce Palmer is also a relatively sympathetic treatment of southern populism's "distinctive and valid criticism of American industrial and financial capitalism."[24]

Although Populists have largely retained their folk hero reputation, southern Progressives are considerably less secure in their status as reformers.

In *Origins of the New South*, Woodward noted the "paradoxical combination of white supremacy and progressivism" and suggested that the Progressive movement failed to fulfill "the political aspirations and deeper needs of the mass of people" in the South.[25] Thereafter southern progressivism fared increasingly well in southern scholarship. During the 1960s progressivism was generally depicted as "an amalgam of agrarian radicalism, business regulation, good government, and urban social justice reforms [that] became in the end a movement for positive government."[26] This interpretation remains popular, of course, although the most recent survey of southern progressivism is far more cautious in its conclusions. Written from a modernization perspective, Jack Temple Kirby's *Darkness at the Dawning* finds southern Progressives divided into two wings, the stronger of which was a rural-based antitrust movement that sought to defend local values while the other was "urban-based, professional-minded, bureaucratizing and centralizing" in thrust. Although Kirby regards segregation and disfranchisement as the "seminal" Progressive reforms, he locates substantial continuity between populism and progressivism and deemphasizes class analysis to stress white consensus on "the great race settlement of 1890–1910."[27]

Other studies have taken a basically different approach to progressivism. In a work on Virginia progressivism published more than a decade ago, Raymond H. Pulley concluded that "the reform impulse sprang from the conserving or reactionary tendencies inherent in the culture of the Commonwealth rather than from a desire to reconcile the state to the march of modern America."[28] As studies of national progressivism have increasingly tended to identify the movement with elitist and corporate capitalist values, Pulley's description of an established leadership, threatened by independent movements, launching a program to restore and buttress the old order has gained broader acceptability. A recent study of the period in a Deep South state reports "Progressive reform in Georgia was conservative, elitist, and above all racist."[29]

This trend in scholarship received its most vigorous and most impressive expression in J. Morgan Kousser's *The Shaping of Southern Politics*. According to Kousser's interpretation, southern progressivism was a reaction to lower class insurgency that threatened the Democratic party's domination of political power in the South. Democratic elites responded with a "revolt against democracy" that sought "the stabilization of society, especially the economy, in the interests of the local established powers, at the expense of the lower strata of society in the South, and sometimes at the expense of out-of-state corporations." The leading proponents of this program of disfranchisement and reform were plantation elites who "bore striking resemblances to antebellum 'patricians.'"[30]

Kousser's study emphasizes the disfranchisement movement and may not offer an adequate interpretation for progressivism as a whole. Yet, if the Redeemers were more closely associated with conservative agricultural values than had once been believed, then it would not be surprising to learn that the Progressive "search for order" contained a strong element of reaction. Modernization theorists have frequently advanced a dual economy thesis which assumes that changes in an economically underdeveloped area would come first to the cities, thereby for a time dividing the modernizing cities from the "traditional" countryside. It may well be that planter oriented rural Progressives endeavored to buttress the old social order with disfranchisement and other programs, that urban Progressive elites promoted various modernizing reforms as Kirby and others have suggested, and that a considerable number of farmers and townsmen retreated into a defense of local values that included a politics of demagoguery and a largely ineffective opposition to northern based corporate enterprise.

In any event, the "synthesis" fashioned during the Progressive era, as George B. Tindall has observed, "governed southern politics through the first half of the twentieth century."[31] Although students of southern politics have devoted relatively little attention to the 1920s, 30s, and 40s, the literature would overwhelmingly support Tindall's observation. During these years, the region solidified its reputation as "the benighted South," "the Nation's No. 1 economic problem," and the home of race-baiting demagogues. V. O. Key, after examining the politics of the period, stated "The South may not be the nation's number one political problem, as some northerners assert, but politics is the South's number one problem."[32] The current state of scholarship on the post-Progressive era strongly suggests that, whatever the positive features of Progressive reform, the results were clearly limited.

Key identified the failures of southern politics with the one-party system. As Key explained, "in the confusions and distractions of one-party politics broad issues of economic philosophy are often obscured or smothered by irrelevant appeals, sectional loyalties, local patriotism, personal candidacies, and, above all, by the specter of the black man." More fundamentally, Key emphasized the success of white elites in the black-belt plantation counties in impressing "on an entire region a philosophy agreeable to its necessities and succeeded for many decades in maintaining a regional unity in national politics to defend these necessities." Although often challenged, socioeconomically privileged whites of the black belt emerged victorious from the crucial political crises in southern history and were the primary architects of the system of white supremacy and disfranchisement that the one-party system rested upon and defended. Normally allied with town merchants, businessmen, and industrialists, plantation-oriented whites induced other groups within southern society "to subordinate to the race question all great social and economic issues that tend to divide people into opposing parties."[33] Even though Key failed to employ "hegemony," "prebourgeois," and other key words and concepts of today, his analysis would not conflict with recent reinterpretations of earlier periods of southern history.

More recent studies have augmented *Southern Politics* without upsetting its general interpretive framework. George B. Tindall, who in *The Emergence of the New South* and other studies has contributed more toward an understanding of southern politics between the wars than any other recent writer, has viewed southern politics from a traditionalist Progressive perspective and has emphasized the "business progressivism" of southern state governments in the 1920s.[34] Blaine A. Brownell has demonstrated that a growth-oriented "white commercial-civic elite" dominated politics in the region's larger cities during the 1920s, and Morton Sosna has traced the activities of the section's tiny reform-minded intelligentsia. Robert A. Garson's *The Democratic Party and the Politics of Sectionalism* is a valuable study of the political animosities that centered around civil rights issues within the national party during the 1940s.[35] Few state studies of southern politics between the wars have appeared.[36]

It is no doubt a tribute to *Southern Politics* that, whereas there are relatively few works dealing with the period Key studied, an outpouring of literature examines southern politics during the years since the book was published. A significant portion of these works investigate the reentry of blacks into southern politics. While the history of blacks as participants in—rather than objects of—southern politics is yet to be written, an impressive number of competent works have examined southern black political behavior since the *Smith* v. *Allwright* decision of 1944. Two Atlanta journalists, Pat Watters and Reese Cleghorn, present probably the most moving account of the black struggle for the ballot; two political scientists, Donald R. Matthews and James W. Prothro, provide the most intensely scholarly study of blacks and New South politics. David J. Garrow's *Protest at Selma* is the best study of the 1965 Voting Rights law, and Steven F. Lawson's *Black Ballots* is perhaps the best overview of the expansion of voting rights in the South.[37]

Another group of studies has analyzed the broader trends in southern politics since *Southern Politics*. *The Changing Politics of the South*, edited by William C. Havard, examines political developments in each of the southern states. Jack Bass and Walter DeVries in *The Transformation of Southern Politics* rely heavily on interviews to draw relatively sanguine conclusions about the course of southern politics since V. O. Key. Hugh D. Graham and I are more cautious about the prospects for two-party competition or for political cleavages along class rather than racial lines in *Southern Politics and the Second Reconstruction*. Earl Black's *Southern Governors and Civil Rights* weighs the impact of black voting on the campaigns and policies of southern chief executives. Donald S. Strong has traced the sources of southern Republicanism in a series of studies.[38] These works have provided valuable insights; certainly more is known about politics in the South since World War II than about any other region. At the same time, each of these studies generally adopts Key's approach and extends his analysis into the more recent period.

Whatever the merits of such a research strategy, it may not be adequate to answer the more fundamental questions posed by recent southern political developments. In 1940 the raison d'etre of southern state governments was the protection of white supremacy and social stability; thirty years later their central purpose was the promotion of business and industrial development. Key emphasized conflict between haves and have-nots, which often took the form of dissension between black belt and hills or city and countryside. But in terms of ideology and public policy, a good argument could be made that the have-nots had lost—or at least were well along the way to losing—the war by the time Key described it. Beginning with Mississippi's Balance Agriculture With Industry program in 1936, all the southern states established industry hunting agencies and structured programs of tax concessions and public support for industrial development. All enacted right-to-work provisions and firmly placed state authority on the side of entrepreneurial and corporate profits.[39] During the same period the southern states in varying degrees vastly improved public education, expanded or originated the merit system in public bureaucracy, and adopted more rational procedures for collecting and disbursing public monies. The elimination of the one-party system, disfranchisement, legislative malapportionment, and de jure segregation was of great importance to the triumph of these policies, but they do not appear to have been closely related to the sporadic battles between the haves and have-nots.

Instead, these developments suggest that the emerging periodization of New South politics may focus on the 1930s or 1940s as a great and, as yet, an ill-understood watershed. Recent interpretations indicate that in fundamental ways there was considerable continuity during the decades following Reconstruction. The labor relations of plantations and mill villages, the social structure with its foundation resting on caste relationships, and an ideology that for want of a better term is usually labeled paternalism may have provided an underlying stability that limited the impact of the undeniable changes that swept across the South during the late nineteenth and early twentieth centuries. These tendencies in the literature are imminently debatable and are apt to fuel an abundance of scholarly controversy. But, then, as V. O. Key observed: "Of books about the South there is no end."[40]

1. C. Vann Woodward, *Origins of the New South, 1877-1913* (Baton Rouge: Louisiana State University Press, 1951); V. O. Key, Jr., *Southern Politics in State and Nation* (New York: Vintage Books, 1949). See Sheldon Hackney, "Origins of the New South in Retrospect," *Journal of Southern History* 38 (May 1972): 191-216.

2. Some of the best of this literature is sampled in Patrick Gerster and Nicholas Cords, eds., *Myth and Southern History* (Chicago: Rand McNally, 1974).

3. Barrington Moore, Jr., *Social Origins of Dictatorship and Democracy: Lord and Peasant in the Making of the Modern World* (Boston: Beacon Press, 1966); William Appleman Williams, *The Contours of American History* (Cleveland: World Publishing Company, 1961); and *The Roots of the Modern American Empire: A Study of the Growth and Shaping of Social Consciousness in a Marketplace Society* (New York: Random House, 1969).

4. Eugene D. Genovese, *Political Economy of Slavery: Studies in the Economy and Society of the Slave South* (New York: Vintage Books, 1965), p. 13; and *The World the Slaveholders Made: Two Essays in Interpretation* (New York: Vintage Books, 1971), p. 125. See also Eric Foner, *Politics and Ideology in the Age of the Civil War* (New York: Oxford University Press, 1980).

5. Genovese, *The World the Slaveholders Made*, p. 230. Genovese comments on the gradual decline of paternalism in the New South in *Roll, Jordan, Roll: The World the Slaves Made* (New York: Vintage Books, 1976), pp. 111, 661.

6. Some of the more important literature is discussed in Harold D. Woodman, "Sequel to Slavery: The New History Views the Postbellum South," *Journal of Southern History* 43 (November 1977): 523-54; and in the exchange between Jonathan M. Wiener, Robert Higgs, and Woodman, "AHR Forum: Class Structure and Economic Development in the American South, 1865-1955," *American Historical Review* 84 (October 1979): 970-1001.

7. Jay R. Mandle, *The Roots of Black Poverty: The Southern Plantation Economy after the Civil War* (Durham: Duke University Press, 1978); and, from a different perspective, Carl N. Degler, *Place Over Time: The Continuity of Southern Distinctiveness* (Baton Rouge: Louisiana State University Press, 1977).

8. Joseph Persky, "Regional Colonialism and the Southern Economy," *Review of Radical Political Economics* 4 (Fall 1972): 70-79. Earlier studies of the colonial nature of the southern economy are numerous. Among the best are Douglas F. Dowd, "A Comparative Analysis of Economic Development on the American West and South," *Journal of Economic History* 16 (December 1956): 558-74; Walter Prescott Webb, *Divided We Stand: The Crisis of a Frontierless Democracy* (New York: Farrar and Rinehart, 1937); Woodward, *Origins of the New South*, pp. 291-320; Howard Odum, *Southern Regions of the United States* (Chapel Hill: University of North Carolina Press, 1936), pp. 353-59. This interpretation has reemerged in a number of recent works, including the most recent survey of southern history: I. A. Newby, *The South: A History* (New York: Holt, Rinehart and Winston, 1978), pp. 287-300. A broader discussion of the literature is Numan V. Bartley, "Another New South?," *Georgia Historical Quarterly* 65 (Summer 1981): 121-37.

9. David R. Goldfield, "The Urban South: A Regional Framework," *American Historical Review* 86 (December 1981): 1009-34. A number of these points are suggested in Blaine A. Brownell and David R. Goldfield, eds., *The City in Southern History: The Growth of Urban Civilization in the South* (Port Washington: Kennikat Press, 1977).

10. Howard N. Rabinowitz, *Race Relations in the Urban South, 1865-1890* (New York: Oxford University Press, 1978).

11. Dwight B. Billings, Jr., *Planters and the Making of a "New South": Class, Politics, and Development in North Carolina, 1865-1900* (Chapel Hill: University of North Carolina Press, 1979), pp. 68, 113, 211, 217, 218.

12. Jonathan M. Wiener, *Social Origins of the New South: Alabama, 1860-1885* (Baton Rouge: Louisiana State University Press, 1978), pp. 72, 223, 227.

13. John Samuel Ezell, *The South Since 1865* (New York: Macmillan, 1963), p. 102. Other textual treatments of the New South contain similar statements.

14. James Tice Moore, "Redeemers Reconsidered: Change and Continuity in the Democratic South, 1870-1900," *Journal of Southern History* 44 (August 1978), p. 367. Among more

important and suggestive state studies that deal with the Redeemer era are William J. Cooper, Jr., *The Conservative Regime: South Carolina, 1877–1890* (Baltimore: Johns Hopkins University Press, 1968); William I. Hair, *Bourbonism and Agrarian Protest: Louisiana Politics, 1877–1900* (Baton Rouge: Louisiana State University Press, 1969); William W. Rogers, *The One-Gallused Rebellion: Agrarianism in Alabama, 1865–1896* (Baton Rouge: Louisiana State University Press, 1970); James T. Moore, *Two Paths to the New South: The Virginia Debt Controversy* (Lexington: University of Kentucky Press, 1974); Roger L. Hart, *Redeemers, Bourbons, and Populists: Tennessee, 1870–1896* (Baton Rouge: Louisiana State University Press, 1975); Edward C. Williamson, *Florida Politics in the Gilded Age, 1877–1893* (Gainesville: University Presses of Florida, 1976).

15. Paul M. Gaston, *The New South Creed: A Study of Southern Mythmaking* (New York: Vintage Books, 1973), pp. 7, 160.

16. Wiener, *Social Origins of the New South*, pp. 187, 218, 219.

17. Billings, *Planters and the Making of a "New South,"* pp. 121–31.

18. Newby, *The South: A History*, p. 290.

19. Sheldon Hackney, *Populism to Progressivism in Alabama* (Princeton: Princeton University Press, 1969), pp. 30, 85, 75.

20. Hart, *Redeemers, Bourbons, and Populists*, pp. 224–35.

21. Robert H. Wiebe, *The Search for Order, 1877–1920* (New York: Hill and Wang, 1967), p. 84. Williams, *The Contours of American History*, pp. 335–38, summarizes a theme that Williams develops more fully in *The Roots of the Modern American Empire.*

22. Lawrence Goodwyn, *Democratic Promise: The Populist Movement in America* (New York: Oxford University Press, 1976).

23. Robert C. McMath, Jr., *Populist Vanguard: A History of the Southern Farmers' Alliance* (Chapel Hill: University of North Carolina Press, 1975).

24. Bruce Palmer, *"Man Over Money": The Southern Populist Critique of American Capitalism* (Chapel Hill: University of North Carolina Press, 1980), p. 221. Two other recent works are Michael Schwartz, *Radical Protest and Social Structure: The Southern Farmers' Alliance and Cotton Tenancy, 1880–1890* (New York: Academic Press, 1976), and Gerald H. Gaither, *Blacks and the Populist Revolt: Ballots and Bigotry in the "New South"* (University: University of Alabama Press, 1977). Scholarly fascination with populism has led to the neglect of other non-Democratic parties. Gordon B. McKinney's *Southern Mountain Republicans, 1865–1900: Politics and the Appalachian Community* (Chapel Hill: University of North Carolina Press, 1978), and Eric Anderson's *Race and Politics in North Carolina, 1872–1901: The Black Second* (Baton Rouge: Louisiana State University Press, 1981) are significant exceptions.

25. Woodward, *Origins of the New South*, pp. 373, 395.

26. George Brown Tindall, *The Emergence of the New South, 1913–1945* (Baton Rouge: Louisiana State University Press, 1967), p. 32. An excellent review of the literature on progressivism that is written from an essentially traditional perspective is Dewey W. Grantham, "The Contours of Southern Progressivism," *American Historical Review* 86 (December 1981): 1035–59.

27. Jack Temple Kirby, *Darkness at the Dawning: Race and Reform in the Progressive South* (Philadelphia: J. B. Lippincott, 1972), pp. 3, 4.

28. Raymond H. Pulley, *Old Virginia Restored: An Interpretation of the Progressive Impulse, 1870–1930* (Charlottesville: University of Virginia, 1968), p. ix.

29. John Dittmer, *Black Georgia in the Progressive Era, 1900–1920* (Urbana: University of Illinois Press, 1977), p. 110.

30. J. Morgan Kousser, *The Shaping of Southern Politics: Suffrage Restriction and the Establishment of the One-Party South, 1880–1910* (New Haven: Yale University Press, 1974), pp. 257, 230, 247.

31. George Brown Tindall, *The Persistent Tradition in New South Politics* (Baton Rouge: Louisiana State University Press, 1975), p. xii.

32. Key, *Southern Politics*, p. 3.

33. Ibid., pp. 255, 9, 315–16.

34. Tindall, *The Emergence of the New South*, pp. 219–284; and Tindall, *The Ethnic Southerners* (Baton Rouge: Louisiana State University Press, 1976), pp. 142–62.

35. Blaine A. Brownell, *The Urban Ethos in the South, 1920–1930* (Baton Rouge: Louisiana State University Press, 1975); Morton Sosna, *In Search of the Silent South: Southern Liberals and the Race Issue* (New York: Columbia University Press, 1977); Robert A. Garson, *The Democratic Party and the Politics of Sectionalism, 1941–1948* (Baton Rouge: Louisiana State University Press, 1974).

36. Exceptions to this statement include David D. Lee, *Tennessee in Turmoil: Politics in the Volunteer State, 1920–1932* (Memphis: Memphis State University Press, 1979); David R. Colburn and Richard K. Scher, *Florida's Gubernatorial Politics in the Twentieth Century* (Tallahassee: University Presses of Florida, 1980); Darlene Clark Hine, *Black Victory: The Rise and Fall of the White Primary in Texas* (Millwood: KTO Press, 1979).

37. Pat Watters and Reese Cleghorn, *Climbing Jacob's Ladder: The Arrival of Negroes in Southern Politics* (New York: Harcourt, Brace and World, 1967); Donald R. Matthews and James W. Prothro, *Negroes and the New Southern Politics* (New York: Harcourt, Brace and World, 1966); David J. Garrow, *Protest at Selma: Martin Luther King, Jr., and the Voting Rights Act of 1965* (New Haven: Yale University Press, 1978); Steven F. Lawson, *Black Ballots: Voting Rights in the South, 1944–1969* (New York: Columbia University Press, 1976).

38. William C. Havard, ed., *The Changing Politics of the South* (Baton Rouge: Louisiana State University Press, 1972); Jack Bass and Walter DeVries, *The Transformation of Southern Politics: Social Change and Political Consequence Since 1945* (New York: Basic Books, 1976); Numan V. Bartley and Hugh D. Graham, *Southern Politics and the Second Reconstruction* (Baltimore: Johns Hopkins University Press, 1975); Earl Black, *Southern Governors and Civil Rights: Racial Segregation as a Campaign Issue in the Second Reconstruction* (Cambridge: Harvard University Press, 1976); Donald S. Strong, *Urban Republicanism in the South* (University: University of Alabama Press, 1960); and "Further Reflections on Southern Politics," *Journal of Politics* 33 (May 1971): 239–56.

39. Only in Louisiana did these policies meet serious resistance; there the Long forces repealed the right-to-work law for industrial workers. James C. Cobb, *The Selling of the South* (Baton Rouge: Louisiana State University Press, forthcoming), is the first general study of southern industrial promotion in the post-World War II era.

40. Key, *Southern Politics*, p. ix.

THE STRANGE CAREER OF THE NEW
SOUTHERN ECONOMIC HISTORY

Gavin Wright

An invitation to survey a decade of research on southern economic history is an invitation to ignore the advice of my teacher, William N. Parker, not to treat history as "the battle of the books." In this field the temptation is particularly strong. Jonathan Wiener begins another recent survey with the following observation: [1]

> The new works on postwar Southern development . . . divide into two basic theoretical approaches: those historians who follow Fogel and Engerman apply neoclassical economic theory and analyze Southern development according to the laws of the market; those who follow Genovese and C. Vann Woodward analyze the South in terms of its constituent classes and see its development as the outcome of conflicts among them. Although these schools by no means exhaust the ways of viewing the problem, they represent much of the important new work.

My hope is to escape the format of history as a class of schools, to review these diverse and often polemical studies with an eye toward what they can tell us about the two preeminent concerns of southern economic history: the development of the regional economy and the welfare of the black population. What I want to show is that "class" and "market" should not be viewed as incompatible opposites. Instead, class power operated chiefly through its influence on the boundaries and terms of various markets. A satisfactory southern economic history should be both a class and a market interpretation.

As though Parker's wisdom and the limits of time and space were not sufficient to justify a relatively abstract treatment, a devastating fire in the Economics Building at the University of Michigan on Christmas Eve, 1981, destroyed all books and notes previously collected for this article. Unfortunate as this incident was, some good may come of it. It has been said that Newton could never have devised his elegantly simple theories if he had been inundated by modern data-generating technology. Sir Walter Raleigh and Fernand Braudel wrote grand histories while in prison. Economists point to the "absence of inhibiting institutions" as a favorable factor in regions of recent settlement. Perhaps a sweeping material loss will serve to clear the

0048-7511/82/0104-0164 $01.00

brain of clutter, revealing to us the main themes of southern economic history in their elegant simplicity.

The Antebellum Economy: The Importance of Asking Good Questions

Economists work with models, and a model is a kind of metaphor. It is in the nature of metaphors that they will be imperfect or incomplete in relationship to the totality of history. The compensating gain is that the model may explicate or clarify some particular set of historical developments or associations. To evaluate a model, therefore, we ought to have a purpose, and my specific purposes are to explain the backwardness of the southern regional economy and "the roots of black poverty" (in Jay Mandle's phrase) since the Civil War. Much of the exasperation of southern history arises from divergence in purposes, or from efforts at characterization without a specific purpose. When we encounter studies with such titles as "How Different Were North and South?" or "The Postbellum South: Continuity or Discontinuity?" we know in advance that we are not going to get satisfying answers.

This is one reason why the long debate over the "efficiency" calculations of *Time on the Cross* has been so unfruitful.[2] Most of the critics have argued, in one way or another, that these figures are not meaningful. The ratio of the market value of outputs to an amalgamation of input values and quantities will have an altogether different character in free and slave systems if these systems foster fundamentally different dynamics of accumulation. Appropriate comparisons of slave plantations and smaller farms within the South will depend upon a choice of behavioral models. But Fogel and Engerman interpret these considerations as allegations of "bias" in their calculations, and continue to treat "efficiency" as though it can usefully be debated in isolation from other topics. They imply that the issues are essentially empirical, but it is now evident that this is not the case: despite protestations, their most recent figures plainly show that the alleged "productivity advantage" for large plantations depends crucially on specialization in cotton relative to corn.[3] If we could agree on a model of the historical process that generated these figures, then we would have something. At that point, whether we choose to call it "efficiency" would be a matter of colossal indifference. One might say that in economic history the model is the message.

The Structural Legacy of Slavery

Over the past ten years a remarkable double-reverse has occurred in prevailing views of the relationship between slavery and economic development. On the basis of national and regional income estimates, Stanley Engerman wrote in 1971 that "discussions of southern backwardness should emphasize adjustments during the war and Reconstruction. . . . [D]ivergence can be attributed to wartime destruction and to social upheaval which prevented rapid recovery from the impact of the Civil War, and not directly to the southern antebellum economic position."[4] This article was part of a systematic dismantling of the traditional economic indictment of slavery, an indictment which traces its heritage to Marxism and to liberal republicanism in about equal parts. Was slave labor inflexible and immobile? No, geographic mobility was high and better adapted to market demands than free labor. Did slavery require a steady diet of virgin soil? No, the rate of land utilization was if anything less than in the free states, and a vast untapped area remained in 1860. Was slavery incompatible with factories and cities? No, case studies show any number of successful counterexamples. Were slaveowners constrained by ideology and the needs of the system in their economic choices? No, they seem to pass every test of rationality. And so on and so on.[5]

The problem with this "indictment" is that it comes too directly from a desire to pass judgment on slavery and reflects an idealized implicit conception of the development process itself. But as research has evolved from simple refutation toward explicit models, the emerging result has been a new appreciation of the lasting structural impact of the antebellum era. A detailed account would be too lengthy, but some central propositions can be listed: (1) slavery reduced the mechanization of farming by offering an alternative way for farm scale to expand; (2) slavery discouraged town-building and investment in infrastructure by providing a form of agricultural wealth, the value of which was independent of local development; (3) slavery worked against the spread of rural markets and farm-town interactions by creating an incentive toward diversification and self-sufficiency on plantations; (4) slavery hindered the early progress of manufacturing by integrating slave women and children into the cotton economy, and by minimizing the incentives to open the region to outside labor flows.[6] This list is only a sampling, but each of these points derives from an explicit model of property rights in labor, and is supported by statistical evidence. Such a list also serves to illustrate the ways in which a "class" interpretation can blend into a "market" interpretation, when the incentives built into certain property rights dictate what sort of markets will emerge and what their scope will be. At the time of emancipation, the southern economy was dispersed, predominantly agricultural, unmechanized, closed to outside labor markets, with few cities and towns, and limited market relationships in general.

Can we say then that these results amount to a vindication of the economic indictment of slavery advanced by Genovese and earlier writers, a modern restatement of an old set of ideas? In some respects this would be fair. An important study by Bateman and Weiss has estimated that rates of return on investments in antebellum manufacturing were extremely high in both North and South (in the neighborhood of 15 to 25 percent), suggesting that reallocation would have raised southern incomes. Much of the best new work on early industrialization has brought out the importance of learning processes and the face-to-face transmission of knowledge and techniques, suggesting that the delay of southern manufacturing was not an innocuous matter of "comparative advantage."[7] The suggestion that "discussions of southern backwardness" should begin with "adjustments during the war and Reconstruction" is surely ill-advised.

But there is some danger in the formulation that the older economic indictment of slavery was "right after all." If economic wisdom has anything to gain from a twentieth-century perspective, it ought to be the understanding that there is no one recipe for economic progress, no single organizational format that will "work" economically, and certainly no simple correspondence between the moral stature and the economic success of particular regimes. The idea that capital accumulation requires week-to-week "flexibility" in labor supply may have seemed true in 1850, but the Japanese success with a very different system shows that it wasn't. In part, the structural legacy of the slave economy proved detrimental to the postbellum South because it was a structure reasonably well-adapted to slavery, "underdeveloped" in terms of a particular scenario for advancement under capitalism. If slavery was doomed, it was doomed by the idea of freedom, which is to say by the very idea which infuses the liberal-republican critique. By accepting as true an analysis which was itself the instrument of historical effect, we lose the benefit of our perspective and run the risk of completely misunderstanding the coming of abolition and its effect. My position is that an *evaluation* of slavery is not a good substitute for understanding the workings of the slave economy: again, the model is the message.

One lingering undertone in the antebellum literature deserves mention: the proposition that the structural differences between North and South resulted not from institutions but from the characteristics of staple crops. Tobacco and cotton are said to require little processing, hence few cities; both crops have long growing seasons, hence limited encouragement to part-time employment; both made ready use of women and child labor, discouraging early industrial activity along English lines.[8] Such factors may well be important and cannot be neatly separated from slavery, since the geography of slavery was itself influenced by crops. But by 1800 the labor systems were set, while the choice of crops was variable; from 1815 onwards, the geography of American farmbelts was continually changing, in both North and South. Within the South it is well-established that family labor patterns differed between slave and free households. Earle and Hoffman have stumbled on the important fact that the late antebellum cost of labor was as high or higher in the South than in the North. But their explanation for this in terms of the seasonality of crops is fallacious, because the geographic location of workers is itself determined by human decisions and market forces: people do not just appear in a locality and then begin responding passively to the demands of the local crop. The real geographic influence was the geography of labor markets, which is exactly where slavery had its most decisive effect.

The "Liberation" of the Southern Economy

The best proof that the structure was influenced by slavery is what happened after the war. There is great potential for historical confusion in the coincidence of massive legal and organizational change with a secular deceleration in cotton demand, and reading the bewildered or self-interested comments of contemporaries does not always help. But I believe that most of the new structural developments in the postwar economy arose from the incentives of the new property rights. Formerly labor was wealth, and wealth was chiefly labor; the location and investment decisions of slaveowners served to augment the value of particular slaves, and slaveowner politics served to keep the value of slave labor high in general. On the plantation, labor was like a fixed cost, and owners strove to raise the output of each slave by spreading the labor across as many acres as possible, making the work year as full as possible, and finding ways to use the young, the old, and the women as well as the men. After emancipation, the "masters without slaves" were primarily *landlords,* whose concern was to raise the value of output per acre, treating labor as a variable cost. Since land is fixed in place, owners now reoriented their investments and their politics toward raising the value of land in particular localities.

Consider how many postbellum tendencies fall into place under this simple model:

1. The allocation of crop acreage switched dramatically toward cotton, which yields output value per acre two to three times that of corn.
2. The ratio of acreage to workers in the cotton belt decreased by somewhere between 30 and 60 percent.
3. Southeastern farmers began using fertilizer in large amounts for the first time, and a whole new commercial fertilizer industry developed.
4. All the southern states completely reversed their positions on immigration, setting up agencies for publicity and recruitment.
5. Railroads were now welcomed into the South by public and private sources.
6. Campaigns to close the southern range to open livestock grazing were initiated by planters.

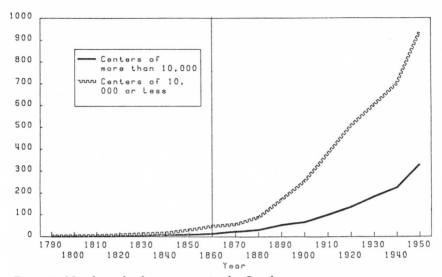

Figure 1. Number of urban centers in the South
Source: Kenneth Weiher, "The Cotton Industry and Southern Urbanization,"
Explorations in Economic History 14 (April 1977), p. 123.

7. Town-building and land promotion activity accelerated, playing a
major role in the early growth of new industries such as cotton textiles
and iron and steel (see Figure 1).

Between 1860 and 1870, the years Engerman identifies as the beginning of
southern backwardness, the number of manufacturing establishments rose by
64 percent, the largest percentage increase in any decade of the nineteenth
century (see Figure 2). This list could be greatly extended, but the drift should
be clear. Since much of this new behavior followed familiar American
developmental lines, a redirection of energies which had been channeled quite
differently before the war, one can appreciate the popularity of the metaphor
that the whole southern economy had been "liberated" by the emancipation
of the slaves.[9]

Is this a "class" interpretation? Indeed it is, but it has little resemblance to
accounts which invest large scattered groups of individuals with common
psychologies and collective strategies. Granted, we are all using metaphors,
which are never entirely "true." But characterizing the rise of the cotton
textile industry as a "revolution from above" by the planter class (as Dwight
Billings does) is not a good metaphor because it is remote from the actual
scope of individual decision-making, and because (in Billings's hands) it
implies that individuals somehow acquire an unchanging class identity early

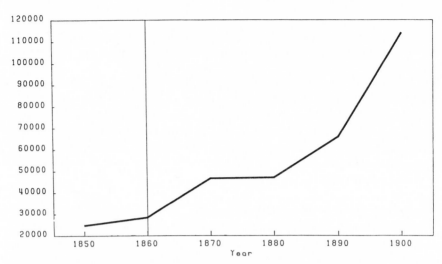

Figure 2. Number of manufacturing establishments, 1850 to 1900
(all southern states)
Source: Donald B. Dodd and Wynelle S. Dodd, *Historical Statistics of the South 1790–1970* (University: University of Alabama Press, 1973).

in life which shapes their behavior ever after.[10] The classic economic conceptions of class are rooted in the factors of production, and from this perspective it is an empty debate whether the "old planter class" was or was not restored to power. They were all a "new class," because the interests associated with their property had changed. When McDonald and McWhiney write that the Civil War made "the great landlord class total masters inside the South," it is a much better metaphor, especially if the accent is on the first syllable.[11]

This interpretation is not inconsistent with microeconomic accounts of the swing toward cotton in terms of the pressures of tenancy, indebtedness, destruction of livestock, fencing laws, and small plots, or the pull of railroads and local marketing facilities. Few of these developments were genuinely innovations or technical breakthroughs. (For example, forthcoming work by Frederick Bode and Donald Ginter will show that tenancy was more common in the antebellum period than was previously thought.) What was new was the pervasive impulse to squeeze more from every acre, an impulse which lay behind many of the "causes" often listed. It even extended to the public sector in that state legislatures had to greatly increase land taxes to restore revenue. This was not simply Republican politics: as J. Mills Thornton has shown, any political party would have faced the same necessity and felt the same backlash.[12] Just as the landowner's desire for land revenue stood behind the determination of plot size and the offers of credit, so the government's need for tax revenue raised the cash requirements of every farm and reinforced the same trend.

Thus the shift into cotton was by no means irrational (a view Wiener mistakenly attributes to me). It was, however, severely injurious to the economic welfare of the region because of its depressing effect on cotton prices: a classic case of individual rationality adding up to suboptimal results in the aggregate. The misconception that "ruling classes" are normally in position to control matters at this aggregate level is precisely what is dangerous about unconstrained class metaphors.

The Geography of Southern Labor Markets

Emancipation released certain economic forces in the South, but did it constitute a "liberation" for the slaves? In fact, there is substantial consensus that planters did have to respond to the desires of the freedmen for more day-to-day independence and family based work organization. Working for someone else was not, of course, their first choice, and the defeat of proposals for land distribution is a good example of class action serving to influence the labor market by denying the freedmen direct access to the means of subsistence. But a labor market did operate, and in the immediate postwar years it was a seller's market. Wiener insists that the decentralization of the plantation be understood in terms of the "concrete process of class conflict" rather than the "abstract logic of the market"; but competitive pressures to adjust working conditions in response to labor scarcity are the essence of the market process. In the presence of the right to quit, there was an inexorable logic by which the centralized plantation labor system had to break down.

A persuasive economic analysis of this logic will appear in a forthcoming work by Gerald Jaynes of Yale University, building in part on the research of Ralph Shlomowitz. If the plantations were to be reorganized on a wage basis, the extreme scarcity of credit virtually required that the bulk of the payment be a postharvest wage. What has not been sufficiently appreciated is that the majority of wage contracts signed under Freedman's Bureau supervision were *share wage* contracts, which is to say that they already contained the postharvest, risk-sharing property of sharecropping. But the gang system cannot coexist with share wages for long, for the simple reason that the work incentive structure is perverse. Knowing in advance that the entire product will be divided on a share basis among a large number of workers, what incentive does any one worker have to exert himself? (Anyone who has ever ordered a restaurant meal knowing that the bill will be divided equally will recognize the problem.) Gradually smaller units of work organization began to be designated, known as "squads," consisting of perhaps ten to twenty hands, typically with some kinship connection. But there was no stopping the devolution process until it reached the smallest unit of social organization, the nuclear family.[13]

These early years of high mobility, experimentation, and institutional change did give way to more stabilized patterns. This change, too, was in large part a market phenomenon. Eric Foner notes that the early labor scarcity was "a question not simply of numbers, but of power. Labor was scarce . . . because those who did work were unmanageable."[14] But labor scarcity never is "a question simply of numbers," but of numbers relative to demand, which in the South depended in turn on the price of cotton. As cotton production expanded after 1866 along a relatively stagnant cotton demand curve, prices fell, and the depression of the 1870s virtually extinguished the ability of laborers to influence working conditions by voting with their feet. The planter class had no power over these global developments, and even if they had such power, stagnation in cotton demand would not have been one of their desiderata. But it was only in the decade of the 1870s that the South emerged as a *low wage* region in a national context.

The question which has been most strenuously debated is whether the typical sharecropping arrangement was a voluntary labor market transaction, or whether it was agreed to only "under duress" from crop liens, debts, and intimidation. Robert Higgs describes the contending forces as "competition versus coercion," and while all writers acknowledge the presence of both forces, it seems evident that the economists believe competition to be more powerful (Higgs, Steven DeCanio, and Joseph D. Reid), while class analysts and legal historians cast their votes for coercion (Wiener, Jay Mandle, Daniel Novak, William Cohen, Pete Daniel).[15] If I had to vote in this election, it would be with the economists. Cases of outright peonage, of brutality and fraud, of trumped-up vagrancy prosecutions and convict labor, were all too common in the postbellum South, but they were not the normal state of affairs and they were not the defining features of sharecropping. There is just too much evidence that farm-to-farm turnover among sharecroppers was high, that black and white farm laborers did move from state to state and employer to employer, and that the attempts of landlords to collude against labor market competition generally failed.

But I do not want to vote, I want to redefine the question. Part of the problem arises because economists are people who understand and appreciate the operation of markets, and they have defined the issue in terms of labor market performance. But they are writing about a century for which the labor market was something to be escaped from. Spending a lifetime on the supply side of a "competitive labor market" was no one's idea of a successful life's work, and the labor market was not seen as the locus of progress for individual workers—for good reason. Instead, farm laborers hoped to use their wages to move out of the labor market through a process involving family labor and the accumulation of wealth. The rungs on the farm tenure ladder were essentially asset-holding categories, from wage labor and sharecropping (no worker input), to "thirds and fourths" (worker provides the mule), to cash tenancy (worker provides all nonland inputs), to farm ownership. These were not jobs to which people were promoted by an employer, but levels of accumulation which individuals had to achieve.

Attachments to families and farm ladder ambitions limited the ability of sharecroppers to take advantage of the competitive labor market. Wage-paying jobs were available to unattached males willing to travel long distances and take their chances. But sharecropping was in essence a family based system, an exchange of a year's assured labor for some family autonomy and an advance on subsistence needs. The whole arrangement revolved around credit relationships which were inherently local in character. What emerged in the South was a kind of geographical dual labor system, in which local markets for family and credit based labor coexisted with longer distance wage labor markets. A forthcoming Stanford dissertation by Warren Whatley presents a model in which the local market adjusts through the average size of sharecroppers' plots, while the wage market ensures that all acreage is utilized. The local markets thus had some links with the outside, but they were poorly integrated with each other.

Behind this structure lie two features of the southern economy: the sparsity of employment opportunities in the rural areas and the high cost of credit, both of which can be traced back to the structural legacy of slavery. Whether we call it "territorial monopoly" or "financial underdevelopment," the evidence is that the isolated rural character of lenders was the major factor behind high southern interest rates.[16] This scarcity of credit was not created by any one class, but the terms and implications of credit to the borrowers were affected by class interests as reflected in the lien laws. The crop lien has been denounced as the cause of nearly every southern misery, but the idea of creating legal rights in a growing crop as a basis for credit is not in itself pernicious. The issue is one of priority, or what financial economists call the "me-first" provisions: who gets what share when receipts are not sufficient to cover claims? Some of the Republican legislatures gave first priority to the laborer's lien, but after Reconstruction priority was assigned to either landlord or merchant. In most states sharecroppers were legally defined as laborers rather than true tenants, with no legal claim on the crop itself. In effect the laborer had made an interest-free contingent loan to the planter, yet he had no security for his loan. The significance of these laws was not that they created quasi-slavery or perpetual servitude to one master, but that they transferred financial risk to the laborers, and hence hindered their efforts to escape the labor market. When a creditor's microeconomic interest in protecting his loan reinforces the landlord's property interest in replenishing the labor market, we have the makings of a class interpretation.[17]

Regional Progress and Black Progress

This leaves till last the most important question: how did these institutions and markets influence the course of southern economic development, and how did regional development relate to black progress? Despite the preeminence of these topics, it is difficult to find explicit interpretations, much less persuasive analysis. The notion that there is some connection between regional and racial backwardness is of course widespread. Gunnar Myrdahl wrote about it in 1944:[18]

> Why is such an extraordinarily large proportion of the Negro people so poor? The most reasonable way to start answering this question is to note the distribution of the Negro people in various regions and occupations. We then find that the Negroes are concentrated in the South, which is generally a poor and economically retarded region. A disproportionate number of them work in agriculture, which is a depressed industry. Most rural Negroes are in Southern cotton agriculture, which is particularly over-populated; backward in production methods; and hard hit by soil exhaustion, by the boll weevil, and by a long time fall in international demand for American cotton. . . . Most of the handicrafts and industries in the South where they have a traditional foothold are declining.

More recently, Robert Higgs has argued that a geographically disadvantaged position within the South was a major part of blacks' economic plight: "To put it bluntly, if too simply, industrialization and urbanization did not occur in the Black Belt."[19]

But there is another formulation of this link, of equally impeccable heritage, which identifies black poverty and subjugation as the central elements in alleged southern "blackwardness." W.E.B. DuBois stated in 1907 that "the economic history of the South is in effect the economics of slavery and the Negro problem," and Nobel-prize economist W. Arthur Lewis argues, "It was racial discrimination in the United States that kept the price of cotton so low; or to turn this around, given the racial discrimination, American blacks earned so little because of the large amount of cotton that would have flowed out of Asia and Africa and Latin America at a higher cotton price." Writers as diverse as Jay Mandle and Brinley Thomas have stressed racial discrimination by northern employers as a cause of black poverty. From a different perspective, Stephen DeCanio and Robert Mellman have argued that average southern *white* incomes were quite close to national

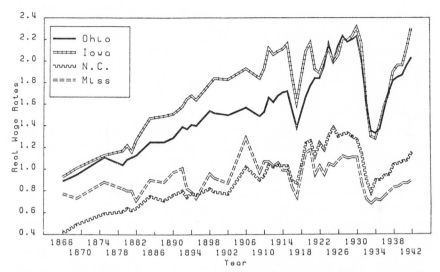

Figure 3. Farm labor wage rates per day without board deflated by WPI 1866 to 1942 (selected states)
Sources: *Crops and Markets* 19 (May 1942): 150–55; U.S. Bureau of the Census, *Historical Statistics of the United States*, Part 1 (Washington, D.C.: 6P0, 1475), pp. 200–02.

norms (ca. 1900), so that most of the regional gap is attributable to low black incomes.[20]

The problem with these interpretations is that they don't look at the labor market as a market. "Per capita income" is not a factor price; it amalgamates land rent, profit, and the return to capital, along with wages, and averages these among all members of the population. When we look directly at the market for labor, however, what we find is that the basic southern wage was far below northern levels, and that this was true for both black and white workers. Consider, for example, the deflated farm wage series displayed in Figure 3. Southern per capita incomes grew, but farm wages show no tendency toward convergence, and Mississippi wages display little trend over the entire period. Southern industrial wages were closely linked to these low wages for farm labor.

What may be more surprising is that the basic southern unskilled wage did not differ greatly between black and white workers. The fact is illustrated in Figure 4 for one industry, but it is supported by a growing body of evidence.[21] This is not merely an artifact of racial occupational categories: segregation was common, and the access to escape routes from the unskilled labor market was highly unequal, but the majority of white southern workers were earning

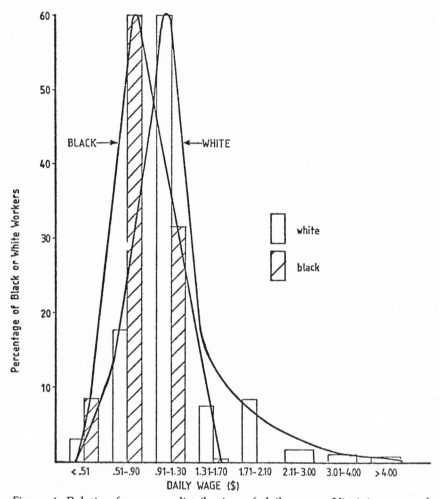

Figure 4. Relative frequency distribution of daily wage, Virginia saw and planning mills, 1900
Source: Virginia Bureau of Labor and Industrial Statistics, 4th Annual Report (Richmond, 1901).

the unskilled wage. My conclusion is that regional "southern backwardness" and "black poverty" have a basic common element: the isolation of southern labor markets from national labor markets. When social critics accused southern employers of using the race issue to divide and subjugate the working class, we can translate this into the statement that both were paid the going wage in the regional market.

Within this market, individual progress was essentially a process of "accu-mulation" in agriculture, or "promotion" in industrial jobs. Racial inequity and racial discrimination were far more glaring in these escape routes from the unskilled labor market. DeCanio's simulation confirms what social and political historians have long argued: that the single most important factor behind racial inequality within the South was the starting point of virtual wealthlessness in 1865. Any group in that position would have been behind for generations, even if discrimination were completely absent. The same study concludes, however, that accumulation was significantly more difficult for blacks than for whites. In industry, racial barriers were if anything worse. Economists like Tom Sowell have pointed to restrictive craft unions and public sector discrimination as mechanisms which stifled competitive pressures, most clearly the extreme racial inequality in public education after disfranchisement. But even competitive nonunionized industries with no legal constraints and with no educational prerequisites had labor policies which were highly racial and highly discriminatory, a fact which Sowell in all his writings has never directly confronted.[22]

The missing right-hand tail on the black wage distribution is a matter of racism and injustice; the low level of the basic wage for both black and white workers is a matter of the painfully slow development of the regional economy. What is most in need of careful study is the development process itself. The temptation to argue that there must be a direct connection between injustice and economic backwardness has been irresistible for many writers (as it was for contemporaries), yet if we may reason by analogy to the case of slavery, it seems likely that this idea has been overdone—if indeed the rela-tionship was not sometimes the reverse. For example, the lethargy and wastefulness of southern agriculture and the failure to diversify away from cotton seemed to be clear examples of exploitive relationships which also sti-fled progress. Closer inspection reveals, however, that alternative crops were even less promising than cotton, and that the slow pace of mechanization was much more a symptom of cheap labor than a cause. Injustices were many, but no feasible program of agricultural reform could have raised southern farm incomes to national norms.[23]

Evaluating southern industrialization is harder. Those writing in the tradi-tion of C. Vann Woodward judge the progress to be much too slow, and argue that "the reasons for the slow rate of industrial development are not far to seek. The South was a colonial economy."[24] But again, most of the identi-fying features of the "colonial economy"—outside ownership, extractive industries, imports of machinery and manufactured goods—are more likely symptoms than causes. This is not of course true of all of the alleged effects of northern influence, but then it is also not the case that industrialization was blocked. North Carolina, which began the postbellum era as the lowest wage state in the nation, had enough industry by the 1920s to push farm wage rates above the levels of the other southern states. Given that the South was a late starter, this gradual low wage industrialization compares favorably to other such cases around the world. When national attention focused on the plight of the southern mill workers in the 1920s, it was rather late in the game and at a point when wages had already advanced well beyond pre-World War I levels. Federal intervention on the side of economic justice in the 1930s and after served to stifle a particular line of evolutionary progress in favor of out-migration.[25]

The plantation areas were not really part of this process, and one can make a case that the destruction of the plantation economy was a necessary prerequisite for both the Civil Rights revolution and the modern economic renaissance of the Deep South. The manner in which this occurred, however, serves to illustrate that history is shaped by class conflict, but classes do not control history as they would like. Whereas the child labor laws, hours limitation, and minimum wages were imposed on the South from outside, the farm programs of the 1930s were virtually written by the planters. The incentives established under the cotton programs led them to move radically away from tenancy and sharecropping toward wage labor systems, setting in motion at the same time an impulse toward mechanization of preharvest operations, even in the midst of depressed conditions. This footloose wage labor, however, was highly responsive to the outside employment opportunities which opened up during World War II, creating the labor shortage which culminated in the perfection of the mechanical cotton picker. The resulting outmigration during the 1950s and early 1960s really closed a chapter in southern economic history, preparing the way for a regional transformation which must have been quite far from the intentions of the planters in their political offensive of a half-century ago.

1. Jonathan Wiener, "Class Structure and Economic Development in the American South, 1865–1955," *American Historical Review* 84 (October 1979): 970.

2. Robert Fogel and Stanley Engerman, *Time on the Cross*, (Boston: Little, Brown, 1974), vol. I, pp. 191–209, vol. II, pp. 126–49; Paul David et al., *Reckoning with Slavery*, (New York: Oxford University Press, 1976), pp. 202–23, 313–20; Robert Fogel and Stanley Engerman, "Explaining the Relative Efficiency of Slave Agriculture," *American Economic Review* 67 (June 1977): 275–96 and subsequent exchange in *American Economic Review* 69 (March 1979): 206–26, and 70 (September 1980): 673–90.

3. See Robert Fogel and Stanley Engerman, "Reply," *American Economic Review* 70 (September 1980), esp. Figure 5(b) on p. 685.

4. Stanley Engerman, "Some Economic Factors in Southern Backwardness in the Nineteenth Century," in *Essays in Regional Economics*, John F. Kain and John R. Meyer eds., (Cambridge, Mass.: Harvard University Press, 1971).

5. See, for examples, Robert S. Starobin, *Industrial Slavery in the Old South*, (New York:

Oxford University Press, 1970); Claudia Dale Goldin, *Urban Slavery in the American South,* (Chicago: University of Chicago Press, 1976); Stanley Engerman, "A Reconsideration of Southern Economic Growth, 1770–1860," *Agricultural History* 49 (April 1975): 343–61; Randall Miller, "The Fabric of Control: Slavery in Antebellum Southern Textile Mills," *Business History Review* 55 (Winter 1981): 471–90; Ronald L. Lewis, *Coal, Iron and Slaves,* (Westport, Conn.: Greenwood Press, 1979).

6. For these points respectively, see Heywood Fleisig, "Slavery, the Supply of Agricultural Labor, and the Industrialization of the South," *Journal of Economic History* 36 (September 1976): 572–97; Gavin Wright, *The Political Economy of the Cotton South,* (New York: Norton, 1978), pp. 121–35; Ralph V. Anderson and Robert E. Gallman, "Slaves as Fixed Capital: Slave Labor and Southern Economic Development," *The Journal of American History* 64 (June 1977): 24–46; Wright, "Cheap Labor and Southern Textiles before 1880," *Journal of Economic History* 39 (September 1979): 655–90. A new study by Claudia Goldin and Kenneth Sokoloff brings out the economic significance of women and child labor in early U.S. industry, though they interpret the role of slavery somewhat differently: "The Relative Productivity Hypothesis," *National Bureau of Economic Research Working Papers* No. 722, 795. The claim by Leonard Curry that the slave South was rapidly urbanizing is not persuasive. His peculiar measurement and choice of dates manage to obscure the facts that the South was not only far less urban than the North at all times, but was increasingly divergent from the national trend during the last two antebellum decades: "Urbanization and Urbanism in the Old South: A Comparative View," *Journal of Southern History* 40 (February 1974): 43–60.

7. Fred Bateman and Thomas Weiss, *A Deplorable Scarcity* (Chapel Hill: University of North Carolina Press, 1981), esp. pp. 99–116; John S. Hekman, "The Product Cycle and New England Textiles," *Quarterly Journal of Economics* 94 (June 1980): 697–717.

8. Claudia Goldin and Kenneth Sokoloff, in "The Relative Productivity Hypothesis," discuss women and child labor requirements. Carville Earle and Ronald Hoffman stress processing in "The Urban South: The First Two Centuries," in *The City in Southern History,* Blaine A. Brownell and David R. Goldfield, eds., (Port Washington, N.Y.: Kennikat Press), and seasonality in "The Foundations of the Modern Economy: Agriculture and the Costs of Labor in the United States and England, 1800–60," *American Historical Review* 85 (December 1980): 1055–94.

9. For description and analysis of these points (citing only recent studies), see Roger Ransom and Richard Sutch, *One Kind of Freedom,* (New York: Cambridge University Press, 1977), pp. 149–70; Kenneth Weiher, "The Cotton Industry and Southern Urbanization," *Explorations in Economic History* 14 (April 1977): 120–40; Gavin Wright, "Freedom and the Southern Economy," *Explorations in Economic History* 69 (March 1979): 90–108; Anderson and Gallman, "Slaves as Fixed Capital," pp. 41–45; David Carlton, "Builders of A New State," in *From the Old South to the New,* Walter Fraser and Winifred B. Moore, eds., (Westport, Conn.: Greenwood Press, 1981); Paul Gaston, *The New South Creed* (New York: Knopf, 1970); Robert L. Brandfon, *Cotton Kingdom of the New South,* (Cambridge: Harvard University Press, 1967); Harold Woodman, *King Cotton and His Retainers,* (Lexington: University of Kentucky Press, 1968); chs. 23–24; J. Crawford King, Jr., "Closing of the Southern Range," *Journal of Southern History* 48 (February 1982): 53–70.

10. Dwight B. Billings, *Planters and the Making of a "New South"* (Chapel Hill: University of North Carolina Press, 1979). A good antidote to Billings is Carlton, "Builders of a New State," which brings out the link between early mills and town-building.

11. Forrest McDonald and Grady McWhiney, "The South from Self-Sufficiency to Peonage: An Interpretation," *American Historical Review* 85 (December 1980): 1115.

12. J. Mills Thornton, "Fiscal Policy and the Failure of Radical Reconstruction in the Lower South," in *Region, Race and Reconstruction,* James M. McPherson and J. Morgan Kousser, eds., (New York: Oxford University Press, 1982).

13. Ralph Shlomowitz, "The Origins of Southern Sharecropping," *Agricultural History* 53 (July 1979): 557–75.

14. Eric Foner, "Reconstruction and the Crisis of Free Labor," in his *Politics of Ideology in the Age of the Civil War* (New York: Oxford University Press, 1980), p. 118. For a similar

theme, see Ronald L. F. Davis, "Labor Dependency among Freedmen, 1865-1880," in Fraser and Moore, eds., *From the Old South to the New*.

15. Robert Higgs, *Competition and Coercion* (Chicago: University of Chicago Press, 1980 — first published 1977); Stephen J. DeCanio, *Agriculture in the Postbellum South* (Cambridge: MIT Press, 1974); Joseph D. Reid, Jr., "Sharecropping as an Understandable Market Response," *Journal of Economic History* 33 (March 1973): 106-30; Jonathan M. Wiener, *Social Origins of the New South* (Baton Rouge: Louisiana State University Press, 1978); Jay Mandle, *The Roots of Black Poverty* (Durham, N.C.: Duke University Press, 1978); Pete Daniel, *Shadow of Slavery* (Urbana: University of Illinois Press, 1972); William Cohen, "Negro Involuntary Servitude in the South, 1865-1940," *Journal of Southern History* 42 (February 1976): 31-60; Daniel A. Novak, *The Wheel of Servitude* (Lexington: The University Press of Kentucky, 1978).

16. Ransom and Sutch, *One Kind of Freedom*, chs. 6-7; John A. James, "Financial Underdevelopment in the Postbellum South," *Journal of Interdisciplinary History* 11 (Winter 1981): 443-54. Interpretations are debated in Gary M. Walton and James F. Shepherd, eds., *Market Institutions and Economic Progress in the New South 1865-1900* (New York: Academic Press, 1981.).

17. Harold Woodman, "Post-Civil War Agriculture and the Law," *Agricultural History* 53 (January 1979): 319-37.

18. Gunnar Myrdahl, *An American Dilemma* (New York: Harper & Bros., 1944), pp. 205-06.

19. Robert Higgs, "Race and Economy in the South, 1890-1950," in *The Age of Segregation: Race Relations in the South, 1890-1945*, Robert Haws, ed. (Jackson: University Press of Mississippi, 1978), pp. 108-09.

20. Booker T. Washington and W.E.B. DuBois, *The Negro in the South* (Philadelphia: G. W. Jacobs & Co., 1907), p. 126; W. Arthur Lewis, *The Evolution of the International Economic Order* (Princeton, N.J.: Princeton University Press, 1978), p. 17; Robert E. Mellman, "A Reinterpretation of the Economic History of the Post-Reconstruction South" (Ph.D. diss., M.I.T., 1975); Stephen J. DeCanio, "Accumulation and Discrimination in the Postbellum South, *Explorations in Economic History* 16 (April 1979): 190-92.

21. Robert Higgs, "Did Southern Farmers Discriminate?" *Agricultural History* 46 (April 1972): 325-28, and "Firm-Specific Evidence of Racial Wage Differentials and Workforce Segregation," *American Economic Review* 67 (March 1977): 236-45; Gavin Wright, "Black and White Labor in the Old New South," in *Business in the New South*, ed., Fred Bateman (Sewanee, Tenn.: The University Press, 1981).

22. For various views on the topics of this paragraph, see Leonard Carlson, "Labor Supply, the Acquisition of Skills and the Location of Southern Textile Mills, 1880-1900," *Journal of Economic History* 41 (March 1981): 65-71; DeCanio, "Accumulation and Discrimination"; J. Morgan Kousser, "Progressivism—for Middle Class Whites Only: North Carolina Education, 1880-1910," *Journal of Southern History* 46 (May 1980): 169-94; Robert A. Margo, "Race Differences in Public School Expenditures: Disfranchisement and School Finance in Louisiana, 1890-1910," *Social Science History* 6 (Winter 1982): 9-34; Thomas Sowell, *Markets and Minorities* (New York: Basic Books, 1981); Paul Worthman, "Working Class Mobility in Birmingham, Alabama, 1890-1914," in *Anonymous Americans*, ed., Tamara K. Hareven (New York: Prentice-Hall, 1971); Gavin Wright, "Black and White Labor in the Old New South."

23. Julius Rubin, "The Limits of Agricultural Progress in the Nineteenth-Century South," *Agricultural History* 49 (April 1975): 362-73.

24. Sheldon Hackney, "Origins of the New South in Retrospect," *Journal of Southern History* 38 (May 1972): 195.

25. Gavin Wright, "Cheap Labor and Southern Textiles, 1880-1930," *Quarterly Journal of Economics* (November 1981): 621-28.

THE EXPLOSION OF FAMILY HISTORY

Mary P. Ryan

Not the least of the novelties of the 1980 presidential election was the attention which politicians and party platforms bestowed on the American family.
An institution whose major role in the campaigns of the past was to inspire
platitudes and garnish a candidate's folksy image became the explicit topic of
political discussion. In more secluded corners of the United States government the family was being subjected to another sort of scrutiny. A memoran-
dum that circulated through the offices of the Department of Health, Education, and Welfare, for example, proposed this remarkably loose definition of
the family: "any combination of individuals who combine in willingness to
meet each other's needs and provide mutual support, emotionally and/or
financially may meet the test of the family."[1] Meanwhile the Bureau of the
Census quietly but audaciously broke with a precedent that dated back to
1790. The category "head of household" was struck from the schedule of the
1980 census of population. The more neutral term "householder" took its
place on the censustaker's form, and beside it could now be found "room-
mate" or "partner" as well as "spouse." When the results of the 1980 census
were tabulated these alterations in the conventional notation of family relationships proved to be more than justified. Only a small fraction (11.5 percent) of the new households formed in the late 1970s sheltered a married
couple, and thus conformed to minimal definitions of a conventional family.[2]
Clearly, the attention which politicians are paying to the family in the 1980s
is inspired by genuine social change and would seem to herald a fundamental
point of transition in American social history.

   Where politicians dare to tread, historians often follow, sooner or later. In
the case of the family, historians have actually taken up an unfamiliar position at the vanguard of public discussion. It was in 1970 with the publication
of three innovative studies, John Demos's *A Little Commonwealth*, Philip
Greven's *Four Generations*, and Richard Sennett's *Families Against the City*,
that historians began an intensive examination of the American family.[3] Each
of these books introduced its novel historical subject with such interpretative
flair and methodological ingenuity (often borrowed from European
demographers and social historians) that together they inspired a hive of
young researchers. Soon studies of the family, often quantitative, localized,
and highly specialized, began to fill the historical journals.

0048-7511/82/0104-0181 $01.00

The growth of family history was stimulated by political concerns as well as scholarly interests. For example, Herbert Gutman's *The Black Family in Slavery and Freedom*, which captured public and professional attention in 1976, was a response to the controversial Moynihan report on the Negro family as much as a rejoinder to a previous body of historical scholarship. Family history was invigorated further in the mid-seventies by a blossoming of feminist scholarship, and the appearance in rapid succession of such illustrious works in the history of American women as Kathryn Sklar's *Catharine Beecher*, Linda Gordon's *Woman's Body, Woman's Right*, Ann Douglas's *The Feminization of American Culture*, and Nancy Cott's *The Bonds of Womanhood*.[4] By the close of the decade questions of reproduction, birth control, abortion, and sexuality had found their way into history books and political debates alike, as family history fed off the popular interest in personal and intimate life which came to define the culture of the 1970s.[5] A decade of rigorous scholarship has provided historians with some valuable intellectual capital, stocks of information and ideas which might bring some clarity to the confusing, fluid, and controversial condition of the contemporary family.

Whatever its scholarly lineage, or political origins, this prodigious research has led to an explosive increase in information about the families of the past. Voyeurs with antiquarian tastes can now be privy to how families loved, labored, dined, died, and mourned together. We have been informed to one degree or another about the family life of not just New England farmers, but also of southern slaves and planters, of immigrants—from Europe, Asia, and Mexico—of capitalists, workers, and the middling sort, of men and women, young and old. In order to acquire this information, family historians have made a wide-ranging and ingenious search for documents which has led them to such serial public records as wills, inventories, censuses, and vital statistics; to such objects of material culture as house plans, home furnishings, and family photographs; to such aggregations of social science data as opinion polls, social surveys, and time budgets; and to such items of folklore as songs, stories, and games. In order to investigate the families of the past, historians have of necessity resorted to new methodologies—demographic, quantitative, and interdisciplinary—and made extensive use of social theory and the concepts of social science. This abundant stock of data, methods, and theory, as well as the mounting stack of books, articles, and even a separate journal of family history, clearly demonstrate that a new and now full-fledged subfield of history has emerged in the space of a decade.[6]

At the same time historians of the family have been making their mark on other and older segments of their discipline. For example, family history has left a vivid imprint on the recent literature about American social structure.

Historians of the working class have been especially quick to discern connections between class and family. Thomas Dublin's study of the Lowell mill girls and Allan Dawley's analysis of the shoemakers of Lynn, Massachusetts demonstrate how America's first generation of factory workers emerged out of a traditional family economy and how worker solidarity was nurtured by kinship as well as trade unionism. According to John Bodnar's account of the advance of organized labor during the 1930s, a concern for family security, as much as the loyalties forged on the job, continued to foster labor militance.[7] The vital links between class and family are not, furthermore, confined to the lower social strata. The work of Paul Johnson, like my own, indicates that the family, acting in collusion with the Protestant church, played a critical role in the formation of an American middle class during the early nineteenth century. Meanwhile, colonial historians have specified those complicated ties of kinship and marriage alliances which were central to achieving and maintaining the status of merchant capitalist.[8]

The history of class formation is only one instance of how the family has moved into the center of contemporary historiography. No longer regarded as merely a by-product of larger historical forces, the family has assumed the status of an active agency in cultural, social, economic, and political changes, all the way from religion to revolution. In fact family historians might well argue, with some justification as well as considerable hubris, that they are situated at a premier vantage point on the whole historical process. Family transitions, those innumerable points in time when one generation succeeds another, are critical historical junctures, moments rife with the possibility of change even as they link the past to the future. For a glimmer of what history might look like as family biography writ large, one can turn to Richard Easterlin's provocative account of the recent demographic history of the United States. Easterlin traces the critical social and economic conditions of our time back to the domestic consciousness, family decisions, and intimate acts which created the postwar baby boom.[9]

It is impossible to do full justice to the wealth, range, and intricacies of family history as it has unfolded over the last decades. Still a crude chronological overview is instructive, if only as a way of identifying the opportunities for research that coexist with the rapid growth of the field. The panorama of family history is now dominated by a vivid and relatively comprehensive picture of the colonial family. At its source and center and still unrivaled in its breadth of vision is John Demos's *Little Commonwealth*. This slim volume, based on data drawn from Plymouth Colony in the seventeenth century, painted a picture not only of the family's size, structure, material surroundings, internal ambience, and relationship to other social formations, but also provided a rare and sophisticated examination of the history of child development. Demos's fine-grained snapshot of the New England family became a moving picture in Philip Greven's *Four Generations*. Through the painstaking process of family reconstitution and systematic comparisons drawn from one generation to the next, Greven plotted the transition from the seventeenth century to the revolutionary era with a precision that had eluded previous historians of the New England mind and polity. Greven's speculations about the relationship between the declining authority of New England fathers and such events as the Second Great Awakening and the American Revolution, like Demos's depiction of Puritan personality development, has inspired a sizeable body of colonial family history and warrants even more research and debate.[10]

From this sound start in early American history, the study of the family has proceeded at a steady pace, but in a rather meandering direction. The movement into the nineteenth century appears rather jolting in retrospect as family history passed not just the watershed of a new century and a new nation but also moved on to a different set of historical questions. Where colonial historians focused on the issue of patriarchal authority as practiced by farmers, their nineteenth-century counterparts dwelt on domesticity and women's sphere, especially as it applied to the urban middle class. But this rich body of evidence about the ideology and emotion invested in the nineteenth-century home is confined to the early part of the century.[11] The picture of the family after 1850 goes out of focus, lost in a flurry of statistics about family size and structure in different American cities.[12] In the twentieth century the image of family history fades almost out of existence. A single recent monograph focuses solely and directly on the family, and this is actually (perhaps significantly) based on divorce records, that is on evidence of family instability. Sociological literature, from the classic *Middletown* to Glen Elder's longitudinal study of the children of the Great Depression provide some direction through this largely vacant landscape of twentieth-century family history. At the same time, on the margins of the social history of the family, for example in the critical essays of Eli Zaretsky and Christopher Lasch, and in studies of mass culture and consuming by Stuart Ewen, Elizabeth Ewen, and Larry May, glimmer some intimations that family history took a new course in the twentieth century.[13] If its theme was patriarchalism in the seventeenth century, and domesticity in the nineteenth, its watchword in the twentieth might be personal life, or the individual's search for a few intimate, intense social and sexual relations. This broad-stroked sketch of family history, 1700 to the present, tells us at least this much: that the field, for all its rapid development, remains an inviting frontier. Indeed almost the entire twentieth century is open scholarly territory.

Until the broken lines and empty spaces of this sketch have been filled in it will remain difficult to discern the overall pattern of family change in the United States. Cautious American historians have left it largely to the Europeanists, the likes of Philippe Ariès, Lawrence Stone, Edward Shorter, and Jean Louis Flandrin, to put forward grand theses of family transformation.[14] In this European model, family change is most often located along two intertwined axes: the degree to which family is isolated from other social formations and the relative intensity of domestic loyalties and affections. Since the pivotal changes along this continuum—the emergence of the privatized, emotionally intense nuclear family—have been dated as early as the sixteenth century in Europe, it is difficult to transplant this time-scheme to the young American nation. It has prompted some historians, such as Shorter, to observe that the American family was "born modern" and thereby deprives U.S. historians of a major turning point in family history. In lieu of a great watershed in family history American historians have made haphazard use of the nebulous concept of modernization and its attendant economic transitions to market and then industrial capitalism, which have been dated anywhere between 1750 and 1900. Such periodization in American family history is both one-dimensional and elastic. For example, the only recent volume which resembles a general survey of American family history, Carl Degler's *At Odds: Women and the Family in America from the Revolution to the Present*, is content to locate the modern family in the 1830s and surmise that it has remained fundamentally unchanged to this day.[15] In sum, the great volume of information and wealth of specialized interpretation which family historians have accumulated over the last decade have not yet been shaped into a coherent and convincing pattern of development over time. The historian's craving for exact periodization remains unsatisfied.

Family history has exploded across the whole panorama of American history like a brilliant display of fireworks. Like fireworks, however, the literature about the family in the past presents a rather motley clustering of images and does not provide the most reliable source of illumination. This disjointed quality of family history is to be expected in such a young field of scholarship and is in part a sign of intellectual health. The field emerged at a time of robust openness and experimentation within the historical profession, as individual scholars set to work on subjects that engaged their interest without always stopping to quibble about the boundaries or legitimacy of their enterprise. Rarely did they even stop to define the subject of their exuberant interest, the family. Some historians let the compilers of historical records define the family for them, as they drew boundaries around the residents of a dwelling unit or the joint listings in marriage and birth records. Those historians who relied on literary or manuscript sources let a common set of linguistic cues—terms like household, home, domesticity, parent, child, husband, and wife—point them to the history of the family. Most of these signals of family history also trigger a personal response among historians. They prompted Christopher Lasch, for example, to recite an ode to domesticity reminiscent of a nineteenth-century lady's magazine. "Men seek a haven in private life in personal relations, above all in the family—the last refuge of love and decency." [16] Lasch stands out among family historians primarily in the lack of guile with which he revealed his personal attitudes about present-day domesticity. More often historians assume a more antiseptic but basically deferential posture toward their subject matter, regarding the family as almost a natural and intrinsically loveable institution. This perspective, which excuses casual references to a "human urge to create families" [17] and generates muffled applause when the family "survives" slavery, industrialization, immigration, or any other historical change, has been called filiopietism by Tamara Hareven. [18]

As Hareven's comment indicates, family historians are becoming more self-conscious about the field of study that has grown up around them. 1982 is an opportune moment to examine carefully the ideological and symbolic associations which historians and their readers inevitably bring to their subject matter. Ideally this self-scrutiny would proceed from a simple but systematic intellectual or cultural history of the family in recent times. [19] In its absence we can make use of the work of anthropologists like David Schneider, who has identified some basic elements of the American family as a symbolic system. Based on field work conducted in the 1960s Schneider argues that Americans perceive the family first of all as a husband, wife, and children who reside together in what they see as a natural, rather than a socially-constructed unit. Secondly, this unit is wedded in the popular mind to expectations of what Schneider terms "diffuse enduring solidarity" or put simply, love. A third critical component of family symbolism envisions a bold social and emotional boundary between the home and the world of work, commerce, and politics. [20]

Although family historians have been quite oblivious to these symbolic nuances of their subject matter, they have, in the course of a decade of empirical research actually uncovered evidence which casts a shadow of doubt on these popular beliefs about the family. First of all, the historical record will not support the assumption that the nuclear family (the fireside tableau of husband, wife, and children) is a natural, exclusive, and universal unit of human residence. Although at any given moment in time most households have sheltered only nuclear relatives, a substantial minority of Americans could always be found sharing a living space with nonkin, be they servants, masters, apprentices, employers, coworkers, boarders, friends, or fellow inmates of public institutions. It is not an exaggeration to estimate that close to a majority of Americans have spent some portion of their life cycles living alone or with those who were not related to them by either blood or marriage. In a number of historical situations, furthermore, demographic conditions—mortality rates, sex ratios, and age distributions—were such that only a minority of the population could be housed within nuclear families. In the Chesapeake colonies during the seventeenth century, for example, most children spent some time living as orphans. Similarly, widowhood was routine in early American mill towns, and bachelorhood was a majority status in the nineteenth-century West. History could have prepared us for the fact that in 1980 fully one in five American dwelling units is classified as a "non-family household."[21]

The second major tenet of popular belief about the family, its association with "diffuse enduring solidarity" or love, is also contradicted by historical evidence. These terms signify a range of feeling which is far too narrow to describe the emotional ambience of the families of the past. Although family relationships routinely provoked intense emotions, they harbor a full spectrum of feelings: anger, bitterness, and hatred as well as love. As contemporary criminologists have noted, and a look at arrest records of the past underscores, the family is second only to the military and the police as the site of violent behavior.[22] What glues these emotionally volatile units together, moreover, is not necessarily love. Edmund Morgan pointed out long ago that the Puritan family was knit together by a system of authority, subordination and formal etiquette.[23] Michael Anderson's examination of the working-class families of nineteenth-century Lancashire led him to postulate that families can be bound together by a calculated exchange of services as well as personal and customary loyalties. American historians of the nineteenth-century working class echo Anderson's "exchange theory" when they speak of the intricate and various "family strategies" whereby the labor and resources of individual family members were pooled and distributed.[24] The historical record also supplies ample evidence that familial support and affection can be ephemeral as well as "enduring." A whole specialty of family history, the study of the life cycle, is devoted largely to examining how families come apart with the passage of time. Breaking up and breaking away are staples of family history occasioned by death or coming of age if not by divorce.[25] All told, family history is replete with tales of disruption and conflict, of generation gaps and the battle of the sexes, as well as enduring solidarity. Conversely, whatever tenuous unity kinsmen or members of households do establish is the result of human action and effort rather than nature.

The third element in Schneider's typology of family symbolism postulates that domestic unity and love construct a barrier against a cold and competitive society. The new family history was actually inaugurated by Philippe

Ariès's brilliant explosion of this myth. Ariès described how, only after 1500, nuclear relatives were slowly and delicately isolated from a dense and extensive web of broader social relations. The pioneers of American family history were also conscious of historical shifts in the boundaries between family and society. In the notion of the "little commonwealth" John Demos carefully described the interdependence of family and community. Although the households of Plymouth Colony were extremely well-defined as the units for holding property, engaging in production, and socializing children and servants, they were also integrally connected to the community—by legal constrictions, social responsibilities, and a general disdain for privacy on the part of the church, the state, and the neighborhood. Subsequently historians have paid lip-service to the issue of the family's boundaries, and occasionally made use of the critical but still vaguely-defined distinction between the public and the private sphere.[26]

Even this rudimentary research is enough to demonstrate that American homes rarely have been as isolated in fact as in symbol. Historians of women as well as the family have taken pains to describe how the household has been integrally tied to the world of work, production, and economics. It hardly bears repeating that for much of American history the farmhouse or the artisan's dwelling-place were the major centers of production, and that household manufacture continued well into the industrial era. Domestic production, be it for sale or family use, furthermore was not always confined within individual households. In northern New England during the colonial period, for example, housewives organized a system for the manufacture and exchange of domestic goods which spanned whole neighborhoods.[27] Neither was consumption always the exclusive responsibility of the family or household. Americans who have lived on the edge of impoverishment, the Irish immigrant in the nineteenth century, for example, and the black poor under slavery and in the ghetto, have regularly shared their humble resources with friends and neighbors as well as extended kin.[28]

Historians have observed social services as well as economic functions moving back and forth across the threshold of the American household. The history of human reproduction, seemingly the most intimate and exclusive responsibility of the domestic sphere, aptly illustrates this phenomenon. After the private act of conception almost every aspect of reproduction links up with the agents and institutions of the larger society. Recent research has demonstrated that through most of U.S. history childbirth itself was not so much a family affair as a woman's ritual. In rural America as late as the 1920s, childbirth was an event at which midwives officiated, where female friends and kin gathered, and from which men were banished. While health professionals and a medical industry now manage the delivery of infants, and although such female rites have largely disappeared, the role of the family in reproduction has hardly been annihilated. In fact, one could argue, quite to the contrary, that for the first time in our history childbirth is becoming truly a family matter, attended by fathers as well as mothers. Even the propagation of the species, the most "natural" and "biological" function commonly assigned to the family, has this complex social history.[29]

Further historical investigation will reveal that a wide array of other social services are recurrently shifting back and forth between the family and other social groups or institutions. These variations do not conform, furthermore, to a simple linear pattern, like the old saw of sociologists which contends that the functions of the family have progressively declined since industrialization. Nor is there much validity to the correlative of this proposition, the notion that the integrity of the family has been progressively undermined by an invasion of experts and bureaucrats. Both the ideology of the so-called helping professions and the policies of the United States government contradict such an impressionistic account of recent family history. American psychologists have operated largely as champions of the isolated family and participated in a concerted campaign to concentrate emotional and social energy within conjugal units. Likewise, "big government" rather than mounting an invasion of the American family has sponsored a domestic revival through low-cost home loans and other incentives to suburban development since World War II. Even functional sociologists have refined their historical formula of late, conceding that the family "has become a specialist in gratifying peoples' psychological needs," a relatively novel domestic assignment which entails the "expansion and spatial separation," not the diminution, of family functions.[30] Historical research is slowly unraveling an ornate pattern in a seamless carpet of social functions and has failed to uncover a discrete and rigid shape called the family.

Yet the determination to erect ideological boundaries between the family and society still persists and testifies to yet another powerful component of American domestic symbolism. Whatever its entanglements with society and politics, the family still looms in the imagination as the primary location of a very special kind of human relationship: it symbolizes a critical emotional boundary. Family contact is expected to be sustained, supportive, reliable, invested with affection and informed by thorough personal knowledge and mutual understanding. The family, to use the sociological expression, is seen as the chief domain of primary relationships. Again the historical record deviates from the domestic symbolism in a variety of ways. First of all, the family is hardly the sole source of personal relations. Through much of American history families were ensconced in small communities where most every social contact linked individuals who knew one another intimately and shared a whole set of traditions and beliefs. In the special case of the New England town such communities actually used the term love to describe the ideal relationship with persons outside the family. When migration and urbanization confined such community experience to a dwindling number of isolated localities, the family did not immediately fall heir to a monopoly on primary relationships. The social history of nineteenth-century America is full of examples of primary relationships which thrived outside the home. Within the middle class women formed loyalties to one another which rivaled conjugal attachments, while their men-folk took to their lodges to indulge in sentimental rituals of male bonding. Working class men, for their part, sought companionship not with wives and children in crowded tenements but in the male fellowship of the tavern, the union hall, the baseball diamond, and the ethnic club. Even in the twentieth century when heterosexual and marital attachments assumed an especially prominent place in popular culture, Americans continued to form intimate friendships around their schools, workplaces, and neighborhoods as well as in the family.[31] The family is neither the lone citadel of reproduction, a retreat from the world of economics and politics, nor a guarded sanctum of sociability. Under sustained scrutiny the boundaries between the family and society, the last cherished symbol of American domestic ideology, seem to shift and shimmer and dance before the historian's eyes, until the image of the family itself becomes blurred almost beyond recognition.

In sum, the rapid accumulation of information about the families of the past now threatens to explode a set of symbols to which Americans have clung at least since the antebellum reign of the cult of domesticity. Cherished associations with the family have lost the patina of universality and the pretense to natural status. In gaining a history, we have, in a sense, lost a symbol. What once appeared to be a concrete institution, a specific set of functions, a warm experience, has become lost in a maze of complicated social relationships. American historians have not yet developed a theory which encompasses these complex relationships. They might take heed, however, of their more theoretically-inclined European colleagues, especially the French, who, from Ariès to the *Annales* school, have played such an important part in the development of family history. A decade of American research lends support, for example, to Jacques Donzelot's proposition that family should be regarded "Not as a point of departure, as a manifest reality, but as a moving resultant, an uncertain form whose intelligibility can only come from studying the system of relations it maintains with the sociopolitical level."[32]

Although this approach to family history may sound as futile as chasing moonbeams, it does not override the need for the kind of detailed empirical studies which have been the mainstay of family history as practiced in the United States. Rather, Donzelot's theoretical directives and a decade of American research challenge us simply to mount studies of the family, no matter how specialized, in a larger social frame. It is time to discard the blinders of domestic ideology and see the family as but one strand in the whole web of relations and institutions that constitute a society. With assistance from social scientists, historians have already begun the project of locating the family in this larger social space. The human ecology school of social geography, for example, can offer many helpful insights and tools of analysis, which historians are beginning to put to good use. In his exploration of the growth and social composition of the suburbs John Modell has revealed how different geographical positions in the metropolitan system can affect such aspects of family behavior as the fertility rate.[33] Further illumination of this critical relationship between the family and the surrounding social spaces is being provided by historians of material culture and architecture. By analyzing inventories of the household furnishings of early modern England and America, Carole Shammas has succeeded in charting the movement of social rituals from public places such as the alehouse to the private fireside. Similarly, an intensive examination of the American architectural record early in this century conducted by Gwendolyn Wright has adumbrated a whole sequence of far-reaching changes in the spatial and material organization of personal life.[34] Yet further guidance through these more open spaces that impinge on the history of the family has been provided by anthropological and sociological literature on social networks. Historians of women and Afro-Americans have been particularly resourceful in employing this interdisciplinary tool, which operates on the principle that primary social loyalties need to be located historically rather than presumed to concentrate within the family. By applying these methods, and by simply widening their focus, historians are beginning to map out the position of the family as a "moving resultant" in a whole galaxy of social relationships.[35]

The family historians of the 1980s would do well to ponder the lessons of today's newspapers as well as yesterday's social science textbooks. Family history is found not just in the quiet recesses of domestic life but also in the center of public controversy. In the past as in the present, family members have repeatedly taken their grievances and their concerns into the streets and before government bodies. The demands of housewives have spilled over into food riots; sexual tension has led to moral reform movements; the longest political struggle of American history, the feminist movement, has often been waged at the critical edge of family history.[36] In her description of feminist designs for cooperative housekeeping and public kitchens, for example, Dolores Hayden has demonstrated that political and social struggles can be mounted at the very portals of the American home, where, in this case, men and women literally broke down the walls of one family system in hopes of building another more to their liking.[37] We have hardly begun to explore this more public and vociferous aspect of family history. An investigation which began, hardly a decade ago, with the naive intention of studying a quiet private corner of the past has opened up this vast and volatile historical vista which can occupy the headlines and the history books for some time to come.

1. Quoted in Catherine M. Allen, "Defining the Family for Post-Industrial Public Policy," in David Pearch Snyder, ed., *The Family in Post-Industrial America* (Boulder, Colo: Westview Press, 1979).

2. Evelyn M. Itagawa, "New Life-Styles: Marriage Patterns, Living Arrangements, and Fertility Outside of Marriage," *Annals of the American Association of Political and Social Science* 451 (January 1981): 15.

3. John Demos, *A Little Commonwealth: Family Life in Plymouth Colony* (New York: Oxford University Press, 1970); Philip J. Greven, Jr., *Four Generations: Population, Land and Family in Colonial Andover, Massachusetts* (Ithaca, N.Y.: Cornell University Press, 1970); Richard Sennett, *Families Against the City: Middle Class Homes of Industrial Chicago, 1872-1890* (Cambridge, Mass.: Harvard University Press, 1970).

4. Herbert G. Gutman, *The Black Family in Slavery and Freedom, 1750-1925* (New York: Pantheon, 1976); Kathryn Kish Sklar, *Catharine Beecher: A Study in American Domesticity* (New Haven: Yale University Press, 1973); Linda Gordon, *Woman's Body, Woman's Right: A Social History of Birth Control in America* (New York: Grossman, 1976); Nancy F. Cott, *The Bonds of Womanhood: "Woman's Sphere" in New England, 1780-1835* (New Haven: Yale University Press, 1977); Ann Douglas, *The Feminization of American Culture* (New York: Knopf, 1977).

5. Richard W. Wertz and Dorothy C. Wertz, *Lying-In: A History of Childbirth in America* (Boston: Free Press, 1977); James Reed, *From Private Vice to Public Virtue: The Birth Control Movement and American Society since 1830* (New York: Basic Books, 1978); James Mohr, *Abortion in America: The Origins and Evolution of National Policy, 1800-1900* (New York: Oxford University Press, 1978); Elaine Tyler May, *Great Expectations: Marriage and Divorce in Post Victorian America* (Chicago: University of Chicago Press, 1980); William Leach, *True Love and Perfect Union: The Feminist Reform of Sex and Society* (New York: Basic Books, 1980).

6. For a numerical accounting of the growth of family history, see Lawrence Stone, "Family History in the 1980's," *Journal of Interdisciplinary History* 12, 1 (Summer 1981): 51–87. Stone's calculation of the extraordinary growth of the field was based on Gerald L. Soliday, ed., *History of Family and Kinship: A Select International Bibliography* (Millwood, N.Y.: Kraus International Publications, 1980). For a taste of the methodological and conceptual range of the new family history, see Michael Gordon, ed., *The American Family in Social Historical Perspective*, 2nd ed. (New York: St. Martin's, 1978) and *The Journal of Family History*, founded in 1976.

7. Thomas Dublin, *Women at Work: The Transformation of Work and Community in Lowell, Massachusetts, 1826-1860* (New York: Columbia University Press, 1979); Alan Dawley, *Class and Community: The Industrial Revolution in Lynn* (Cambridge, Mass.: Harvard University Press, 1976); John Bodnar, "Immigration, Kinship, and the Rise of Working-Class Realism in Industrial America," *Journal of Social History*, 13 (Fall 1980): 44–64; Barbara M. Tucker, "The Family and Industrial Discipline in Ante-Bellum New England," *Journal of Labor History* 21 (Winter 79–80): 55–74.

8. Paul Johnson, *A Shopkeeper's Millenium: Society and Revivals in Rochester, New York, 1815-1837* (New York: Hill and Wang, 1978); Mary P. Ryan, *Cradle of the Middle Class: The Family in Oneida County, New York, 1790-1865* (New York: Cambridge University Press, 1981); Peter Dobkin Hall, "Marital Selection and Business in Massachusetts Merchant Families, 1700-1900" in Gordon, ed., *American Family*, pp. 101-14.

9. These implications of a generational approach to history are suggested in Norman Ryder, "The Cohort as a Concept in the Study of Social Change," *American Sociological Review* 30, 1 (December 1965): 1843-61; Richard Easterlin, *Birth and Fortune: The Impact of Numbers on Personal Welfare* (New York: Basic Books, 1980).

10. Daniel Blake Smith, *Inside the Great House: Planter Family Life in Eighteenth Century Chesapeake Society* (Ithaca, N.Y.: Cornell University Press, 1980); Linda Auwers, "Fathers, Sons and Wealth in Colonial Windsor, Connecticut," *Journal of Family History* 3 (Summer 1978): 136-50; Ralph J. Crandall, "Family Types, Social Structure and Mobility in Early America, Charleston, Massachusetts, A Case Study," in Virginia Tufte and Barbara Myerhoff, eds., *Changing Images of the Family* (New Haven: Yale University Press, 1979); John Waters, "The Traditional World of the New England Peasants: a View of Seventeenth-Century Barnstable," *New England Historical and Geneological Register*, January 1976, pp. 19-32; Lois Green Carr and Lorena S. Walsh, "The Planter's Wife: The Experience of White Women in Seventeenth-Century Maryland," in Gordon, ed., *American Family*, pp. 263-88.

11. Cott, *The Bonds of Womanhood*; Sklar, *Catharine Beecher*; Mary Beth Norton, *Liberty's Daughters: The Revolutionary Experience of American Women, 1750-1800* (Boston: Little, Brown, 1980); Barbara Welter, "The Cult of True Womanhood, 1820-1860," *American Quarterly* 18 (1966): 151-74.

12. See, for example, Michael Katz, *The People of Hamilton Canada West: Family and Class in a Mid-Nineteenth Century City* (Cambridge, Mass.: Harvard University Press, 1975), ch. 5; Clyde and Sally Griffen, *Natives and Newcomers: The Ordering of Opportunity in Mid-Nineteenth Century Poughkeepsie, New York* (Cambridge, Mass.: Harvard University Press, 1978); Sennett, *Families Against the City*; R. A. Burchell, *The San Francisco Irish, 1848-1880* (Berkeley: University of California Press, 1980), ch. 5; Virginia Yans-McLaughlin, *Family and Community, Italian Immigrants in Buffalo, 1880-1930* (Ithaca, N.Y.: Cornell University Press, 1977).

13. May, *Great Expectations*; Glen H. Elder, Jr., *Children of the Great Depression* (Chicago: University of Chicago Press, 1974); Robert and Helen Lynd, *Middletown: A Study in Modern American Culture* (New York: Harcourt, Brace, 1929); Stuart Ewen, *Captains of Consciousness: Advertising and the Social Roots of Consumer Culture* (New York: McGraw-Hill, 1976); Larry May, *Screening Out the Past* (New York: Oxford University Press, 1980); Elizabeth Ewen, "City Lights: Immigrant Women and the Rise of the Movies," *Signs* 5 (Spring 1980): 45-66, supplement; Eli Zaretsky, *Capitalism, the Family and Personal Life* (New York: Harpers, 1976).

14. Philippe Ariès, *Centuries of Childhood*, trans. Robert Baldick (New York: Knopf, 1965); Lawrence Stone, *The Family, Sex and Marriage in England 1500-1800* (London: Weidenfeld and Nicolson, 1977); Edward Shorter, *The Making of the Modern Family* (New York: Basic Books, 1975); Jean Louis Flandrin, *Families in Past Time* (Cambridge, England: Cambridge University Press, 1979).

15. Carl Degler, *At Odds: Women and the Family in America from the Revolution to the Present* (New York: Oxford University Press, 1980).

16. Christopher Lasch, *Haven in a Heartless World: The Family Besieged* (New York: Basic Books, 1977), preface.

17. Degler, *At Odds*, p. 127.

18. Tamara Hareven, "Family and Work Patterns of Immigrant Laborers in a Planned Industrial Town, 1900-1930" in Richard L. Ehrlich, ed., *Immigrants in Industrial America 1850-1920* (Charlottesville, Va.: University Press of Virginia, 1977), pp. 47-66. See Yans-McLaughlin, *Family and Community* for an example of the "celebration of survival" approach. For an example of a more subtle perspective on family "adaptation" to immigration and indus-

trialization, see Caroline Golab, "The Impact of the Industrial Experience on the Immigrant Family: the Huddled Masses Reconsidered," in Ehrlich, ed., *Immigrants*, pp. 1–33.

19. Flandrin, *Families in Past Time*, pp. 11–19, 145–74; Mark Poster, *Critical Theory of the Family* (New York: Continuum, 1978).

20. David M. Schneider, *American Kinship: A Cultural Account*, 2nd ed. (Chicago: University of Chicago Press, 1980).

21. See Carr and Walsh, "The Planter's Wife"; Daniel Walkowitz, *Worker City, Company Town* (Urbana: University of Illinois Press, 1978), pp. 112–15. Rudy Ray Seward, *The American Family, A Demographic History* (Beverly Hills, Calif.: Sage, 1978). Historians are beginning to recognize that these variations in the relationship between kinship and residence are far more interesting than the early generalizations of the Cambridge School about the long history of relatively small nuclear families in the West. See Peter Laslett and Richard Wall, eds., *Household and Family in Past Time* (New York: Cambridge University Press, 1972).

22. Richard J. Gellis and Murray A. Straus, "Violence in America," *Journal of Social Issues* 35 (1979): 15–40; Research on family violence in America is now underway by Linda Gordon and Elizabeth Pleck, among others.

23. Edmund S. Morgan, *The Puritan Family, Religion and Domestic Relations in Seventeenth-Century New England* (New York: Harper and Row, 1966).

24. Michael Anderson, *Family Structure in Nineteenth-Century Lancashire* (Cambridge, England: Cambridge University Press, 1971). See essay by Claudia Goldin and Michael Haines in Theodore Hershberg, ed., *Philadelphia: Work, Space, Family, and Group Experience in the Nineteenth Century* (New York: Oxford University Press, 1981).

25. Tamara Hareven, "Cycles, Courses and Cohorts: Reflections on Theoretical and Methodological Approaches to the Historical Study of Family Development," *Journal of Social History* 12 (Fall 1978): 97–109.

26. Philippe Ariès, "The Family and the City," *Daedalus* 106, 2 (Spring 1977): 227–35; Richard Sennett, *The Fall of Public Man* (New York: Knopf, 1977).

27. Elizabeth Pleck, "Two Worlds in One: Work and Family," *Journal of Social History* 10 (Winter 1976): 178–90; Laurel Thatcher Ulrich, "A Friendly Neighbor: Social Dimensions of Daily Work in Northern Colonial New England," *Feminist Studies* 6 (Summer 1981): 392–406.

28. Carol Stack, *All Our Kin* (New York: Harper and Row, 1974); Elizabeth Pleck, *Black Migration and Poverty: Boston, 1865–1900* (New York: Academic Press, 1979), esp. pp. 188–92.

29. Wertz and Wertz, *Lying-In*; Judy Barrett Litoff, *American Midwives, 1860 to the Present* (Westport, Conn.: Greenwood Press, 1978); Catherine M. Scholten, "On the Importance of the Obstetric Art, Changing Customs of Childbirth in America 1750–1825," *William and Mary Quarterly* 34 (July 1977): 426–46.

30. Gwendolyn Wright, *Building the American Dream: A Social History of Architecture in America* (New York: Pantheon, 1981), ch. 5; Mary P. Ryan, *Womanhood in America from Colonial Times to the Present*, 2nd ed. (New York: Franklin Watts, 1979), ch. 5; Bert Adams, quoted in Howard M. Bahr, "Changes in Family Life in Middletown, 1924–77," *Public Opinion Quarterly* 44 (Spring 1980): 35–52.

31. Caroll Smith-Rosenberg, "A Female World of Love and Ritual," *Signs* 1 (August 1976): 1–29; Bruce Laurie, "Nothing by Compulsion: Life Styles of Philadelphia Artisans, 1820–1850," *Labor History* 15 (Summer 1974): 337–66; Jon Kingsdale, "The Poor Man's Club: Social Function of the Urban Working Class Saloon," *American Quarterly* 25 (October 1973): 473; Claude Fischer et al., *Networks and Places* (New York: Free Press, 1977), p. 51.

32. Jacques Donzelot, *The Policing of Families*, trans. Robert Hurley (New York: Pantheon, 1979), p. xxv.

33. John Modell, "Suburbanization and Change in the American Family," *Journal of Interdisciplinary History* (Spring 1977): 621–46.

34. Gwendolyn Wright, *Moralism and the Model Home: Domestic Architecture and Cultural Conflict in Chicago, 1873–1913* (Chicago: University of Chicago Press, 1980); Carole Shammas, "The Domestic Environment in Early Modern England and America," *Journal of Social History* 14 (Fall 1980): 3–19.

35. For an excellent application of this method, see James Borchert, "Urban Neighborhood and Community: Informal Group Life, 1850–1960," *Journal of Interdisciplinary History* 11, 4 (Spring 1981): 67–133.

36. William Leach, *True Love and Perfect Union: The Feminist Reform of Sex in Society* (New York: Basic Books, 1980).

37. Dolores Hayden, *The Grand Domestic Revolution: A History of Feminist Designs for American Homes, Neighborhoods and Cities* (Cambridge, Mass.: M.I.T. Press, 1981); Barbara Leslie Epstein, *The Politics of Domesticity: Women, Evangelism and Temperance in Nineteenth-Century America* (Middletown, Conn.: Wesleyan University Press, 1981).

SEXUALITY IN NINETEENTH-CENTURY AMERICA: BEHAVIOR, IDEOLOGY, AND POLITICS

Estelle B. Freedman

In the past decade, as historians have explored the "private side" of history, the subject of sexuality has attracted increasing scholarly attention. Well before Michel Foucault argued that the nineteenth century had witnessed an expansion of sexual discourse that created new categories of sexualities, social historians were reinterpreting not only the discourse on sexuality in nineteenth-century America, but changing patterns of sexual behavior as well. During the 1970s, when family historians identified changing rates of fertility and illegitimacy, they raised new questions about the frequency of marital intercourse and the possible use of contraceptives and abortion. When feminist historians explored the meanings of sexuality and reproduction in women's lives, they sparked lively debates about the relationship between ideology and behavior and about the regulation of female sexuality by the medical profession. Soon studies of prostitution, homosexuality, and sexual utopians expanded the scope of this historical inquiry. By the 1980s, public policy debates over abortion, adolescent sex, and homosexuality inspired a new interest in the origins of state regulation of sexuality.[1]

Within this growing literature, historians have focused for the most part on two broad subjects: sexual ideology and sexual behavior, or, as Carl Degler has summarized this distinction, "What Ought to Be and What Was."[2] Particularly for the nineteenth century, scholars have explored attitudes about proper sexual conduct, usually found in published advice literature, and the actual sexual practices that people engaged in, usually deduced from quantitative sources but also found in legal records and personal papers. Too often, however, historians have explained the relationship between ideology and behavior by asking whether or not ideas influenced individual sexual practice.

My reading of the literature on sexuality in nineteenth-century America has made me uneasy with the limitations of these two categories. By thinking only of ideas and behaviors, historians fail to recognize an important third category, one that might be labeled "sexual politics." The subject matter in this category includes political efforts to transform sexual thought or practice (for example, moral reform, antiprostitution, or birth control movements), while the interpretations take into account relationships of power, particularly those based on class or gender.

A second problem is the assumption that ideology precedes and then influences behavior, more or less effectively. The implied causality may be misleading. For example, by looking first at nineteenth-century sexual advice literature, which often advocated male self-control and female passionlessness, and then at the decline in white marital fertility rates, the latter can be seen as evidence that couples internalized these ideals, engaged less frequently in intercourse, and thus had fewer children. In contrast, by looking first at behavioral change, namely the means by which the decline in white, marital fertility was achieved, an alternative hypothesis emerges. For if the decline in fertility resulted from the separation of sexuality from its reproductive function—through the use of contraception and abortion, for example—then the main question for nineteenth-century sexual history is not whether repression was effective, but rather whether and how the growing importance of non-procreative sexuality influenced sexual ideas and politics. Indeed, recent literature on sexual behavior, ideology, and politics reveals that the increasing visibility of erotic sexuality, separate from procreation, presented a central problem for nineteenth-century society.

Sexual Behavior

Historians who examine nineteenth-century sexual behavior take two demographic facts as starting points. One is the steady decline in white marital fertility rates, from 7.04 births in 1800 to 3.56 births in 1900.[3] The other is a two-phased shift in premarital pregnancy rates—first, a decline from a late eighteenth-century high of almost 30 percent of all births to a mid-nineteenth-century low of under 10 percent; and second, by the close of the century, an increase to approximately 20 percent of all births.[4]

The decline in marital fertility rates has important implications for the history of sexual behavior. Most explanations correlate this decline with urbanization, industrialization, or the availability of land.[5] These social and economic considerations undoubtedly influenced individual decisions to limit family size, but the question remains—*how* did couples achieve this reduction? According to Daniel Scott Smith, nineteenth-century women insisted on abstinence from intercourse within marriage in order to reduce the frequency of childbirth. Carl Degler agrees that women influenced the decision to control fertility, but he also provides extensive evidence that married, middle class white women might have used contraceptives or abortion, as well as abstinence, to do so. As James Mohr shows, increasing numbers of married, middle class women turned to abortion at mid-century. It is not clear whether the subsequent criminalization of abortion led to a reduction in its use, to greater reliance on contraceptives, or to both. From the work of Linda Gordon and others we know that information about contraceptive techniques, including douching, condoms, and withdrawal, was available in early nineteenth-century medical and popular health literature.[6] Women exchanged such information through their correspondence, and men no doubt learned of the techniques from visiting either prostitutes or doctors. Efforts to suppress birth control information, exemplified by the passage of the Comstock Law in 1873, may have been, in fact, a reaction to increased use. And despite Comstock's crusade, contraceptive information continued to circulate in medical if not popular texts.[7]

Fluctuations in premarital pregnancy rates have further implications for understanding the frequency of intercourse and use of contraceptives. Daniel Scott Smith and Michael Hindus argue that premarital pregnancy rates declined in the early nineteenth century when young people internalized an ideology of sexual continence and thus reduced the frequency of intercourse. By the late nineteenth century, increasingly autonomous young adults engaged in premarital sex and used contraceptive devices, indicating a new willingness to separate sexuality and reproduction.[8]

These studies of fertility, premarital pregnancy, and contraception pose a number of questions about sexual behavior. Did marital fertility decline not because married couples engaged in intercourse less frequently, but rather because they used contraception or abortion? Did doctors and druggists provide contraceptive information to married couples throughout the century? Did unmarried couples have greater access to contraceptives and abortion in the early nineteenth century, thus keeping the premarital pregnancy rates low, but less access in the latter part of the century, when such information may have gone "underground"? If the answers to these questions are positive, then the frequency of marital and premarital intercourse may have remained constant or even increased over the century, but the meaning of intercourse may have been changing as its reproductive function declined, thus allowing the erotic component of sexuality to emerge more clearly.

These questions, however, are based solely on evidence of the fertility of white, native-born Americans, particularly those living in the Northeast. The very few available studies of immigrants, southern whites, and blacks suggest that their fertility rates remained high during the nineteenth century, indicating either more frequent intercourse or less contraceptive use.[9] The most extensive research concerns slavery and focuses largely on whether it was masters or slaves who shaped sexual behavior on the plantation.[10] Most scholars agree that while older assumptions about black promiscuity are inaccurate, slaves did have a unique sexual system that drew upon certain African customs and resembled preindustrial sexual patterns elsewhere. They condoned premarital intercourse, accepted "illegitimate" births, and valued stable unions with frequent intercourse. It is not clear whether incentives for slave reproduction came from white masters or black slaves, but it is clear that reproduction was not the sole purpose of intercourse among blacks. As Genovese shows, slaves regarded love as a central motive for sex and marriage. Finally, most writers agree that sexual relations between masters and female slaves were less frequent than abolitionists claimed, in part because women resisted their masters and in part because of mutual interest in maintaining the integrity of the slave families.[11]

Although few investigations of working class sexual practices have appeared to date, several recent studies of prostitution provide clues that men engaged in pre- or extramarital intercourse. In mining and cattle towns, for example, working class, black and immigrant women (many of them Latin American or Asian) supported themselves as prostitutes for at least a few years of their lives. As families began to settle in these communities, the once-tolerated "red-light districts" came under attack, and prostitution went underground.[12] As in eastern cities, however, the opponents of prostitution remained conscious of its survival, and thus of the possibility of sexual experience that was entirely divorced from reproduction.

In addition to quantifying the frequency of marital and premarital intercourse, historians have begun to ask qualitative questions about how individuals experienced their sexuality and the personal identities they attached to it. Some of this research focuses on women in an attempt to discover whether they enjoyed or disliked marital intercourse. A small but growing literature investigates the meaning of same-sex love.

In answer to the question "Were women passionless?" historians such as Linda Gordon suggest that women may well have experienced an aversion to sex, not only because of powerful proscriptions on female passion but because women had good reason to fear the physical consequences of pregnancy and childbirth. And when men paid inadequate attention to female sexual pleasure, women had further reason to avoid intercourse. Carl Degler champions an alternative view. Drawing on the earliest available survey of female sexuality, he argues that married, middle class white women did exhibit sexual desire and that a significant proportion experienced orgasm. To further support his case Degler cites the private writings of nineteenth-century feminists who clearly expressed passionate desires. But the responses to the survey Degler uses can be calculated differently, as Carroll Smith-Rosenberg shows, to find that a majority of the respondents engaged in intercourse with their husbands more frequently than the women themselves wished. More importantly, the survey reveals that most of these women believed procreation, and not pleasure, was the purpose of intercourse.[13] Unfortunately, the study tells nothing about female sexual experience outside the white, middle classes.

Sexual experience, of course, is not confined to heterosexual intercourse. William Shade speculates that the decline in marital fertility may have been accompanied by an increase in masturbation and lesbianism. This view assumes a constant level of sexual activity that finds various forms of expression over time, an assumption that is difficult to support. Shade cites, for example, the shrill crusade against female masturbation in the nineteenth century.[14] (A similar attack upon masturbation by young men had originated at least a century earlier.) In the 1880s, many doctors condemned the widespread practice of masturbation by women of all classes, and some linked the practice to friendships among girls. At the same time, educators became suspicious of "smashing," or same-sex crushes, at women's schools. These public outcries do not in themselves indicate an increased level of masturbation or lesbianism, but there is some evidence to confirm that women engaged in both practices in the late nineteenth century. During the 1920s, Katharine B. Davis surveyed 2,200 women about their sex lives and found that a majority of those born after 1850 reported masturbating to orgasm, while one out of five college-educated women had some lesbian experiences.[15]

Intimate relationships between women friends had been considered acceptable since at least the eighteenth century. As Smith-Rosenberg explains, such "homosocial" relationships emerged naturally within the separate female sphere. In a recent examination of these intensely sensuous "romantic friendships," Lillian Faderman concludes that throughout the nineteenth century these attachments remained nonsexual. She argues that even those women who formed "Boston Marriages" (lifelong companionships in shared households) in the late nineteenth century had so internalized the ideal of passionlessness that they could not engage in genital sexuality. But Faderman repeatedly mistakes ideology for behavior, assuming, for instance, that fictional depictions of passionlessness provide an accurate guide to actual behavior. Whatever these couples may have done in private, Faderman argues convincingly that neither they nor the society termed these relationships "lesbian." At the beginning of the century, most legal and medical authorities could not imagine sexual relations between two women because female sexuality was, by definition, linked to reproduction. After 1900, however, these authorities recognized the possibility of female homosexuality and increasingly labeled it pathological.[16]

Same-sex love between men in nineteenth-century America has received less scholarly attention than has the subject of female relationships, but abundant documentary evidence confirms its existence. In his collection, *Gay American History*, Jonathan Katz published the records of both passionate male friendships and explicitly sexual relationships. The documents support the views of British writers such as Jeffrey Weeks that a distinct male homosexual identity and an urban gay subculture emerged toward the end of the nineteenth century.[17] At that time, as Faderman agrees, sexologists and medical authorities began to categorize homosexuality as a permanent, biological condition. As a result, they argue, those who engaged in homosexual acts increasingly took on homosexual identities. Though stigmatized, they could now find each other and begin to develop a unique sexual subculture.

Just as nineteenth-century writers identified women as "The Sex," most historians have limited their inquiries about sexual experience largely to the study of women. Aside from those men who visited brothels or left records of their homosexual activities, we have learned very little about either middle or working class men's sexuality. It is not yet clear whether sources such as medical records, divorce cases, diaries, and letters will provide sufficient evidence for generalizing about male sexual experience—a crucial task for understanding the separation of procreative and erotic sexuality.[18] Until historians investigate these sources, the most "private side" of history remains one-sided, and our understanding of nineteenth-century sexual behavior remains incomplete.

Sexual Ideology

The results of new research on sexual behavior—a decline in white marital fertility rates, evidence of contraceptive use, abortion, prostitution, and indications of both male and female homosexuality—provide an important background for understanding both dominant and alternate sexual ideologies of the nineteenth century. Despite wide variations in the content of published advice literature, a central tension runs throughout nineteenth-century sexual ideology—that is, whether sex "ought to be" a procreative or an erotic act. The evidence of behavioral change strongly suggests that the procreative function of sex declined over the century; but studies of sexual ideology reveal intensive efforts on the part of some to affirm that sex served reproductive ends and to contain the troubling potential of the erotic.

Before exploring this central tension, however, it is important to recognize the diversity of sexual advice found in the writings of clergy, doctors, and moral reformers from the late eighteenth to the late nineteenth centuries. Aimed at an audience of white, middle class women and men, this literature prescribed two basic virtues, male continence and female purity, which distinguished it from earlier texts. The former ideal required men to exert their will in order to control their natural lust; the latter ideal assumed an innate passionlessness on the part of women.[19] The principles of continence and purity, however, had a wide range of practical meanings. Some marriage manuals called for moderate conjugal intercourse, with female orgasm, while others called for abstinence for both sexes. Moreover, sexual ideals changed over the course of the century.[20]

Historians have arrived at divergent interpretations of male continence and female purity in part because they have read different authors, from different generations, and in different contexts. For example, the antebellum health reformer Sylvester Graham, the subject of a useful biography by Stephen Nissenbaum, represents an extreme case; Graham believed that any sensual excitement, including marital sex, depleted men's bodies. His prophylaxis for the "pathology of desire" included moderate diet, simple clothing, chaste reading, and minimal contact between the sexes.[21] In contrast, William Leach examines the writings of those he considers feminist reformers—an unspecified group of later nineteenth-century liberal women and men—and concludes that they did not repudiate sexual passion. Rather, authors such as Lester Ward and Elizabeth Cady Stanton "looked upon desire, passion, and feeling in both sexes within marriage as essentially beneficent and healthy forces."[22] Had Leach read the works of still other nineteenth-century feminists, such as advocates of social purity, he would have found abundant evidence that sexual restraint remained a powerful theme.

Discussions of female purity reveal similar distinctions. Nancy Cott identifies the cultural sources of an ideal of female passionlessness in texts on etiquette, morality, and religion published in the late eighteenth and early nineteenth centuries. Medical texts incorporated these views and many American doctors adopted the British physician William Acton's model of the asexual woman. Yet middle class women were also exposed to quite different sexual advice. As Carl Degler argues, many nineteenth-century authors, both male and female, encouraged women to experience physical pleasure in sex, and several doctors urged husbands to provide this pleasure. What these texts may indicate, however, is a change in the late nineteenth century rather than a contradiction of Cott's work on the earlier period. As Degler himself acknowledges, one can find almost any opinion in medical texts, including the ideal of passionlessness.[23]

Whether nineteenth-century authors viewed sexual desire as a disease or encouraged passionate sex for both spouses, during most of the century they agreed that procreation was the ultimate purpose of sexual activity. Thus, with the exception of a few radicals, they considered any means of birth control "unnatural." Even feminists, Linda Gordon shows, preferred to keep sexuality and reproduction linked; thus they rejected the use of artificial contraceptives that might separate the two. Similarly, any nonprocreative sexual act constituted an unnatural "abuse," and hence excessive marital sex, masturbation, and homosexual acts came to be seen as causes of physical and mental decline. For example, nineteenth-century authorities revived Tissot's notion that masturbation led to insanity, where earlier proscriptions had been based on the argument that masturbation interfered with conjugal sex; masturbation, along with sodomy (a term sometimes used to refer to all non-procreative sexual acts) changed from a sin to a disease that endangered both body and mind. Although this consensus on procreative sexuality began to break down at the end of the century, for most nineteenth-century Americans, to speak of sex was to speak of procreation.[24]

Recent work on utopian communities highlights the tension between procreation and eroticism that lay just beneath the surface of sexual thought. Both Lawrence Foster and Louis Kern show how the sexual ideals of Shakers, Oneidans, and Mormons elaborated upon the dominant sexual ideology at its most difficult oppositions: those of procreation versus erotic sexual activity and social versus individual control over sexuality.[25]

The struggle to incorporate both procreation and eroticism in utopian sexual life produced a variety of solutions. Shakers totally proscribed intercourse, thus rejecting procreation entirely, but they did allow for sensual expression through ritual dances, visions, and trances. At Oneida, procreation had a limited place, for in John Humphrey Noyes's regimen of "coitus reservatus," men preserved their semen by learning to avoid ejaculation during intercourse. Erotic pleasure, however, could be enjoyed by both men and women. The Mormons, in contrast, identified sex entirely with procreation.[26]

As in the larger society, the theme of self-control pervaded utopian sexual thought. According to Kern, male self-control served as an antidote to the "threat of the autonomous individual." But social control—the subordination of the individual to the community—played a large role in each utopian system. Shakers closely surveilled members' physical activity; Oneidans employed mutual criticism to enforce sexual norms and institutionalized a system of selective breeding known as stirpiculture. Mormons both elevated polygamy to a social duty and achieved some eugenic control by requiring church approval for men's choice of wives. Thus, despite the societal emphasis on the internalization of sexual restraint, utopians tried to keep sexuality a communal concern and emphasized the social benefits of both eroticism and procreation. In this sense they harked back to an earlier era of community control over sexuality. Their ideas suggest as well that Americans feared uncontrolled erotic sexuality as something that threatened to place the individual beyond the control of the community.[27]

In fact, many historical explanations of the ideal of male continence reinforce the conclusion that sexual control represented a means of assuaging fears of anarchy during a period when hierarchical restraints upon individual mobility were being removed. Both David Brion Davis and Ronald Walters use this argument, the former to explain the association of sex and death in American fiction, and the latter to explain the rhetoric of northern male abolitionists who attacked unrestrained lust among southern male slave-holders.[28] For abolitionists and others, control of the body offered a check upon individualism that would both reduce the threat of unrestrained use of power and insure the progress of civilization.

As in utopian communities, in the society at large sexuality provided an important link between self-control and social control. As Walters points out, when individuals channeled eroticism to serve reproductive ends, they contributed to the growth of a healthy, or eugenic, population. Perfectionist thought in the antebellum period originally fostered this view, and the introduction of Darwinism later in the century made the link between self-control and eugenic progress central in American sexual ideology.[29]

Toward the end of the century, one set of ideas—those of the Free Lovers—did challenge the dominant sexual ideology. Although these "sex radicals," who Hal Sears and Linda Gordon discuss, did oppose contraception and believe in the importance of self-control, they differed from most Victorians in two important ways. For one, writers such as Moses Harmon and Angela Heywood developed a critique of marriage that involved greater procreative and erotic choices for women. They believed women had the right to determine when to bear children *and* the right to experience erotic pleasure. Moreover, they insisted that the crucial, and often missing, element in sexual relations was love, which they saw as the only proper motivation for both procreation and pleasure. The sex radicals differed in a second important way when, as anarchists or libertarians, they stood firmly against state control of sexuality. Thus they opposed Anthony Comstock's notion of using the federal government to suppress information about sexuality and they rejected the goals of those eugenicists who advocated state intervention in mating and motherhood.[30]

Although recent histories have shown that nineteenth-century sexual ideology was not uniform, they do suggest that a set of common concerns about the meaning of nonprocreative sexuality prevailed. Procreation remained the most highly valued goal of sex, while erotic desire evoked ambivalence at best, and fear of disease and social anarchy at worst. Most Victorian authors emphasized the need to control eroticism, but their means for doing so ranged from abstinence to moderation to elaborate utopian designs for allowing individual pleasure within social boundaries.

What remains to be investigated is whether there were ideologies other than these white, middle class views that are so accessible through printed advice literature. Was there, for instance, a full-fledged defense of a sexual underground, or demimonde, such as that described for Victorian England? Or was there a distinct urban working class or ethnic view of sexuality? [31] By identifying such possible alternatives, it will become clearer whether there were in fact competing sexual ideologies in the nineteenth century or if, as we now tend to assume, a powerful middle class world view dominated sexual thought throughout American society.

Sexual Politics

It is difficult and somewhat artificial to draw a sharp line between ideology and politics, and much of the literature discussed here has as its purpose the interpretation of sexual ideas. But the subject of sexual politics differs from descriptions of the content of sexual thought because it asks basically political questions: Whose interests did ideas serve? By what means did notions of sexual propriety come to predominate? By which social groups were they enforced? In other words, what relationships of power were at stake? The answers to these questions generally involve class, age, and gender.

The role of class in determining Victorian sexual norms appears in the earliest literature on nineteenth-century sexual history, particularly but not exclusively in discussions of male sexuality. In his 1963 essay on sexual ideology and the social system in nineteenth-century England, Peter Cominos argued that Victorians associated economic success, or class mobility, with sexual sublimation. He identified the symbolic importance of sperm as a metaphor for accumulated capital and argued that sexual control came to be identified with the education of a gentleman. Not incidentally, this system rested upon a double standard that required the availability of working class women who, as prostitutes, safeguarded the ideal of purity in the middle class family. [32]

For the United States, G. J. Barker-Benfield uses similar arguments in characterizing antimasturbation literature and medical views of women as part of a "Spermatic Economy." In this closed energy system, each expenditure of sperm depleted the amount of energy a man had for productive economic tasks and capital accumulation. Thus, a man who wished to achieve upward class mobility within the competitive marketplace would have to preserve his resources through sexual self-control as well as control of female sexuality. The economic logic of this interpretation has been challenged, since consumption was also crucial to the developing market economy, but the symbolic power of the spending-saving metaphor, whether in Victorian pornography or in antimasturbation literature, cannot be dismissed. [33]

A more convincing analysis of the relationship between class and sexual ideology appears in the work of Charles Rosenberg. Sexual repression, he explains, supported particular class aspirations within a bureaucratizing society "by helping to create a social discipline appropriate to a middle class of managers, professionals and small entrepreneurs."[34] In addition, Rosenberg suggests that in America, as in England, middle class men differentiated themselves from the lower classes, and especially from domestic servants, by adopting the value of continence. The implication here is that the working class had a different set of sexual values, though it is not yet clear whether and how these views came in conflict with those of the middle class.

A few historians have looked at generational conflicts to explain changing sexual attitudes and practices. In their analysis of premarital pregnancy rates, for example, Smith and Hindus argue that during the late eighteenth century young people gained autonomy from parental controls by engaging in premarital intercourse; since marriage usually followed pregnancy, premarital sex could often assure them their own choice of mates. They also suggest that when young men no longer inherited land or crafts, they adopted sexual restraints, not only because self-control instilled habits of thrift and patterns of deferred gratification, but also because it helped young men avoid the economic burden of families. At the same time, young women could use their sexual purity as a bargaining point in the marriage market.[35]

Other historians have employed a less functionalist analysis to explain constraints on young people's sexuality. According to R. P. Neuman, the nineteenth-century association of masturbation with insanity should be seen as an aspect of parental struggles for control over adolescents who desired personal autonomy. Both Carroll Smith-Rosenberg and Mary Ryan have explored the symbolic meaning of autonomous young men in Jacksonian America. Smith-Rosenberg concentrates on male moral reformers who viewed the pubescent male as a symbol of uncontrolled individuality and used masturbation as a code for both autonomy and homosexuality. The male reformers, she argues, projected their fears of social change and sexual pollution upon the "loose" young urban men who were beyond the control of patriarchal fathers. As Ryan's study of a New York community reveals, class, age, and gender could converge in moral crusades; female moral reformers targeted young male clerks and college students as the source of licentiousness and attempted to place community controls over their sexual autonomy.[36]

The bulk of political interpretation of sexuality concentrates on gender and attempts to determine whether female purity, or passionlessness, served the interests of men (particularly doctors) or of women themselves. The strongest argument for the view that men attempted to control female sexuality in their own interests appears in studies of male medical authorities. Barker-Benfield, for instance, argues that doctors expressed a symbolic fear of women as absorbers of male sperm and thus employed radical obstetrics and gynecology (including ovariotomy, clitorodectomy, and uterine cauterization) to control unruly women.[37] Short of imputing conspiratorial motives to doctors, some historians who read the conservative medical literature have been struck by the projection of physical infirmity onto the female body. Michel Foucault explains this "hysterization" of women as one of several mechanisms by which sexual discourse spread throughout the society, but Smith-Rosenberg and Sarah Stage find a more precise meaning in the prevalent identification of women with their reproductive organs. For one, such biological determinism kept women securely in the home at a time when increasing numbers sought to enter the public sphere. In addition, the projection of sexual pathology onto women may have freed men to assume positions of strength.[38]

Critics of this point of view, such as Regina Morantz, argue that doctors did not single out women for treatment of the reproductive organs. Men, too, suffered from neurasthenia, worried about masturbation and seminal emissions, and occasionally had their genitals cauterized.[39] Still, men visited doctors of their own sex, something few women could do, and these doctors treated men's genitals almost entirely for sexual complaints such as venereal disease, masturbation, and impotence. For the most part, doctors prescribed individual will or self-control to cure men, while they prescribed medical and surgical interventions for a wide range of female complaints, whether or not the complaints were sexual in nature.

The recent studies of utopian communities contribute to the interpretation that men attempted to institutionalize control over female sexuality. Kern in particular argues that men used sex to maintain patriarchal power in the Shaker, Oneida, and Mormon communities. He detects a central fear of women's sexual and maternal power in Noyes's system: men had the power to select sexual partners, prevent ejaculation, and control breeding; women remained the weaker vessels, permitted to have orgasms that drained their vital energies, while denied the power derived from autonomous sexuality and motherhood.[40] But Kern's sweeping criticism of all three communities for subordinating women fails to explain the appeal these groups had for female members. And his interpretation does not rest on personal testimony that either men or women experienced a hierarchy of gender in these utopian communities.

Other historians, although not disputing the dominance of males, argue that Victorian sexual ideas could serve women's self-interest and at times provide leverage in their dealings with men. Several variations on this theme occur, ranging from the suggestion that women caricatured their sexual roles in order to escape from them, as in the case of hysteria, to the proposition that women achieved autonomy by denying their sexual desires.[41] In between lies the bulk of interpretation—that women attempted to utilize a repressive ideology in order to gain personal meaning and political influence.

A number of feminist historians argue that women who accepted the ideal of passionlessness may have done so in order to achieve greater personal freedom. Nancy Cott explains that passionlessness served to elevate women closer to moral equality with men. Others have reasoned that the physical consequences of intercourse, including potential venereal infection and debilitation from repeated childbearing, could make "prudery" a useful tool for women to gain freedom from reproduction or from unsatisfactory sexual relationships. And, as Linda Gordon shows, feminists emphasized women's right to say no to sex as a means of achieving female control over reproduction.[42]

Both Daniel Scott Smith and Carl Degler assume that women did in fact achieve such control within the context of the nineteenth-century family. Smith terms this control "domestic feminism" and believes it led to the decline of white marital fertility rates and ultimately to women's increased power in society. But Smith's reasoning about female sexual control, based solely on quantitative evidence, is suspect; it fails to ask whether women or men determined frequency of intercourse and whether the control of fertility has any implications for female independence in the public sphere. Degler attempts to provide documentation on both of these points with extensive qualitative evidence, some of which seems to contradict his earlier argument that women enjoyed sexual passion, now proving that they sought to avoid it. In the end, however, he concludes that women did limit sex in marriage, not from an aversion to sexual expression but as a means of gaining autonomy.[43] Thus sexual ideology and reproductive strategy may have converged to serve women's personal interests.

Although it is not clear whether middle class women did in fact refrain from intercourse except for the purpose of reproduction, many supported social movements that attacked men's ability to have sexual intercourse without taking responsibility for its reproductive consequences. In their campaigns against the double standard, women resisted the separation of sexuality and reproduction because they perceived it as antithetical to their interests. Thus, female moral reform associations in Jacksonian America attacked male licentiousness, waged a war on "seducers," and called for female control over the nation's sexual mores.[44] In the late nineteenth century, women left the home in the name of domesticity, proselytizing for a single sexual standard through the social purity movement and the Women's Christian Temperance Union. Degler calls these efforts "organizing to control sexuality"—especially men's nonreproductive sexuality. Through them women increasingly came to demand political power, as organizations such as the W.C.T.U. supported woman suffrage in the name of "Home Protection" and as a means of defending the single sexual standard.[45]

Most feminist historians interpret temperance and social purity as efforts to overturn women's subordinate domestic status, arguing that sexual control served women's interests. Barbara Epstein shares these views, but her recent book includes a criticism of reformers' insistence on a single sexual standard. Epstein argues that even if domesticity and purity did enhance women's power, it did so at the cost of their adhering to a "rigid and antisexual moral code" that required a loss of sexual self-assertion.[46] What Epstein does not consider is the possibility that those who attacked men's sexual behavior did not necessarily remain asexual themselves, either in marriage or with friends. She overlooks, for instance, W.C.T.U. President Frances Willard's passionate relationships with other women. Nonetheless, Epstein offers an important revision of the dominant interpretation of social purity and her book represents a significant step toward the integration of political and sexual history.

Nineteenth-century women's political response to the double standard has also been criticized for its role in encouraging state intervention in sexual matters. In the 1880s, both male and female purity crusaders supported legislation to raise the age of consent; moreover, some of them tolerated the antilibertarian tactics of moralists like Anthony Comstock. Both Mary Ryan and Judith Walkowitz have recently drawn parallels between women engaged in moral reform and antiprostitution in the nineteenth century and the current New Right efforts to achieve state regulation of sexual expression. The historical evidence for this parallel seems to be stronger for Britain, where, as Walkowitz shows, social purity took a decidedly antilibertarian turn after the 1880s.[47] Whether this holds for the United States has yet to be argued convincingly, but the question will undoubtedly influence future research on the politics of sexuality.

Conclusion

Recent investigations of sexuality in nineteenth-century America raise as many new questions about sexual behavior, ideology, and politics as they begin to answer. Because historians have focused largely on women's sexual behavior and on middle class sexual ideas, we have an incomplete and possibly distorted vision of how most people acted or thought. Because the analysis of sexual politics has been, for the most part, an implicit one, historians have not yet fully explored its possibilities. We need to know more about men, about the working class, and about the sexual underworld in nineteenth-century American cities; we need to explore the meaning of medical problems, such as venereal disease, for sexual thought; and we need to look more closely at the sexual experiences of those who articulated a politics of sexuality in the late-nineteenth century. Only after much imaginative research has uncovered a fuller historical record will it be wise to generalize about the direction and causes of change in nineteenth-century sexual history.

Nonetheless, the studies reviewed in this essay do point toward a hypothesis that bears further exploration. Over the course of the nineteenth century, as white American women bore fewer and fewer children, the reproductive function of sexuality became less central. Although some middle class Victorians may have heeded advice to limit sexual intercourse, others experienced sexuality as a nonprocreative act. The evidence of contraceptive use, abortion, and homosexuality, of a tension over eroticism within American sexual ideology, and of the political defense of a sexuality limited to reproduction all suggest that Americans struggled to come to terms with the potential of an erotic, nonprocreative sexuality. Thus, although the ideological support for the separation of sexuality and reproduction did not appear until the twentieth century, the process itself began much earlier.[48] The nineteenth-century conflict over nonreproductive sexuality provides an important context for understanding both the political campaigns to regulate sexuality at the end of the century and the preoccupation of modern sexual ideology with the erotic.

Most men and women living in nineteenth-century America were not conscious of the growing importance of nonreproductive sexuality, while many of those who were resisted the separation of reproduction and sexuality. White, middle class women, including feminists, may have feared that they would lose what limited social influence they had as mothers or that men would enjoy the benefits of erotic sexuality while women continued to take the reproductive risks. Some middle class men associated the erotic with the lower classes and sought to differentiate themselves by practicing sexual restraint. On the other hand, some utopians and radicals sought ways to incorporate the erotic within the sexual lives of both women and men; others attempted to control reproduction. Meanwhile, innumerable women and men—including couples who used contraception and abortion, some blacks and immigrants, prostitutes and their clients, homosexuals, and those who masturbated or had adulterous sexual relationships—unknowingly participated through their actions in the creation of new categories of sexuality.

By the 1880s, defenders of an older sexual order called for "reform"— criminalization of abortion, suppression of birth control information and of prostitution, condemnation of adultery, and, in general, the subordination of selfish (erotic) desires to a particular vision of the social good. Their voices still echo in contemporary America.[49] A thorough understanding of the historical circumstances that motivated these demands may contribute not only to a more accurate account of nineteenth-century society, but also to a more effective response to the sexual politics of our own time.

I am grateful to Peggy Pascoe for bibliographic assistance in the preparation of this essay, and to the following people for their helpful comments on earlier drafts: John D'Emilio, Susan Johnson, Susan Krieger, Sue Lynn, Elaine Tyler May, Diane Middlebrook, Peggy Pascoe, Elizabeth Pleck, Paul Robinson, Barbara Rosenblum, and Mary Ryan.

1. Michel Foucault, *The History of Sexuality: An Introduction*, vol. 1 (New York: Random House, Pantheon Books, 1978). For earlier surveys of historical literature on sexuality in America, see John C. Burnham, "American Historians and the Subject of Sex," *Societas* 2 (August 1972): 307–16; Ronald G. Walters, "Sexual Matters as Historical Problems: A Framework of Analysis," *Societas* 6 (Summer 1976): 157–75. On the interest in sexual history during the 1970s, see Stephen Nissenbaum, *Sex, Diet, and Debility in Jacksonian America: Sylvester Graham and Health Reform* (Westport, Conn.: Greenwood Press, 1980), p. xii. On the current interest in the politics of sexuality, see Ellen Ross and Rayna Rapp, "Sex and Society: A Research Note from Social History and Anthropology," *Comparative Studies in Society and History* 23 (January 1981): 72; "Sexuality in History," a special issue of the *Radical History Review* 20 (Spring-Summer 1979). On England, see Jeffrey Weeks, *Sex, Politics, and Society: The Regulation of Sexuality Since 1800* (London: Longman, 1981).

2. Carl N. Degler, "What Ought to Be and What Was: Women's Sexuality in the Nineteenth Century," *American Historical Review* 79 (December 1974): 1467–90.

3. Daniel Scott Smith, "Family Limitation, Sexual Control, and Domestic Feminism in Victorian America," in *Clio's Consciousness Raised*, eds., Mary S. Hartman and Lois Banner (New York: Harper and Row, 1974), p. 123.

4. Daniel Scott Smith and Michael S. Hindus, "Premarital Pregnancy in America, 1640–1971: An Overview and Interpretation," *Journal of Interdisciplinary History* 5 (Spring 1975): 537–70.

5. Summaries of historical interpretations of the decline in fertility rates appear in Carl N. Degler, *At Odds: Women and the Family in America from the Revolution to the Present* (New York: Oxford University Press, 1980), pp. 181–89; Michael B. Katz and Mark J. Stern, "Fertility, Class, and Industrial Capitalism: Erie County, New York, 1855–1915," *American Quarterly* 33 (Spring 1981): 63–70.

6. Smith, "Domestic Feminism"; Degler, *At Odds*, chs. 8–10; James C. Mohr, *Abortion in America: The Origins and Evolution of National Policy, 1800–1900* (New York: Oxford University Press, 1978), chs. 3–4; Linda Gordon, *Woman's Body, Woman's Right: A Social History of Birth Control in America* (New York: Grossman, 1976), chs. 2–3. Additional evidence of the use of abortion and contraception appears in John S. Haller, Jr. and Robin M. Haller, *The Physician and Sexuality in Victorian America* (Urbana: University of Illinois Press, 1974), esp. pp. 113–24; Michael A. LaSorte, "Nineteenth-Century Family Planning Practices," *Journal of Psychohistory* 4 (Fall 1976): 163–84. The increased use of birth control by English middle class couples is argued in Joseph A. Banks and Olive Banks, *Feminism and Family Planning in Victorian England* (New York: Schocken Books, 1964); Patricia Branca, *Silent Sisterhood: Middle-Class Women in the Victorian Home* (London: Croom and Helm, 1975); F. Barry Smith, "Sexuality in Britain, 1800–1900: Some Suggested Revisions," in *A Widening Sphere: Changing Roles of Victorian Women*, ed., Martha Vicinus (Bloomington: Indiana University Press, 1977), pp. 182–98.

7. According to Wilson Yates, there was a "continual flow of information from the medical profession to the public" between 1831 and 1900; even after 1873, medical journals provided a platform for discussing contraception. See Wilson Yates, "Birth Control Literature and the Medical Profession in Nineteenth-Century America," *Journal of the History of Medicine and Allied Sciences* 31 (January 1976): 44.

8. Smith and Hindus, "Premarital Pregnancy."

9. On immigrant rates, see Peter R. Shergold, "The Walker Thesis Revisited: Immigration and White American Fertility, 1800–1860," *Australian Economic History Review* 14 (September 1974): 168–89; Tamara K. Hareven and Maris A. Vinovskis, "Marital Fertility, Ethnicity, and Occupation in Urban Families: An Analysis of South Boston and the South End in 1880," *Journal of Social History* 8 (Spring 1975): 69–93; Degler, *At Odds*, pp. 220–22; Richard H. Steckel, "Antebellum Southern White Fertility: A Demographic and Economic Analysis," *Journal of Economic History* 40 (June 1980): 350; Michael R. Haines, "Fertility and Marriage in a Nineteenth-Century Industrial City: Philadelphia, 1850–1880," *Journal of Economic History* 40 (March 1980): 151–58. Katz and Stern, "Fertility," argue that class, rather than ethnicity, explains the differential rates in the New York county they studied. For differential rates of childbearing by black women, see Wilson H. Grabill, Clyde V. Kiser, and Pascal K. Whelpton, "A Long View," in *The American Family in Social-Historical Perspective,* ed. Michael Gordon (New York: St. Martins Press, 1973), pp. 389–91.

10. Robert Fogel and Stanley Engerman argue in *Time on the Cross: The Economics of American Negro Slavery* (Boston: Little, Brown, 1974) that slaves' sexual mores approximated those of white, middle class Victorians. Their critics on this point include Herbert G. Gutman, *Slavery and the Numbers Game: A Critique of Time on the Cross* (Urbana: University of Illinois Press, 1975), pp. 88–164; Herbert Gutman and Richard Sutch, "Victorians All? The Sexual Mores and Conduct of Slaves and Their Masters," in *Reckoning With Slavery: A Critical Study of the Quantitative History of American Negro Slavery,* eds. Paul A. David, Herbert G. Gutman, Richard Sutch, Peter Temin and Gavin Wright (New York: Oxford University Press, 1976), pp. 134–62; Eugene D. Genovese, *Roll, Jordan, Roll: The World the Slaves Made* (New York: Random House, Pantheon Books, 1974). Cheryll Cody's study of one plantation, "A Note on Changing Patterns of Slave Fertility in the South Carolina Rice District, 1735–1865," *Southern Studies* 16 (Winter 1977): 457–63, supports Fogel and Engerman's interpretation.

11. Genovese, *Roll, Jordan, Roll,* pp. 459–72; Gutman and Sutch, "Victorians All?," esp. pp. 136, 142. The possibilities for studying Native American sexuality are suggested in Martin B. Duberman, Fred Eggan, and Richard Clemmer, "Documents in Hopi Indian Sexuality: Imperialism, Culture, and Resistance," *Radical History Review* 20 (Spring-Summer 1979): 99–130.

12. Lucie Cheng Hirata, "Free, Indentured, and Enslaved: Chinese Prostitution in Nineteenth-Century America," *Signs* 5 (Autumn 1979): 3–29; Marion S. Goldman, *Gold Diggers and Silver Miners: Prostitution and Social Life on the Comstock Lode* (Ann Arbor: University of Michigan Press, 1981); George M. Blackburn and Sherman L. Ricards, "The Prostitutes and Gamblers of Virginia City, Nevada: 1870," *Pacific Historical Review* 48 (May 1979): 239–58; Carol Leonard and Isidor Wallimann, "Prostitution and the Changing Morality in the Frontier Cattle Towns of Kansas," *Kansas History* 2 (Spring 1979): 34–53. For a discussion of the treatment of prostitutes, see Estelle B. Freedman, *Their Sisters' Keepers: Women's Prison Reform in America, 1830–1930* (Ann Arbor: University of Michigan Press, 1981), chs. 1–2. On prostitution in England, see Judith R. Walkowitz, *Prostitution and Victorian Society: Women, Class, and the State* (New York: Cambridge University Press, 1980). For the Progressive era in the United States, see Mark Connelly, *The Response to Prostitution in the Progressive Era* (Chapel Hill: University of North Carolina Press, 1980); Ruth Rosen, *The Lost Sisterhood: Prostitution in America, 1900–1918* (Baltimore: Johns Hopkins University Press, 1982).

13. Gordon, *Woman's Body,* pp. 105–06; Degler, "What Ought to Be"; Degler, *At Odds*, ch. 11; Carroll Smith-Rosenberg, "A Richer and a Gentler Sex," paper presented at the Berkshire Conference on the History of Women, Bryn Mawr, Pennsylvania, June 1976.

14. William G. Shade, "'A Mental Passion': Female Sexuality in Victorian America," *International Journal of Women's Studies* 1 (January-February 1978): 15. On doctors' concerns about female masturbation, see James Reed, *From Private Vice to Public Virtue: The Birth Control Movement and American Society Since 1830* (New York: Basic Books, 1978), pp. 159–60; Hal D. Sears, *The Sex Radicals: Free Love in High Victorian America* (Lawrence: Regents Press of Kansas, 1977), pp. 188–89; Carroll Smith-Rosenberg, "Puberty to Menopause: The Cycle of Femininity in Nineteenth-Century America," in *Clio's Consciousness Raised,* eds. Hartman and Banner, pp. 23–37.

15. Shade, "Mental Passion," pp. 16–17; Vern L. Bullough and Martha Voght, "Homosexuality and Its Confusion with the Secret Sin in Pre-Freudian America," *Journal of the History of Medicine and Allied Sciences* 28 (April 1973): 150; Lillian Faderman, *Surpassing the Love of Men: Romantic Friendship and Love Between Women from the Renaissance to the Present* (New York: William Morrow, 1981), p. 291; Nancy Sahli, "Smashing: Women's Relationships Before the Fall," *Chrysalis* 8 (Summer 1979): 17–28.

16. Carroll Smith-Rosenberg, "The Female World of Love and Ritual: Relations Between Women in Nineteenth-Century America," *Signs* 1 (Autumn 1975): 1–29; Faderman, *Surpassing the Love of Men*, pp. 147–253. On the question of whether women's loving friendships were sexual, see Blanche Wiesen Cook, "Female Support Networks and Political Activism: Lillian Wald, Crystal Eastman, Emma Goldman," in *A Heritage of Her Own*, eds. Nancy F. Cott and Elizabeth H. Pleck (New York: Simon and Schuster, Touchstone, 1979), pp. 412–44; and "The Historical Denial of Lesbianism," *Radical History Review* 20 (Spring-Summer 1979): 60–65; Judith Schwarz, " 'Yellow Clover': Katharine Lee Bates and Katharine Coman," *Frontiers* 4 (Spring 1979): 59–67; Leila J. Rupp, " 'Imagine My Surprise': Women's Relationships in Historical Perspective," *Frontiers* 5 (Fall 1980): 61–70. On cross-dressing women who may have been lesbians, see Jonathan Katz, *Gay American History: Lesbians and Gay Men in the U.S.A.* (New York: Thomas Y. Crowell, 1976), pp. 209–79.

17. Katz, *Gay American History* (a second collection of documents is forthcoming from Harper and Row); Jeffrey Weeks, *Coming Out: Homosexual Politics in Britain from the Nineteenth Century to the Present* (London: Quartet Books, 1977), chs. 1–3; Kenneth Plummer, *The Making of the Modern Homosexual* (London: Hutchinson, 1981). On the emergence of homosexual subcultures in twentieth-century America, see John D'Emilio, "Gay Politics, Gay Community: San Francisco's Experience," *Socialist Review* 55 (January-February 1981): 77–104; and *Sexual Politics, Sexual Communities: The Making of a Homosexual Minority in the U.S., 1940–1970* (Chicago: University of Chicago Press, forthcoming).

18. Several recent studies suggest the possible uses of divorce records as evidence of adultery, sexual fantasies, and sexual complaints: Marion Goldman, "Sexual Commerce on the Comstock Lode," *Nevada Historical Society Quarterly* 21 (Summer 1978): 105; Robert L. Griswold, "Apart But Not Adrift: Wives, Divorce, and Independence in California, 1850–1890," *Pacific Historical Review* 49 (May 1980): 279–80; Elaine Tyler May, *Great Expectations: Marriage and Divorce in Post-Victorian America* (Chicago: University of Chicago Press, 1980), ch. 6.

19. The printed advice literature that stressed these themes, especially after 1830, is analyzed by Barbara Welter, "The Cult of True Womanhood, 1820–1860," *American Quarterly* 18 (Summer 1966): 150–74; Michael Gordon, "From an Unfortunate Necessity to a Cult of Mutual Orgasm: Sex in American Marital Education Literature, 1830–1940," in *Studies in the Sociology of Sex*, ed. James M. Henslin (New York: Appleton-Century-Crofts, 1971), pp. 53–77; Ronald G. Walters, *Primers for Prudery: Sexual Advice to Victorian America* (Englewood Cliffs, N.J.: Prentice Hall, 1974); Haller and Haller, *Physician and Sexuality;* Degler, "What Ought to Be"; Nissenbaum, *Sex, Diet, and Debility.*

20. On inconsistent and changing ideals, see Charles E. Rosenberg, "Sexuality, Class and Role in Nineteenth-Century America," *American Quarterly* 35 (May 1973): 131–53; R. P. Neuman, "Masturbation, Madness, and the Modern Concepts of Childhood and Adolescence," *Journal of Social History* 8 (Spring 1975): 1–27.

21. Nissenbaum, *Sex, Diet, and Debility,* esp. ch. 7.

22. William Leach, *True Love and Perfect Union: The Feminist Reform of Sex and Society* (New York: Basic Books, 1980), p. 95.

23. Nancy F. Cott, "Passionlessness: An Interpretation of Victorian Sexual Ideology, 1790–1850," *Signs* 4 (1978): 219–36; Haller and Haller, *Physician and Sexuality,* pp. 97–98; Degler, "What Ought to Be," and *At Odds,* ch. 11.

24. On the taboo against nonprocreative sex, see Louis J. Kern, *An Ordered Love: Sex Roles and Sexuality in Victorian Utopias* (Chapel Hill: University of North Carolina Press, 1981), pp. 32–33; Walters, *Primers for Prudery,* p. 44; Bullough and Voght, "Homosexuality," esp. p. 154; Gordon, *Woman's Body,* ch. 5; Peter L. Tyor, " 'Denied the Power to Choose the

Good': Sexuality and Mental Defect in American Medical Practice, 1850–1920," *Journal of Social History* 10 (June 1977): 473–75. New ideas about masturbation are discussed by Bullough and Voght, "Homosexuality"; Nissenbaum, *Sex, Diet, and Debility,* esp. pp. 30, 110; Robert H. MacDonald, "The Frightful Consequences of Onanism: Notes on the History of a Delusion," *Journal of the History of Ideas* 28 (July–September 1967): 423–31.

25. Lawrence Foster, *Religion and Sexuality: Three American Communal Experiments of the Nineteenth Century* (New York: Oxford University Press, 1981); Kern, *Ordered Love.*

26. Kern, *Ordered Love,* esp. pp. 41–46, 110, 146, 284; Foster, *Religion and Sexuality,* esp. pp. 47, 94, 227. For an interpretation of changing Mormon sexual ideas, see Klaus J. Hansen, "Mormon Sexuality and American Culture," *Dialogue* 10 (Autumn 1976): 45–56.

27. Kern, *Ordered Love,* esp. pp. 21–26, 78–79, 93–98, 133, 156, 288; Foster, *Religion and Sexuality,* esp. pp. 13, 47, 92, 98, 227, 235–37; Hansen, "Mormon Sexuality."

28. David Brion Davis, *Homicide in American Fiction, 1798–1860: A Study in Social Values* (Ithaca, N.Y.: Cornell University Press, 1957), pp. 153–56, 205; Ronald G. Walters, "The Erotic South: Civilization and Sexuality in American Abolitionism," *American Quarterly* 25 (May 1973): 180, 189, 198. On abolitionist sexual thought, see also Lewis Perry, " 'Progress, Not Pleasure, Is Our Aim': The Sexual Advice of an Antebellum Radical," *Journal of Social History* 12 (Spring 1979): 354–66.

29. Walters, "Erotic South," pp. 198–201; Kern, *Ordered Love,* pp. 299–300. Similarly, Foucault (*History of Sexuality,* pp. 104, 139–46) identifies population control as one means by which sexuality serves to regulate both the individual body and the social body. These analyses, however, do not distinguish between the relationship of men and that of women to reproduction, a crucial distinction for most nineteenth-century sexual theorists and for contemporary feminists.

30. Sears, *Sex Radicals,* esp. pp. 66, 120, 132, 175–79, 210, 234; Gordon, *Woman's Body,* ch. 5.

31. On the sexual underground and class-defined sexuality in England, see Steven Marcus, *The Other Victorians: A Study of Sexuality and Pornography in Mid-Nineteenth Century England* (New York: Basic Books, 1966); Ronald Pearsall, *The Worm in the Bud: The World of Victorian Sexuality* (Toronto: Macmillan, 1969); Fraser Harrison, *The Dark Angel: Aspects of Victorian Sexuality* (London: Sheldon Press, 1977); Leonore Davidoff, "Class and Gender in Victorian England: The Diaries of Arthur J. Munby and Hannah Cullwick," *Feminist Studies* 5 (Spring 1979): 87–141; Weeks, *Sex, Politics, and Society,* ch. 4.

32. Peter T. Cominos, "Late Victorian Sexual Respectability and the Social System," *International Review of Social History* (2 parts), 8 (1963): 18–48 and 216–50. Davidoff, "Class and Gender," explores the sexual relationships between upper class men and working class women, particularly servants.

33. Ben Barker-Benfield, "The Spermatic Economy: A Nineteenth-Century View of Sexuality," in *The American Family in Social-Historical Perspective,* ed. Michael Gordon (New York: St. Martins Press, 1973), pp. 336–72. Degler, *At Odds,* pp. 292–93, summarizes the criticisms of the economic logic. On pornography, see Marcus, *Other Victorians.*

34. Rosenberg, "Sexuality, Class, and Role," p. 132.

35. Smith and Hindus, "Premarital Pregnancy."

36. Neuman, "Masturbation"; Carroll Smith-Rosenberg, "Sex as Symbol in Victorian Purity: An Ethnohistorical Analysis of Jacksonian America," *American Journal of Sociology* 84 (Supplement 1978): S212–S247; Mary P. Ryan, "The Power of Women's Networks: A Case Study of Female Moral Reform in Antebellum America," *Feminist Studies* 5 (Spring 1979): 66–86.

37. G. J. Barker-Benfield, *The Horrors of the Half-Known Life: Male Attitudes Toward Women and Sexuality in Nineteenth-Century America* (New York: Harper and Row, 1976), part 2; Haller and Haller, *Physician and Sexuality,* pp. 38–40; Ann Douglas Wood, " 'The Fashionable Diseases': Women's Complaints and Their Treatment in Nineteenth-Century America," in *Clio's Consciousness Raised,* eds. Hartman and Banner, pp. 1–22.

38. Foucault, *History of Sexuality,* pp. 104, 146; Carroll Smith-Rosenberg, "Puberty to Menopause: The Cycle of Femininity in Nineteenth-Century America," in *Clio's Consciousness*

Raised, eds. Hartman and Banner, pp. 23–37; and "The Hysterical Woman: Sex Roles and Role Conflict in Nineteenth Century America," *Social Research* 29 (Winter 1972): 652–78; with Charles Rosenberg, "The Female Animal: Medical and Biological Views of Woman and Her Role in Nineteenth-Century America," *Journal of American History* 20 (September 1973): 332–56; Wood, "Fashionable Diseases"; Sarah Stage, *Female Complaints: Lydia Pinkham and the Business of Women's Medicine* (New York: W. W. Norton, 1979), pp. 74–75.

39. Regina Morantz, "The Lady and Her Physician," in *Clio's Consciousness Raised*, eds. Hartman and Banner, pp. 38–53. A similar argument is made by Gail Pat Parsons, "Equal Treatment for All: American Medical Remedies for Male Sexual Problems: 1850–1900," *Journal of the History of Medicine* 32 (January 1977): 55–71.

40. Kern, *Ordered Love*, pp. 180–84, 203, 224–89.

41. The former interpretation appears in Smith-Rosenberg, "Hysterical Woman," and in Haller and Haller, *Physician and Sexuality*; the latter appears in Degler, *At Odds*, p. 258, and Leach, *True Love*, pp. 36–37.

42. Cott, "Passionlessness"; Gordon, *Woman's Body*, ch. 5; Haller and Haller, *Physician and Sexuality*, pp. xii, 102.

43. Smith, "Domestic Feminism"; Degler, *At Odds*, pp. 271, 273.

44. Carroll Smith-Rosenberg, "Beauty, the Beast, and the Militant Woman: A Case Study in Sex Roles and Social Stress in Jacksonian America," *American Quarterly* 23 (1971): 562–84; Ryan, "Power of Women's Networks."

45. David J. Pivar, *Purity Crusade: Sexual Morality and Social Control, 1868–1900* (Westport, Conn.: Greenwood Press, 1973); Ruth Bordin, *Women and Temperance: The Quest for Power and Liberty, 1873–1900* (Philadelphia: Temple University Press, 1981); Barbara Epstein, *The Politics of Domesticity: Women, Evangelism and Temperance in Nineteenth-Century America* (Middletown, Conn.: Wesleyan University Press, 1981); Degler, *At Odds*, ch. 12.

46. Epstein, *Politics of Domesticity*, p. 85.

47. Walkowitz, *Prostitution*, esp. pp. 236–49; and "The Politics of Prostitution," *Signs* 6 (Autumn 1980): 123–35; Ryan, "Power of Women's Networks." In the United States, at least some feminists opposed Comstock, as did Free Love advocates (Sears, *Sex Radicals*, p. 115).

48. On twentieth-century ideas, see, e.g., David M. Kennedy, *Birth Control in America: The Career of Margaret Sanger* (New Haven: Yale University Press, 1970); Nathan Hale, *Freud and the Americans: The Beginnings of Psychoanalysis in the United States, 1876–1917* (New York: Oxford University Press, 1971); Gordon, "Marital Education Literature"; John C. Burnham, "The Progressive Era Revolution in American Attitudes Towards Sex," *Journal of American History* 59 (March 1973): 888–908; Paul Robinson, *The Modernization of Sex* (New York: Harper and Row, 1976); Gordon, *Woman's Body*; Howard I. Kushner, "Nineteenth-Century Sexuality and the 'Sexual Revolution' of the Progressive Era," *Canadian Review of American Studies* 9 (1978): 34–49; Reed, *From Private Vice to Public Virtue*; Christina Simmons, "Companionate Marriage and the Lesbian Threat," *Frontiers* 4 (Fall 1979): 54–59.

49. On the politics of sexuality in the contemporary New Right, see Rosalind Petchesky, "Antiabortion, Antifeminism, and the Rise of the New Right," *Feminist Studies* 7 (Summer 1981): 206–46.

EXPANDING THE PAST: RECENT SCHOLARSHIP ON WOMEN IN POLITICS AND WORK

Elaine Tyler May

During the last two decades, women's history has emerged as a flourishing field. Among all the "new histories," it holds center stage where theoretical debates and methodological innovations are taking place. One reason for the current flurry of intellectual ferment in the field is that women's history is in a critical stage of transition. The first task was to uncover women's buried past and place the female experience on the map of history. The next task is to redraw the map. Now that women are beginning to surface in the historical literature, it is necessary to correct the distortions and rethink several of the guiding principles of historical inquiry. Although women's history is still a relatively new field, it has already begun to move beyond the first task and into the next. At this point, the major challenge is not simply to point out what women have done in the past, but what ultimate difference it makes in our total understanding of the historical experience. This requires altering our conceptual framework and expanding our basic definitions.[1]

Two of the areas where women's history is expanding the boundaries of scholarship are politics and work. Historians have generally assumed that these realms of activity are part of public life, or the "male" sphere. Consequently, the role of women in these endeavors has often been slighted or ignored. Recent scholarship has not only documented women's participation, it has challenged the presumed division between public and private life.[2] In the process, it has pointed toward new definitions of politics and work. From a body of literature which is by now quite large and fertile, I have selected several studies for the purpose of this review which move us toward an expanded view of work and politics in the context of nineteenth- and twentieth-century United States history.

Women and Politics

Politics involves the use of power in civil society. Natalie Davis has noted that "power can lodge in dangerous nooks and crannies. . . . [I]t needs to be examined in its full complexity."[3] Women were using power in various "nooks and crannies" long before they had the vote. As early as the Revolution, they utilized their power within society to affect the political process.

Studies by Linda Kerber and Mary Beth Norton expand the stage of Revolutionary activism from the battlefields and meeting halls to the sidelines, homes, and streets, where extensive female involvement took place. Kerber points out that routine tasks such as purchasing were politicized. Wearing homespun or boycotting tea were not only symbolic political acts, they spurred the domestic economy at the expense of the British. Women were also active petitioners during the Revolutionary years; they supplied the army with clothing and blankets, and policed local merchants suspected of hoarding scarce commodities. Such actions were clearly political, and the women were aware of the importance of their efforts. As Rachel Wells boasted, "I have Don as much to Carrey on the warr as maney that Sett Now at the healm of government." [4]

Yet after the war, as state governments began to codify laws, women were excluded from the body politic. In fact, some rights that they had prior to the Revolution were eroded in its wake. It became more difficult, for example, for wives to control their own property during the first half-century of the Republic. And although the franchise expanded for men and primogeniture declined, coverture, which denied wives legal identity because they were "covered" by their husbands, was perpetuated.

In an effort to understand this exclusion, Kerber analyzed the ideological assumptions that accompanied the founding of the nation. Women were not simply ignored; they were kept in a subordinate position. Measures that would have given them more personal autonomy, such as property rights or easy divorce, were resisted. Kerber's work has important implications, for it suggests that according to the founders of the nation, the republican polity could withstand decentralized authority and a broadening of the base of citizenship only if the family held firm as a bastion of patriarchal authority. By reinforcing traditional gender roles, and giving "Republican Mothers" the charge of training responsible citizens, the Founding Fathers hoped to prevent rampant egalitarianism from plunging the Republic into social chaos. [5]

After the Revolution, middle class white women began to carve an identity out of their domestic sphere. Republican Motherhood gave them a quasi-political role based in the family, which promised influence but denied direct access to political power. It also provided them with the task of moral guardianship, which could be taken outside the home and into the broader society. The concept of domesticity nourished a rich public life for women in voluntary associations, churches, and reform crusades. As guardians of public morals, many entered civic life in an effort to make the entire society "homelike." [6] Gradually, women became aware of their "bonds": those that oppressed as well as united them. In the early nineteenth century, a full-blown feminist movement did not emerge, but as Nancy Cott argues, consciousness of their unique place in society was a necessary precondition for political activism.[7] What is most important about early movements such as temperance, evangelism, and abolitionism is that the participating women did not reject the ideology of domesticity when they moved into the public arena; they embraced it. When they finally began to challenge inequalities based on sex, most nineteenth-century feminists who articulated the women's rights position claimed that their special status entitled them to full participation in the affairs of the nation.

How, then, did women begin to mobilize on their own behalf when they were excluded from the political process and still tied to the ideology of domesticity? Nineteenth-century America, with a weak central government and a proliferation of voluntary associations of all kinds, provided an environment conducive to women's organizing on behalf of a wide variety of causes and issues. Sara Evans and Harry Boyte have suggested that such "free social spaces," or "incubators for democratic social movements" are necessary for political insurgency to develop.[8] During the first half of the nineteenth century, the abolition movement, as well as churches, charities, and reform crusades, provided the necessary social spaces for middle class women who were eager to expand their roles beyond the home. Blanche Glassman Hersch's study of female abolitionists, Barbara Berg's examination of women's voluntary associations, and Barbara Leslie Epstein's work on evangelical reform and temperance document the way in which women politicized the ideology of domesticity to further their own interests.[9]

The antislavery crusade is a case in point. Many of the women who became active in abolitionism argued that the institution of slavery was antithetical to the values of domesticity: it tore families apart and trampled female virtue. But in the process of organizing on behalf of slaves, they became aware of their own inferior status. Their subordination became even more apparent as female abolitionists faced hostility, harassment, and ostracism when they attempted to speak in public, thereby violating one of the implicit codes of female conduct. But it was more than recognition of their subordinate status that gave rise to the women's rights movement. It was the fact that in the antislavery crusade, they gained essential organizing skills along with the recognition of their strengths and capabilities. If the ideology of domesticity provided the initial justification for their involvement in the public arena, the abolition movement provided the free social space necessary for women to mobilize on their own behalf.[10]

For those who participated in these movements, moving into public endeavors did not involve relinquishing the home as a female preserve. Even the women's rights movement after 1848, which challenged the notion of separate spheres, was divided on the issue of female status. While some feminists called for basic equality with men, others claimed that women were morally superior to men and therefore deserving of special status. Many of the most vocal leaders of the movement advocated women's entry into the public arena on the grounds that their special female domestic qualities would bring a positive influence into politics. According to several accounts of the suffrage movement, it was the moral superiority argument that was later taken up by conservative elements within the Progressive movement, which eventually brought women the vote but little else in the way of meaningful advance.[11] There is some truth to this view. But as Ellen DuBois has argued, at the time when the women's rights movement first emerged in the antebellum period, feminists saw the vote as the major means for achieving equality. Suffrage would advance women's status, and at the same time allow them to bring a fundamentally different perspective into politics. Yet while suffragists challenged the male monopoly in the public arena, they still maintained that the private sphere had a distinct female character.[12] Nineteenth-century feminism rested in large measure on the assumption that women should enter the political world without losing their unique claim to domesticity.

By the late nineteenth century, this domestic ideology provided the foundation for women's involvement in a wide variety of activities, ranging from temperance to settlement work. Although temperance has generally been viewed as a conservative issue directed against immigrants and their places of public mingling (and certainly this was part of it), recent studies by Ruth Bordin and Barbara Leslie Epstein have uncovered a strong feminist undercurrent within temperance organizations. In addition to providing a means of protection against drunk and abusive men, temperance was also in large part an effort on the part of many women to assert themselves politically. It mobilized thousands on the grass roots level and propelled them into numerous other political movements, from socialism to suffrage.[13]

The new scholarship on politics in the nineteenth century points to a number of suggestive interpretations. It overturns earlier views of the Victorian era that portrayed women as victimized by the ideology of domesticity, confining them to the home and turning them into weak and frail creatures. While it is certainly true that rigid role prescriptions did exist, it is also clear that women politicized domesticity for their own purposes. The question of overall strategy, however, remains somewhat oblique. Estelle Freedman argues that women were most effective when they built separate institutions, while William Leach suggests that the main thrust of nineteenth-century feminism was to forge a compatible relationship with men through egalitarian marriage. Carl Degler claims that the family has consistently been "at odds" with the women's movement, while Daniel Scott Smith found the home providing an important arena for "domestic feminism" where women gained control over reproduction.[14] These controversial issues still beg for a resolution. Yet at the very least, all studies provide a common denominator: "women's sphere" gave women power and leverage, which they were often able to use in the public as well as the private realm.

Here we have one of the most important insights yielded by scholarship on women in politics. It indicates the complex ways in which public and private life interact, and demonstrates the fact that political activity can take a wide variety of forms. Many women certainly made use of their "domestic" role in their efforts to achieve social change. Yet for all it has yielded, this body of scholarship leaves a critical issue unresolved: not all women, nor all men, adhered to the same sex-role ideology. White middle-class feminists held certain assumptions that ethnic and working class women did not necessarily share. Aside from a few notable moments when cross-class alliances were successful, the "lady" and the "mill girl" rarely came together in the nineteenth-century women's movement.[15] It was one thing for middle class women to mobilize *on behalf of* their less fortunate sisters, as they did in prison reform, antiprostitution crusades, charity organizations, and abolitionism.[16] But it was another thing to mobilize *with* them.

Mari Jo Buhle's recent study of the Socialist movement explores the problem of uniting women across class and ethnic lines. In the nineteenth-century Socialist movement, immigrant women were class conscious but hostile to feminism. They hoped socialism would free female wage earners to return to hearth and home, whereas native-born middle class feminists called for women's right to labor as an important part of the Socialist program. The two groups never came together in an effective coalition, even after the formation of the Socialist party in the early twentieth century.[17] Other efforts to forge cross-class alliances in the early twentieth century, such as the Women's Trade Union League, also ultimately failed.[18] Buhle's study provides an outstanding example of the way in which women's politics must be viewed in a broad context. Much more research will need to be done before we will understand the complex way in which gender interacts with other determinants such as race and class to form political coalitions and power bases.[19]

So far, we know quite a bit more about the impact of gender on politics in the nineteenth century than in the twentieth century. Part of this has to do with the fact that it is much easier to identify women's politics before they gained access to the political process through the vote. The twentieth century poses much more difficult problems because women seem to blend into the political scene. In addition, the male and female spheres began to overlap as more women entered the paid labor force, and the ideology of domesticity based on female virtue gave way in the face of the "moral revolution." As the

Victorian culture which provided the context for nineteenth-century activism waned, the women's movement as a visible political force declined. Most studies see organized feminism dying in 1920 when the vote was achieved.[20]

Twentieth-century feminism poses a major challenge for historians of women. As yet there is no clear consensus on what the term "feminism" actually means. Does it apply only to organized movements for equal rights, or can it be used to refer to any individual woman's efforts to gain equality or personal advancement? The literature is divided on this point. The twentieth century presents particular difficulties because efforts on the part of women to create and take advantage of new opportunities did not necessarily correspond to organized political activities. Joyce Antler's research on Lucy Sprague Mitchell—a woman who strove for a fulfilling career as well as equality in marriage—suggests that the struggle for sexual equality, while not obvious in the public realm, may have been alive and well in women's individual lives.[21] Yet we do not know how widespread this consciousness was, or if it was connected to larger political goals.[22]

Women's rights organizations did not entirely disappear; but they seemed to flounder on strategy. After the achievement of the vote, the National American Woman Suffrage Association transformed itself into the League of Women Voters, a nonpartisan and essentially nonfeminist "good government" group. During the 1920s, the National Women's Party was the only national group that called itself a feminist organization. Controversy surrounding such issues as protective legislation and the Equal Rights Amendment prevented consensus among women's organizations.[23] Meanwhile, many women continued to contribute to local political movements, and several rose to national prominence in the New Deal, where they helped shape social welfare legislation.[24] Yet aside from a few exceptions, feminism was not a major issue for most female organizations, or for the women directly involved in politics.

The question still remains, why did the momentum for women's rights collapse after the vote was achieved? Why did feminism as a widespread sentiment lay dormant for over forty years? This is an issue that begs for more historical attention, for it was not until the 1960s that a mass movement emerged again. Sara Evans locates the roots of the rebirth of feminist activism in the Civil Rights and student movements of the 1960s. As in the abolition crusade, women in Civil Rights and the New Left discovered their own strengths and gained the skills and experience necessary for forging a massive grass-roots feminist movement. The new women's movement, unlike its nineteenth-century predecessor, refuted the ideology of domesticity, which was considered an obstacle to gaining full equality. But many of the same processes that mobilized women in the nineteenth century, from neighborhood gatherings to local church and student groups, continued to generate the environments in which feminist consciousness and activism could be cultivated.[25]

Yet the new movement, for all its gains on the grass roots level, has also met tremendous opposition from women who find their sense of identity and fulfillment in traditional notions of womanhood. It still remains difficult to mobilize women on feminist issues across class and racial lines, much as it did in the nineteenth century. When questions pertaining to family and sex roles surface in the political arena, women are likely to become very active, but not necessarily as feminists. Many, in fact, feel that feminism threatens their womanhood. The Equal Rights Amendment and abortion have brought many women into national prominence as political foes on opposite sides of these issues. As in the past, some struggle for their rights, while others seek to protect their privileges. Here we have another challenge facing historians of women. Because most of the scholarship on women's politics has focused on feminism, we know very little about the way in which gender considerations influenced the political attitudes of those who remained aloof from feminism.[26]

The task for the future, then, is to explore more fully the ways in which women have formulated their political views. Already there is a solid foundation upon which to build. Recent scholarship has documented a wide range of political activity in areas that extend far beyond the voting booths and legislative halls. It has also demonstrated that gender, along with race, class, and ethnicity, influences ideology and behavior. By uncovering women's participation in politics, women's history has expanded the boundaries of what we call the political world.[27]

Women and Work

As with politics, scholars have often viewed work in a narrow context. Historians have generally accepted a definition of labor deeply rooted in American culture: work is something that is paid. As such, it usually takes place in the "public" arena, where men are dominant and women are either absent or peripheral. But work does not only take place in the labor force, nor is it necessarily compensated with wages. According to the common view, as the country industrialized productive labor shifted outside the home to the factories, fields, shops, and offices where men toiled, leaving women at home. Although wives and daughters may have performed chores such as cleaning, cooking, or child rearing, these functions were not considered essentially productive, and most women were assumed to be economic dependents. Yet women's labors inside and outside the home have been essential in providing for the well-being of their families. Private life has interacted with public life to determine the type of work both sexes have performed.

The unpaid work of women in the home has been essential for men's and families' economic lives. Several scholars, including Ann Oakley, Rae André and Heidi Hartmann, have documented the importance of housework as a productive endeavor.[28] Child care, food purchase and preparation, cleaning, laundry, and household management have usually been the responsibility of women and have enabled men to pursue different tasks. In addition, women have often determined how far wage-earners' wages would stretch. As Susan J. Kleinberg has shown in her study of late nineteenth-century Pittsburgh, wives' labors in the home enabled families to survive under extremely difficult conditions, and their management of household budgets determined to a large extent the quality of life a steel worker's earnings would provide.[29]

Women's domestic functions often served to advance the careers of their husbands. Sociologists have pointed to the "two-person career," a term describing the hidden but necessary services provided by wives of business or corporate executives which propel the upward mobility of their husbands. Sometimes these functions amount to full-time jobs in entertainment and public relations. Employers have been known to interview wives when they make hiring or promotion decisions.[30] In all these ways, women's skills and services help to determine the career patterns of their husbands. Although none of this should come as a surprise, its importance in terms of historical investigation is profound, for it alters a basic assumption that has guided explorations into the study of work and mobility—that the wage is the fundamental indicator of productive labor in a capitalist society. Capitalism and individualism, two principles central to American thought, rest on the notion that work in industrial society is done by individuals for pay. Yet women's economic endeavors do not always fit into this mold.

Recent scholarship has demonstrated that even after industrialization, the family remained an economic unit in which all adults (and frequently children) contributed to household support. Scholars of European history have shown that industrialization did not suddenly or dramatically alter preindustrial work and gender roles. Joan Scott and Louise Tilly, for example, found women moving back and forth between domestic and paid labor in the period of early industrialization, in order to meet family needs.[31] This work, plus similar research on the United States, revised the previous assumption that industrialization removed the work place from the home and left women as dependents in a "leisure" realm. There is some truth to this view in certain contexts, notably affluent urban women of the nineteenth and twentieth centuries. But neither these wives, nor southern plantation mistresses, were necessarily "leisured"—their work lives were determined by their status, and often included numerous managerial as well as domestic tasks. Some women did comprise a "leisure class," but as Thorstein Veblen and others since have noted, even these women were expected to acquire certain skills and habits of conspicuous consumption in order to advance the status of their husbands and families.[32]

Aside from these few exceptions, most women have worked, as have most men. Once this essential fact is fully incorporated into the historical literature, it will bring about a major expansion of the common definition of work. Nonpaid labor in the home is only one of many economic endeavors women have pursued which have gained little scholarly attention. One reason for this is that their work is often hidden from view. Piecework at home, street market endeavors, taking in boarders, or doing sewing and laundry for others rarely appeared on documents indicating occupational status. This type of earning was not likely to be noted by census takers who considered these workers "housewives." Yet all of these market endeavors were ways in which women continued preindustrial patterns of productivity by making their domestic work pay.[33]

In spite of the underrepresentation of women in occupational statistics, we now know a great deal about their economic pursuits.[34] But uncovering their contribution to production is only one side of the question. To fully understand the economic process, it is essential to explore women's place in it, in terms of opportunity, compensation, and working conditions. In other words, once we know not only what women have done, but how their labor has been valued, we will have a clearer picture of how the system operates as a whole. Further, we can gain insight into economic power relationships and the way in which labor is either rewarded or degraded. Since so much of our national thinking as well as historical writing has stressed the virtue of work, the relationship between the worker and the productive system needs to be understood in all its complexity. In this context, the experiences of women can be extremely enlightening.

Women's productive endeavors are shaped by a variety of determinants. Family needs, ethnic traditions, and labor market conditions combine to affect the nature of their work. During the 1830s and 40s, for example, young single native-born women left the farms to participate in factory work. Thomas Dublin's study of the New England textile mills examines this experience. Although they gained some measure of economic independence, conditions were far from ideal. The women organized numerous strikes and protests over wage cuts, speed-ups, and long hours. These efforts were futile against the power of the companies, and when immigrants began to offer an even cheaper source of labor, most of the young native-born mill workers left the factories.[35]

For immigrant women, ethnic and family values often had a profound effect on their economic endeavors. Since work outside the home usually paid better than work inside the home, the extent to which daughters, sisters, or wives were encouraged to take jobs helped determine the occupational mobility of the men in their families. Mobility studies have shown that the family context has had a great deal to do with occupational patterns, especially intergenerational mobility. But the effect of gender roles has not been quite so apparent. Several scholars of immigrants have suggested that various notions concerning women's proper place may have made a significant difference.[36] For example, because Italian families placed a high value on wives remaining at home, children may have left school in order to enter the labor force and help support their families. These children would forfeit the advantages of higher education. In contrast, Jewish women had been accustomed to gainful employment in Europe, and readily entered the American paid labor force so that their children would have occupational advantages as a direct result of their mothers' employment. Gender role variations among different ethnic groups, then, may well have been an important factor affecting differential mobility.[37]

The family context not only determined whether or not a woman would work outside the home, it often influenced how long she held a job and the kind of employment she pursued. Until very recently, and with the notable exception of blacks, most women who held jobs spent only a few years in the labor force prior to marriage. They as well as their families and employers expected them to leave their jobs when they married. Moreover, their jobs were usually extensions of their roles in the home, such as textile work, domestic service, teaching, or nursing. There are several characteristics of these occupations that relate to domestic duties. First, they are usually underpaid. Since women's work in the home has generally been devalued, its extensions in the labor force have also been devalued.[38] Secondly, since women were not expected to remain in the labor force, their jobs usually required little skill or training and offered little possibility for advancement.

A number of recent studies show how these factors worked against staying in the labor force. David Katzman's study of domestic service, and research on wage-earning women by Leslie Woodcock Tentler and Susan Estabrook Kennedy, suggest that these workers were rarely motivated to stay at their jobs because the conditions and compensation were so poor. Winifred Wandersee has argued that employment outside the home often reflected a commitment to family values rather than an indication of a shift toward autonomy or self-realization, which also inhibited long-term participation in the paid labor force.[39] The same factors also served to minimize women's participation in labor organizations.

It has long been assumed that women have been among the most difficult employees to organize. Yet recent scholarship has shown that under certain circumstances, they organized effectively and forcefully. In the Lowell mills they were in the forefront of the ten-hour day movement. In Lynn shoe factories, "lady stitchers" were a major force in the massive 1860 shoemakers' strike, which, according to Allan Dawley, may not have occurred at all and certainly would have been less effective without their participation. Meredith Tax's study of women in the labor movement shows that in the 1880s and 1890s in Chicago, 37,000 female workers organized a powerful movement, gained the backing of middle class reformers, and won major gains.[40]

Women have shown themselves to be effective union members. Yet their efforts usually failed to sustain strong and lasting organizations. Part of the problem was that most were temporary workers, segregated into unskilled or semiskilled occupations which weakened their power base. But perhaps the most important factor was that many male-dominated unions made concerted efforts to keep them out of the ranks of organized labor. By refusing to allow them in the unions, or by making their participation difficult by holding meetings in saloons or at hours when family responsibilities made it impossible for them to attend, union leaders prevented many women from joining the labor movement. Rather than striving for better pay and conditions for all workers, the unions feared that women would bring down wages and hinder union effectiveness. By accepting the system's devaluation of women's work, unions hindered women's unionizing efforts and contributed to their marginal status in the ranks of labor.[41]

The devaluation of female labor has pervaded the economic system and affected the way in which corporate capitalism has evolved in this country. In the nineteenth century, most studies agree that with the possible exception of mill work in the early part of the century, and a few professional occupations later, most jobs for women were underpaid and offered little opportunity for advancement. Some occupations, such as teaching children, achieved low status precisely because they were filled by women and appeared as extensions of domestic tasks. As industry expanded in the cities in the twentieth century, new types of white-collar jobs became available, bringing more middle class women into the paid labor force. Yet these positions remained sex-segregated and outside the central rungs of the corporate hierarchy. A secretary could advance to become an executive secretary, but not an executive. A male clerk, however, might rise through the ranks.

Clearly, the rewards for most of these jobs were meager. Perhaps this is one reason why paid work remained a temporary experience for women throughout the first half of the twentieth century. Leslie Woodcock Tentler's study of white wage-earning women during these decades shows that most left their jobs when they married. As late as 1930, over 90 percent of all wives remained out of the paid labor force. And although opportunities seemed to be gradually improving, both Lois Sharf and Ruth Milkman have suggested that the Depression effectively dampened any possibilities emerging in the early twentieth century which might have propelled women toward full participation in the labor force. During the Depression, they remained in poorly paid occupations and often became the sole wage-earners for their families if their husbands were out of work, to nobody's satisfaction.[42]

During World War II, when women entered war industries, they were urged to give up their jobs when the soldiers came home. Yet after the war, wives continued to enter the labor force because two household incomes were often necessary to maintain the constantly rising standard of living. Although their wartime work demonstrated that they could do any type of labor, and many now held their jobs for more than a few years, they still remained in sex-segregated jobs with low pay and few opportunities for advancement. The segmentation of the labor market by gender has remained constant throughout the twentieth century.[43]

Studies of women's work have opened the way for new approaches to the investigation of mobility, household economy, and the organization of production. We have seen that the low status afforded domestic labor not only devalued housework, it also influenced the kinds of occupations women entered outside the home and the low status and compensation that came with them. It contributed to segregation in a limited range of occupations, and inhibited female workers from organizing into unions. At the same time, recent research has clearly demonstrated that the low status given female labor does not reflect its importance to the nation's productive potential. Recognizing the extent and variety of women's work yields an expanded definition of work as well as a greater understanding of the economic system which historians can no longer ignore.

Conclusion

The task of women's history is to continue to question the basic concepts upon which historical inquiry builds. Already the field has taken great strides in that direction. Scholarship on women has expanded our view of the political world. It has brought political history beyond the voting booths and legislative halls and into the streets, churches, and homes, where a great deal of activism has taken place. In the process, it has yielded innovative approaches to grass-roots politics as well as public policy, and suggested new theoretical dimensions for the study of insurgent movements. But a great deal more work needs to be done before we will fully understand the dynamics of political belief and behavior. Historians of women must continue to explore the relationship between gender and politics, which will utlimately force all scholars of the political process to do the same.

Similar efforts need to be made in historical investigations of the economy.

Recent research has challenged commonly held beliefs about mobility, domestic work, labor force participation, and union organizing which have guided historical inquiry in the past. The new scholarship calls for a closer look at the interaction of public and private life, and for a rethinking of assumptions concerning individual achievement. Many of these recent studies have raised questions about individualism as one of the central tenets of American thought as well as historical investigation. When women's economic endeavors are taken into consideration, it becomes clear that the achievements of individuals are determined to a great extent by the relationship between men's and women's work. Women's productive functions have often taken place in a collective context, where combined resources and energies comprise the economic unit. Even the type of work they performed was frequently determined by family rather than individual considerations. Their work in turn affected the social mobility of husbands, brothers, and fathers, as well as the total economic well-being of their households. Scholars need to move beyond assumptions of individualism to understand not only women's experiences but men's as well.

At this point, having created a tremendous amount of intellectual turbulence, women's history must move beyond its current stage of transition. Now that women have been brought out of the shadows, the next step is to take a new look at the total picture, from a vantage point that includes both sexes, and within a context that considers gender as a fundamental category for historical investigation.[44] There is still a long way to go. In spite of the wealth of new scholarship, very little of it has filtered down in large synthetic works covering general themes and issues in American history. Frances Fitzgerald in her 1979 study of history text books noted that "texts have not actually found many women in America, but they have replaced their pictures of Dolley Madison with photographs of Susan B. Anthony." Rarely has the overall conceptualization been revised to include women or gender in the total picture. Typical is a disappointing text with the promising title *Men, Women and Issues in American History* (1975), which is organized around the lives of seventy-five men and nine women. Yet in the last few years, the outpouring of scholarship from the field of women's history has generated new efforts to weave new conceptualizations into the historical fabric.[45] The process has definitely begun, and will continue as more scholars become sensitive to the issues and approaches pioneered by historians of women.

I would like to thank Joyce Antler, Nancy Cott, Sara Evans, Eric Foner, Estelle Freedman, Lary May, Riv-Ellen Prell, Omri Shochatovitz, Judith Smith, and Stephan Thernstrom for ideas, suggestions, and very helpful criticisms.

1. Scholars in European as well as American history have advanced this view. See, for example, Gerda Lerner, *The Majority Finds Its Past: Placing Women in History* (New York: Oxford University Press, 1979); Natalie Zemon Davis, " 'Women's History' in Transition: The Euro-

pean Case," *Feminist Studies* 3, 3/4 (Spring-Summer 1976): 83–93; Joan Kelly-Gadol, "The Social Relations of the Sexes: Methodological Implications of Women's History," *Signs* 1, 4 (Summer 1976): 809–23; Susan J. Kleinberg, "The Systematic Study of Urban Women," in *Class, Sex, and the Woman Worker*, eds. Milton Cantor and Bruce Laurie (Westport, Conn.: Greenwood Press, 1977), pp. 20–42; Carroll Smith-Rosenberg, "The New Woman and the New History," *Feminist Studies* 3, ½ (Fall 1975): 185–98; Mary Beth Norton, "American History — Review Essay," *Signs* 5, 2 (Winter 1979): 324–337; Ann D. Gordon, Mari Jo Buhle, and Nancy E. Schrom, "Women in American Society: An Historical Contribution," *Radical America* 5, 4 (July-August 1971): 3–66; Ellen Du Bois, Mari Jo Buhle, Temma Kaplan, Gerda Lerner, and Caroll Smith-Rosenberg, "Politics and Culture in Women's History: A Symposium," *Feminist Studies* 6, 1 (Spring 1980): 26–64; Berenice Carroll, ed., *Liberating Women's History: Theoretical and Critical Essays* (Urbana: University of Illinois Press, 1976); Nancy Schrom Dye, "Clio's American Daughters: Male History, Female Reality," and Jane Tibbitts Schulenburg, "Clio's European Daughters: Myopic Modes of Perception," both in Julia A. Sherman and Evelyn Torton Beck, *The Prism of Sex: Essays in the Sociology of Knowledge* (Madison: University of Wisconsin Press, 1979), pp. 9–53; Carl N. Degler, "What the Women's Movement Has Done to American History," *Soundings* 64, 1 (Winter 1981): 403–21. For an excellent overview of the field, see the introduction to Nancy F. Cott and Elizabeth H. Pleck, eds., *A Heritage of Her Own: Toward a New Social History of American Women* (New York: Simon and Schuster, 1979), pp. 9–24.

2. Several studies have begun to question how separate the spheres actually were, even in the Victorian era. See, for example, Ellen Rothman, "Sex and Self-Control: Middle-Class Courtship in America, 1770–1870," *Journal of Social History* (forthcoming); E. Anthony Rotundo, "Body and Soul: Changing Ideals of American Middle-Class Manhood, 1770–1920," *Journal of Social History* (forthcoming); Steven Stowe, "Mastery and Doubt: Becoming a Man in the Planter Class," paper presented at the annual meeting of the Organization of American Historians, Detroit, 1981.

3. Davis, "'Women's History' in Transition," p. 90. For an elaboration of this definition of politics, see Eric Foner's introduction to *Politics and Ideology in the Age of the Civil War* (New York: Oxford University Press, 1980).

4. Mary Beth Norton, *Liberty's Daughters: The Revolutionary Experience of American Women, 1750–1800* (Boston: Little, Brown, 1980); Linda Kerber, *Women of the Republic: Intellect and Ideology in Revolutionary America* (Chapel Hill: University of North Carolina Press, 1980). See also Norton, "Eighteenth-Century American Women in Peace and War: The Case of the Loyalists," *William and Mary Quarterly* 3rd ser., 33 (July 1976): 386–409; Joan Hoff Wilson, "The Illusion of Change: Women and the American Revolution," in *The American Revolution: Explorations in the History of American Radicalism*, ed. Alfred A. Young (Urbana: University of Illinois Press, 1976). Quote is from Kerber, *Women of the Republic*, p. 33.

5. Kerber, *Women of the Republic*, esp. ch. 5.

6. Frances Willard used the term when she called on temperance women to "make the whole world HOMELIKE." Quoted in Mari Jo Buhle, *Women and American Socialism, 1870–1920* (Urbana: University of Illinois Press, 1981), p. 65.

7. Nancy F. Cott, *The Bonds of Womanhood: "Women's Sphere" in New England, 1780–1835* (New Haven, Conn.: Yale University Press, 1977).

8. Sara Evans and Harry Boyte, "Free Social Spaces — Schools for Democratic Revolt," in *Leaders From Below*, ed. Colin Greer (Princeton, N.J.: Pilgrim Press, forthcoming). The general theory of democratic insurgency is also explored by Lawrence Goodwyn in *Democratic Promise: The Populist Movement in America* (New York: Oxford University Press, 1976).

9. Blanche Glassman Hersch, *The Slavery of Sex: Feminist-Abolitionists in America* (Urbana: University of Illinois Press, 1978); Barbara J. Berg, *The Remembered Gate: Origins of American Feminism, The Woman and the City, 1800–1860* (New York: Oxford University Press, 1978); Barbara Leslie Epstein, *The Politics of Domesticity: Women, Evangelism, and Temperance in Nineteenth-Century America* (Middletown, Conn.: Wesleyan University Press,

1981). See also Carroll Smith-Rosenberg, "Beauty, the Beast, and the Militant Woman: A Case Study in Sex Roles and Social Stress in Jacksonian America," *American Quarterly* 23 (1971): 562–84; Nancy F. Cott, "Young Women in the Second Great Awakening in New England," *Feminist Studies* 3, ½ (Fall 1975): 15–29; Ann M. Boylan, "Evangelical Womanhood in the Nineteenth Century: The Role of Women in Sunday Schools," *Feminist Studies* 4, 3 (October 1978): 62–80; Mary P. Ryan, "The Power of Women's Networks: A Case Study of Female Moral Reform in Antebellum America," *Feminist Studies* 4, 1 (Spring 1979): 66–86.

10. Hersch, *Slavery of Sex*; Gerda Lerner, *The Grimke Sisters from South Carolina: Pioneers for Woman's Rights and Abolition* (New York: Schocken, 1969).

11. See, for example, William O'Neill, *Everyone Was Brave: The Rise and Fall of Feminism in America* (Chicago: Quadrangle, 1969); Alan Grimes, *The Puritan Ethic and Woman Suffrage* (New York: Greenwood Press, 1967).

12. Ellen DuBois, *Feminism and Suffrage: The Emergence of an Independent Women's Movement in America, 1848–1869* (Ithaca, N.Y.: Cornell University Press, 1978). See also DuBois, "The Radicalism of the Woman Suffrage Movement: Notes Toward the Reconstruction of 19th Century Feminism," *Feminist Studies* 3, ½ (Fall 1975): 63–71.

13. Epstein, *Politics of Domesticity*; Ruth Bordin, *Woman and Temperance: The Quest for Power and Liberty, 1873–1900* (Philadelphia: Temple University Press, 1981). See also Jed Dannenbaum, "The Origins of Temperance Activism and Militancy Among American Women," *Journal of Social History* (December 1981); and also the discussion of the WCTU in Buhle, *Socialism*.

14. Estelle Freedman, "Separatism as Strategy: Female Institution Building and American Feminism, 1870–1930," *Feminist Studies* 5, 3 (Fall 1979): 512–29; and *Their Sisters' Keepers: Women's Prison Reform in America, 1830–1930* (Ann Arbor: University of Michigan Press, 1980); William Leach, *True Love and Perfect Union: The Feminist Reform of Sex and Society* (New York: Basic Books, 1980); Carl Degler, *At Odds: Women and the Family in America from the Revolution to the Present* (New York: Oxford University Press, 1980); Daniel Scott Smith, "Family Limitation, Sexual Control, and Domestic Feminism in Victorian America," *Feminist Studies* 1 (Winter-Spring 1973): 40–57.

15. Gerda Lerner, "The Lady and the Mill Girl: Changes in the Status of Women in the Age of Jackson, 1800–1840," *Midcontinent American Studies Journal* 10 (Spring 1969): 4–15, revised in Cott and Pleck, eds., *Heritage*, pp. 182–96.

16. See Freedman, *Their Sisters' Keepers*; Berg, *The Remembered Gate*; Lerner, "The Lady and the Mill Girl."

17. Buhle, *Socialism*.

18. Nancy Schrom Dye, *As Equals and As Sisters: Feminism, The Labor Movement, and the Women's Trade Union League of New York* (Columbia, Mo.: University of Missouri Press, 1980); Elizabeth Jameson, "Imperfect Unions: Class and Gender in Cripple Creek, 1894–1904," in *Class, Sex*, eds. Cantor and Laurie, pp. 166–202; Robin Miller Jacoby, "The Women's Trade Union League and American Feminism," *Feminist Studies* 3, ½ (Fall 1975): 126–40.

19. For a few of several approaches to culture and politics, see Herbert Gutman, "Work, Culture and Society in Industrializing America, 1815–1919," *American Historical Review* 78 (June 1973): 531–88; Paul Johnson, *A Shopkeeper's Millenium: Society and Revivals in Rochester, New York, 1815–1837* (New York: Hill and Wang, 1978).

20. See, for example, O'Neill, *Everyone*; Andrew Sinclair, *The Better Half: The Emancipation of the American Woman* (New York: Harper and Row, 1965); Eleanor Flexner, *Century of Struggle* (New York: Atheneum, 1970), first published by Harvard University Press, Cambridge, Mass., 1959; Page Smith, *Daughters of the Promised Land: Women in American History* (Boston: Little, Brown, 1970), ch. 20.

21. Joyce Antler, "Feminism As Life Process: The Life and Career of Lucy Sprague Mitchell," *Feminist Studies* 7, 1 (Spring 1981): 135–57. See also Estelle Freedman, "The New Woman: Changing Views of Women in the 1920's," *Journal of American History* 61, 2 (September 1974): 372–93.

22. For a discussion of women's pursuit of educational and occupational goals, see Frank Stricker, "Cookbooks and Law Books: The Hidden History of Career Women in Twentieth-

Century America," *Journal of Social History* 10 (Fall 1976): 1–19, also in Cott and Pleck, eds., *Heritage*, pp. 476–98.

23. Nancy Cott's current work in progress on twentieth-century feminism explores many of these issues: see "The Problem of Feminism in the 1920's," Isabella MacCaffrey Lecture, Harvard University, May 1981; and "The Crisis of Transition in Feminism in the United States," paper presented at Radcliffe College, May 1982. Donald Meyer is also pursuing these questions in a comparative framework: see "Feminism in Italy, Sweden, and the United States, 1870–1970," paper presented at the American Historical Association, San Francisco, December 1978. His current manuscript in progress, "Sex and Freedom in Four Countries," also includes the Soviet Union.

24. For one example of women's sustained participation in a local movement, see Ronald Lawson and Stephan E. Barton, "Sex Roles in Social Movements: A Case Study of the Tenant Movement in New York City," *Signs* 6, 2 (Winter 1980): 230–47; Susan Ware, *Beyond Suffrage: Women in the New Deal* (Cambridge, Mass.: Harvard University Press, 1981).

25. Sara Evans, *Personal Politics: The Roots of Women's Liberation in the Civil Rights Movement and the New Left* (New York: Knopf, 1979).

26. Studies of women's ideology generally focus on notions of womanhood, such as Barbara Welter's, "The Cult of True Womanhood: 1820–1860," *American Quarterly* 18, 2 (1966): 151–74; or on "women's sphere" over time, such as Sheila Rothman's *Woman's Proper Place: A History of Changing Ideals and Practices, 1870 to the Present* (New York: Basic Books, 1978). Or they focus on feminist ideology, such as Aileen Kraditor's, *Ideas of the Woman Suffrage Movement, 1890–1920* (New York: Columbia University Press, 1965); or Gayle Graham Yates's, *What Women Want: The Ideas of the Movement* (Cambridge, Mass.: Harvard University Press, 1975). A few recent studies have begun to analyze antifeminism among women, but either they investigate the current political scene without a historical perspective, or they critique the Left for its failure to respond to the familial values which now provide the banner of the Moral Majority. See, for example, Susan Harding, "Family Reform Movements: Recent Feminism and its Opposition," *Feminist Studies* 7, 1 (Spring 1981): 57–75; Wini Breines, Margaret Cerullo, and Judith Stacey, "Social Biology, Family Studies, and Antifeminist Backlash," *Feminist Studies* 4, 1 (February 1978): 43–67; Catherine Arnott, "Feminists and Anti-Feminists as True Believers," *Sociology and Social Research* 57, 3 (1977): 300–06; Kent L. Tedin et al., "Social Background and Political Differences Between Pro- and Anti-ERA Activists," *American Political Quarterly* 5, 3 (1977): 395–408; David W. Brady and Kent L. Tedin, "Ladies in Pink: Religion and Political Ideology in the Anti-ERA Movement," *Social Science Quarterly* 56 (March 1976): 564–75; Barbara Easton, "Feminism and the Contemporary Family," in Cott and Pleck, eds., *Heritage*, pp. 555–77; Linda Gordon and Allen Hunter, "Sex, Family, and the New Left: Anti-Feminism as a Political Force," *Radical America* 11, 6–12, 1 (November 1977–February 1978): 9–25. Antifeminism in Britain has received some historical attention, see Brian Howard Harrison, *Separate Spheres: The Opposition to Women's Suffrage in Britain* (London: Holmes and Meier, 1978).

27. The discipline of political science has suffered from a narrowness of vision that has also characterized much of political history. For critiques of the literature in political science, see Susan C. Bourque and Jean Grossholtz, "Politics an Unnatural Practice: Political Science Looks at Female Participation," *Politics and Society* 4 (Winter 1974): 225–66; Virginia Sapiro, "Research Frontier Essay: When are Interests Interesting? The Problem of Political Representation of Women," *American Political Science Review* 75, 3 (September 1981): 701–16.

28. Rae André, *Homemakers: The Forgotten Workers* (Chicago: University of Chicago Press, 1981); Ann Oakley, *Woman's Work: The Housewife, Past and Present* (New York: Pantheon, 1975); Heidi I. Hartmann, "The Family as the Locus of Gender, Class and Political Struggle: The Example of Housework," *Signs* 6, 3 (Spring 1981): 366–94; Joann Vanek, "Time Spent in Housework," *Scientific American* (November 1974): 116–21. For a defense of women's work in the home, see Arlene Rossen Cardozo, *Women at Home* (Garden City, N.J.: Doubleday, 1976).

29. Susan J. Kleinberg, "Technology and Women's Work: The Lives of Working Class Women in Pittsburgh, 1870–1900," *Labor History* 17, 1 (Winter 1976): 58–72.

30. Rosabeth Moss Kanter, *Men and Women of the Corporation* (New York: Basic Books, 1977), ch. 5; Hanna Papanek, "Men, Women, and Work: Reflections on the Two-Person Career," *American Journal of Sociology* 78 (January 1973): 90–96.

31. Louise Tilly and Joan Scott, *Women, Work and Family* (New York: Harper and Row, 1978).

32. Thorstein Veblen, *The Theory of the Leisure Class* (New York: New American Library, 1976 edition).

33. Christine Stansell, "Class, Poverty, and the Struggle for the Streets: Women and Children of the Laboring Poor in New York City, 1815–1860," *Feminist Studies* (forthcoming); Judith Smith, "The Transformation of Family and Community Culture in Immigrant Neighborhoods, 1900–1940," in *Labor History and the New England Working Class*, eds. Donald Bell and Herbert Gutman (Urbana: University of Illinois Press, forthcoming).

34. Overviews of women's work in the paid labor force include Robert W. Smuts, *Women and Work in America* (New York: Columbia University Press, 1959); and Elizabeth F. Baker, *Technology and Women's Work* (New York: Columbia University Press, 1964). Recent studies include Alice Kessler-Harris, *Out to Work* (New York: Oxford University Press, 1982); and Barbara Mayer Wertheimer, *We Were There: The Story of Working Women in America* (New York: Pantheon, 1977).

35. Thomas Dublin, *Women at Work: The Transformation of Work and Community in Lowell, Massachusetts, 1826–1860* (New York: Columbia University Press, 1979). See also Dublin, "Women, Work, and the Family: Female Operatives in the Lowell Mills, 1830–1860," *Feminist Studies* 3, 2 (Fall 1975): 30–39; and "Women, Work and Protest in the Early Lowell Mills: 'The Oppressing Hand of Avarice Would Enslave Us,'" in Cantor and Laurie, eds., *Class, Sex*, pp. 43–63; Lise Vogel, "Hearts to Feel and Tongues to Speak: New England Mill Women in the Early Nineteenth Century," in Cantor and Laurie, eds., *Class, Sex*, pp. 64–82.

36. Barbara Klaczynska, "Why Women Work: A Comparison of Various Groups — Philadelphia, 1910–1930," *Labor History* 17, 1 (Winter 1976): 73–87; Carol Groneman, "'She Earns as a Child, She Pays as a Man': Women Workers in a Mid-Nineteenth Century New York City Community," in Cantor and Laurie, eds., *Class, Sex*, pp. 83–99; Judith E. Smith, "Our Own Kind: Family and Community Networks in Providence," *Radical History Review* 17 (Spring 1978): 99–120, also in Cott and Pleck, eds., *Heritage*, pp. 393–411; Virginia Yans-McLaughlin, "Italian Women and Work: Experience and Perception," in Cantor and Laurie, eds., *Class, Sex*, pp. 101–43; Elizabeth H. Pleck, "A Mother's Wages: Income Earning Among Married Italian and Black Women, 1896–1911," in Gordon, ed., *The American Family*, pp. 490–510; Laurence A. Glasco, "The Life Cycles and Household Structure of American Ethnic Groups: Irish, Germans, and Native-Born Whites in Buffalo, New York, 1855," *Journal of Urban History* 1 (May 1975): 339–64, also in Cott and Pleck, eds., *Heritage*, pp. 268–89. See also the *Journal of Urban History* 4, 3 (May 1978), a special issue devoted to immigrant women and the city, which includes articles by Carol Groneman on the Irish in New York; Janice Reiff Webster on Scandinavian women in Seattle; Corinne Azen Krause on Italian, Jewish, and Slavic women in Pittsburgh; Maxine Seeler on the education of immigrant women in the early twentieth century; Julia Kirk Blackwelder on employed women in three twentieth-century cities.

37. For a study of differential mobility, see Stephan Thernstrom, *The Other Bostonians* (Cambridge, Mass.: Harvard University Press, 1973).

38. Gerda Lerner, "Just a Housewife," in Lerner, *Majority*, pp. 129–44; Heidi Hartmann, "Capitalism, Patriarchy, and Job Segregation by Sex: The Historical Roots of Occupational Segregation," *Signs* 1 (1975): 137–69.

39. David M. Katzman, *Seven Days a Week: Women and Domestic Service in Industrializing America* (New York: Oxford University Press, 1978); Leslie Woodcock Tentler, *Wage-Earning Women: Industrial Work and Family Life in the United States, 1900–1930* (New York: Oxford University Press, 1979); Susan Estabrook Kennedy, *If All We Did Was to Weep at Home: A History of White Working-Class Women in America* (Bloomington, Ind.: Indiana University Press, 1979); Winifred D. Wandersee, *Women's Work and Family Values, 1920–1940* (Cambridge, Mass.: Harvard University Press, 1981).

40. See Dublin, *Women at Work*; Alan Dawley, *Class and Community: The Industrial Revolution in Lynn* (Cambridge, Mass.: Harvard University Press, 1976), pp. 80–83; Meredith Tax, *The Rising of the Women: Feminist Solidarity and Class Conflict, 1880–1917* (New York: Monthly Review Press, 1980). For a discussion of women in the Paterson silk industry strike, see Delight Dodyk, "The Operatives of Paterson's Silk Mills: A Study in Women's Industrial Experience in the Early Twentieth Century," paper presented at the New Jersey Historical Commission's 13th Annual New Jersey History Symposium, Trenton, December 5, 1981.

41. Dye, *As Equals and As Sisters*; and "Feminism or Unionism? The New York Women's Trade Union League and the Labor Movement," *Feminist Studies* 3, ½ (Fall 1975): 111–25; Roslyn L. Feldberg, " 'Union Fever': Organizing Among Clerical Workers, 1900–1930," *Radical America* 14, 3 (May–June 1980): 53–67; Alice Kessler-Harris, "Organizing the Unorganizable: Three Jewish Women and their Union," *Labor History* 17, 1 (Winter 1976): 5–23; and " 'Where are the Organized Women Workers?,' " *Feminist Studies* 3, ½ (Fall 1975): 92–110.

42. Tentler, *Wage-Earning Women*; Lois Scharf, *To Work and To Wed: Female Employment, Feminism, and the Great Depression* (Westport, Conn.: Greenwood Press, 1980); Ruth Milkman, "Woman's Work and the Economic Crisis: Some Lessons from the Great Depression," *The Review of Radical Political Economics* 8, 1 (Spring 1976): 73–91, 95–97, shorter version in Cott and Pleck, eds., *Heritage*, pp. 507–41.

43. Valerie Kincade Oppenheimer, *The Female Labor Force in the United States* (Westport, Conn.: Greenwood Press, 1970); Juanita M. Kreps, *Women and the American Economy: A Look to the 1980's* (Englewood Cliffs, N.J.: Prentice-Hall, 1976); William Henry Chafe, *The American Woman: Her Changing Social, Economic, and Political Roles, 1920–1970* (New York: Oxford University Press, 1972); Mary P. Ryan, *Womanhood in America: From Colonial Times to the Present* (New York: Watts, 1975), chs. 5, 6, 7. See also Chafe, *Women and Equality: Changing Patterns in American Culture* (New York: Oxford University Press, 1977); Karen Anderson, *Wartime Women: Sex Roles, Family Relations, and the Status of Women During World War II* (Westport, Conn.: Greenwood Press, 1981). For an analysis of the sexual segregation in the professions, see Joan Jacobs Brumberg and Nancy Tomes, "Women in the Professions: A Research Agenda for American Historians," *Reviews in American History* 10, 2 (June 1982): 275–96.

44. Although most of the work on gender has focused on women, some scholars have begun looking carefully at male roles. See, for example, Peter N. Stearns, *Be A Man! Males in Modern Society* (New York: Holms and Meier, 1979); Peter Gabriel Filene, *Him/Her/Self: Sex Roles in Modern America* (New York: Harcourt, Brace, Jovanovich, 1974); G. J. Barker-Benfield, "The Spermatic Economy: A Nineteenth-Century View of Sexuality," in *The American Family in Social-Historical Perspective*, ed. Michael Gordon, 2nd ed. (New York: St. Martins Press, 1978); Rotundo, "Body and Soul"; Stowe, "Mastery and Doubt." For a number of innovative essays, see Elizabeth H. Pleck and Joseph H. Pleck, eds., *The American Man* (Englewood Cliffs, N.J.: Prentice-Hall, 1980).

45. Frances Fitzgerald, *America Revised: History Schoolbooks in the Twentieth Century* (Boston: Atlantic Little Brown, 1979), p. 93; Howard H. Quint and Milton Cantor, eds., *Men, Women and Issues in American History*, 2 vols. (New York: Dorsey Press, 1975). For a new text which integrates women into the fabric of American history, see Mary Beth Norton et al., *A People and a Nation: A History of the United States* (Boston: Houghton Mifflin, 1982).

WELL-TRODDEN PATHS AND FRESH BYWAYS: RECENT WRITING ON NATIVE AMERICAN HISTORY

Reginald Horsman

Books on Native American history are still being sought by publishers, but the excitement of the late 1960s and the early 1970s has died down. The battle between those attacking and those defending white policies is less often seen in simplistic form, and solid monographs are now more common than impassioned pleas. There has generally been an improvement in the quality of writing on the American Indian, and though most books are still written from a white perspective a sensitivity to the Native American point of view is gradually percolating from the scholarly monographs through the general texts. Even nonspecialists now realize that Indians have to be viewed as more than "savage," "noble," or "doomed" obstacles to progress on the North American continent.

Yet, while there is a new sensitivity and more solid contributions, traditional areas of interest and traditional methodology still loom large in Native American historiography. In spite of the frequent requests for new approaches and new themes, much effort has been devoted in recent years to reworking familiar topics. The most influential historical trends of the past ten years have largely bypassed Native American history. Only a minority of books have attempted to take Indian history out of its traditional framework by introducing new themes and new approaches. In the essays on contemporary historical writing in the recent *The Past Before Us* there is a striking lack of influential works on Native American history.[1] The new social history has helped transform writing on black history, but Native American history too often remains parochial. There are vigorous controversies among its practitioners, but these arguments have little impact on historians in other fields.

Much of the writing on the American Indian is still concerned with white perceptions of and policies toward Native Americans. The white image of the Indian has a perennial fascination for historians, and for the most part recent books in this area have been cast in a familiar mold. The most ambitious of these works, at least in chronological scope, is Robert F. Berkhofer's *The White Man's Indian*, which surveys white views of the Indian from first contact to the present. While this study touches perceptively on most aspects of

0048-7511/82/0104-0234 $01.00

literary, scientific, and even popular images of the Indian, and though it provides an excellent introduction to recent literature, it is too short to do much more than suggest the depth and variety of white perceptions of the Indian. Also, its general theme does not allow Berkhofer the opportunity to produce the Indian-centered history he asked for in his earlier writings.[2]

Berkhofer's detached analysis has little in common, at least in spirit, with Richard Drinnon's *Facing West*, which also ranges over the whole sweep of American history from New England in the 1630s to the Vietnam War. While Berkhofer strives for absolute cultural relativism, Drinnon has no hesitation in condemning what he perceives as a continuous history of white racism. For Drinnon, racism began long before it was given a formal structure, and he argues that it stemmed from psychic and sexual repression. He traces a direct link between racism toward the Indian and American attitudes and policies in the Pacific since the turn of the century. The book brings to the subject some of the passion and commitment that was more familiar ten years ago.[3]

Historians have long been attracted to those dramatic early colonial years when Europeans first encountered the inhabitants of the New World, and writers have continued to rework that period in recent years. Bernard Sheehan's *Savagism and Civility* is cast in a tradition that received its first full expression in the writings of Roy Harvey Pearce. Sheehan dissects English views of the Indian at the time of the very first contacts in Virginia. His interest is in how the English view of the Indian can be explained in terms of a dichotomy between Indian "savagery" and English "civility." Sheehan has a fine command of the sources, and his analysis is sophisticated, but the model is a common one.[4] White horror and self-examination when confronted with Indian "savagery" has become an over-familiar historical theme. H. C. Porter's *The Inconstant Savage* is involved with much the same period as Sheehan's work, but it is more descriptive, more diffuse, and much less sophisticated in its analysis. In undiscriminating detail Porter presents the English view of the Indian from the early sixteenth century to 1660. He has compiled a vast amount of information, but his book lacks perceptive analysis and it is difficult to imagine that it will often be read from cover to cover.[5]

Of the various books concerned with the image of the Indian at the time of the first English contact the most original in its conclusions is Karen Ordahl Kupperman's *Settling with the Indians*. Kupperman deals with the clash of English and Indian cultures from 1580 to 1640. She argues that the English in dealing with the Indians were moved not by an incipient or overt racism but by considerations of class. Status, she argues was all-important to the Englishmen of these years, and they were able to perceive many Indians as lower-class Englishmen not as irredeemable savages.[6] Her argument is not completely convincing, but it is refreshing to read an author who tries to break away from existing paradigms for white–Indian relationships in the early seventeenth century.

In recent years white policy has been an even more popular topic than the white image of the Indian. The approach and methodology has generally been traditional, but there has been a gradual and welcome shift in areas of concentration. This has still left some glaring gaps, but these gaps are fewer and less broad than they were ten years ago. Major interest has shifted from the pre- to the post-Civil War period. Yet, even within this move there are some anomalies. The last few decades of the nineteenth century and the New Deal era are now benefiting from extensive research, but there is still a paucity of work on the first decades of this century and on the years since 1945.

Several of the recent works on the years from 1860 to 1900 have dealt in one way or another with aspects of white exploitation of the Indians, and have been concerned with the ways in which the government, unwillingly or not, played into the hands of special interests that wished to obtain resources in the possession of the Indians. David Nichols has shown how the Indian Office was vulnerable to corrupt pressures, and H. Craig Miner, William Unrau, and William T. Hagan have demonstrated how from the mid-nineteenth century to the early twentieth century Indian resources were coveted and appropriated by a variety of special interests. The good intentions of reformers were often overwhelmed by greed and by a white government that failed either to protect Indian interests or to build Indian prosperity. Even those measures which were promoted and defended as reforms for the benefit of the Indians eventually became a means by which more resources were lost. A different approach to this problem, and a welcome effort to expand the methodology of Native American history, is presented in Leonard A. Carlson's *Indians, Bureaucrats, and Land*, which explains how the reform-inspired Dawes Act eventually resulted in still more Indian suffering. Carlson makes good use of quantitative data and the cliometric techniques of the new economic history to show that Indian farming declined as a result of the allotment policies of the Dawes Act.[7]

Another historian who has brought new techniques to the study of Native American history in the late nineteenth century is Paul Stuart. In his institutional history of the Indian Office from 1865 to 1900 Stuart has made use of formal organizational theory. The book suffers from the narrowness common to such structured internal studies, but is a hopeful sign that, like Carlson, Stuart has been willing to break out of the straightjacket of the usual approaches to Native American history.[8]

American Indian policies and the motives that inspired them do not lack defenders. Some downplay the eventual results of white policies toward the

Indians, and place emphasis on the good intentions of those who inspired and helped shape governmental Indian policy. Among those who argue that reformers and many in government service were moved by a genuine feeling that their actions would help the Indians, the most prominent and knowledgeable is Francis Paul Prucha. Prucha has continued to add to his already prolific scholarly output on Indian history. His knowledge ranges over the whole course of white policies from the Revolution to the present, and his work is marked by careful scholarship, an extensive knowledge of the sources, and a willingness to believe the best of those who inspired, framed, and carried out white policies toward the Indians. While admitting that the reformers were ethnocentric, Prucha defends their motives. He sees in American Indian policy a strong humanitarian ingredient stemming in large measure from the Christian evangelical tradition, and is less concerned with the consequences of governmental and private actions than with the good intentions of the white "friends of the Indian."

The range of Prucha's interests can be followed in his essays in *Indian Policy in the United States.* Most of these essays have been published or presented before, but together they form a useful introduction to the ideas that have both helped shape and have arisen from Prucha's larger works. Two of Prucha's other recent books cast light on reform and humanitarian sentiment in the years from the Civil War through the first decade of the twentieth century. His *American Indian Policy in Crisis* is concerned with Christian reformers in the years from 1865 to 1900, and *The Churches and the Indian Schools, 1888–1912* is useful not only for understanding Indian education but also for aspects of anti-Catholicism at the turn of the century.[9]

The flurry of interest in the last decades of the nineteenth century has unfortunately not been matched by books on the first decades of the twentieth century. The only well-developed field in twentieth-century Indian policy is that of the shaping of New Deal policies under John Collier and the controversies that swirled around the Indian Reorganization Act of 1934. In the last decade the assumptions regarding Collier's policies and New Deal reforms have been challenged by a number of detailed scholarly interpretations. Historians have found much to criticize in what has long been regarded as a much needed change in American Indian policy. The possible lines of this revisionism were suggested as long ago as 1968 in Lawrence C. Kelly's work on the Navajo, but in recent years the pace of the revisionism has increased and Collier's policies have undergone a major reappraisal. Donald L. Parman has dealt specifically with the impact of the New Deal on the Navajo and with the ways in which the Navajo resisted both governmental efforts at stock reduction and the Indian Reorganization Act, and Kenneth R. Philp, in his biography of Collier, while not completely rejecting earlier praise of Collier's work, presents a far more balanced view of his policies than has previously been available.[10]

With the publication of Graham D. Taylor's study of the administration of the Indian Reorganization Act in the ten years after its adoption, the reappraisal of Collier's policies and the Indian New Deal has become comprehensive. Taylor argues that many Indians were unprepared for the new tribal governments desired by Collier and his aides. Collier, he contends, approached the Indians from a white viewpoint that had too little understanding of and sympathy for actual Indian experience. As a result Collier encountered resistance which was complicated by Indian factionalism. Even policies designed to revive Indian tribal integrity and Indian culture were based on a white image of what being an Indian meant. The revisionist view of New Deal policies is now well-integrated into scholarly thought on governmental Indian policy.[11]

Indian policy studies of the 1930s are now common but the years since that time have been sadly neglected. The origin and politics of termination, the dramatic shifts in governmental policy, the white backlash, and a host of other subjects all need basic research and writing by historians. It is, of course, an area in which historians need great sensitivity. Native Americans and their leaders have very strong views on the events of the past thirty-five years and the written record has often to be melded with oral history at both the local and the national level.

To investigate those twentieth-century areas that the historians of governmental Indian policy have neglected, it is necessary to turn to some of the books written by those who have specialized in the history of Indian societies. In recent years some histories of individual tribes have begun to go beyond the established formula of wars, warriors, and treaties to deal with the more pressing problems of the twentieth century. There has also been a greater willingness to integrate anthropological concepts and a sensitivity to Indian values into the better tribal studies, and there has been a greater interest in the history of previously neglected tribes. For the most part, however, historians still write of Indian societies in lineal tribal histories stretching over several centuries.

Among the recent tribal histories that have broken new ground, W. David Baird's *The Quapaw Indians* is particularly useful in that it both discusses the history of a small, neglected tribe and deals effectively with the tribe in the twentieth century. Some of the recent accounts of better known tribes have also stressed the modern period. The Navajo have been the focus of attention in several of the books on New Deal Indian policy, and a new general history, by Peter Iverson, focuses on the recent history of the tribe. Both Edmund J. Danziger's study of the Lake Superior Chippewa and Roy W. Meyer's history of the Indians of the Upper Missouri carry the discussion of the tribes from prehistoric times into the twentieth century. Danziger devotes over half of his book to the latter period and combines manuscript research and personal interviews in a way that is still quite rare among historians of Native Americans. Like so many other tribal histories, however, Danziger's work suffers from its attempt to cover centuries in a limited space.[12]

Neglected tribes of the Great Lakes and prairie regions are being written about with increasing frequency in recent years, although not all of these histories reflect the latest tendencies in Native American studies. Patricia Ourada's history of the Menominees is a useful overview of the history of a tribe that has long needed a comprehensive account. More cultural in their approach are two ethnohistorical studies by scholars trained as anthropologists. Martha Royce Blaine's history of the Ioway and James Clifton's study of the Potawatomi are rich in cultural details on the internal history of the tribes, and Clifton's work has the additional advantage of a coverage that reaches the 1960s. More traditional in approach is R. David Edmunds's history of the Potawatomi, which presents a detailed account of white-Potawatomi contact and tribal history to the 1840s.[13]

Even in dealing with tribes that have often been written about, historians have in recent years extended their discussion to less familiar topics. The long neglected history of Indian-black interrelationships has attracted considerable attention in recent years. Slavery among the Cherokee has been discussed in books by Theda Perdue and R. Halliburton, Jr., and David F. Littlefield, Jr., has written about Cherokee freedmen. Littlefield has been particularly prolific in this area. In the past five years he has also written books on Chickasaw freedmen, on blacks and Creeks, and on blacks and Seminoles.[14] This whole subject has by no means been exhausted, but at least the groundwork for future studies has been established.

The Cherokee have long been one of the most discussed Indian tribes, and the interest shows no sign of abating. John Philip Reid has demonstrated that it is possible to bring a fresh approach even to supposedly well-worn materials in his *A Better Kind of Hatchet*, a book which while dealing with Cherokee-white relations presents an original discussion of Cherokee legal history in the eighteenth century. More familiar in their approach are the essays in *The Cherokee Indian Nation*, edited by Duane H. King, but the essays are concerned with anthropological as well as historical questions.[15]

While historians have gradually expanded the histories of single tribes in both area and time, and while they have continued to write sound traditional accounts of conflict, such as Donald E. Worcester's recent history of the Apaches,[16] they have generally been reluctant to synthesize tribal histories into regional accounts. Historians are still frequently bound by white concepts of a "tribe" or "nation" with a supposedly unified power structure and a history evolving in a typical white pattern. Regional histories that demand the examination of a number of tribes hold the potential of allowing comparisons both of the changing patterns of Indian tribal societies and of the vagaries of white policy, but they have seldom achieved this.

Efforts at regional history in recent years have concentrated on the South. J. Leitch Wright, Jr. has written an account of the Indians of the Old South from first contact into the eighteenth century. His book, which is written from the perspective of a historian, concentrates more on external relationships than Charles Hudson's book on the southeastern Indians from before white contact to the present. Hudson summarizes and synthesizes a vast amount of writing on the tribes of the region, and stresses broad areas of Indian culture rather than the evolving historical record. Less unified, and somewhat less ambitious in its coverage, is a recent collection of essays on the southeastern Indians since Removal. In this volume, edited by Walter I. Williams, historical topics are for the most part dealt with by anthropologists.[17] The potential of regional Indian history awaits full realization; it might well produce more effective results than the now routine format of describing the history of a single tribe for several centuries.

Successful biographies of individual Indians are much rarer than excellent histories of individual tribes. In the past, the emphasis has usually been on Indian warriors, and publishers are still attracted by such accounts. There is often a difficulty in finding sufficient source material for full-length biographies of pre-twentieth-century figures, and it is surprising that there have not been more attempts at collections of scholarly, well-written essays on individual Indians. Two recent efforts have approached the task in slightly different ways. In his *American Indian Leaders* editor R. David Edmunds has attempted to present a full spectrum of Indian leadership from the 1740s to the 1970s. The contributions include both peace and war leaders. Of eleven sketches only two are from the twentieth century, but these—Peter Iverson's essays on Carlos Montezuma and Peter MacDonald—are particularly useful. H. Glenn Jordan and Thomas M. Holm have tried another approach. They state that their volume has the intention of avoiding the usual emphasis on warriors, and that it aims at exposing readers to those Indians "who sought compromise and accommodation." They do, however, include some familiar names.[18] Much remains to be done with the essay form as a route to Indian biography, for full-scale biographies of eighteenth- and nineteenth-century leaders will continue to present research problems.

Most historians of Indian history are not writing the "Indian-centered" history that was often asked for in the early 1970s, but an increasing number of books have integrated a sympathy for Indian society and Indian values into studies of white-Indian interaction. There has also been the steady development of a vigorous subfield of the relationship of Indians to their environment. A fair amount of this writing has been produced not by academic historians but by geographers and those in related environmental fields.

Indian-white relationships in early Canada have seen fruitful attempts at a more imaginative approach to Native American history. A fine beginning was made in 1974 when geographer Arthur J. Ray successfully blended a knowledge of economic and ecological factors into his study of Indians in the fur trade. In 1978 the same author teamed with Donald B. Freeman in an analysis of relations between the Indians and the Hudson's Bay Company in the years to 1763. This book uses not only geographic and anthropological models but also a computer analysis of the company's account books. While it is not as effective as Ray's earlier book, it at least opens the possibility of ways in which new analytical frameworks and new methodologies can be used to investigate familiar topics. That the history of the fur trade can be examined in a variety of new ways is shown by Jennifer Brown's study of the fur trade company families, which by extending the new interest in the history of women and the family to this area gives new insights on Indian-white relationships. On a more general level, French-Indian relationships in early Canada have been analyzed revealingly in Cornelius J. Jaenen's study of the sixteenth and seventeenth centuries. Jaenen shows great sensitivity in illustrating how the differing values of the Indian and French societies affected their relationship.[19]

Of the new areas of interest one of the liveliest has been the discussion of the relationships of the Indians to their environment, and the interaction of environmental factors and cultural change. Calvin Martin was one of the first to write innovative articles in this area, and in his recent study of Indian-animal relationships and the fur trade he has further developed the area of biohistory. His provocative study concludes with a controversial discussion of the Indian attitude toward their environment. Martin's fresh and vigorous approach is difficult to copy, and other works on the Indians and their environment have ranged from detailed monographs to general studies for a broad public: geographer Gary C. Goodwin has written of pre-Revolutionary Cherokee patterns of cultural change in relationship to the natural environment; Howard S. Russell ranges far and wide in an area of study unfamiliar to most historians to discuss Indian food production and consumption in New England before white contact; and Robert F. Heizer and Albert Elsasser have surveyed the complex relationships of California's many tribes to their different environments. A useful introduction to the subject of ecological factors in Native American history is Christopher Vecsey and Robert W.

Venables's *American Indian Environments*, a collection of ten essays on ecological issues and Indians in their environment.[20] At the moment even university press publications on the American Indians range from traditional blood-and-thunder accounts of warrior chiefs to sophisticated analyses of Indian cultures and social organization drawing upon anthropological and other social science theories and using new computer techniques. Too much is still plodding in approach and traditional in method. Native American history needs jolting out of the well-worn ruts in which it often travels. Some excellent books are being written, but there have been few breakthroughs. Native American history has never quite thrown off the parochial air that dominated it when it was merely a subfield of an equally parochial frontier history. In recent years the field has enjoyed a burst of enthusiasm and interest, and a new sensitivity to the Indian point of view. What it needs now is a little more freshness and originality, and more young historians who will bring to it some of the new approaches and techniques that have begun to transform writing on other areas of American history.

1. Michael Kammen, ed., *The Past Before Us: Contemporary Historical Writing in the United States* (Ithaca, N.Y.: Cornell University Press, 1980).

2. Robert F. Berkhofer, *The White Man's Indian: Images of the American Indian from Columbus to the Present* (New York: Knopf, 1978). I have discussed some of Professor Berkhofer's earlier work as well as other writing on Native American history to the mid-1970s in "Recent Trends and New Directions in Native American History," in *The American West: New Perspectives, New Dimensions*, ed. Jerome O. Steffen (Norman: University of Oklahoma Press, 1979), pp. 124–51.

3. Richard Drinnon, *Facing West: The Metaphysics of Indian-Hating and Empire-Building* (Minneapolis: University of Minnesota Press, 1980).

4. Bernard W. Sheehan, *Savagism and Civility: Indians and Englishmen in Colonial Virginia* (Cambridge, Eng.: Cambridge University Press, 1980).

5. H. C. Porter, *The Inconstant Savage: England and the North American Indian, 1500–1660* (London: Duckworth, 1979).

6. Karen Ordahl Kupperman, *Settling with the Indians: The Meeting of English and Indian Cultures in America, 1580–1640* (Totowa, N.J.: Rowman and Littlefield, 1980).

7. David A. Nichols, *Lincoln and the Indians: Civil War Policy and Politics* (Columbia: University of Missouri Press, 1978); H. Craig Miner and William E. Unrau, *The End of Indian Kansas: A Study of Cultural Revolution, 1854–1871* (Lawrence: Regents Press of Kansas, 1978); H. Craig Miner, *The Corporation and the Indian: Tribal Sovereignty and Industrial Civilization in Indian Territory, 1865–1907* (Columbia: University of Missouri Press, 1976); William T. Hagan, *United States-Commanche Relations: The Reservation Years* (New Haven: Yale University Press, 1976); Leonard A. Carlson, *Indians, Bureaucrats, and Land: The Dawes Act and the Decline of Indian Farming* (Westport, Conn.: Greenwood Press, 1981). Paul Wallace Gates, ed., *The Rape of Indian Lands* (New York: Arno Press, 1979) is a useful collection of previously published articles on the loss of Indian lands.

8. Paul Stuart, *The Indian Office: Growth and Development of an American Institution, 1865–1900* (Ann Arbor: UMI Research Press, 1979).

9. Francis Paul Prucha, *Indian Policy in the United States: Historical Essays* (Lincoln: University of Nebraska Press, 1981); *American Indian Policy in Crisis: Christian Reformers and the Indian, 1865–1900* (Norman: University of Oklahoma Press, 1976); and *The Churches and the Indian Schools, 1888–1912* (Lincoln: University of Nebrasks Press, 1979).

10. Lawrence C. Kelly, *The Navajo Indians and Federal Indian Policy, 1900–1935* (Tucson: University of Arizona Press, 1968); Donald L. Parman, *The Navajos and the New Deal* (New Haven: Yale University Press, 1976); Kenneth R. Philp, *John Collier's Crusade for Indian Reform, 1920–1954* (Tucson: University of Arizona Press, 1977).

11. Graham D. Taylor, *The New Deal and American Indian Tribalism: The Administration of the Indian Reorganization Act, 1934–45* (Lincoln: University of Nebraska Press, 1980). See also Laurence M. Hauptman, *The Iroquois and the New Deal* (Syracuse, N.Y.: Syracuse University Press, 1981).

12. W. David Baird, *The Quapaw Indians: A History of the Downstream People* (Norman: University of Oklahoma Press, 1980); Peter Iverson, *The Navajo Nation* (Westport, Conn.: Greenwood Press, 1981); Edmund Jefferson Danziger, *The Chippewas of Lake Superior* (Norman: University of Oklahoma Press, 1978); Roy W. Meyer, *The Village Indians of the Upper Missouri: The Mandans, Hidatsas, and Arikaras* (Lincoln: University of Nebraska Press, 1977).

13. Patricia K. Ourada, *The Menominee Indians: A History* (Norman: University of Oklahoma Press, 1979); Martha Royce Blaine, *The Ioway Indians* (Norman: University of Oklahoma Press, 1979); James A. Clifton, *The Prairie People: Continuity and Change in Potawatomi Indian Culture, 1665–1965* (Lawrence: Regents Press of Kansas, 1977); R. David Edmunds, *The Potawatomis: Keepers of the Fire* (Norman: University of Oklahoma Press, 1978).

14. Theda Perdue, *Slavery and the Evolution of Cherokee Society, 1540–1866* (Knoxville: University of Tennessee Press, 1979); R. Halliburton, Jr., *Red Over Black: Black Slavery Among the Cherokee Indians* (Westport, Conn.: Greenwood Press, 1977); Daniel F. Littlefield, Jr., *The Cherokee Freedmen: From Emancipation to American Citizenship* (Westport, Conn.: Greenwood Press,1978); *The Chickasaw Freedmen: A People without a Country* (Westport, Conn.: Greenwood Press, 1980); *Africans and Creeks: From the Colonial Period to the Civil War* (Westport, Conn.: Greenwood Press, 1979); and *Africans and Seminoles: From Removal to Emancipation* (Westport, Conn.: Greenwood Press, 1977).

15. John Philip Reid, *A Better Kind of Hatchet: Law, Trade, and Diplomacy in the Cherokee Nation during the Early Years of European Contact* (University Park: Pennsylvania State University Press, 1976); Duane H. King, ed., *The Cherokee Indian Nation: A Troubled History* (Knoxville: University of Tennessee Press, 1979).

16. Donald E. Worcester, *The Apaches: Eagles of the Southwest* (Norman: University of Oklahoma Press, 1979).

17. J. Leitch Wright, Jr., *The Only Land They Knew: The Tragic Story of the American Indians in the Old South* (New York: Free Press, 1981); Charles Hudson, *The Southeastern Indians* (Knoxville: University of Tennessee Press, 1976); Walter L. Williams, ed., *Southeastern Indians Since the Removal Era* (Athens: University of Georgia Press, 1979).

18. R. David Edmunds, ed., *American Indian Leaders: Studies in Diversity* (Lincoln: University of Nebraska Press, 1980); H. Glenn Jordan and Thomas M. Holm, eds., *Indian Leaders: Oklahoma's First Statesmen* (Oklahoma City: Oklahoma Historical Society, 1979), p. 11. Among recent biographies of Indians, Gary E. Moulton's, *John Ross: Cherokee Chief* (Athens: University of Georgia Press, 1978) and Kenny A. Franks's, *Stand Watie and the Agony of the Cherokee Nation* (Memphis: Memphis State University Press, 1979) are nonanalytical in their approach. Ella E. Clark and Margot Edmonds's, *Sacagawea of the Lewis and Clark Expedition* (Berkeley: University of California Press, 1979) and Hugh A. Dempsey's, *Red Crow, Warrior Chief* (Lincoln: University of Nebraska Press, 1980) have weaknesses as scholarly biographies.

19. Arthur J. Ray, *Indians in the Fur Trade: Their Role as Trappers, Hunters, and Middlemen in the Lands Southwest of Hudson Bay, 1660–1870* (Toronto: University of Toronto Press, 1974); with Donald B. Freeman, *"Give Us Good Measure": An Economic Analysis of Relations between the Indians and the Hudson's Bay Company before 1763* (Toronto: University of Toronto Press, 1978); Jennifer Brown, *Strangers in Blood: Fur Trade Company Families in Indian Country* (Vancouver: University of British Columbia Press, 1980); Cornelius J. Jaenen, *Friend and Foe: Aspects of French-Amerindian Cultural Contact in the Sixteenth and Seventeenth Centuries* (New York: Columbia University Press, 1976). See also Patricia Dillon

Woods, *French-Indian Relations on the Southern Frontier, 1699–1762* (Ann Arbor: UMI Research Press, 1980) for a useful account of Indian-French interaction in French Louisiana.

20. Calvin Martin, *Keepers of the Game: Indian-Animal Relationships and the Fur Trade* (Berkeley: University of California Press, 1978); Gary C. Goodwin, *Cherokees in Transition: A Study of Changing Culture and Environment Prior to 1775* (Chicago: University of Chicago, Department of Geography, 1977); Howard S. Russell, *Indian New England before the Mayflower* (Hanover, N.H.: University Press of New England, 1980); Robert H. Heizer and Albert B. Elsasser, *The Natural World of the California Indians* (Berkeley: University of California Press, 1980); Christopher Vecsey and Robert W. Venables, eds., *American Indian Environments: Ecological Issues in Native American History* (Syracuse, N.Y.: Syracuse University Press, 1980).

THE HISTORY OF AMERICAN MEDICINE: A FIELD IN FERMENT

Ronald L. Numbers

The term "medical history" has long meant different things to different people. To the medically trained scholars who founded the field, medical history involved primarily the study of what physicians, usually famous ones, did and thought. Although some of these pioneers also explored the cultural context of medical history, they jealously guarded their field against pretenders. For example, Erwin H. Ackerknecht, a physician-historian, once noted condescendingly that a history of antebellum medical schools was not *really* medical history because it did not deal with "the history of medicine proper, that is, the history of diseases and their treatment."[1] In recent decades, however, as more and more nonphysicians have entered the field, its scope has broadened to embrace health as well as sickness, patients as well as practitioners, behavior as well as belief, social relations as well as scientific change. In view of these developments, some historians have suggested substituting "history of health care" for "history of medicine."[2] My own feeling is that either label will do, as long as "medicine" is taken in its broadest sense to include both preventive and curative activities.

The designation "medical historian" has provoked similar dispute. The physician-historian Henry Sigerist, one of the first full-time medical historians in the United States, defined a medical historian as "a *physician*, trained in the research methods of history, who takes an active part in the life of his time and is in close touch with the medical problems of his time."[3] Because most historians of American medicine have not been physicians, they have often hesitated to call themselves medical historians, and a few of the leading contributors to the field scarcely think of themselves as such. Even the late Richard H. Shryock, one of the most respected medical historians of the century, did not regard persons like himself, trained only in history, as "professional medical historians." That title he reserved for those "*physicians* who have been enabled, by the establishment of special chairs and institutes, to give much or all of their time to historical studies."[4]

The Intellectual Origins of American Medical History

Since the founding of the Institute of the History of Medicine at Johns Hopkins University in 1932, professional physician-historians have found

0048-7511/82/0104-0245 $01.00

academic homes primarily within medical schools.[5] Consequently, they have oriented their research toward the interests and needs of the medical profession. Although some of them have occasionally written on American topics—see, for example, Sigerist's *American Medicine* (1934) and Ackerknecht's *Malaria in the Upper Mississippi Valley, 1760–1900* (1945)—they have tended to investigate less provincial affairs and to leave the American scene to scholars trained in American history.

At first, American historians questioned the legitimacy of medicine as a proper subject for study, an attitude illustrated by the experience of Shryock, the first American historian to write extensively about medicine. After serving as a technician in the Army Medical School during World War I, he enrolled as a graduate student in the University of Pennsylvania Department of History, hoping to write a dissertation on the history of public health in America. When he informed the professor of American history of his intentions, the professor coolly replied: "an interesting subject, Mr. Shryock, but not history."[6] Thus rebuffed, he selected a more conventional topic; but soon after receiving his Ph.D. in 1924, he shifted his attention back to medical matters. Throughout the middle third of the century he served as the principal model for nonphysicians aspiring to careers in medical history.

Fortunately for the growth of the field, the situation Shryock found at Pennsylvania did not long prevail in the leading departments of history. The change came about largely through the efforts of a small group of American social and intellectual historians led by Arthur M. Schlesinger and Dixon Ryan Fox, editors of the twelve-volume *History of American Life* (1927–1944), who in the 1920s launched a crusade "to free American history from its traditional servitude to party struggles, war and diplomacy and to show that it properly included all the varied interests of the people."[7] Neither Schlesinger nor Fox personally devoted much attention to medical history, but both helped to create a climate of opinion receptive to such innovations and encouraged their students to cultivate the field. Before leaving Columbia University for the presidency of Union College, Fox directed what appear to be the first two dissertations written on American medical history: Courtney Robert Hall's biography of Samuel Latham Mitchill and Henry Burnell Shafer's history of the medical profession in antebellum America.[8]

Schlesinger exerted an even greater influence on the field, perhaps second only to Shryock's. During his tenure at Harvard University, which lasted into the 1950s, at least three of his students—George W. Adams, John B. Blake, and Leonard K. Eaton—wrote dissertations on medical subjects that were later published as books, and a fourth, Donald Fleming, wrote a biography of William H. Welch after leaving graduate school. A number of Schlesinger's students, including several who never wrote about medicine themselves, in turn trained a second generation of scholars interested in American medical history.[9]

Already by the early 1960s nonphysicians had thus emerged as the dominant force within American medical historiography. In addition to the Schlesinger school, there were over a half-dozen other American historians working on medical topics, among the most prominent of whom were Whitfield J. Bell, Jr., John C. Burnham, David L. Cowen, Horace H. Cunningham, John Duffy, and James Harvey Young. Indiscriminately lumped together as "social historians of medicine," they often wrote in the manner of cultural and intellectual historians. Although they rarely occupied chairs in medical history or taught in medical schools, they set the standards for acceptable scholarship and redefined the boundaries of the field. Physician-historians, most of whom were neither trained nor employed as historians, continued to produce local, institutional, and biographical studies, but they increasingly found themselves outside the mainstream of American medical history.

The Shape of the Field, 1962-1981

In order to identify as objectively as possible recent developments in the writing of American medical history, early in 1982 I sent a questionnaire to sixty-five members of the American Association for the History of Medicine, a voluntary society founded in 1925 and open to anyone interested in joining. All sixty-five had published books or articles on the history of medicine in America. I asked them to list the five books, excluding anthologies, published between 1972 and 1981 that had "made the greatest contribution to our understanding of American medicine (broadly conceived)" and to indicate which of the five they deemed most outstanding. To facilitate comparison, I asked them to do the same for books published during the previous ten years. By early March I had received thirty-three useable responses, the results of which are tabulated in Table 1. All but four of the respondents were nonphysicians. Two of the four physicians held Ph.D.'s in history as well as M.D. degrees. Most of the respondents (64 percent) were in mid-career; 9 percent were under age thirty-one, 27 percent were over sixty. Although I applied no statistical tests, my impression is that neither age nor medical training made a significant difference in the responses given.

In a field widely thought to be dominated by physicians, it is striking that only one book listed in Table 1, George W. Corner's history of the Rockefeller Institute, was written by a physician. Sixteen of the authors on the list received their training in departments of history, and nearly half of these could trace their pedigree back to Schlesinger, four (Cassedy, Kett, Reed, and Ettling) through Donald Fleming. The remaining four authors did their graduate work in a variety of disciplines, ranging from epidemiology

Table 1. Leading Contributions to American Medical History, 1962–1981

Published between 1962 and 1971	Ranked in Top 5 by:	Ranked Number 1 by:
1. C. Rosenberg, *Cholera Years* (1962)	82%	42%
2. R. Stevens, *American Medicine and the Public Interest* (1971)	64	15
3. R. Shryock, *Medicine in America* (1966)	52	15
4. J. Kett, *Formation of the American Medical Profession* (1968)	39	3
5. J. H. Young, *Medical Messiahs* (1967)	33	0
6. T. Bonner, *American Doctors and German Universities* (1963)	27	0
7. J. Burrow, *AMA: Voice of American Medicine* (1963)	24	0
8. G. Corner, *History of the Rockefeller Institute* (1964)	18	0
9. J. Cassedy, *Charles V. Chapin* (1962)	15	0
9. G. Grob, *State and the Mentally Ill* (1966)	15	0
9. N. Hale, *Freud and the Americans* (1971)	15	0

Published between 1972 and 1981		
1. W. Rothstein, *American Physicians in the Nineteenth Century* (1972)	58%	15%
2. T. Savitt, *Medicine and Slavery* (1978)	33	9
3. M. Vogel, *Invention of the Modern Hospital* (1980)	33	3
4. G. Grob, *Mental Institutions in America* (1973)	27	0
5. B. Rosenkrantz, *Public Health and the State* (1972)	24	6
6. J. Ettling, *Germ of Laziness* (1981)	24	0
7. E. R. Brown, *Rockefeller Medicine Men* (1979)	21	3
8. S. Strickland, *Politics, Science, and Dread Disease* (1972)	18	3
9. R. Numbers, *Almost Persuaded* (1978)	15	0
9. J. Reed, *From Private Vice to Public Virtue* (1978)	15	0
9. M. Walsh, *"Doctors Wanted: No Women Need Apply"* (1977)	15	0

(Stevens) to political science (Strickland) and sociology (Brown and Rothstein). Not one of the twenty-one came out of a graduate program in the history of medicine. Eleven of the nineteen living authors taught in departments of history, two (Rosenkrantz and Stevens) had primary appointments in history of science departments, and another two (Numbers and Savitt) worked in medical schools. Thus whatever arrangements prevailed for general medical historians, those working in American medical history have received, and continue to receive, their greatest patronage from history departments, a situation that may help to explain the readiness with which they have strayed from physician-oriented history.

Forty books published between 1962 and 1981 appeared on three or more questionnaires. Of this number only six were written by physicians:

James Bordley, III and A. McGehee Harvey, *Two Centuries of American Medicine, 1776-1976* (1976)

George W. Corner, *A History of the Rockefeller Institute, 1901-1953* (1964)

Harry F. Dowling, *Fighting Infection: Conquests of the Twentieth Century* (1977)

Peter C. English, *Shock, Physiological Surgery, and George Washington Crile: Medical Innovation in the Progressive Era* (1980)

David F. Musto, *The American Disease: Origins of Narcotic Control* (1973)

George Rosen, *Preventive Medicine in the United States, 1900-1975* (1976)

The authors of three of these books—Corner, Dowling, Bordley, and Harvey—were eminent physicians interested primarily in chronicling the achievements of medicine. Rosen earned a doctorate in sociology as well as in medicine, Musto, a master's degree in history. Only one of the top forty books on American medicine published in the past twenty years, English's biography of Crile, was written by a person possessing both an M.D. and a Ph.D. in history.

It may be significant, although I am not sure, that all of these physician-authored books focus on the twentieth century. Even the Bordley and Harvey volume, an old-fashioned celebration of medical progress that begins with the American Revolution, devotes over half of its pages to the period after World War II and seven-eighths of its space to the past hundred years. But lest anyone conclude that physician-historians monopolize twentieth-century medical history because of their technical expertise, I should point out that half of the books listed in Table 1, all but one written by nonphysicians, also focus on the twentieth century. It may be true that nonphysicians writing about the twentieth century have shied away from discussing the internal history of medicine, but then so have physician-historians like Corner, Musto, and Rosen.

To determine if similar patterns of authorship existed for articles on American medical history as well as for books, I asked the historians receiving my questionnaire to list the most influential articles published during the past two decades. Although a number of respondents chose not to answer this question, the responses I did receive are, I believe, suggestive. Five of the six articles most frequently mentioned were by Charles Rosenberg:

"The Practice of Medicine in New York a Century Ago," *Bulletin of the History of Medicine* 41 (1967): 223-53. [mentioned 11 times]

"The Therapeutic Revolution: Medicine, Meaning, and Social Change in Nineteenth-Century America," *Perspectives in Biology and Medicine* 20 (1977): 485-506. [7]

"Social Class and Medical Care in 19th-Century America: The Rise and Fall of the Dispensary," *Journal of the History of Medicine* 29 (1974): 32-54. [7]

"Inward Vision and Outward Glance: The Shaping of the American Hospital, 1880-1914," *Bulletin of the History of Medicine* 53 (1979): 345-91. [4]

"Pietism and the Origins of the American Public Health Movement: A Note on John H. Griscom and Robert M. Hartley," *Journal of the History of Medicine* 23 (1968): 16-35. Written with Carroll Smith-Rosenberg. [4]

This list and Table 1 suggest that Rosenberg now occupies the position once held by Shryock as the leading practitioner of American medical history. Trained as an undergraduate in history at the University of Wisconsin, where the physician-historian Ackerknecht introduced him to the history of medicine, he went on to study with Richard Hofstadter in the Department of History at Columbia University and to spend a year as a fellow at the Institute of the History of Medicine affiliated with the Johns Hopkins Medical School. His education thus embraced the best of both American and medical history. His first book, *The Cholera Years*, by far the most admired book in the field published since 1961, received the unqualified praise of both communities. In this, as well as in his other writings, he has convincingly demonstrated the interdependence of medical and cultural history. His insistence on situating medical developments within their cultural context and on exploring connections between ideas and institutions has helped to tear down the artificial barrier that an older generation had erected between the internal and external history of medicine. His work on the history of therapeutics, conceded by many to be the most perceptive analysis of this historically treacherous subject ever published, showed that lack of medical training need not deter an industrious and intelligent historian from tackling technical medical topics.

Of the eighteen "most influential" articles listed by more than one respondent, four were by physician-historians:

Robert P. Hudson, "Abraham Flexner in Perspective: American Medical Education, 1865-1910," *Bulletin of the History of Medicine,* 56 (1972): 545-61. [mentioned 7 times]

Edward C. Atwater, "The Medical Profession in a New Society: Rochester, New York (1811-60)," *Bulletin of the History of Medicine* 47 (1973):

221-35; and "The Physicians of Rochester, N.Y., 1860-1910: A Study in
Professional History, II," *ibid.* 51 (1977): 93-106. [3]

Gert H. Brieger, "American Surgery and the Germ Theory of Disease,"
Bulletin of the History of Medicine 40 (1966): 135-45. [2]

George Rosen, "The First Neighborhood Health Center Movement—Its
Rise and Fall," *American Journal of Public Health* 61 (1971): 1620-35. [2]

Two features of this list are noteworthy. In view of the medical training and
experience of the authors, it is curious that three of the four describe social,
rather than technical, developments. It is also significant, I think, that all four
earned graduate degrees in addition to their M.D.'s. Rosen, as mentioned
earlier, held a Ph.D. in sociology; Brieger, Hudson, and Atwater studied at
the Johns Hopkins Institute of the History of Medicine, with Brieger earning a
Ph.D. and Hudson and Atwater M.A.'s. Does this suggest that the time has
passed when a physician untrained in history or the social sciences is likely to
make a meaningful contribution to medical history? If so, it would not be surprising. After all, medical history is one of the few remaining academic fields
in which amateurs still expect to participate on an equal basis with professionals.

The predominance of nonphysicians in the history of medicine and the proliferation of studies on its socioeconomic aspects rather than on its internal
development have lately provoked a strong reaction among physician-
historians and sympathizers who worry, as the editor of the *Journal of the
History of Medicine* put it, that academically trained historians are writing
"medical history without medicine." He feared that scholars trained in
historical seminars rather than in clinics and laboratories would tend to
ignore "basic medical science and clinical methods and concepts." [10] Using
more picturesque language, the editor of the *Bulletin of the History of
Medicine* complained that the present generation of American medical
historians was reducing the great doctors of the past to bits of "flotsam on a
great economic or social current." [11]

Those for whom medical history was more of a hobby than a career
especially resented the ascendancy of nonphysicians. "[T]he obvious fact that
the history of medicine seems to be coming under the control of Ph.D.'s" has
created a "malaise or exasperation among certain M.D.'s," observed an
amateur physician-historian in 1979. The takeover by historians untrained in
clinical medicine, he thought, boded ill for the field because nonphysicians,
who learned about medicine from written sources rather than from experience, lacked the sensitivity to interpret the past correctly. [12] The Ph.D.'s, for
their part, often showed little appreciation for the physician turned historian.
To them, physicians practicing history made about as much sense as
historians practicing medicine.

It would be inaccurate, however, to leave the impression that the community of medical historians is neatly divided between M.D.'s and Ph.D.'s. There have always been historians who encouraged the participation of physicians, as well as physicians who supported the professionalization of medical history. Besides, if anything, there are three, not two, distinct interest groups. On one hand are the practicing physicians for whom history is an avocation. Many in this group identify with the type of inspirational medical history written by Sir William Osler, who believed that the great doctors of the past could serve as positive models for the present. In 1969 some of these physician-historians formed the American Osler Society, an exclusive body that meets alternately with the American Association for the History of Medicine (AAHM) and the American College of Physicians.

On the other hand are the academically trained historians, including most of the historians of American medicine, who typically reside in departments of history. They write medical history not to inspire the present generation of health professionals but to understand the past for its own sake or, in some instances, to illuminate present concerns. They may or may not belong to the AAHM; if they do, it is often less central to their professional lives than the Organization of American Historians or the American Historical Association.

Between the practicing physicians and the academic historians is a comparatively small group of historians trained in both medicine and history. These scholars generally teach in medical schools in departments of medical history or medical humanities and attach a great deal of value to their role as medical educators. Although they may teach some nonmedical students, their primary pedagogic goal is to train "humanist" physicians, a task for which they believe themselves uniquely qualified. "[T]he physician-professional-historian is undoubtedly the best qualified person to teach medical history," declared one of them recently, at the same time acknowledging that non-physicians could probably do a competent job of teaching "in fields related to medicine, especially those areas related to the social history of medicine which do not require any professional medical training."[13] A few years ago these medical educators organized their own informal society, with admission by invitation only; they continue as well to provide leadership in the AAHM at a level disproportionate to their numbers.

New Directions

Critics of medical history, both inside and outside the field, have frequently complained that its cultivators place too much emphasis on heroic physicians and medical milestones and too little on the social context in which healing takes place. If these criticism fairly reflect American medical historiography before the 1970s—and I suspect they do not—they certainly are no longer valid, especially if we look beyond the cadre of self-proclaimed medical historians to the larger community of scholars who write about the history of health care in America.

If we compare the books on American medical history published during the ten years preceding 1972 with those published since, we see considerable continuity of interest. Medical historians continued to write biographies of famous doctors and nurses,[14] accounts of medical institutions,[15] studies of public-health reform,[16] and analyses of public-policy debates.[17] But in at least three traditional areas of research—physicians, hospitals, and public health—the scholarship of the 1970s and early 1980s markedly advanced our understanding of the past, in each instance by broadening the search for causal explanations.

According to Table 1, the most important book of the past decade was William G. Rothstein's *American Physicians in the Nineteenth Century: From Sects to Science.* In it the author, a sociologist, recast the entire history of the medical profession in the nineteenth century. Instead of focusing on professional leaders, he looked at "the behavior of the majority of the professionally trained physicians." Instead of explaining their actions in altruistic terms, he stressed their economic self-interest. And, most radical of all, instead of distinguishing between the body of orthodox practitioners (allopaths) and their sectarian competitors, he treated the allopaths as merely another sect, albeit the largest and most powerful one.[18]

Rothstein's work was not without its flaws—most notably its Whiggish distinction between medically valid and invalid therapies and its arbitrary definition of sects—but its blemishes were scarcely so offensive as to warrant the outrage and scorn with which some physician-historians greeted it. One, quoting Friedrich Engels, judged Rothstein's muted economic interpretation to be "almost identical to the materialist conception of history." Another belittled his book as "a provocative paradox of historiographical and medical naïveté." A third described it as illustrating "the point that a non-medical historian should be very careful before getting into technical concepts, practices and areas."[19] Such criticism smacked of a double standard: winking at the historical slips of physicians while damning nonphysicians for the most trivial of medical errors.

During the past century the general hospital emerged as the most visible symbol of modern medicine; yet historians until very recently overlooked this development. There were, to be sure, numerous chronicles of individual institutions, but no analyses of the unprecedented growth of hospitals between 1875 and 1925 or of their transformation from a marginal to a central role in the provision of health care. This dismal record improved dramatically with the back-to-back appearance of two landmark studies of the general hospital: Morris J. Vogel's history of Boston hospitals in the late nineteenth and early twentieth centuries and David K. Rosner's study of hospitals in New York and Brooklyn.[20] Both authors treated the hospital more as a social than a medical institution, and both emphasized change rather than progress. In place of the prevailing notion that scientific and technological advances (e.g., anesthesia and the x-ray) gave birth to the modern hospital, they pointed to a host of equally important social, political, and economic factors and argued that institutional change often preceded technological innovation. Although neither Vogel nor Rosner denied the significance of medical science and technology, they left the impression that such influences were of secondary consequence. Such radical revisionism prompted Charles Rosenberg to warn historians not to let the glitter of socioeconomic interpretations blind them to the positive role played by scientific medicine.[21]

Mental hospitals, or insane asylums as they used to be called, attracted great historical attention during the 1970s, often on the part of persons disillusioned with institutionalized care for the mentally ill and convinced that such institutions served as agents of social control rather than human betterment. Although reassessment of the asylum—and the very notion of mental illness—began before the 1970s, American historians tended to remain outside the debate until 1971, when David J. Rothman published *The Discovery of the Asylum*, a widely read work that likened the antebellum insane asylum to the penitentiary. In contrast to those who viewed the asylum as a benevolent reform, Rothman portrayed it primarily as an instrument of social control.[22]

Foremost among the scholars who challenged Rothman was Gerald N. Grob, who in 1973 published a comprehensive history of mental institutions in America before 1875. There and elsewhere Grob maintained that the asylum represented a response to real social and medical needs and should not be seen simply as an agency "by which dominant elites restrained deviant groups . . . thereby ensuring their own hegemony." He agreed with Rothman that the asylums failed to fulfill their early promise but attributed this failure to temporary setbacks, not to "an inevitable consequence of institutional solutions."[23]

The rewriting of public health history in the 1970s closely paralleled that of hospital history. Although historians of public health had produced some useful biographical and community studies prior to the 1970s, much of the work in this area, like that dealing with hospitals, contained little analysis, overemphasized progress, and slighted the context in which reform took place. Glimmers of a more sophisticated approach to public health appeared in Stuart Galishoff's 1975 monograph on Newark during the Progressive era.[24] But it was Judith Walzer Leavitt's analysis of the politics of health reform in Milwaukee that set the standard for studying public health at the local level. Rather than simply describing the activities of the city health department in fighting disease, improving sanitation, and regulating food, Leavitt (like Galishoff, an urban historian) examined the processes by which change occurred, paying as close attention to the activities and motivations of the opponents of reform as to those of the proponents.[25]

Despite the understandable inclination of public-health historians to concentrate on local communities—especially urban ones—some have produced valuable state and regional studies. The best examples of such works are Barbara Gutmann Rosenkrantz's history of the Massachusetts State Board of Health and John Ettling's splendidly written history of the Rockefeller Foundation's efforts to eradicate hookworm disease in the South. In a refreshing departure from the current fashion of emphasizing economic motivation, Ettling stressed instead the religious roots of the antihookworm campaign, cleverly drawing parallels between county hookworm dispensaries and southern tent revivals and describing hookworm as the medical equivalent of sin.[26]

Some of the most exciting—if not always the most reliable—medical history to come out of the past decade has focused on subjects previously on the periphery of medical history (e.g., blacks and women) and on relationships previously unexamined (e.g., between medicine and capitalism). Although medical historians writing before the 1970s occasionally wrote about the health care of black Americans, the civil rights movement and the resulting explosion of interest in Afro-American history directed unprecedented attention to the topic, particularly to the questions of whether blacks were biologically different from whites and how such differences, if they existed, affected black history. In the best-informed attempt to answer these questions, Todd L. Savitt, a medical student turned southern historian, examined the health status of slaves in antebellum Virginia. In addition to determining patterns of illness and access to health care, he looked at the ways in which diet, dress, housing, and labor may have affected their health. The result was not only the most comprehensive analysis of sickness and health among blacks, but perhaps the most comprehensive medicohistorical study of any segment of the American population.[27] The 1970s failed, however, to produce much in the way of scholarship about the role of blacks as providers of health care or about health care among other minority groups.

Like blacks, women remained on the margins of medical history until the 1970s, when the feminist movement discovered the ideological importance of the field. The first angry outburst at the way women had suffered in the past came from two radical scholars outside of history, Barbara Ehrenreich, a biologist, and Deirdre English, a social worker. In the early 1970s they collaborated on two widely circulated pamphlets that accused male physicians of actively suppressing women health workers and of fostering "sexist ideology and sexual oppression."[28]

Simultaneously with the publication of these accusations there appeared an influential essay by Ann Douglas Wood, a specialist in American literature, who described relationships between nineteenth-century physicians and their women patients in terms of "psychological warfare." Male physicians, she alleged, gave vent to their "agressively hostile male sexuality and superiority" by subjecting their female victims to treatments with "injections, leeches, and hot irons." In contrast, women physicians, who were just entering the profession, sought to free their sisters from male control and to provide more humane treatment.[29] A few years later, G. J. Barker-Benfield, a historian, brought out a psychoanalytical study of the attitudes of nineteenth-century male physicians toward women, provocatively titled *The Horrors of the Half-Known Life*, and Richard and Dorothy Wertz published a history of childbirth in America in which they attributed the elimination of midwives to the strivings of male physicians to satisfy their economic and "psychosexual needs."[30] Although these early studies often read more like polemics than history, and frequently displayed a shocking disregard for the factual integrity of medical history, they nevertheless played a positive role in directing attention away from elites and in suggesting new directions for historical investigation.

One of the first women historians to call for an end to polemics was Regina Markell Morantz, who argued cogently that the medical experiences of women could be properly understood only when placed in historical context. Her own work demonstrated how this could be done. For example, to determine whether the medical practices of nineteenth-century women physicians differed from those of male physicians, she and Sue Zschoche compared the obstetrical records of two Boston hospitals, one run by female doctors, the other by males. Contrary to the assertions of Wood and others, they found striking similarities in both medical theory and practice.[31] In a similarly constructive way Carroll Smith-Rosenberg went beyond the rhetoric of sexual oppression to show how the sometimes negative beliefs of male physicians toward women helped to legitimize their professional role.[32]

The groundswell of interest in women's history produced a series of excellent studies of women as healers: doctors, nurses, and midwives. As indicated above, the demise of the midwife came, for some feminists, to symbolize the perversity of male physicians. However, in an illuminating monograph on the post-Civil War midwife, Judy Barrett Litoff, following a line of argument earlier suggested by Frances E. Kobrin, revealed a complex story in which social and cultural factors contributed as much to the decline of midwifery as did the arguments and activities of physicians.[33]

Mary Roth Walsh's history of women physicians, *"Doctors Wanted: No Women Need Apply,"* also corrected many myths. Using the Boston area as a case study, she showed that, contrary to almost universal belief, women enjoyed a "golden age" as physicians in the late nineteenth century, before sexual quotas reduced their access to medical schools. Surprisingly, rising professional standards for physicians seemed to have had little effect on the number of women doctors.[34]

For nearly a century the history of nursing was customarily written for nurses by nurses. In the 1970s, however, historians discovered the nurse and introduced critical analysis into nursing history. In a radical departure from traditional historiography, Barbara Melosh drew on the techniques of cultural, feminist, and labor history to rewrite the history of nursing since 1920. Generally ignoring professional leaders, who she believed represented a minority position among nurses, she emphasized instead the work experiences of "ordinary nurses" and their "shop-floor culture," giving us one of the finest examples of medical history written from the bottom up.[35]

Whereas Melosh came across as being more radical in method than tone, other historians have adopted an explicitly political stance in writing about American medicine. Linda Gordon's "Marxist-Feminist" analysis of the American birth-control movement, *Woman's Body, Woman's Right,* gives what one sympathetic reviewer has described as "a concrete picture of how certain economic and political forces within American capitalism have influenced the relationship of women and medicine."[36] According to their own account, Marxist historians of medicine see physicians "not as disembodied intellects, but as social products of a specific culture," and they view medical knowledge "as ideology in the service of an elite, with no more claim to objectivity than political or philosophical ideas." Thus, for example, they do not ask how medical scientists discovered a disease, but why they invented it.[37]

American medical historians of radical persuasion have tended to concentrate not so much on the invention of diseases as on the development of a medical system in the service of capitalism. In an influential 1973 essay on "the use of medical education reform to establish modern professional elitism in medicine," Gerald E. Markowitz and David K. Rosner argued that the much-applauded reforms of the early twentieth century "centralized, bureaucratized, modernized and expanded medicine and medical education in the interests of physicians' own professional needs and with little regard for the needs of the public." In a similar vein, Howard S. Berliner viewed the Carnegie-funded Flexner Report of 1910 as "an attempt by the capitalist class" to solidify the position of a medical elite, not as a praiseworthy effort to upgrade medical education and improve medical care.[38]

In *Rockefeller Medicine Men: Medicine and Capitalism in America,* the most controversial medical history of the past decade, E. Richard Brown, a sociologist and health planner, gave this argument its fullest treatment to date. With an eye constantly on the present, he traced the roots of the current "crisis" in health care back to the turn of the century, when the Carnegie and Rockefeller foundations donated millions of dollars to develop "a medical system to meet the needs of capitalist society," specifically the maintenance of a healthy work force and the legitimation of the human misery they were creating. In Brown's hands, scientific medicine emerged "not as the determining force in the development of modern health care but as a tool developed by members of the medical profession and the corporate class to serve their perceived needs." [39]

Although much of the work of these radical historians has been too long on polemics and too short on evidence to suit my taste, they have, I believe, exposed some important ties between medicine and society, and they have forced some of the more timid of us to expand our historiographical horizons. They have also dragged medical history out of its ivory tower and thrust it into the public arena. If the recently published studies by Rosner (on New York hospitals) and Melosh (on nursing)—both long on scholarship and short on polemics—are harbingers of things to come, we can expect some of the most stimulating medical history of the 1980s to come from this quarter.

Second Thoughts

In 1971 Charles Rosenberg called for a "new emphasis" in the history of medicine, a shift away from the intellectual life of physicians to their activities as healers and as members of a profession. Medical historians, he said, needed to place medicine in its social and cultural context and to explore the ways in which socioeconomic factors might have influenced medical developments. [40] Rosenberg's call, as we have seen, did not go unheeded. In fact, during the following decade American medical historians devoted so much attention to nonintellectual factors that even the social-history advocates began to express concern. As early as 1977 Gerald N. Grob noted "an excessive preoccupation with socioeconomic determinants" and an inability on the part of many social historians of medicine to deal intelligently with the history of disease. John B. Blake, a Schlesinger student, observed that the fascination of American medical historians with social issues and irregular healers was creating "a distorted view not only of scientific history but also of the professional history that is their central concern." And by 1979 even Rosenberg was urging medical historians not to underestimate the importance of medical science and other intellectual currents. [41]

To a certain extent these warnings are well taken. Compared with the abundance of first-rate studies on the social and cultural aspects of American medicine, the past decade produced few comparable accounts of theory and practice, disease, or basic research.[42] I do, however, question the notion that regular physicians and their activities should be the "central concern" of American medical historians. Our primary goal, as I see it, is to explain the changing patterns of sickness and health in America, the part played by physicians in alleviating suffering and prolonging life being only one facet of the record.

The publications of the British physician-historian Thomas McKeown on declining mortality rates in England and Wales, as well as recent epidemiological studies, suggest that nutrition, sanitation, and personal life-style have had—and continue to have—a greater effect than curative medicine on health and longevity. If this is true, then we should be worrying far more about the historical neglect of diet, housing, and personal hygiene than about the temporary eclipse of physicians.[43]

Another glaring gap in the literature of American medicine is the absence of a critical survey that synthesizes existing scholarship. Since Francis R. Packard brought out his fact-filled *History of Medicine in the United States* at the turn of the century, few historians have had the courage to undertake such a task. Richard Shryock made an elegant beginning in *Medicine and Society in America*, but failed to carry the story beyond 1860. John Duffy marked the Bicentennial with a survey called *The Healers*, a convenient summary for the general reader, but left many areas unexplored and unanalyzed.[44] Thus we have no suitable interpretation of American medicine to offer students and other scholars interested in learning about the subject.

I began this essay by pointing to the long-standing difficulty of defining medical history and its practitioners. The developments of the past decade have, if anything, exacerbated the problem. The discovery of medicine by historians of women and blacks, professionals and laborers, urban society and southern culture, has all but erased any boundaries that may previously have distinguished the field of American medicine. Personally, I welcome the change. Medical history is too important to be left to "medical historians."

1. Erwin H. Ackerknecht, Review of *Medical Education in the United States before the Civil War*, by William Frederick Norwood, *Quarterly Review of Biology* 20 (1945): 96.

2. Susan Reverby and David Rosner, "Beyond 'the Great Doctors,'" in *Health Care in America: Essays in Social History*, eds. Reverby and Rosner (Philadelphia: Temple University Press, 1979), p. 3.

3. Quoted in Gert H. Brieger, "The History of Medicine and the History of Science," *Isis* 72 (1981): 538. Italics added.

4. Richard H. Shryock, "The Historian Looks at Medicine," *Bulletin of the Institute of the History of Medicine* 5 (1937): 890. Italics added. Ironically, Shryock later became the first, and only, nonphysician to direct the Johns Hopkins Institute of the History of Medicine.

5. On the preprofessional period of American medical history, see Whitfield J. Bell, Jr., "The Writing of American Medical History before Professionalization," *Transactions and Studies of the College of Physicians of Philadelphia* 42 (1974): 49–60.

6. Whitfield J. Bell, Jr., "Richard H. Shryock: Life and Work of a Historian," *Journal of the History of Medicine and Allied Sciences* 29 (1974): 18.

7. Arthur M. Schlesinger, *In Retrospect: The History of a Historian* (New York: Harcourt, Brace & World, 1963), p. 113. See also Dixon Ryan Fox, *Ideas in Motion* (New York: D. Appleton-Century, 1935), pp. 81–82, 87.

8. As far as I can tell, these are the first published dissertations on American medical history: Courtney Robert Hall, *A Scientist in the Early Republic: Samuel Latham Mitchill, 1764–1831* (New York: Columbia University Press, 1934); Henry Burnell Shafer, *The American Medical Profession, 1783 to 1850* (New York: Columbia University Press, 1936); Helen E. Marshall, *Dorothea Dix: Forgotten Samaritan* (Chapel Hill: University of North Carolina Press, 1973); St. Julien Ravenel Childs, *Malaria and Colonization in the Carolina Low Country, 1526–1696* (Baltimore: Johns Hopkins Press, 1940); William Frederick Norwood, *Medical Education in the United States before the Civil War* (Philadelphia: University of Pennsylvania Press, 1944), completed as a dissertation in 1939.

9. A. Hunter Dupree, "The History of American Science—A Field Finds Itself," *American Historical Review* 71 (1968): 867. A partial list of second-generation Schlesinger students who have written on medical history includes Thomas N. Bonner (Ray Allen Billington), James H. Cassedy (Donald Fleming), John Ettling (Fleming), Nathan G. Hale, Jr. (Henry F. May), Joseph F. Kett (Fleming), Judith Walzer Leavitt (Richard C. Wade), William Frederick Norwood (Erik M. Eriksson), Ronald L. Numbers (A. Hunter Dupree), and James Reed (Fleming).

10. [Leonard Wilson], "Medical History without Medicine," *Journal of the History of Medicine* 35 (1980): 5–7. See also [Wilson], "Schizophrenia in Learned Societies: Professionalism vs. Scholarship," *ibid.* 36 (1981): 5–8.

11. Lloyd G. Stevenson, "A Second Opinion," *Bulletin of the History of Medicine* 54 (1980): 135.

12. Gordon W. Jones, Letter to the Editor, *Journal of the History of Medicine* 34 (1979): 457–58; see also Jones, Review of *Lying-in: A History of Childbirth in America*, by Richard W. Wertz and Dorothy C. Wertz, *ibid.*, pp. 113–14.

13. Guenter B. Risse, "The Role of Medical History in the Education of the 'Humanist' Physician: A Reevaluation," *Journal of Medical Education* 50 (1975): 463. For a recent opinion by a physician-historian of the qualifications needed for writing medical history, see Gert H. Brieger, "History of Medicine," in *A Guide to the Culture of Science, Technology, and Medicine*, ed. Paul T. Durbin (New York: Free Press, 1980), pp. 165–66.

14. See, e.g., Helen E. Marshall, *Mary Adelaide Nutting: Pioneer of Modern Nursing* (Baltimore: Johns Hopkins University Press, 1972); James O. Breeden, *Joseph Jones, M.D.: Scientist of the Old South* (Lexington: University Press of Kentucky, 1975); Gerald N. Grob, *Edward Jarvis and the Medical World of Nineteenth-Century America* (Knoxville: University of Tennessee Press, 1978); Peter C. English, *Shock, Physiological Surgery, and George Washington Crile: Medical Innovation in the Progressive Era* (Westport, Conn.: Greenwood Press, 1980).

15. On medical schools, see, e.g., Martin Kaufman, *American Medical Education: The Formative Years, 1765–1910* (Westport, Conn.: Greenwood Press, 1976); and *The University of Vermont College of Medicine* (Hanover, N.H.: University Press of New England, 1979); Ronald L. Numbers, ed., *The Education of American Physicians: Historical Essays* (Berkeley: University of California Press, 1980). On medical societies, see, e.g., James G. Burrow, *Organized Medicine in the Progressive Era: The Move Toward Monopoly* (Baltimore: Johns Hopkins University Press, 1977); Ronald L. Numbers, *Almost Persuaded: American Physicians and Compulsory Health Insurance, 1912–1920* (Baltimore: Johns Hopkins University Press, 1978).

16. See, e.g., John Duffy, *A History of Public Health in New York City, 1866–1966* (New York: Russell Sage Foundation, 1974).

17. On pesticides, see James Whorton, *Before Silent Spring: Pesticides and Public Health in Pre-DDT America* (Princeton: Princeton University Press, 1974); Thomas R. Dunlap, *DDT: Scientists, Citizens, and Public Policy* (Princeton: Princeton University Press, 1981). On drugs, see David F. Musto, *The American Disease: Origins of Narcotic Control* (New Haven: Yale

University Press, 1973). On medical research, see Stephen P. Strickland, *Politics, Science, and Dread Disease: A Short History of United States Medical Research Policy* (Cambridge: Harvard University Press, 1972). On government health insurance, see Monte M. Poen, *Harry S. Truman versus the Medical Lobby: The Genesis of Medicare* (Columbia: University of Missouri Press, 1979); Ronald L. Numbers, ed., *Compulsory Health Insurance: The Continuing American Debate* (Westport, Conn.: Greenwood Press, 1982).

18. William G. Rothstein, *American Physicians in the Nineteenth Century: From Sects to Science* (Baltimore: Johns Hopkins University Press, 1972). On osteopathic physicians, see Norman Gevitz, *The D.O.'s: Osteopathic Medicine in America* (Baltimore: Johns Hopkins University Press, 1982).

19. Reviews of *American Physicians in the Nineteenth Century*, by William G. Rothstein: J. B. deC. M. Saunders, *Journal of Medical Education* 48 (1973): 298; Chester R. Burns, *Journal of the American Medical Association* 223 (1973): 1166; George Rosen, *Clio Medica* 9 (1974): 162.

20. Morris J. Vogel, *The Invention of the Modern Hospital: Boston, 1870-1930* (Chicago: University of Chicago Press, 1980); David K. Rosner, *A Once Charitable Enterprise: Hospitals and Health Care in Brooklyn and New York, 1885-1915* (Cambridge, England: Cambridge University Press, 1982). See also Charles Rosenberg, "And Heal the Sick: Hospital and Patient in 19th Century America," *Journal of Social History* 10 (1977): 428-47; and "Inward Vision & Outward Glance: The Shaping of the American Hospital, 1880-1914," *The Bulletin of the History of Medicine* 53 (1979): 346-91.

21. Charles Rosenberg, "The Origins of the American Hospital System," *Bulletin of the New York Academy of Medicine* 55 (1979): 17.

22. David J. Rothman, *The Discovery of the Asylum: Social Order and Disorder in the New Republic* (Boston: Little, Brown, 1971). See also Rothman's sequel, *Conscience and Convenience: The Asylum and Its Alternatives in Progressive America* (Boston: Little, Brown, 1980).

23. Gerald N. Grob, "Rediscovering Asylums: The Unhistorical History of the Mental Hospital," in *The Therapeutic Revolution: Essays in the Social History of American Medicine*, eds. Morris J. Vogel and Charles Rosenberg (Philadelphia: University of Pennsylvania Press, 1979), p. 136; Gerald N. Grob, *Mental Institutions in America: Social Policy to 1875* (New York: Free Press, 1973). See also Richard W. Fox, *So Far Disordered in Mind: Insanity in California, 1870-1930* (Berkeley: University of California Press, 1978).

24. Stuart Galishoff, *Safeguarding the Public Health: Newark, 1895-1918* (Westport, Conn.: Greenwood Press, 1975).

25. Judith Walzer Leavitt, *The Healthiest City: Milwaukee and the Politics of Health Reform* (Princeton: Princeton University Press, 1982).

26. Barbara Gutmann Rosenkrantz, *Public Health and the State: Changing Views in Massachusetts, 1842-1936* (Cambridge: Harvard University Press, 1972); John Ettling, *The Germ of Laziness: Rockefeller Philanthropy and Public Health in the New South* (Cambridge: Harvard University Press, 1981).

27. Todd L. Savitt, *Medicine and Slavery: The Diseases and Health Care of Blacks in Antebellum Virginia* (Urbana: University of Illinois Press, 1978). See also Kenneth F. Kiple and Virginia Himmelsteib King, *Another Dimension to the Black Diaspora: Diet, Disease, and Racism* (Cambridge, England: Cambridge University Press, 1981). On blacks and human experimentation, see James H. Jones, *Bad Blood: The Tuskegee Syphilis Experiment* (New York: Free Press, 1981).

28. Barbara Ehrenreich and Deirdre English, *Witches, Midwives, and Nurses: A History of Women Healers*, 2nd ed. (Old Westbury, N.Y.: Feminist Press, 1973); and *Complaints and Disorders: The Sexual Politics of Sickness* (Old Westbury, N.Y.: Feminist Press, 1973). See also their later volume, *For Her Own Good: 150 Years of the Experts' Advice to Women* (Garden City, N.Y.: Anchor Press/Doubleday, 1978).

29. Ann Douglas Wood, "'The Fashionable Diseases': Women's Complaints and Their Treatment in Nineteenth-Century America," *Journal of Interdisciplinary History* 4 (1973): 25-52.

30. G. J. Barker-Benfield, *The Horrors of the Half-Known Life: Male Attitudes Toward*

Women and Sexuality in Nineteenth-Century America (New York: Harper & Row, 1976);
Richard W. Wertz and Dorothy C. Wertz, *Lying-in: A History of Childbirth in America* (New
York: Free Press, 1977).

31. Regina Markell Morantz, "The Perils of Feminist History," *The Journal of Interdisciplinary History* 4 (1974): 649–60; and with Sue Zschoche, "Professionalism, Feminism,
and Gender Roles: A Comparative Study of Nineteenth-Century Medical Therapeutics," *Journal of American History* 67 (1980): 568–88.

32. Carroll Smith-Rosenberg, "Puberty to Menopause: The Cycle of Femininity in
Nineteenth-Century America," *Feminist Studies* 1 (1973): 58–72. See also Smith-Rosenberg,
"The Hysterical Woman: Sex Roles and Role Conflict in 19th-Century America," *Social
Research* 39 (1972): 652–78; and with Charles Rosenberg, "The Female Animal: Medical and
Biological Views of Woman and Her Role in Nineteenth-Century America," *The Journal of
American History* 60 (1973): 332–56; John S. Haller, Jr., and Robin M. Haller, *The Physician
and Sexuality in Victorian America* (Urbana: University of Illinois Press, 1974); Sarah Stage,
Female Complaints: Lydia Pinkham and the Business of Women's Medicine (New York: W. W.
Norton, 1979).

33. Judy Barrett Litoff, *American Midwives: 1860 to the Present* (Westport, Conn.: Greenwood Press, 1978); Frances E. Kobrin, "The American Midwife Controversy: A Crisis of Professionalization," *The Bulletin of the History of Medicine* 40 (1966): 350–63. See also Jane B.
Donegan, *Women & Men Midwives: Medicine, Morality, and Misogyny in Early America*
(Westport, Conn.: Greenwood Press, 1978).

34. Mary Roth Walsh, *"Doctors Wanted: No Women Need Apply": Sexual Barriers in the
Medical Profession, 1835–1975* (New Haven: Yale University Press, 1977).

35. Barbara Melosh, *The Physician's Hand: Work Culture and Conflict in American Nursing*
(Philadelphia: Temple University Press, 1982). For other examples of the new nursing history,
see Jane E. Mottus, *New York Nightingales: The Emergence of the Nursing Profession at
Bellevue and New York Hospital, 1850–1920* (Ann Arbor, Mich.: UMI Research Press, 1980);
Susan Reverby, "The Search for the Hospital Yardstick: Nursing and the Rationalization of
Hospital Work," in *Health Care in America*, pp. 206–25.

36. Martha H. Verbrugge, "Women and Medicine in Nineteenth-Century America," *Signs* 1
(1976): 968; Linda Gordon, *Woman's Body, Woman's Right: A Social History of Birth Control
in America* (New York: Grossman, 1976). For an excellent account of the birth-control movement that pays more attention than Gordon to the medical profession, see James Reed, *From
Private Vice to Public Virtue: The Birth Control Movement and American Society since 1830*
(New York: Basic Books, 1978). See also James C. Mohr, *Abortion in America: The Origins
and Evolution of National Policy, 1800–1900* (New York: Oxford University Press, 1978).

37. Terry M. Parssinen and Karen Kerner, "Development of the Disease Model of Drug
Addiction in Britain, 1870–1926," *Medical History* 24 (1980): 294–95. For a much-cited exam-
ple of this type of history, see Karl Figlio, "Chlorosis and Chronic Disease in Nineteenth-
Century Britain: The Social Constitution of Somatic Illness in a Capitalist Society," *Social
History* 3 (1979): 167–97.

38. Gerald E. Markowitz and David Karl Rosner, "Doctors in Crisis: A Study of the Use of
Medical Education Reform to Establish Modern Professional Elitism in Medicine," *American
Quarterly* 25 (1973): 107; Howard S. Berliner, "A Larger Perspective on the Flexner Report,"
International Journal of Health Services 5 (1975): 573–92.

39. E. Richard Brown, *Rockefeller Medicine Men: Medicine and Capitalism in America*
(Berkeley: University of California Press, 1979), pp. 4, 127. For typical responses to Brown, see
Howard S. Berliner, Review of *Rockefeller Medicine Men* and Other Books, *The Bulletin of the
History of Medicine* 54 (1980): 131–34; Lloyd G. Stevenson, "A Second Opinion," *ibid.*, pp.
134–40; E. Richard Brown and Daniel M. Fox, "Deuce-Ace Book Reviewing: A Third
Opinion," *ibid.*, pp. 589–93; Harold Y. Vanderpool, Letter to the Editor, *ibid.* 55 (1981):
434–37; Saul Benison, "Ideology *über alles:* An Essay Review," *The Journal of the History of
Medicine* 37 (1982): 83–90.

40. Charles E. Rosenberg, "The Medical Profession, Medical Practice and the History of

Medicine," in *Modern Methods in the History of Medicine,* ed. Edwin Clarke (London: Athlone Press, 1971), pp. 22–35.

41. Gerald N. Grob, "The Social History of Medicine and Disease in America: Problems and Possibilities," in *The Medicine Show: Patients, Physicians and the Perplexities of the Health Revolution in Modern Society,* ed. Patricia Branca (New York: Science History Publications, 1977), p. 2; John B. Blake, "Homeopathy in American History: A Commentary," *Transactions and Studies of the College of Physicians of Philadelphia,* 5, 3 (1981): 92; Rosenberg, "Origins of the American Hospital System," p. 17.

42. For exceptions to this generalization, see Elizabeth W. Etheridge, *The Butterfly Caste: A Social History of Pellagra in the South* (Westport, Conn.: Greenwood Pub. Co., 1972); Ettling, *Germ of Laziness;* Alfred W. Crosby, Jr., *Epidemic and Peace, 1918* (Westport, Conn.: Greenwood Press, 1976); Harry F. Dowling, *Fighting Infection: Conquests of the Twentieth Century* (Cambridge: Harvard University Press, 1977). For a pioneering effort to determine therapeutic practices, see J. Worth Estes, "Therapeutic Practice in Colonial New England," in *Medicine in Colonial Massachusetts, 1620–1820,* eds. Philip Cash, Eric H. Christianson, and J. Worth Estes (Boston: Colonial Society of Massachusetts, 1980), pp. 289–383.

43. Thomas McKeown, *The Modern Rise of Population* (New York: Academic Press, 1976); and *The Role of Medicine: Dream, Mirage, or Nemesis?* (Princeton: Princeton University Press, 1979). Several historians have explored the ideology of personal health reform: Stephen Nissenbaum, *Sex, Diet, and Debility in Jacksonian America: Sylvester Graham and Health Reform* (Westport, Conn.: Greenwood Press, 1980); James Whorton, *Crusaders for Fitness: A History of American Health Reformers, 1830–1920* (Princeton: Princeton University Press, 1982); Ronald L. Numbers, *Prophetess of Health: A Study of Ellen G. White* (New York: Harper & Row, 1976). Among the few historical studies that touch on diet and health are Etheridge, *The Butterfly Caste;* Savitt, *Medicine and Slavery;* and Kiple and King, *Another Dimension to the Black Diaspora.* Leavitt's *The Healthiest City* represents one of the first attempts by an American medical historian to test the applicability of McKeown's thesis to America; see also, Judith Walzer Leavitt and Ronald L. Numbers, "Sickness and Health in America: An Overview," in *Sickness and Health in America: Readings in the History of Medicine and Public Health,* eds. Leavitt and Numbers (Madison: University of Wisconsin Press, 1978), pp. 3–10.

44. Richard Harrison Shryock, *Medicine and Society in America: 1660–1860* (New York: New York University Press, 1960); John Duffy, *The Healers: The Rise of the Medical Establishment* (New York: McGraw-Hill, 1976). John S. Haller, Jr., *American Medicine in Transition, 1840–1910* (Urbana: University of Illinois Press, 1981), is more a collection of discrete essays than a coherent overview. Unfortunately, I have not yet had the opportunity to read Paul Starr, *The Social Transformation of American Medicine* (New York: Basic Books, 1982), which covers the period from 1760 to the present.

CLIO AS PHYSICIST AND MACHINIST

Nathan Reingold

For the historians of science and technology in the United States, 1971 was an *annus mirabilis*. At the time, we did not realize it. An obvious great event of the previous year was the conference at Northwestern University on the nineteenth-century sciences in America whose proceedings appeared in the following year.[1] For a number of us, the conference was a great surprise because so many cared enough to come to Evanston. Although 1971 was not like Newton's great year of 1665–1666 in witnessing overwhelming intellectual feats, it was a year in which the output of articles and books jumped considerably, including a number of works of very high quality in an impressive array of intellectual modes and on a wide range of topics.[2]

Important works had, of course, appeared earlier. In the previous year Raymond P. Stearns published the culmination of a lifetime of research and an epitome of an older mode, *Science in the British Colonies of America*. A more modish work of 1970 was the undeservedly neglected *Dollars for Research: Science and its Patrons in Nineteenth-Century America* by Howard S. Miller. As early as 1966, A. Hunter Dupree, a pioneer practitioner, proclaimed that the field had found itself, arousing an antipathy among "regular" historians of science that still lingers.[3] But despite the appearance of fine articles and books, a sense of pessimism had spread, a feeling of lost momentum.

As late as the Bicentennial, Brooke Hindle could write off the study of the pre-1789 period as a closed historiographic incident. Yet in that year Herbert Leventhal published his *In the Shadow of the Enlightenment: Occultism and Renaissance Science in Eighteenth-Century America*, clearly showing the influence of Keith Thomas's work on the decline of magic in England. Three years previously Joan Hoff-Wilson sounded a quite different note in her "Dancing Dogs of the Colonial Period: Women Scientists," not only bringing a new gender into the story but calling for a rethinking of what "science" is. Two years after Hindle wrote, Neil Longley York presented a fresh interpretation of technology in Revolutionary America.[4] The history of colonial science and technology is alive and well.

To return to 1971, in that year Daniel J. Kevles presented two articles on the World War I period that heralded his splendid treatment of that era in his later book, *The Physicists*, easily the most significant work on the history of science in the United States in the last decade. 1971 also saw the publication of two fine pieces of history clearly within the scope of Kevles's as yet unpublished book. In the *American Historical Review* Stanley Coben wrote on the varied factors involved in the transfer of quantum mechanics to the United States. Ronald Tobey raised interesting questions about the mind-set of leaders of the scientific community in *The American Ideology of National Science, 1919–1930.*[5]

But in 1971 the history of technology probably had the richest harvest. Seymour Chapin presented a fascinating article on how patent administration and law influenced the process of research and development. The question of the social responsibilities of engineers yielded Edwin Layton's classic study, *The Revolt of the Engineers.* Another classic work, a fine example of how to do a biography of an inventor-engineer, was the study of Elmer Sperry by Thomas P. Hughes. And there were many other articles and books of note in the class of 1971.[6]

Although high quality and the wide range of topics continued in the years immediately after 1971, there was a drop in absolute numbers, as though the scholarly community involved was drawing a breath after the prodigious labors involved. The year 1976 witnessed a great upsurge in publications of all sorts, but with a greater variability in quality.[7] After the inevitable drop in 1977, contributions rose, often of very good quality and exhibiting diverse approaches to a widening range of topics. In fact, since January 1, 1980 enough articles and books of moment have appeared to justify a review article solely on the output of the eighties. I am referring to a bibliography approaching the one hundred mark by the time of publication of this essay.

The upsurge has not gone without notice. The third issue (April 1981) of a new newsletter, *History of Science in America: News and Views,* gave a partial listing of workers in the field numbering 143; the last issue of 1981 bluntly raised the prospect of a specialized society with a specialized journal.[8] To those of us interested in professionalization as a process, it was almost as if our notes were coming alive to haunt us. An even greater wonder followed, perhaps in part a response to the roughly 40 percent representation of American topics in the 1981 meeting of the History of Science Society. The March 1982 issue of *Isis* carried an editorial "On American Science" calling on the practitioners of the specialty not to "forget the wide, Sartonian vision of the republic of learning."[9] On reading these words, I was undecided if this was a coming of age or the onset of senescence. The growth of the study of the history of science and technology in the United States owes very little to George Sarton's vision or to its elaboration by a generation of self-anointed heirs. The historians involved were not heirs to Sarton's positivistic vision of the history of human progress being the history of science, nor were they enthralled by his implicit definition of the history of science being the account of successive approximations to an absolute truth. Neither did they accept Sarton's view of history of science as being part of the scientific enterprise.

Rather than a recital of published contributions of the last decade or so, complete with gold stars and demerits, I want to give a kind of intellectual, nonquantitative demography to explain the relations of this specialty to developments in broader disciplinary groupings, specifically American history and the history of science. There is also a need to discuss the tangled differences and similarities of the historians of science and the historians of technology. These are not merely matters of turf but often relate to disputes on conceptual issues and even current public policies.

Most of the historians who began specializing in the study of American events in science, technology, and medicine in the fifteen or twenty years after the end of World War II initially came from United States history. They were clearly part of a movement well under way to define the history of the nation in broader terms than by the conventional foci on the political, the constitutional, and the military. Among the more prominent and influential examples were Arthur M. Schlesinger, Sr., Richard H. Shryock, and Merle Curti.

The origins of the positions of these three individuals and similarly minded scholars is quite complex, perhaps a result of successive pushes for various "new" histories in the preceding half century. My impression is that Americans who specialized in the study of European and other histories similarly tended to a broader view of the scope of historical research—more so than their colleagues overseas. One thinks of Preserved Smith or remembers that Henry Guerlac of Cornell, one of the really important pioneers of professional history of science in this country, did his Harvard thesis under Crane Brinton, not George Sarton. After World War II, when the national mood placed so great an emphasis on the sciences that NSF and NIH were willing to give increasing support to their study in the historical mode, there were American historians more than willing to benefit from a modest slice of the new funds.

Quite different from the "regular" historians of science—neither Guerlac (except for a war history) nor his students worked on American topics—the Americanists (as I shall designate them) were consciously working within the traditions of a particular national history, and striving to add to its scope. Historians of science, in contrast, quite often came from the sciences, and a substantial portion retained institutional and emotional ties with the scientific community. Some viewed history of science as a necessary tool in reforming science education; some viewed themselves as providing a "bridge" to the general public to assure understanding and support for research and development; some consciously sought to educate future scientists in order to avoid the mistakes of the past; and some sincerely believed they were applying their scientific knowledge—doing science—when they studied the past. In varying degrees, many of these historians of science of the 1945–1965 era deviated from Rabb's description of history as a discipline.[10] They were trying to form a new field between history and science, benefiting from both but perhaps closer to the latter. All too often, they invoked unexamined concepts like "world scientific community" and "world view," or tacitly accepted Robert Merton's "norms of science" even as their writings helped undermine such intellectual constructs.

Americanists had no such illusions, but the idea of a national history was all too often unexamined in the rush to investigate particulars. They saw American history (and therefore themselves) as necessarily broad in an interdisciplinary sense; they tended to scorn the conventional history of science concern with the best science as Whiggish and to relish research forays among the literary remains of the "little men" (later women) of science and even into the murky reaches of the thoughts and actions of those on the margins of the world of research. Implicitly, their attitudes became in some degree what we now regard as "anthropological," although I doubt that derived from any significant study of the contributions from that field. In this respect the Americanists were close to and at home in the emerging American Studies movement. Over the years the *American Quarterly* has published a sprinkling of articles on the sciences, and its former annual bibliography had a section on science and technology as early as 1958.

If the history of science and technology in the United States had an assured, if modest, role in the American Studies movement, its relation to the field of American history was equivocal. In contrast to the *American Quarterly*, the *Journal of American History* only introduced a science and technology breakdown in its listing of current articles in the last decade. In my experience, all too many historians of science and technology, whether Americanists or not, were (are?) notably sensitive about whether fellow historians or scientists recognized the merits of their work.[11] It was a serious problem for many, transcending even the realities of the job market.

It is now clear that in the early years (1945–65) many of us were far too optimistic about the growth of the study of history of the sciences in America, propelled no doubt by the sense of euphoria so widely present in this country before the effect of the Viet Nam war became painfully apparent. Even before then, a dip in achievements was sensed, no doubt more a product of personal circumstances than of any objective trend. But afterwards, the growth of other historical specialities in United States history in the late sixties and early seventies provided a new basis for self-doubts among Americanists. At the time of the Bicentennial, a number of informal, unpublished forays into college and secondary school texts by historians of science and technology in the United States disclosed a near omission or reliance on outmoded sources. Of course, there is no objective measure of what should appear in such works or in general works on the collegiate level. Nevertheless, the need for missionary work still exists.

On the other hand, the impact of the newer research of Americanists is apparent in a number of areas, particularly intellectual history.[12] Evolution's arrival and impact, the role of biology in racial attitudes, the part played by modern physics in the international politics of World War II and its sequel, and the rise of the American university [13]—all are now studied with an eye to the activities and once arcane folkways of scientists. Many other evidences exist of impact. There are traces in art historian Barbara Novak's *Nature and Culture*. Unexpectedly, the urban historian Thomas Bender called attention to the changing place of the sciences in American communities. Even more surprising was how a lawyer used historical results to support an argument on the constitutional status of science.[14] Unless one seeks positivistic hegemony in the mode of George Sarton, there is every reason for optimism on the effects of the writings produced since 1971, even of the last three decades.

The most visible trend in the last decade is the influx of investigators from the history of science into the study of American topics, both scientific and technological. Whether American or not, the history of the sciences has always attracted individuals from diverse professions. Scientists, engineers, philosophers, various species of social scientists, journalists, and literary historians have all contributed, sometimes substantially. History of science is almost inevitably interdisciplinary, a characteristic not without its perils in practice.[15] The coming of "proper" historians of science to American topics in significant numbers since, let us say, 1968 raises questions about training, attitudes, and goals. And these hinge on how and why the history of science has changed in the last generation.

As a consequence of their differing origins from the Americanists, historians of science in the early period of professionalization of the field were markedly internalistic in their orientation. Although mindful of the perils of Whig history (Herbert Butterfield was also a pioneer in the modern history of science), many, but not all, of these scholars tended to idealize theory and theoreticians, to stress the autonomous nature of the growth of science since the seventeenth century (exceptions were noted as unfortunate deviations from the desired ideal), and often to accept, with qualifications, the ideology of science as given in such statements as Merton's on the norms of science. This kind of history of science was a peculiar form of intellectual history. If there was a theoretical framework for internal history, it was provided by the contents of the science itself and the ideology voiced by spokesmen for science. It was universalistic, and clearly minimized concern for particulars of environments, whether national, regional, or local. Exceptions disclosed by historical research rarely resulted in calls for questioning of this framework, only for alertness against contemporary repetitions. In this framework, social or institutional history was looked down on. Up until its publication in 1971, Roger Hahn's superb *The Anatomy of a Scientific Institution: The Paris Academy of Sciences, 1666-1803* was decried by some of the elders of the community of "regular" historians of science as an unfortunate aberration of a promising young scholar.[16]

Applied areas like technology and medicine showed up in occasional pieces concerned with purported intersections of theory and practice, but rarely did they become principal areas of concern, as in the case of many Americanists. Those fields clearly could not support an ideology of purity of theory and of theory invariably propelling practice. Necessarily, technology and medicine ranked lower on the implicit hierarchy of many historians of science. When the climate of opinion changed, younger historians would find Mary Douglas's anthropological accounts of dietary taboos analogous to the reactions of older scientists, historians, and philosophers to involvement with applications and to various calls for relevance.[17] Yet, some younger scholars from "straight" history of science backgrounds brought a thin knowledge of the national scene to American topics, as did their advisors in many instances.[18]

Fortunately for the Americanists, in the early days they were not in history of science groups but in American history and largely invisible to the general historians of science. To be fair, the Americanists were tolerated as a minor, aberrant group. They were like the scholars concerned with other "exotic" scientific cultures—Islam, the Soviets, China, Japan—worthy but clearly not in the mainstream. That was located in Western Europe; to be more exact, in Western Europe since the Renaissance. To be even more precise, the dominant ideology unconsciously limned by regular historians of science probably originated in the late nineteenth century.[19] And if the historians of exotic cultures persisted in wondering whether social, economic, and other external factors influenced the growth of the content of science, it merely mirrored the aberrant and minor status of their regions of study—clearly not a matter for those concerned with the great, universalistic pure theory oriented science of Western Europe. As colonials, literally for some or symbolically for others, their science was by definition derivative and inferior.

Even before 1971, the model of science implicitly or explicitly animating much of history of science was in question in many quarters. Non-Western

European topics were booming; in a few years the Canadians would start a society for the history of science and technology in their country. More important than the interest in the formerly exotic areas was the spread of concern for "external" topics accompanied in many instances by unconcern for the supposed purity of a self-generating body of concepts and data. In short, many of the younger historians and some of their teachers were coming closer to where the Americanists had always been. The changes did not come from the influence of the Americanists.

It was a process of becoming historicized, of replacing the body of science and its supposed norms with another frame or frames of reference. Trends in history in general and in the issues of the day were decisive. For the old assumptions of universal laws of nature and the discipline they supposedly imposed on the behavior of scientists, many historians of science tacitly substituted a kind of culturalism—a viewing of science and scientists in the contexts of their societies. For some the new view countered the decline of the old certainties of science and its histories of an activity necessarily universal and inevitably benign because uncontaminated by the sordid. For many the new viewpoint provided a basis for correcting old distortions even as it hopefully yielded an accurate, new picture of scientists and science in their social contexts. For others the new contextual history was a way of avoiding the sterility of internal history, the dogmas of the scientific community, the irrelevance of philosophy of science, and the service intellectualism of many modes of the social sciences.

To a large extent, the historians of science—whether of the United States or elsewhere—more or less followed the path taken by many of their fellow historians to intense "local" or case studies. Having spurned the universalism of science as their grand theory, many were hesitant or ambiguous about what Merton designated theories of the middle range. Despite strong opposition, many historians accepted the idea of the social construction of knowledge. Cutting down on the area of focus, rather than applying theory, grand or middle, gave the historian a broader context for investigation within a narrower, achievable span. Underlying the narrowing of focus were three assumptions: (1) the "real" action occurred locally, within a limited time and space span; (2) the "real" action had to be more multicausal than allowed by older views of science; (3) only from the local could the historians derive and/or test generalizations of broader applicability. What this means concretely is visible in a number of leading works in the history of science and technology in the United States since 1971.

For example, one can compare Anthony F. C. Wallace's *Rockdale*, Daniel J. Kevles's *The Physicists*, and Merritt Roe Smith's *Harpers Ferry Armory and the New Technology*.[20] Although written by a cultural antropologist with notable historical interests, Wallace's book was immediately and deservedly hailed by historians of technology as a masterpiece.[21] His treatment of how the machinery in a small textile mill area in antebellum Pennsylvania affected both capitalists and workers is engrossing. But Wallace was after bigger game, as his subtitle clearly indicated:

> The growth of an American village in the early Industrial Revolution: An account of the coming of the machines, the making of a new way of life in the mill hamlets, the triumph of evangelical capitalists over socialists and infidels, and the transformation of the workers into Christian soldiers in a cotton-manufacturing district in Pennsylvania in the years before and during the Civil War.

Perhaps not the grand theory called for by Walters's comments on Geertz,[22] *Rockdale* is not simply a local history nor a field report on a tribal group. Wallace's use of local records and of the census enumerations (as the notes of field anthropologists) is simply outstanding, whatever one finally makes of the validity of his thesis. Despite the census and local records, far too much hinges on records of the mill owners, their families, and friends for descriptions of and judgments on the workers. There is also the obvious question of whether data from a few mills in the Delaware Valley justifies a thesis meant for all of the United States. Finally, Wallace ends with the Civil War, but the mills continued in operation afterwards, the last one closing only after World War II. Would a longer time span suggest a different thesis? The qualities of the book are such that it will remain a great contribution no matter what future researchers conclude about Wallace's grand generalization. What produces that effect is the presence of a broader vision than usual in writings on the history of technology.

Kevles's book does not have one grand thesis to prove. Rather, he postulates two persisting basic motivations underlying the actions of scientists in the United States since about 1880. "Best-science elitism" was "the construction of an institutional pyramid, oriented towards the advancement of abstract physics, open to talent at the bottom, and commanded at the heights by a best-science elite" (p. 44). "Political elitism" was related but distinctly different. It called for "direct governmental support [of science] with only nominal governmental control . . . on the assumption that they [scientists] were a select group who deserved to exercise power with only limited accountability" (p. 53). Leaving aside the lack of sustained development of the two concepts and that one can argue against specifics in Kevles's text, the book works in an unexpected manner. It is not an intense "local" study of a particular professional group, despite some fine passages of that nature. Rather, Kevles has produced a grand, sweeping narrative on the evolution of national science policies, displaying a great control of sources and of the details of each episode with a relative indifference to the roles of other scientific, technical, and medical groups in developing national policies. Kevles presents what amounts to an integrated sequence of local case studies of policy formulation. Quite like the great histories of the last century, *The Physicists* supports Lawrence Stone's views on the revival of narrative. Kevles's success underlines the deficiencies in the outlook of the older conventional history of science by demonstrating the fruitfulness of looking at science nationally in the normal style of general historians.

A third outstanding work is Merritt Roe Smith's *Harpers Ferry Armory and the New Technology: The Challenge of Change.* A "local" study but one based on a lesser range of local sources than *Rockdale,* Smith's book is the latest and best work on the "American System of Manufacturing," the style of manufacturing, particularly involving metal products, leading to mass production in the United States. Smith's account, based largely on his own work but also on the writings of a number of other scholars, is a conclusive demonstration of the atypical environment of military procurement that yielded true interchangeable parts in the decades before the Civil War. He does not obviously lean on Mumford's idea of the role of war in technological change, nor does Smith much concern himself with how this technique eventually spread to parts of the civilian industrial sector. Descriptions of machinery and processes are exemplary yet lacking in the personal drama conveyed by Wallace's textile equipment in *Rockdale.*

To most readers of *Harpers Ferry Armory,* the great and impressive surprise was its author's showing how local inhabitants (a "junto") successfully resisted intrusion of new techniques for many years. Unlike Wallace, Smith had little in the way of local sources, but benefited from records of Army Ordnance in the National Archives. In a carefully understated way, Smith countered any idea of technological imperatives in history, implicitly arguing for the importance of local cultural patterns. Perhaps because of its author's restraint in theorizing, *Harpers Ferry Armory* is the most convincing of the three works in establishing its point of view.

Yet neither it nor *The Physicists* is the most exciting in the sense of heuristic power. Despite any qualms about Wallace's general thesis or his specific judgments, *Rockdale* is so extraordinarily provocative, it may influence us far longer than the other two. For example, the book is comparable to E. P. Thompson's *The Making of the English Working Class* (1963). Both are accounts of how radical or deviant trends among the working class are deflected from militancy by firm action of an upper class aided by a form of Protestantism. Because Rockdale's evangelical mill owners are tough but paternalistic (not merely dog-eat-dog laissez-faire types), democratic, believers in upward mobility, and remain in close physical proximity to their workers, class warfare is avoided. Wallace's work tacitly takes an anti-Marxist stance, almost arguing for American exceptionalism. The mills and their machinery play a different role in his valley than in British analogs, blocking the development of the United States equivalent of a Labour Party or of a Marxist tradition.

Rockdale's success from the perspective of another discipline was more than a bit disconcerting to at least some historians of technology,[23] stimulating all too familiar status-anxiety pangs. By now the Americanists working on science are less prone to such emotions, perhaps because apparent success breeds complacency. (I include myself in this description.) The history of technology's start, in a formal sense with the founding of the Society for the History of Technology and its journal, *Technology and Culture*, was accompanied by assertions of being twenty years behind the history of science. Recent assertions cut the gap to fifteen years, not much progress in roughly a quarter century.

Comparisons with history of science refer to such parameters as size of community, number of special teaching and research programs, and number of publications. Making such counts are hazardous because of problems of defining the countable units, but even crude informal surveys show a disparity favoring the historians of science. Even more important than numbers is a subjective sense among many historians of technology that somehow science is rated higher on many scales of values than is technology. There is even a sense of being looked down on by historians of science. And they dearly want technology and its history to loom large both in scholarly discourse and in the world of current affairs.

The latest annual report of the National Science Board of the National Science Foundation has a quotation from Louis Pasteur on its title page reading in part: "There are not two sciences. There is ONLY ONE SCIENCE and the application of science, and these two activities are linked as the fruit is to the tree."[24] Let us disregard the highly probable possibility that Pasteur and the National Science Board may not assign identical meanings to these words. The "one science" most likely refers to something very specific— probably a Comtean formulation in late nineteenth-century European thought. But such a belief in the unification of knowledge has deep roots in the western tradition, persisting to this era. Mirroring this trend in many western countries, not only the United States, is a tendency to lump under "science" (or cognate terms) both theory or systems of knowledge and the knowledge and actions involved in many aspects of industry, medicine, and agriculture. There is a widespread assumption that these aspects are or should be, somehow or other, part of, or related to, "science." A further tacit assumption follows: that it is knowledge that is all important for practice (like the tree to the fruit), and since basic (the most theoretical or general) knowledge is the highest form of knowledge, it and its creators and possessors necessarily have intellectual, institutional, and ideological primacy. A train of arguments of this nature clearly functions, in the minds of those so inclined, as a justification for the necessary autonomy of science from ordinary social processes and can, by extension, justify a role for technology as an exogenous, deterministic force functioning best when untrammeled by nontechnical, therefore irrelevant, social constraints. Even historians of technology, who do not go so far because of a belief in technology as a special kind of social history, tacitly fall back to this position when defending the separateness of history of technology from the history of science.

As Americanists never recognized that separation, the tendencies in that direction among a number of historians of technology are serious causes for alarm in theory. In practice, the leading scholars involved tend to agree. Americanists are notable for their avoidance of the theory/practice bifurcation in their belief in the existence of a wider cultural nexus. In some quarters there is a strong drive to merge the study of science, technology, and medicine,[25] not only because of beliefs in the unity of knowledge and in the existence of a cultural nexus, but also because of a recognition of similarity or identity of the processes observed in knowledge validation, social interactions, and relations with the broader society. The science/technology or theory/practice division is seen as a social accounting artifact deriving from the interaction of current fashions with traditional patterns of thought and behavior. Rarely does the division truly match intellectual and institutional realities. Just think of "pure" minded universities scrambling to get into the big money of genetic engineering.

The historians of technology do have a point—if only a limited one—in their outrage over quotations like Pasteur's. Technology, they insist, is not applied science with its implication of "merely" before "applied" and the further conclusion that technology is inferior and less important than science.[26] Technology has unique aspects derived from experience, not from theory. It devises knowledge differing from science in important particulars. Technology's history should and does include aspects absent from accounts of scientific fields. Historians of technology have sometimes reluctantly conceded the existence of science-based or high-technology industries and have perhaps balanced that admission by attempts at bringing under their tent traditional crafts and large-scale practical ventures antedating the industrial revolution. Smith's and Wallace's books, among others, extended the scope of the field to the workers on the shop floor.

Perhaps the most important cause of the insistence that technology is not applied science is a strong dissent from the national research and development policies prevailing since the World War II period. These are condemned as basic research centered and dominated by the scientists even though one of the principal architects was a notable engineer, Vannevar Bush, and engineering programs ("development") far out-bulk basic science in funding. In adopting such positions, historians of technology were arguing for the prerogatives of engineers against the claims of scientists. Often involved were assumptions that the policies ascribed to Bush were elitist and less democratic in the sense that scientists purportedly placed disciplinary concerns ahead of society's needs. Given the ample literature of professionalization of engineering showing its practitioners as quintessential organizational men, one can doubt assertions of the inherently democratic nature of engineering.[27]

In their attempts at achieving independence from history of science, the historians of technology are influenced by and sorely handicapped by their relationship to professional engineering. It was an easy step to equate technology with engineering. Funds and jobs for the specialty came partly from that source. In many writings the differences between scientists and engineers became a well-worn, unexamined cliché. It was a convenient way of disregarding science-based or high technology industries, as well as a momentary lapse of memory about craftsmen and industrial workers. What we do know is that engineers tend to come from different, lower social strata than scientists.[28]

Like the historians of science, historians of technology have a problem in defining their specialty's relationships to factors other than knowledge, whether scientifically or empirically derived, but the problem takes a very particular form. There are strong pressures from the museum world and from industrial archaeology to make physical objects (instruments, tools, production devices, and structures) the center of attention, to define technology as being concerned with the generation and use of things or systems of things. Among historians of science, scientific instrumentation is regarded as understudied, and there is a growing awareness of a need to investigate the craft of experimentation.[29] But this in no way compares with the thing-worship present in some quarters of the history of technology. Historians of technology interested in technology as knowledge or as systems, such as Edwin T. Layton or Thomas P. Hughes, have to argue that artifacts are valuable as evidence of human intentions and their outcomes in response to pressure from thing-worshippers.[30]

Despite scholars like Lynn White, Lewis Mumford, and John U. Nef, historians of technology in America are much more likely than historians of science in America to be overwhelmingly United States-centered. (Nor is it accidental that the exceptions tend to be those historians concerned with technology as knowledge.) Technology was widely viewed as necessarily national or local, not international. The massive presence of a rising conventional history of science specialty forced Americanists to look overseas. Margaret Rossiter's work on agricultural chemistry is an obvious example.[31] The past success of the American economy encouraged concentration by historians of technology on United States events, often in a nationalistic mode. In contrast, the historians of science in America, faced with the indifference of the generality of historians of science, had to tackle historiographic issues to explain why conditions for early science in the United States did or did not resemble conditions in Britain, France, and Germany and why study of the conditions was worthy. During the Bicentennial meeting of the Society for the History of Technology, dubious nationalistic assertions occurred— like antebellum American workers being simply more industrious than their European counterparts to help explain the appearance of the American System.[32] Similar statements about superior inventiveness still appear in the literature, as do comments derived from Chandler's "visible hand" about superior managerial skills. Such works as Edward W. Constant II's *The Origins of the Turbojet Revolution* is a hopeful harbinger of a more balanced, comparative history.[33] If not, the persistence of industrial distress in the United States in the face of Japanese and German success may give rise to the negative of the nationalistic history, a literature of a lost cause, technical and economic, myopically imparting "lessons" from the past.

By far the most visible trend in the history of technology is a refinement of the standard product of this specialty. Influenced by the writings of economic historians and others before 1960, historians of technology now commonly turn out articles and monographs giving the origins, introductions, and various consequences of particular devices or entire areas of technological advance—either in biographical, corporate, or broader industrial settings. The best recent example is Reese V. Jenkins's *Images and Enterprise: Technology and the American Photographic Industry, 1839–1925.* Precedents are in the works of Hunter on steamboats, Anderson on refrigeration, Passer on the electrical manufacturers, to mention but a few.[34] One can predict the visible hand, the bottom view from the shop floor, and the impact on consumers will regularly appear in later works in this genre. In other words, many historians of technology now practice an updated, sophisticated, version of what one cliometrician recently dismissed as "good old economic history."

Prophecy is not my strong point, but review articles stimulate that vice. Americanists will face creative tensions in adjusting to pressures to merge or not merge with American history, the history of science (now broadly defined), and even various programs with titles like "Science, Technology, Society, and Values." They will not solve that problem nor wholly shake tensions imparted by the situation. There is a great need for careful studies of the obscure members of scientific and technical professions. Almost all our existing generalizations are from the top. Popularization is not well served by studies emanating from sociology and even American literature. It is a topic sorely needing a fresh viewpoint.

Having earlier displayed my lack of reverence for George Sarton and his view of science, I must confess to seeing a virtue in two aspects compared to what developed later among his successors. Sarton insisted on viewing all the science of a period in juxtaposition (the ONE SCIENCE of Pasteur?). There is currently far too great a tendency for overspecialization. There is a real need to view science and technology as interacting elements of a larger system, not as distinct, independent systems of disciplinary specialties. Thinking over the scramble to cash in on genetic engineering makes one more sympathetic to the ideal of a pure science or a basic theory. Much of the kind of history produced by Americanists or by others interested in what used to be called externalist history is devoted to demonstrating complex motivations in scientists other than simply the addition to our knowledge. I now wonder whether historians of my ilk underestimated the power and worthiness of the ideal.

As to the scientists and engineers involved, we historians have to develop a typology of roles played by the objects of our investigations. Except as great investigator or empire builder, we have difficulty in assigning functions to individuals. Why does the scientific community regularly produce historians, philosophers, popularizers, managerial technicians, and even a few genuine mystics? The various roles of engineers are especially ill-served by the history of technology.

I have a wistful desire for a fresh revival of the study of the published writings of scientists and engineers but not in the mode of good old internal history — often second-rate philosophy or second-rate science struggling to be more than ahistorical. Let us think of the writings of scientists and engineers as a peculiar form of literature requiring analysis of genres, explication of rhetorics, and unearthing of underlying structures. If that sounds formidably off-putting, let me conclude by asserting that not only is the history of science and technology in this country an important, still undeveloped area for research, it is also a great delight, being filled with unlikely characters, improbable events, and moments of great comedy. It is simply fun. I do not advise using such language when applying for grants and fellowships, but I hope American historians will respond to those sentiments by reading what now exists and what will appear in the next decade.

1. George H. Daniels, ed., *Nineteenth-Century American Science: A Reappraisal* (Evanston, Ill.: Northwestern University Press, 1972).

2. I am indebted to my colleague Marc Rothenberg for the use of the manuscript of his forthcoming bibliography of secondary works in the history of the sciences (except medicine) in the United States.

3. Raymond P. Stearns, *Science in the British Colonies of America* (Urbana: University of

Illinois Press, 1970); Howard S. Miller, *Dollars for Research: Science and Its Patrons in Nineteenth-Century America* (Seattle: University of Washington Press, 1970); A. Hunter Dupree, "The History of American Science—A Field Finds Itself," *American Historical Review* 71 (1966): 866–74; Stephen G. Brush, "The Rise of Astronomy in America," *American Studies* 20 (1979): 41–67.

4. For Hindle's comments, see his introduction to the volume he edited: *Early American Science* (New York: Science History Publications, 1976). Herbert Leventhal, *In the Shadow of the Enlightenment: Occultism and Renaissance Science in Eighteenth-Century America* (New York: New York University Press, 1976); Joan Hoff-Wilson, "Dancing Dogs of the Colonial Period: Women Scientists," *Early American Literature* 7 (1973): 225–35; Neil Longley York, "Technology in Revolutionary America, 1760–1790" (Ph.D. dissertation, University of California, Santa Barbara, 1978).

5. Daniel J. Kevles, " 'Into Hostile Camps': the Reorganization of International Science in World War I," *Isis* 62 (1971): 47–60; "Federal Legislation for Engineering Experiment Stations: the Episode of World War I," *Technology and Culture* 12 (1971): 182–89; and *The Physicists: The History of a Scientific Community in Modern America* (New York: Knopf, 1978); Stanley Coben, "The Scientific Establishment and the Transmission of Quantum Mechanics to the United States, 1919–32," *American Historical Review* 76 (1971): 442–66; Ronald C. Tobey, *The American Ideology of National Science, 1919–1930* (Pittsburgh: University of Pittsburgh Press, 1971).

6. Seymour L. Chapin, "Patent Interferences and the History of Technology: A High-Flying Example," *Technology and Culture* 12 (1971): 414–46; Edwin T. Layton, Jr., *The Revolt of the Engineers: Social Responsibility and the American Engineering Profession* (Cleveland: Case Western Reserve University Press, 1971); Thomas P. Hughes, *Elmer Sperry: Inventor and Engineer* (Baltimore: Johns Hopkins University Press, 1971). A list of some of the other works of note from 1971 would have to include Donald deB. Beaver, "Altruism, Patriotism, and Science: Scientific Journals in the Early Republic," *American Studies* 12 (1971): 5–19; Paul F. Boller, Jr., "The New Science and American Thought," in *The Gilded Age*, rev. ed., ed. H. Wayne Morgan (Syracuse: Syracuse University Press, 1971), pp. 239–57; Sally G. Kohlstedt, "A Step Towards Scientific Self-Identity in the United States: The Failure of the National Institute, 1844," *Isis* 62 (1971): 339–62; Margaret W. Rossiter, "Benjamin Silliman and the Lowell Institute: The Popularization of Science in Nineteenth-Century America," *The New England Quarterly* 44 (1971): 602–26; Robert E. Kohler, Jr., "The Origin of G. N. Lewis's Theory of the Shared Pair Bond," *Historical Studies in the Physical Sciences* 3 (1971): 343–76; John S. Haller, Jr., *Outcasts from Evolution: Scientific Attitudes of Racial Inferiority, 1859–1900* (Urbana: University of Illinois Press, 1971); James H. Cassedy, "Applied Microscopy and American Pork Diplomacy: Charles Wardell Stiles in Germany, 1898–1899," *Isis* 62 (1971): 5–20.

7. See George W. Black, Jr., *American Science and Technology: A Bicentennial Bibliography* (Carbondale: Southern Illinois University Press, 1979). This lists only articles, not books, appearing in 1976, including a number not prepared for the Bicentennial.

8. The newsletter is edited by Clark A. Elliott of the Harvard University Archives and is available on request from him. It is supported by voluntary contributions from the readers, a fact saying much about the feelings of those working in the field.

9. Arnold Thackray, "On American Science," *Isis* 73 (1982): 7–10. The quotation is from the concluding peroration.

10. Theodore K. Rabb, "Coherence, Synthesis, and Quality in History," *Journal of Interdisciplinary History* 12 (1981): 315–32.

11. This is fairly obvious, apparently; David Hollinger even briefly noted it in his comments at a History of Science Society session in Los Angeles in December 1981. The feelings are probably a kind of growing pain of a relatively new historical specialty.

12. This appears in a muted form in John Higham and Paul K. Conkin, eds., *New Directions in American Intellectual History* (Baltimore: Johns Hopkins University Press, 1979).

13. To this list can be added military and naval history, business history (especially for high technology sectors), agricultural history, and the history of philanthropy. The listing is not exhaustive and says that science and technology are widely and significantly present in modern

societies. This does not imply either omnipresence or some kind of scientific-technological determinism. On the contrary, what is emerging largely underscores how national cultures and subcultures define the nature and extent of science and technology within each cultural unit.

14. Barbara Novak, *Nature and Culture: American Landscape and Painting, 1825-1875* (New York: Oxford University Press, 1980); Thomas Bender, "Science and the Culture of American Communities: the Nineteenth Century," *History of Education Quarterly* 16 (1976): 63-77; Steven Goldberg, "The Constitutional Status of American Science," *University of Illinois Law Forum* (1979): 1-33.

15. For an example of perils, see Nathan Reingold, "Science, Scientists, and Historians of Science," *History of Science* 19 (1981): 274-83.

16. Roger Hahn, *The Anatomy of a Scientific Institution: The Paris Academy of Sciences, 1666-1803* (Berkeley: University of California Press, 1971).

17. Mary Douglas, *Purity and Danger: An Analysis of Concepts of Pollution and Taboo* (London: Routledge and Kegan Paul, 1966). Despite her sparkling demonstration that penguin meat is not kosher, I am not an admirer of Mary Douglas in the sense of those, particularly in Great Britain, who see her as a great liberator of history of science—principally because I was never a believer in what she is supposedly delivering us from.

18. To cite one example, Peter Buck's *American Science and Modern China, 1876-1936* (Cambridge, England: Cambridge University Press, 1980) is notably deficient in its displayed knowledge of what was transpiring in the research and development communities in the United States. It also neglects the best source for the topic of the book, the archives of the Rockefeller Foundation.

19. Arthur P. Molella and Nathan Reingold, "Theorists and Ingenious Mechanics: Joseph Henry Defines Science," *Science Studies* 3 (1973): 323-51.

20. Anthony F. C. Wallace, *Rockdale: The Growth of an American Village in the Early Industrial Revolution* (New York: Knopf, 1978); Kevles, *Physicists;* Merritt Roe Smith, *Harpers Ferry Armory and the New Technology: The Challenge of Change* (Ithaca, N.Y.: Cornell University Press, 1977).

21. David A. Hounshell, "On the Discipline of the History of American Technology," *Journal of American History* 67 (1981): 854-65.

22. Ronald G. Walters, "Signs of the Times: Clifford Geertz and Historians," *Social Research* 47 (1980): 537-56.

23. Hounshell's article is the most explicit statement known to me.

24. National Science Board, *ONLY ONE SCIENCE, Twelfth Annual Report* (Washington: National Science Foundation, [1981]).

25. Arnold Thackray, "Science, Technology, and Medicine," *Journal of Interdisciplinary History* 12 (1981): 299-314.

26. This point is made repeatedly in an interesting report on history of technology in the United States: Svante Lindquist, *The Teaching of History of Technology in USA—A Critical Survey in 1978.* Report TRITA-HOT-5003 (Stockholm Papers in History and Philosophy of Technology, Royal Institute of Technology Library, 1981). A sprightly account of the specialty, it is filled with quotations and other information but not wholly sensitive to the nuances observed. Well worth reading.

27. Daniel Hovey Calhoun, *The American Civil Engineer: Origins and Conflict* (Cambridge: Technology Press, 1960); Monte A. Calvert, *The Mechanical Engineer in America, 1830-1910: Professional Cultures in Conflict* (Baltimore: Johns Hopkins University Press, 1967); Edwin T. Layton, Jr., "Science, Business, and the American Engineer," in *The Engineer and the Social System,* eds., R. Perruci and J. E. Gerstl (New York: Wiley, 1969); Raymond H. Merritt, *Engineering in American Society, 1850-1875* (Lexington: University Press of Kentucky, 1969); Bruce Sinclair, *A Centennial History of the American Society of Mechanical Engineers, 1880-1980* (Toronto: University of Toronto Press, 1980); Clark C. Spence, *Mining Engineers and the American West: The Lace-Boot Brigade, 1849-1933* (New Haven: Yale University Press, 1970).

28. The most recent summary of such statistics in general is Clark A. Elliott's "Models of the American Scientist: A Look at Collective Biography," *Isis* 73 (1982): 77-93. See also Elliott's

introduction to his *Biographical Dictionary of American Science: The Seventeenth through the Nineteenth Centuries* (Westport, Conn.: Greenwood Press, 1979).

29. That partly explains why *The Papers of Joseph Henry* gives Henry's experimental records in meticulous detail. In their eagerness to give science's history in the form of scientific thought, historians of science in the past not only shortchanged social and institutional history, they sometimes were most cavalier in dealing with *the* professional activity of many scientists— experimentation.

30. Note the final footnote to Thomas P. Hughes, "Convergent Themes in the History of Science, Medicine, and Technology," *Technology and Culture* 22 (1981): 550-58.

31. Margaret W. Rossiter, *The Emergence of Agricultural Science: Justus Liebig and the Americans, 1840-1880,* Yale Studies in the History of Science and Medicine, 9 (New Haven: Yale University Press, 1975).

32. For particularly egregious examples, see *Technology and Culture* 20 (1979): 10-11.

33. Edward W. Constant II, *The Origins of the Turbojet Revolution* (Baltimore: Johns Hopkins University Press, 1980).

34. Reese V. Jenkins, *Images and Enterprise: Technology and the American Photographic Industry, 1839-1925* (Baltimore: Johns Hopkins University Press, 1975); Louis C. Hunter, *Steamboats on the Western Rivers: An Economic and Technological History* (Cambridge: Harvard University Press, 1949); Oscar Edward Anderson, Jr., *Refrigeration in America: A History of a New Technology and Its Impact* (Princeton: Princeton University Press, 1953); Harold Clarence Passer, *The Electrical Manufacturers, 1875-1900: A Study in Competition, Entrepreneurship, Technical Change, and Economic Growth* (Cambridge: Harvard University Press, 1953).

THE HISTORY OF EDUCATION

Laurence Veysey

Until the late 1950s writing in the history of American education remained imprisoned in the mold of a triumphal, unexamined progressivism. It recorded the growth of public school systems since the days of Horace Mann with no regard for social or intellectual context aside from the rhetorical invocation of "advancing democracy." In retrospect this way of writing about the subject was called the Cubberley tradition, after its greatest exemplar, Ellwood P. Cubberley, long-time dean of the School of Education at Stanford University. Cubberley's role was typical in that the history of education was then written mainly by educators rather than by historians. Yet the difference mattered less than one might suppose, for many historians were themselves submerged in the same progressive assumptions.

Then fresh breezes stirred, associated with the names of Lawrence A. Cremin (*The Transformation of the School*, 1957) and Bernard Bailyn (*Education in the Forming of American Society*, 1960). Cremin's was a pseudoliberation. Boldly announcing the need for a fresh beginning, he could not really divorce himself from what he still described as the "wonderful" world of Cubberley. His work, right down to the latest volume in his multivolume history of American education, continued a tradition of triumphantly chronicling the growth of something abstractly called education, uncritical treatment of the school reformers, and failure to ask interesting questions.[1] Cremin's volumes were encyclopedic in the bad sense, with endless biographical sketches of minor people who never come alive, yet practically nothing on what schools were actually like. Their conceptual framework was one of conventional holistic nationalism. Immigrant-native conflict received almost no attention (and it is odd to come across a work published in 1980 that used the term "Americanization" without quotation marks).

Bernard Bailyn called for a redefinition of educational history away from the narration of the rise of formal school systems and toward an identification with the entire concept of acculturation. His manifesto became endlessly cited thereafter in the opening paragraphs of journal articles in a dutiful but abstract ritual of strange persistence within the subdiscipline (it is still going on). Bailyn's dictum, however, did not really move most scholars in the field

0048-7511/82/0104-0281 $01.00

to change their ways. His formula would have led them to embrace an anthropological perspective in the style of Ruth Benedict or David Riesman. But in the 1960s that style was generally going out of fashion.

Thus neither of the major names so often invoked in connection with the rising vitality of educational history actually led the field toward the kinds of important changes that swept through it as the 1960s advanced. Instead, the best of educational history was captured by the spirit of the "new" social history, with its insistent emphasis on ethnicity, class, and gender as focal points for interpretation. Since neither Bailyn nor Cremin represented that spirit they were soon left far behind, a discrepancy amounting to a curious phenomenon. In no other subfield of historical writing does there seem to be such a striking disjuncture between the explicit celebration of "influence" (particularly in the case of Bailyn) and the actual currents of influence, which were those generally affecting the younger generation in American society and scholarship in the mid-1960s.

Before exploring the real breakthrough that occurred, it would be well to place the field more firmly in its institutional setting. During the late 1950s a self-conscious effort was made by the Fund for the Advancement of Education, a subsidiary of the Ford Foundation, to improve the quality of scholarship and teaching in the field of the history of education, since it was widely perceived to be appallingly bad. The Fund addressed itself directly to academic institutions, where leading universities, undergoing a heady period of academic expansion, easily became convinced that trained historians should be attached to their schools of education. The usual form this took was of a joint appointment in the history department and the education school. As with other such joint appointments, their youthful holders were stuck in a potentially uneasy situation. One ear had to be kept tuned to the appraisal of the professional school, limiting one's freedom of self-definition as a scholar—yet schools of education often remained notoriously indifferent toward history, even while they honored the connection; on the other hand, history departments could regard the joint appointees as somehow marginal from their own standpoint. The holders of joint appointments in history and education, who appeared in fair numbers during the early 1960s, thus found themselves oddly isolated. Some of them were not even in American history, but in the history of education in Europe or other parts of the world. The History of Education Society and its journal, *The History of Education Quarterly* (founded 1960) provided a meeting-ground for such scholars, though all its prominent members did not hold these joint appointments.

The study of the history of education has not achieved the degree of coherence or of burgeoning support (beyond the initial impetus) to allow it to generate its own clearcut intellectual focus. Thus the repetitive invocations of

Bailyn's name in scholarly articles may amount to a kind of fig-leaf. For instance, the international scope of the field could allow for exciting work in comparative history, but in fact little of it has taken place.[2] Journal articles on education in other societies instead deal with random times, themes, and locales, producing a highly scattered and thin impression. Again, the history of higher education has been formally included in the Society's scope, and occasional sessions in it are offered at annual meetings, but it has been distinctly to one side of the subfield, amounting to a protospecialty of its own (and thus discussed separately in this essay). The requirements of education schools may still affect this neglect.

Thus the core of the field is still the history of public school systems in the United States. Only in this area is there the richness of accumulated scholarship that leads to significant schools of thought and the excitement of sustained debate. The word "system" holds a central place in the vocabulary of educational historians, regardless of their sometimes fierce differences of interpretation. And this word resonates in connection with the rise of systems of public schools. In this fundamental respect the scope of the field has changed much less from the days of Ellwood P. Cubberley than its practitioners would like to imagine. Guilt feelings over this have existed, stemming from the memory of Bailyn's dictum of 1960. But, as at a conference in December 1980, called "Beyond the System," and sponsored by Teachers College, Columbia, outreach takes the form of examining the histories of related institutional agencies such as charity organizations, penny newspapers, and programs for adults and the handicapped. In practice, therefore, the history of education continues to define itself as a subspecialty within the larger category of the history of bureaucracy.

Inside these considerable limits, the field flamed into vigorous life during the second half of the 1960s, fed by the scholarship of the newly trained generation, a substantial share of whom had been temporary understudies of Bailyn at Harvard. For the first time there were genuinely brilliant people in the history of education who were not held back by their mixed ties to departments of history and schools of education. Perhaps their balancing act mattered relatively little after all, except for vetoing any pronounced following of Bailyn's dictum, because, as compared with law schools for instance, schools of education had a weak and formless tradition. The result could be real freedom to think for oneself in historical terms, so long as one confined one's attention to the expected subject matter, systems or agencies of education.

In the late 1960s, many young historical scholars found themselves being informally influenced by Marxism, the "new" social history, or both in some combination. The result—the conceptual engulfment of educational history from "outside"—was nothing but gain, for it made the field relevant to

American history in the larger and most contemporary sense. The younger leftist scholars, led by Michael Katz (*The Irony of Early School Reform*, 1968), were quickly termed "revisionists."

The revisionists accepted the subject matter defined by Cubberley, but turned the old success story of the history of American public school systems into one of appalling failure, and additionally discovered that the leaders of the public school movement, both in the nineteenth and twentieth centuries, were class-biased, racist, and sexist. The school systems were seen as bureaucratic monuments to those values. The most systematic historical account of American education written from a revisionist standpoint (*Schooling in Capitalist America*, 1976), and for several years the nub of excited controversy among leading scholars in the subdiscipline, was not written by trained historians, but by educators Samuel Bowles and Herbert Gintis, who taught economics from a Marxian perspective. An interesting attempt to integrate the history of school systems with the overall economic and social history of industrializing America, no book better captures the flavor of the revisionist movement as applied to the entire historical sweep, emphasizing social class as well. Though Katz wrote with more subtlety, his scholarship remained anchored in a single period, the mid-nineteenth century.

Bowles and Gintis often lapsed into simplistic arguments, especially in assuming an overly rational quality in the thinking of the creators of public schools and in assuming that their aims were effectively realized, for instance in such areas as vocational education. But they brought an analytical perspective, compelling despite its over-neatness and excesses, into an area of history that had never had one. To put this another way, now there was a hypothesis to test—that the development of public school systems in all time periods closely followed from and reflected the expansion of the capitalist industrial economy. Such an explanation may be questioned, for it minimized the school systems as self-serving bureaucracies detached from any goal larger than their own survival and expansion, but it raised central critical questions where none had existed before. The argument that it stirred was extremely healthy for the field of the history of education. The same basic analysis may also be found in a more recent book of similar chronological breadth and greater attention to empirical nuance, *Schooled to Order*, (1979) by David Nasaw.

Other scholars who were generally part of the revisionist movement focused in more depth upon the actual history of the school bureaucracies from the new point of view, as for instance David Tyack (*The One Best System*, 1974). Tyack stressed ethnicity more than class as the defining variable of conflict, and placed more emphasis upon the professionalization of school administrations in major cities after 1890; whereas for Katz the die had been cast in all the fatefully negative directions in antebellum Massachu-setts. But Tyack scrutinized the school men only somewhat less severely. Still other revisionist scholars performed a muckraking operation on intellectual history, as in Clarence J. Karier's provocative treatment of John Dewey, whom Bowles and Gintis had notably refrained from attacking (in Karier et al., *Roots of Crisis*, 1973), and Paul Violas's study of the thinking of Charles Horton Cooley, Edward A. Ross, and Jane Addams (also in *Roots of Crisis*). On the level of intellectual history as on that of school administration, the motive of social control rather than the provision of individual opportunity was seen by these writers to dominate the expansion of American public education.

The revisionist onslaught was generally over by 1976. It was responded to, not so much by efforts at direct refutation (with a single exception to be noted), as by a tendency among prominent younger scholars to dissociate themselves from its excesses while still accepting much of its agenda—the exploration of school history with sensitivity to questions of class, ethnicity, and (to a lesser extent) gender. Solid monographs, more modest in scope and somewhat influenced by revisionism but without its bitter animus against the middle class, began to draw the highest praise. Among these were books by Marvin Lazerson (*The Origins of the Urban School*, 1971), Carl Kaestle (*The Evolution of an Urban School System*, 1973), and Stanley K. Schultz (*The Culture Factory*, 1973) that began to answer the historian's hunger for knowledge of what had really gone on at the local level, and that made use of archival research.

What had started in response to the social protests of the mid-1960s filtered upward into academia, eventually resulting in a much better grasp of social reality as applied to the history of education. It was this crucial element that had always been missing from the field before. Judging by the chronology of all the books that have been mentioned thus far (and I do not attempt to men-tion all the important works of recent years), this empirical quest proceeded quite independently alongside the formulation of the revisionist analytical perspective. Both were the parallel products of that initial mood of radical social protest. But when the air had cleared by the late 1970s, those who had done their empirical homework were bound to fare best in the judgment of their fellow historians, even if they lacked the overall vision of Bowles and Gintis. Thanks to scholars like Lazerson and Kaestle, American school history had attained a respectable density of accomplishment.

Perhaps only a neoconservative would think it worthwhile to expend energy in a frontal assault upon revisionism—as Joseph Kett observed, the entire controversy over revisionism was deeply politicized.[3] Diane Ravitch, however, willingly stepped into the antagonist's role. Thanks to private funding, a great many historians were sent copies of her lengthy review, "The Revisionists Revised" (1977). Writing in a lucid, acerbic style, Ravitch maintained that the heart of the revisionist argument lay in the claim "that American schools have been an *intentional, purposeful* failure." She attacked three major "analytical devices" of the revisionists: their use of the concept of social class "in a deterministic manner," their positing of an exact correspondence between the aims of policy-makers and the effects of their policies, and their assumption that the structure of an institution (bureaucracy) determines its purposes. But the revisionists had not seen schools to be an intentional, purposeful success in terms of their promoters' goals; the judgment of failure was that of outsiders and critics. Ravitch had to twist the language to make her opponents seem absurd. In opposing an emphasis on social class, Ravitch flew in the face of the "new" social history altogether, not just the New Left, and appeared to be calling for a return to a Tocquevillean, consensus-oriented view of the American past. And an alternative version of revisionism, which defined the immigrant "victims" of school systems more in ethnic than in class terms, was left unconfronted.[4] Ravitch's last two points were much better taken. Revisionists did have an overly rational view of history, and a review of Katz's language on bureaucracy sustains her interpretation, though Katz and others took pains to show that behind bureaucracy lay a particular set of values.[5]

Both sides in the controversy were adept at marshaling arguments and evidence. The core of the dispute, although not acknowledged by Ravitch, lay in the contrast between versions of history that sympathetically identify themselves on the one hand with the perspective of bureaucratic administrators and their upper-middle class clients and on the other with the bottom levels of the society, whether defined ethnically or in class terms. The essence of revisionism was sympathy for immigrants—particularly for Catholic immigrants who, unlike the Jews, had little regard for education but were forced to attend school. From this basic shift of sympathy flowed all the argumentation.

Historians often passionately overidentify themselves with groups involved in the conflicts about which they are writing—whether nation-states, elites within them, or the downtrodden. History abounds in conflicts where neither side is unambiguously heroic or attractive in terms of modern sensibilities (the Romans versus the early Christians, the Puritans versus the Stuart establishment). Michael Katz at least was willing briefly to face this, pointing out the dilemma posed by working class authoritarianism, in which the traditional ambience of the Roman Catholic church in America was not a negligible factor.[6]

But what of the schools' success or failure from any point of view? Historians of education, whether revisionist or not, have understandably fallen into the trap of magnifying the historical role of their subject matter, of exaggerating the impact of schools upon the culture and the values of various groups in America. Bowles and Gintis, in their otherwise sweeping and comprehensive analysis, practically ignored the family, the peer group, and the mass media as agents of acculturation. But so do nearly all writers in the subdiscipline, whatever their persuasion. It may be that historians of education ought to be writing histories of the movies, or, like Joseph Kett (*Rites of Passage*, 1977), histories of the idea of childhood and adolescence. Retaining the sense of subject matter bequeathed by Ellwood P. Cubberley, most educational historians remain vulnerable to the charge that they are living in a somewhat unreal world so far as the lives of most people are concerned. Someone ought to explore the hypothesis that, far from being either sinister or benign, twentieth-century high schools mainly serve as locales for peer group rendezvous and for tax-supported child care. On a subtle level, the fascinating work of the maverick historian of education Daniel Calhoun (*The Intelligence of a People*, 1973) asked some of these unsettling questions about the state of the larger culture, though it took off from an abstract notion ("intelligence") that is dangerously insecure in view of the way it has been shown to be intertwined with cultural bias. But in spite of the fact that the history of education remains tied far too much to the study of the motives of school administrators and reformers, its temporary gains in the period 1968–1976 were not at all slight.

* * *

The history of colleges and universities does not mesh well with the history of school systems. (Nor have these zones of education articulated easily in actual fact.) As bureaucratic history, the history of higher education is more arcane; as intellectual history, it is far more viable and important. To put this in a slightly different way, it is harder to reduce the history of higher education to social history, though the attempt has been made. If intellectual history deserves to survive, then surely the thinking of university professors has formed an increasingly large part of it. Again, there is a much greater case for the relevance of academia to the central political history of the society as the twentieth century has advanced, even if such a case can easily be overstated.[7]

At first, in the postwar period, there was the same need for a liberation from progressivism in the history of higher education as in school history. Higher education is a subject specialty within schools of education, and the predictable kind of textbook along the older lines employed for such courses was *Higher Education in Transition* (1958), by John S. Brubacher and Willis Rudy. Yet it would be unfair to dismiss progressivism as if it were confined to that level. At some point it merges into a utilitarian perspective—the view that universities have existed for the aim of social service—an outlook of undeniable importance that can be divorced from the cruder teleological assumptions built into the old progressivism. Actually, such a utilitarian point of view has underlain the meticulous scholarship of a number of books that would be on anyone's shelf as prime building blocks in the field. One thinks of Merle Curti and Vernon L. Carstensen's *The University of Wisconsin* (1949) and of Hugh Hawkins's *Between Harvard and America* (1972).

An equal need has existed for liberation from another scholarly tradition that affected only the history of higher education, the custom of aging professors writing celebratory histories of their local campuses. Most such volumes were on the same level as antiquarian local history in general, except that they were written by academics who should have known better. At their best, they might contain enough shrewdness, despite self-censorship, to constitute important primary material. The minor industry of local campus history has continued because it functions independently of the scholarly mainstream; the product of local institutional pressures, volumes of this kind are a bit rarer now, but only because publication costs make it harder for some kinds of books to get into print.

As of the late 1950s and early 1960s, the field cried out for an approach that would transcend both progressivism or utilitarianism and the antiquarian chronicling of particular colleges and universities. Richard Hofstadter and Walter P. Metzger moved toward a more sophisticated kind of intellectual history in *The Development of Academic Freedom in the United States* (1955), but did not record the real variety of major intellectual forces within the university; their subject matter, academic freedom, lent itself to treatment as a kind of morality play, a mode they did not entirely renounce. Frederick Rudolph's *The American College and University* (1962) brought a fresh skepticism to the scene, though he found no organizing principle. My own book, *The Emergence of the American University* (1965), treating the period 1865–1910, tried to go further, both in the study of intellectual history as applied to higher education and in the study of the consequences of the developing university bureaucratic structure upon individuals. In it I identified three major schools of thought on the nature of the ideal university in America, to which I gave the labels utility, research, and culture. None of them was completely fulfilled, as the bureaucracy growing up silently alongside them often threatened to engulf them all. Writing too early to be influenced by the "new" social history, I sympathized with the more purely intellectual goals of the university.

The only more recent book to attempt a similar comprehensive overview of the subject is Burton J. Bledstein's *The Culture of Professionalism* (1976). Bledstein reverted to the utilitarian tradition but turned it upside down, blaming the influence of the university for many of the ills of the recent American elite. Brilliant in its initial chapters, Bledstein's book chose poor examples of academic administrators to make its points, relied too heavily on those examples, and lacked discrimination in identifying and dealing with the various academic traditions. Indeed, it refused to take those traditions seriously, hence amounted to an indirect attack upon intellectual history altogether. But it does deserve to be read.

Academic history possesses an incredible complexity. Monographs inevitably are its sturdiest basis. Achievements on this level are widely scattered as are the academic disciplines they range over. Biographies can have an importance which they usually lack in the history of school systems.[8] But brilliant as they may be, a greater challenge lies in the reconstruction of the histories of entire academic disciplines. There has been something of a push toward such histories in recent years. Bruce Kuklick's *The Rise of American Philosophy* (1977), though it deals only with Harvard (despite the title), manages to intermingle institutional and intellectual history as do few other works. Ideally, the balanced history of academic disciplines would serve as a welcome antidote to the magnification of individual campuses in isolation, the tendency that is still the bane of the field.

Such histories of disciplines compete, however, with the more amateurish histories of the same fields written by academic participants who are not trained historians. The third volume in the American Academy of Arts and Sciences history series has opted to include essays by these amateurs, with the result that this may be a less useful overview of knowledge than that offered in its first two books. Although both are collections of essays by different authors, with a perspective tending toward the establishmentarian and an emphasis on science at the expense of the humanities, there is no better place yet to go for a sense of the cutting-edge of inquiry in relation to the history of American academic scholarship than these two earlier volumes.[9]

In the pre-Civil War period, the history of American colleges is closely bound into the history of American Protestant religion. The trend in recent scholarship has been to try to make the colleges of the early nineteenth century seem more intellectually respectable and more socially useful than was formerly thought.[10] This argument downplays the stifling quality of evangelical religion and overplays the importance of the social mobility of villagers in an age of rapid urbanization and immigration. One remains skeptical of how far it can be carried.[11]

Inevitably the field must continue to focus on the late nineteenth and twentieth centuries, when universities of undeniable importance have existed in an American setting. The largest question remains the articulation of the internal intellectual histories of the disciplines with the social relations of the

American university. It cannot be done by verbal sleight-of-hand, as with the earlier Progressives' teleological slogans about the social functions of education. We must face the fact that universities may be *relatively* useless, especially when they are the most exciting places intellectually. The history of higher education will remain the study of an elite, though increasing access to the B.A. degree is certainly an important theme in the twentieth century. It may be important frankly to recognize this and to begin comparing various sectors of the academic elite with nonacademic elite groups in American society. Such an approach would get us away from crude attacks on the university and yet be more realistic than to pretend that professors have been just ordinary folks. Let us begin seriously to compare professors with lawyers, doctors, government bureaucrats, and businessmen.

It is possible that the caliber of scholarship will decline in all fields of American history during the next twenty years, as potential fresh blood is denied entrance. Even so, history of education has undergone a transformation from a sterile enclave into an area of research that holds important keys to an understanding of the industrialization process. Though there is much yet to be done, we have a number of fine books to read as we face the darker days ahead.

1. See Lawrence A. Cremin, *The Wonderful World of Ellwood Patterson Cubberley* (New York: Teacher's College Press, 1965), and *American Education: The National Experience, 1783-1876* (New York: Harper and Row, 1980).

2. Fritz Ringer is an exception. See his *Education and Society in Modern Europe* (Bloomington: Indiana University Press, 1979). But even Ringer's work primarily limits itself to comparisons between different European societies.

3. Joseph Kett, "On Revisionism," *History of Education Quarterly* 19 (1979): 229-35.

4. Diane Ravitch, "The Revisionists Revised," *Proceedings of the National Academy of Education* 4 (1977): 1-84; quotes from pp. 7, 11, 13 (her italics). For an earlier, more reasonable estimate of the revisionists, see Marvin Lazerson's essay review of Katz, Greer, and Spring, in *Harvard Educational Review* 43 (1973): 269-83.

5. See Michael Katz, *Class, Bureaucracy and Schools* (New York: Praeger, 1971), pp. xxii-xxiii.

6. Ibid., pp. 16, 135-36, 139.

7. See Laurence Veysey, "Higher Education as a Profession: Changes and Continuities," in *The Professions in American History*, ed. Nathan O. Hatch (Notre Dame: University of Notre Dame Press, forthcoming). In an unabashedly polemical vein, see also, Veysey, "Book Re-Views," *American Journal of Education* 90 (1981): 103-06.

8. See, e.g., Dorothy Ross, *G. Stanley Hall* (Chicago: University of Chicago Press, 1972); David Hollinger, *Morris R. Cohen and the Scientific Ideal* (Cambridge, Mass.: M.I.T. Press, 1975); Fred Matthews, *Quest for an American Sociology* (Montreal: McGill-Queen's University Press, 1977).

9. The first two volumes in the series are Sanborn C. Brown and Alexandra Oleson, eds., *The Pursuit of Knowledge in the Early American Republic* (Baltimore: Johns Hopkins University Press, 1976); and Oleson and John Voss, eds., *The Organization of Knowledge in Modern America, 1860-1920* (Baltimore: Johns Hopkins University Press, 1979).

10. See David Allmendinger, *Paupers and Scholars* (New York: St. Martins Press, 1975); Stanley M. Guralnick, *Science and the Ante-bellum American College* (Philadelphia: American Philosophical Society, 1975).

11. For the continuing flavor of this argument, see David B. Potts, "Curriculum and Enrollments: Some Thoughts on Assessing the Popularity of Antebellum Colleges," *History of Higher Education Annual* 1 (1981): 88–109.

THE STATE OF LEGAL HISTORY

James Willard Hurst

Law has been both a distinctive institution in United States history, and a material factor playing on and influenced by other factors of that history. Until about the last forty years, however, historians paid relatively little attention to legal elements in the country's experience, and worked within only a narrow conception of the scope of legal history. The last generation has witnessed a substantial growth in the literature, expressing enlarged ideas of the socially relevant subject matter of the field. The expanded definition ranges more widely over (1) time, (2) place, (3) institutional context, and (4) legal agencies studied. The fourth dimension of this growth reflects the other three and forms the core character of legal history as a new-shaped specialty.

Work on legal history in this country before the 1940s tended to a relatively narrow focus on place. Most study went into legal activity along the Atlantic seaboard, largely neglectful of varied roles of law in the continental expansion of the United States. There was, of course, a good deal of attention given to federalism, but mostly in terms of constitutional doctrine and related aspects of politics. Although marked economic and cultural sectionalism mingled with the development of a national economy and elements of a national culture, it is only within recent years that students of legal history have begun to explore ways in which legal doctrine and uses of law may have shaped or responded to sectional experiences and patterns different from or in tension with interests taking shape on a national scale. The country is too big and diverse to warrant assuming that what holds for New England, the Middle Atlantic, or Southern coastal states holds for all of the South, the Mississippi Valley, the Plains, the Southwest, or the Pacific Coast. In fact, an early, instructive lesson in regional differences in legal history was provided in 1931 by studies distinguishing development of water law in areas of generous and of limited rainfall; but until recently such essays had few counterparts. Moreover, from the 1880s on, the growth of markets of sectional or national reach under the protection of the federal system gave impetus to expanded roles of national law, ranging into quite different realms of policy from those embraced within the bounds of pre-1860 state common law or state statute law of corporations and private franchises. Legal historians have only lately begun to come abreast of the last hundred years' development of law made by the national government.

0048-7511/82/0104-0292 $01.00

Allied to limitations of place in earlier work in legal history were limitations of time. To an extent disproportionate to social realities, research centered on the colonial years, on the first years of the new states, and on the creation of a national constitution. Until the 1940s students badly neglected the nineteenth century, though in important respects that century did at least as much to determine the character of twentieth-century society in the United States as the colonial years or the late eighteenth century. Specialized studies have now revealingly appraised relations of law to the economies of selected states between 1800 and 1860. But the Civil War and the headlong pace, depth, and diversity of change from the 1880s into the 1920s produced a new economy and a new society. Historians have just begun to examine that critical span of growth and default in public policy. Tardy attention to such later periods may reflect a mistaken notion that history resides only in a distant past. So far as that bias exists, it does not withstand analysis. Obviously the closer students come to their own times, the more danger that their readings may be skewed by confusions, feelings, and interest peculiar to their immediate experience. But the hazard points to cautions in technique, not to a justification for limiting the proper subject matter of inquiry. What historians study is the time dimension of social experience, a dimension that extends into the present as well as the past. Indeed, the generation since the end of World War II has seen a period of creative and destructive disjunctions in developing roles of law that is at least as important as any other in the prior record.

Early in the twentieth century Roscoe Pound challenged legal scholarship to seek deeper insights through a sociological jurisprudence which might put law into realistic context with other institutions. Legal historians have been slow to respond to the challenge. The most distinguished scholarship of earlier years largely treated law as a self-contained system, with prime attention given to its internal structure and procedures and scant attention to its working relations to the environing society. So far as research has broken out of those bounds, it has tended to give most attention to relations of law to the changing character of the private market. Even in that domain we lack studies of concrete particulars, of where and how law may have helped or hindered in meeting functional requisites of market operations. Emphasis on law-market relations fits the reality—that the private market has been central to ideas and styles of action which have determined the location and character of prevailing political power in the country, especially over the last 150 years. But, beyond that range, social reality requires that legal historians pay more attention to the interplay of law and the family and sex roles, the bearing of law on the church, on tensions between conventional morality and individuality, on education, and on the course of change in scientific and technological knowledge. Particularly since the 1880s social developments have fostered a society of increasing interlock of processes and relations. Demands on public policy regarding the good order of social relations have tended to mount to an extent and over a range which legal historians have yet to match in their studies. To press the point is not to imply an exaggerated estimate of law's importance. To the contrary, more institutionally sophisticated study of legal history is likely to yield modest estimates of the comparative impact of law and of other-than-legal institutional factors. What such study may produce is better answers to Roscoe Pound's probing question about the limits of effective legal action. But only broad concern with law's operational ties to other components of social order will lead to the contributions the study of legal history should make to an illuminating sociology of law.

The most immediate as well as most stringent effect in limiting the range of work in legal history has been the preoccupation of students with courts and judicial process. Indeed, to put the matter so understates the limitation, for in fact historians have not been mainly concerned with courts, but specifically with the reported opinions and judgments of appellate courts. Of course courts have been important in the system of law. From about 1810 to 1890 judge-made (common) law provided a great bulk of standards and rules for market operations (in the law of property, contract, and security for debt), for domestic relations, and for defining familiar crimes against person and property. Even so, from the late eighteenth through the nineteenth century legislation dealing with government structure and with grants of franchises and corporate charters to private persons formed a large part of legal order; from the 1880s on, statute law and rules and regulations made by executive and administrative officers under broadening currents of power delegated by legislators grew to become the predominant body of public policy dealing particularly with the economy.

Nonetheless, in the face of growth of the legislative components of legal order, work in legal history has long been inclined to put disproportionate, indeed more often than not nearly exclusive, emphasis on the activity of appellate courts. There have been understandable reasons for this bias, but they do not justify it. Appellate court opinions typically offer more explicit and available identification and rationalization of public policy choices than do statutory or administrative materials. Court cases present relatively sharply drawn dramas of confrontation; the well marked roles of plaintiffs and defendants at least give more appearance of explaining the relevant interests and issues than the often more diverse, confused, imperfectly stated positions taken in the pulls and hauls of legislative process and the maneuvering of special interests as these play on legislators and administrators. Responsive to different social functions, legislative and executive or administrative lawmakers are likely to deal with diffuse or varied concerns, not as well defined as those aligned in lawsuits.

Some commentary distinguishes "law" from "government." This formula may have contributed to the idea that "law" consists simply in what courts do. There may be an imputation in the distinction that once we step outside the area of judicial action we confront only arbitrary exercises of will—that statutes and executive or administrative rules and precedents do not provide principled or predictable lines of public policy. Facts do not bear this out. Over spans of years legislative and administrative processes have produced sustained rankings of values and predictable regularities of choice. For example, there has been no whimsical or sheer flux of will in developed patterns of statute and administrative law dealing with the organization of markets, with public health and sanitation, safety on the job, allocation of costs incident to industrial accidents, or with taxation. Of course these bodies of law have reflected a good deal of push and pull among contending interests. But such maneuvering has been no less present, if more below the surface, of much common law development. As with the substance of public policy, so it has been with procedures for making it. The observer can identify and predict continuities in development of legislative and administrative procedures as well as of judicial procedures in such matters as setting terms of notice or hearing to affected interests, fixing relations of legislative committees to their parent bodies, and arranging modes of making administrative rules or orders.

The tendency to identify "law" with courts may have stemmed in part from roles of judges in reviewing actions of other legal officers. A norm of our system has been that aggrieved individuals or groups should be able to seek a remedy in court against official actions which exceed authority conferred by constitutions or by statutes. In this sense law created and operated by judges has had an existence apart from activities of other legal agencies. But this fact does not justify disproportionate attention to judicial process. In practice, relatively little legislative or administrative action has come under judicial review. Mostly, legislatures and administrators set and enforce their own limits on themselves, defined by their own doctrine and precedents in interpreting relevant constitutional and statutory provisions. In addition, administrative law making stands under scrutiny in legislative hearings and through the process of legislative appropriations. Outside spheres of official action, it is true that in the nineteenth century courts predominated in structuring private relationships, as through the law of contract and property. But in the twentieth century statute and administrative law enter largely into the governance of private relations; "law" in this domain can no longer be identified simply with what judges do.

If one implicitly identifies "law" with commands, the more likely focus is courts, which seem the distinctive source of judgments or decrees. In two ways this approach distorts reality. Even if we focus on commands, for the past 100 years at least the bulk of legal commands have rested on statute books, administrative rules or regulations, or have been embodied in administrative precedents. Granted, from the 1790s to the 1870s administrative law making had a limited role compared to the surge of common law growth. But even in that earlier time the statute books contained a substantial volume of binding standards and rules. From the 1880s the trend accelerated to more and more governance of affairs through statutory and administrative directions; by the 1980s lawyers were turning most of the time to legislation or delegated legislation, or to administrative case law to find what the law might command their clients to do or not to do.

More important than identifying the source of the command aspects of law, however, is to take account of great areas of public policy in which command has been less to the fore than the positive structuring of relationships, and in which statutory and administrative outputs have always dominated. The power of the public purse has resided firmly in the legislature; judges have never had authority to levy taxes, and only by indirection and to a marginal extent have their judgments determined for what public money should be spent. Resource allocation through public taxing and spending has long been a major source of impact on the society. In the nineteenth century, Congress—and state legislatures under delegation from Congress—set terms for disposing of a vast public domain, an immensely important style of legal allocation of resources in times when a cash-scarce economy found it hard to raise money by taxes. Statutory provision of tax exemptions and selectivity in taxable subjects were also means for promoting favored lines of economic activity. In the twentieth century growth in general productivity created unprecedented liquidity in the economy, with direct money subsidies from government assuming the dominant role that land grants had in the nineteenth century. By conditions set on government grants in aid, and by elaborating exemptions, credits, and deductions under individual and corporate income taxes, twentieth-century tax and appropriations law became of major importance in regulating and channeling economic activity and affecting the distribution or allocation of purchasing power. Public policy also affected resource allocation by legislative and administrative action controlling, or at least materially influencing, the supply of money (including supply of credit), and (for better or worse) deflationary or inflationary trends in the economy. Courts have had only marginal involvement in these matters, which legal historians have neglected in proportion to the exaggerated attention they have given judicial process.

Narrow identification of law with commands—and of commands with courts—ignores other major sectors of legal action than those involved in direct allocation of resources. Even from the late eighteenth century legislative grants of patents, of special action franchises (as for navigation improvement), and provision of corporate charters were important means of promoting as well as legitimating and to some degree regulating forms of private collective action. Government licensing, always within statutory and administrative frameworks, carried on to play a salient role in the twentieth century. From the late nineteenth century the character of the society was shaped much by activities of business corporations, and, especially in the twentieth century, by the influence of lobbies pursuing profit and nonprofit goals; the structure and governance of corporations and of pressure groups derived primarily from private initiatives, but also could not be divorced from statutory and administrative law which profoundly affected the scope given to private will. Moreover, overlapping the resource-allocating, licensing, and regulatory roles of law, yet with their own special character, were uses of law to promote or channel advances in science and technology. Here, again, one encounters a major sector of modern legal history, built more from legislative and administrative than from judicial contributions, which would be ignored insofar as one identifies "law" and legal history with courts and with commands issuing from courts.

Until recent years legal historians wrote as if their subject defined itself within narrow jurisdictional limits of place, time, and institutional reference. However, over the last forty years broader currents of ideas have begun to move through the area. Livelier concern with roles of law in dealing with social adjustments and conflicts has fostered fresh attention to theory. Legal historians have been appraising issues of (1) consensus or want of consensus on values, (2) pluralism expressed through bargaining among interests, and (3) social and economic class dominance in legal order.

Critics have found want of realism or sophistication in a good deal of work in legal history, which they read as portraying the United States as a society of substantial harmony, based on almost universally shared values, marked by little or no use of law by the powerful to oppress the weak. Much of the criticized work is not as naive as the criticism would suggest. It is no new discovery that law has often involved severe conflicts over power and profit, or that the realities of conflict have not always been plain on the surface of events. These themes sounded in Federalist Number Ten, in the attacks leveled by Madison and Jefferson on Hamilton's programs, and in Calhoun's Disquisition on Government. On the other hand, conflict has never been the whole of law's story. A substantial part of social reality has been the presence of some broadly shared values which have shaped or legitimated uses of law. Wholesale denial of that could hardly stand against stubborn facts which show that this has been, overall, a working society; an operational society can only rest on some substantial sharing of values.

The real issue in appraising the social history of law is not to establish consensus or no consensus as the single reality, but to determine how much consensus, on what, among whom, when, and with what gains and costs to various affected interests. Law has embodied values shared among broad, yet diverse sectors of interests. The course of events has borne witness, for example, to long-held, broadly sustained faith that social good follows from an increase in general economic productivity measured in transactions in private markets. Similar faith has accorded legitimate roles to the private market as a major institution for allocating scarce economic resources. Over most of the country's past people have shown a belief that they would benefit in net result from advances in scientific knowledge and in technological capacity to manipulate the physical and biological environments. These articles of faith have come under rising challenge in the past fifty years. But the challenges themselves evidence the felt reality of earlier consensus, even as new public policies bearing on the environment attest emergence of some new areas of value agreement. In some criticism of "consensus history" there seems to lurk confusion between recognizing facts and evaluating the social impact of the facts. The critics plainly disapprove some values which broad coalitions of opinion embodied in past public policy. But to disapprove now of a shared value of the past is not to disprove that people in the past in fact shared the value. To recognize the realities of shared values does not require that we disregard all grounds of skepticism toward consensus. Constructive criticism will weigh the history of public policy with consideration of the parts played in affairs by force, indoctrination, despair, and indifference.

To the extent that it has been effective, legal order in the United States has rested on successful assertion of a monopoly of physical force in legal agencies and their ability to fix terms on which private persons may properly wield force. The constitutional ideal is that public force be used only for public good. An important task for legal historians is to probe the amount of fiction and reality in the pursuit of this constitutional ideal. The record shows uses of law which have put the force of law at the disposal of private greed for power and profit. The record also shows that in considerable measure law has been too weak, incompetent, or corrupt to prevent uses of private force against workers, the poor, or racial or ethnic minorities. Recognition of realities of consensus should not ignore these dark aspects of the legal record.

People may be brought to accept public policy through indoctrination against their best interests, under guidance and for the benefit of special interests. Because of the legitimacy which the idea of constitutional government has tended to confer on legal order, law may be a useful instrument for such manipulation. Past politics has shown the effectiveness of rallying slogans based on law, including appeals to "law and order," to "freedom of contract," and to "due process and equal protection of the laws." Historians need to be aware that, while law may rest on consensus, law may be used to build consensus, and to do so in service to diverse special interests.

Apparent agreement on values embodied in law may reflect not so much positive consent or wish as resigned or despairing acceptance of superior force, directly or indirectly applied. Thus, immigrants' acceptance of "Americanization" may have sprung from a sense of insecurity and lost roots rather than from positive commitment. Again, it is difficult to grapple with the element of "class war" in the context of a society in which so much combat among interests has stayed within bounds of regular processes of the market, of politics, and of the law. Another factor which may have diluted the effect of common will has been the presence of contradictions among shared values. The course of antitrust policy is a notable example. Since the Sherman Act a substantial public opinion has accepted the idea of using law to give positive protection to the competitive vitality of the private market. On the other hand, people have learned to prize a rising material standard of living, and to associate this satisfaction with fruits of large-scale production and distribution; these attitudes have developed in continuing tension. Government has given firm institutional embodiment to antitrust programs. But public policies, not only toward the antitrust effort, but also regarding tariffs, patents, taxes, and public spending have failed to withhold governmental subsidies from or mount effective challenges to the growth and entrenchment of concentrations of private control in markets. In such varied respects the country's experience cautions legal historians to explore the origins and quality of will behind apparent sharing of values.

There is another element in apparent policy consensus to which critics of "consensus history" do not give due weight. This has developed into a society of increasing diversity and numbers of roles and functions. Amid this complexity most people have in fact probably been indifferent to particular uses of law to affect allocations of gains and costs among specialized interests; most people have not sought specific involvement in specific decisions of public policy. Instead they have tacitly if not explicitly shared a value distinctive to the legal order—acceptance of certain regular, legitimated, peaceful processes for making decisions, whatever the particular substance of the decisions taken. Public budgets provide an outstanding example. For the most part voters do not send members to the legislature under specific mandates to spend so many dollars on public health inspection of food processors, or on university libraries, police radio transmitters, or any other of the myriad items of appropriations acts. The voters are content that their votes legitimate a public process for deciding on all these particulars. True, indifference to the particulars may sometimes rest on indoctrinated ignorance. But, more likely, it rests on valid, rational perceptions of self interest; as creatures of limited time, energy, and capacity, most individuals can not busy themselves in helping decide how every competition of focused interests should be worked out. Thus a valid indifference toward many substantive specifics in uses of law has probably been a continuing element in a real consensus which accepts legal processes. The reality of this consensus has grown with the need of it, as the society has grown more diverse in the experiences its members encounter.

Growth in diversity and interlock of relations in the United States has emphasized uses of law to channel and legitimate bargains struck among competing interests. The significance of legal processes for the operations of a pluralist society is attested to by the accommodations evident in state session laws and in the federal Statutes at Large in the nineteenth century, and in both statute law and administrative regulations of the twentieth century. In the growth of common law bargaining uses of law have been less overt, and within the close bounds of propriety, but they have been present nonetheless. Resort to political parties and party politics have been woven into activities of formal legal agencies in such bargaining to give a generally centrist character to pursuit of major interest adjustments.

More open to dispute than the general acceptance of interest bargaining through law have been assessments of the social results and the social and political legitimacy of such uses of legal process. Some observers may have read the bargaining record too complacently, taking the law's contributions to have been only to the public good; there is some of this tone even in the sophistication of Federalist Number Ten. But as early as the Disquisition on Government (1831) Calhoun pointedly questioned whether bargaining might amount to no more than creation of artificial majorities based on selfishly opportunistic coalitions. Modern criticism of faith in the general benefits of a pluralist social-legal order have suggested several useful cautions to legal historians. First, over sizeable periods of time and ranges of interests, inequalities in practical as well as in formal legal power have barred or severely limited access to the bargaining arena for Indians, blacks, and other disadvantaged ethnic groups, women, and the poor in general. Moreover, inequalities have limited those who did enter the arena; bargaining power was often in gross imbalance, as for example between big business and small business, between urban creditors and rural debtors, and between employers and workers. Further, apart from excluded or generally disadvantaged sectors of society, some interests have been so diffuse or unorganized as to have only limited say about what went on. This was the position in the late nineteenth century in relations of farmers and small businessmen with the railroads, and in the twentieth century in dealings of consumers with big firms supplying mass markets. In this respect white middle class people who in other ways shared profits of dominance over less advantaged groups were themselves disadvantaged. The most subtle, but probably most harmful limitation on the bargaining process derived from the sharply focused self interest which typically provided the impetus in resorts to legal processes. Perceptions of self interest usually brought to bear will to initiate and sustain uses of law to serve particular ends. What did not enter perception did not stir will. In an increasingly diverse, shifting society, even among relatively sophisticated and powerful individuals and groups, perceptions of interest tended to concentrate on rather short-term adjustments, specialized and intricate in detail. Such factors fostered narrowly pragmatic uses of law which were likely to slight broad reaches of cause and effect and long-term impacts. The second half of the twentieth century showed some tardy realization of these limitations of interest bargaining. Thus there were moves to invoke law to regulate the course of technological change and even of scientific inquiry, as well as to reassess social gains and costs from operations of the private market.

For all the qualifications, there were positive aspects in the history of interest bargaining through law. There were disquieting trends toward increased concentration of private and public power. Nonetheless, the society continued to show a considerable dispersion of different types of practical power, and a material challenge for legal historians was to improve our understanding of the qualities and defects of legal processes in affecting both concentration and dispersion. Interest bargaining through law seems to have contributed to creating socially productive elaboration of the division of labor within and outside of market processes. Finally, harsh experience with abuses of various types of legal order has suggested no convincing alternative that seems likely to improve on interest bargaining within constitutional legal processes as a means toward a legal and social order that will be at once efficient and humane. The principal alternatives that history offers have involved narrowly based, centralized authority, which typically has fallen into abuse without serving either efficiency or humanity. Overall, our experience teaches that a just and efficient society needs more guidance for policy than mere bargaining among a plurality of interests may supply, but that the society cannot afford to do without a substantial bargaining component in its legal order.

Some interpret United States legal history as a record of uses of law by a narrow sector of society to help get and control the principal means of production so as to dominate all other social sectors for the gains that concentrated wealth and power afford. In this view all else in the law which does not seem to fit this reading of events—constitutional structures, Bill of Rights guarantees, or generalized legal rights of property, contract, and individual security—is only a facade for the real, tight monopoly held by an inner circle of private powerholders.

This critique carries useful insights for legal historians who do not accept its ultimate thesis. Concentrated private wealth has used and abused its influence on law to its own advantage. It has fostered or accepted, though it may not always have initiated, exclusion of disadvantaged minorities from the circle of effective interest bargainers. It has proved capable of subverting to its ends the organized physical force of the law. Short of resort to overt force, sustained, gross inequalities in private command of wealth and income have promoted unjust uses of law to serve special interests. Concentrated private control in large business corporations has brought into question the legitimacy of the private market as an institution for healthy dispersion of power.

However, United States legal history seems too rich and diverse to be understood simply as recording the success of a small class of controllers of the means of production in dominating the whole course of the society. That interpretation underestimates the realities of shared values and interest bargaining, neglects the extent to which public policy embodied in law has responded to functional needs of life in society, and fails to appreciate some more profound limitations on the success of efforts to create a social order at once effective and humane.

An analysis which rates the country's legal history as simply a product of ruling class domination must deal with the fact that some broadly shared values have had important roots other than in the distribution of control of means of production. Thus from the adoption of the First Amendment separation of church and state developed into a substantially unchallenged premise of public policy. Into this item of consensus went influences derived from the sectarian diversity of the country, memories of religious wars and persecution abroad, and an individualistic outlook on life born of mixed parentage in religious, economic, and cultural factors that reached back some centuries. Another salient example is the great impress on public policy of broadly shared values which grew out of the experience of growth in science and technology. True, this experience was affected by the market. But it involved reckonings not limited simply to those of a market calculus. Technical and science based confidence that material advance would boundlessly improve the quality of life did as much to sustain faith in the social merits of the market as market activity did to promote faith in science and technology. Continuing exposure to what people saw as evident benefits from additions to their technological command of nature made them the more receptive to change brought by technology; the idea that such change might properly call for some legal regulation was therefore the slower to emerge.

Further, a ruling class interpretation of the country's legal history under-rates the extent to which interest bargaining through law has curbed private operation of means of production. Public policy in this domain was often defective in content and in execution. Nonetheless, out of interest group bargaining within legal processes emerged substantial regulations protecting workers, consumers, and small and moderate sized business firms in matters of health, safety, collective bargaining, honest dealing, and maintenance of some extent of competition in market. By the 1970s one could not realistically define the structure and governance of even the largest business corporations without adding to provisions of corporation law proper a range of legal con-trols external to corporation law in matters of finance, credit, marketing practices, taxation and accounting, labor relations, stockholder relations, and impacts on the environment.

Apart from expansion of legal controls, another aspect of affairs puts in question a diagnosis which explains legal history in terms of big business dominance. Through the nineteenth century and into the twentieth a large proportion of legal contests among competing interests seems to have been intraclass rather than interclass collisions among different segments of entre-preneurial property owners who, though of varying means, all played capi-talist roles. This appraisal fits much of the development of law dealing with creditor-debtor relations, the money supply, regulation of insurance and banking, relations between corporate promoters and managers and investors, and with antitrust protection of the market. In these aspects law has often reflected a degree of fractionalization of capitalist interests substantial enough to put in question the dominance of a high capitalist sector. To all of this, one must add account of the more or less distinct impact of political processes.

Another dimension of legal history which a ruling class interpretation slights has been the response to what broad sectors of opinion have perceived to be functional requisites of a working society. Population growth and con-centration, broader and more complex market operations, and effects of advancing technology multiplied the pressures of functional considerations, especially from the 1880s. Such pressures seem to have been material, for example, in the development of law dealing with public health and sanitation, with promotion of predictable regularities in market transactions, and with organizing and administering a supply of basic facilities for transport, water supply, and the generation of electric power. Of course the capitalist context often puts its distinctive stamp on these developments. But comparison with operations in noncapitalist societies suggests the presence of pressures likely to attend large-scale, bureaucratized, technically intricate social arrange-ments as such. So far as care for function took on a character specially adapted to capitalism, legal historians need to learn more about the concrete particulars of uses of law to serve those functional needs.

Finally, legal history needs to take due account of how far much of what happens in society is grounded in the fact that under all kinds of social organization, capitalist, socialist, or whatever, humans are limited beings. We need to be cautious about fixed definitions of "human nature"; exploitation has often sought to justify itself by appeals to that "nature." But the stubborn fact remains that we are creatures of limited physical, intellectual, and emotional capacity, with limited ability to transcend sense of self or of the groups to which we feel near, and with limited courage and energy of will. Within such limitations we confront overwhelming detail and density of experience, sometimes moved by changes which in pace, range, depth, and intricacy outstrip our understanding. To our limitations as individuals we must add limits set, sometimes below awareness, by cultural inheritance and mass emotion. Out of this mixture which makes up our human predicament as individuals and as members of social groups, history tells how much has happened from unchosen, unplanned, often unperceived accumulations of events and their consequences. Probably these elements account for more legal history than all of the deliberate strivings which our vanity likes to dwell on. Here perhaps we confront limits of effective legal action that are more deeply rooted than any ruling class theory can measure.

Yet law has been a major instrument for combatting mindless and chaotic experience. Hardly any aspect of legal history more poignantly bears on our human situation than resort to legal processes to move against the daunting forces of individual and social drift and inertia. But this is an aspect which legal historians have tended to leave unexamined. By definition an interpretation which reads legal history in terms of dominant and dominated sectors of society deals largely with conscious and deliberate striving. Thus, along with all other interpretations that turn on estimates of will, it omits the great darkness which surrounds all striving. Realism calls for including in the story the influences of existential fears and insecurities. Whatever the particular organization of power in society, general experience teaches that under any system people will feel the impacts of greed, lust for power over others, fear of the stranger, and yearning for individual and group security against primitive fears of what lies in the surrounding murk and muddle. However imperfectly seen or realized, some responses to such threats and challenges have appeared in the country's legal history. Those responses are deep in constitutional structures and in provisions of the Bill of Rights, in uses of law to allocate resources so as to advance knowledge and provide education, and in creation of legal standards and rules which may foster empathy among individuals who stand to each other in no close ties of blood, kin, clan, religion, race, or nationality. True, the law's responses have been conditioned by many features of this particular social context—in the setting of North

America, with its social growth timed in the surge of the commercial and industrial revolutions and the rise of the middle class, its values stamped as predominantly white, middle class, and capitalist, Christian, individualist, and pragmatic. But there is a substratum of meaning here which study of such contextual particulars does not reach. No more will that substratum be reached by a ruling class interpretation. Law has nothing to do with creating these ineluctable terms of existence. But the presence or absence of response to them through law, and the qualities or deficiencies of response provide inescapable dimensions of legal history, whether or not legal historians have the sensitivity to see this.

AMERICAN INTELLECTUAL HISTORY:
ISSUES FOR THE 1980s

David A. Hollinger

The study of American intellectual history now confronts a series of opportunities and dilemmas that are too often obscured by the tendency of historiographical discussion to dwell on such ephemeral issues as this field's relative status in the profession, the morale of its practitioners, and the exact location of its boundaries with other fields. Basic to all three of these distractions is a lamentable preoccupation with professional rather than intellectual challenges. Challenges of these two kinds are of course connected, but even challenges defined primarily by the dynamics of the profession are most appropriately met by directly addressing intellectual challenges, instead of the other way around. American intellectual history should be approached not as a distinctive population of practitioners whose interests are at stake but as an intellectual expanse occupied periodically by scholars operating out of many networks and possessed of a variety of skills—an expanse that is the property of no one, even of scholars who spend enough of their time in it to become known as "intellectual historians." We would do well to see this expanse as a *commons* instead of an estate. The opportunities and dilemmas found there are best recognized in the context of what has been taking place on this commons in recent years.

The study of American intellectual history is surely one of the most diverse, eclectic, and loosely organized of the subdisciplines of American history that retain a single name, and that form the basis for undergraduate courses and for major headings in indexes of dissertations and of scholarly monographs. This has always been so, but what counts as "American intellectual history" is now a more open question than ever before. Teaching and scholarship were once sustained in part by the notion that there exists a distinctive American intellectual tradition: courses could be organized around this tradition, and monographs could be written on episodes in its growth and transformation. Whatever else this tradition might encompass, it was known to include the thought of the Puritans, Edwards, Franklin, the Founding Fathers, the Transcendentalists, and the Pragmatists. With the waning of belief in the reality of a distinctive national tradition, at least one with this old cast of characters, the field of American intellectual history lost its hold on

0048-7511/82/0104-0306 $01.00

what was once thought to be a challenging and durable set of specific problems. The result can be seen in both teaching and scholarship.

A given syllabus may be organized around popular culture or the history of "intellectuals," around uniquely American preoccupations and cultural products or American participation in intellectual movements common to the extended culture of modern Europe, around "social thought" or literary culture, around political ideologies or religious-philosophical world views, to list only the most obvious of the choices on which the teaching of this field is currently based. Although one can be reasonably certain that a course in diplomatic history will address Woodrow Wilson's decision to enter World War I, or that a course in economic history will take up the Panic of 1819, similar predictions are risky for intellectual history, especially with reference to the period since the Civil War. The people and problems studied by Morton White in 1949 and Henry May in 1959 are no longer assumed to be basic. The textbooks of Ralph Henry Gabriel, Merle Curti, and Stow Persons have exercised little influence during the past two decades. A once-standard anthology edited by Perry Miller has been out of print for years.[1] Nowadays, Bruce Barton and Benjamin Spock are as likely to be assigned as are Thorstein Veblen and Reinhold Niebuhr, and often for good reasons.

Scholarly works manifest this same diversity. While the field's grasp on a set of specific problems embedded in a single national tradition has loosened, "intellectual history" has turned up in many places. "We no longer need intellectual history" as a specialty, one leading historian has proposed with reference to European as well as American studies, "because we have all become intellectual historians."[2] There are studies of aspects of feminism, antislavery, and education, for example, that deal primarily and self-consciously with ideas, and are easily received as contributions to intellectual history. One can argue that American intellectual history is not really a "field" at all, but merely the extension into the field of American history of a particular way of doing history.

Yet references to American intellectual history as a field have persisted even while more and more historians have become comfortable with the study of ideas. These references now refer more decisively than ever to a methodologically defined entity. Among historians of the United States, at least, intellectual history has come during the last ten or fifteen years to be more, not less, distinct from its sibling subdisciplines. Commentaries on American intellectual history have always addressed its "aims and methods," but not since the days when Perry Miller and Henry Nash Smith were considered innovative has this field been so consistently understood to be a *kind* of history rather than a set of problems to which a given mode of analysis has a natural relation.

This understanding has sharpened primarily with reference to three basic commitments long associated with intellectual history, but cast into more bold relief during the last ten or fifteen years while subject to some skepticism from the profession at large. To specify these commitments is not to define the "essential nature" of intellectual history, if there is such a thing. As K. M. Minogue has recently observed, "intellectual history . . . is, of almost all academic activities, one of the most resistant to reduction to form." [3] The three commitments to which I have alluded simply indicate the interests and sensitivities for which the study of American intellectual history has recently been a vehicle.

One commitment is to *thinking* itself, a human activity that demands historical study no less than migrating, fighting, building, multiplying, praying, farming, and a host of other activities that make up the events historians study. This proposition might seem so banal as to be beyond dissent, but there remain some historians who regard mental activity as important only when it can be shown to be a cause or a consequence of "real" events "outside the mind." Although Bernard Bailyn is too sophisticated for a formulation as bald as that, his 1981 presidential address to the American Historical Association betrays this bias: Bailyn contrasts the "interior" worlds of "attitudes, beliefs, fears, and aspirations" to "the exterior world of palpable historical events," and insists that "in the end the question historians must answer is the relation" of the former to the latter.[4] Historians who depict acts of mind as "events," too, may have only a semantic quarrel with Bailyn, but a more substantial issue in priorities divides Bailyn from those who would focus on these events, rather than treat them as considerations relevant to the order of "palpable" events.

The commitment to the historical significance of thinking has been strongly affirmed, however, by another recent president of the American Historical Association, William J. Bouwsma. What we need, asserts Bouwsma, is more "studies in the construction of meaning." Such studies are not the possession only of scholars who have called themselves intellectual historians, but such scholars have made their "greatest impact on historiography" when addressing "the history of meanings." Although Bouwsma toys with the possibility that this "history of meanings" could take the place of an "intellectual history" he believes has been too cerebral in its sense of how meanings are created, he vindicates interests and sensitivities with which the study of intellectual history has been persistently identified. Central to his prescriptions is "the concept of man as an animal who must create or discern meaning in everything he does"; historical scholarship would do well to focus less on "what happens to people," he insists, and more on "what human beings have made out of that experience."[5] This was exactly the advice of Perry Miller, who did more than any other single scholar to indicate to Americanists the possibilities of intellectual history as a distinctive enterprise.[6]

The sense-making efforts that most engaged Miller's attention were made by what we have come to call "intellectual elites." This belief in the historical significance of thinking done by people who were reasonably good at it, who specialized in it, or were at least expected by groups within their society to take the lead in doing it, is the second of the commitments for which the study of American intellectual history has been a vehicle. Indeed, the scholars who label their own work as "intellectual history" are more often than not devoted to the study of the discourse of these out-and-out "thinkers." Studies of this kind have sometimes been oblivious to what may have been going on in the minds of "ordinary" people, or have assumed uncritically that much of the population shared, at least in rudimentary form, the ideas articulated by society's leading intellectuals. Recent scholarship has been less casual regarding the relation of elites to the populations surrounding them. Still, some historians are convinced that whatever we need to know about the American past, we are not going to learn it by studying the likes of Jonathan Edwards, Josiah Royce, and F. Scott Fitzgerald. One might imagine that individuals who actually made *arguments* about the issues of their day, or who expressed through art a distinctive sensitivity to the dimensions of these issues, would be appropriate candidates for historical study, yet it is exactly here that skepticism about the orientation of American intellectual history has become the most strident and moralistic. Laurence Veysey has implied that scholars involved in the study of intellectual elites may have reason to suffer "guilt" for their pursuit of "the most arcane thought processes of exceptional individuals."[7]

If virtue attends upon the study of ideas held in common by large populations, the third in this list of commitments ought to carry with it the guarantee of a clean conscience. This third item is the operating assumption that social action necessarily takes place within a framework of meanings that serve to enable and to restrict what people do. The behavior of statesmen and strikers, pioneers and whaling men, bureaucrats and poets is to be understood at least partly in terms of ideas common to publics of which they were members. The meanings men and women associate with their actions "form the very structure" of their "social world," Gordon Wood reminded readers of *New Directions in American Intellectual History*, although he granted that the insight is hardly "new." Since ideas define and help to create social life, adds Wood, "it makes no sense to treat ideas mechanically as detached 'causes' or 'effects' of social events and behavior."[8] This concern with the enabling and delimiting functions of structures of meaning has been advanced with particular reference to political languages by Quentin Skinner and

J. G. A. Pocock, two methodologists of intellectual history quoted extensively during the last decade by Americanists.[9] This third commitment, like the others, is subject to some skepticism. It violates a distinction that some historians continue to find indispensable: "social realities" are one thing, and the presumably epiphenomenal worlds of thought are another.[10]

If these three intellectual commitments now endow the professional study of American intellectual history with what shape it has, it does not follow that everyone involved in that study has invested equally in each of the three, nor that given practitioners are more interested in these commitments than they are in the particular topics on which they work. It would be a mistake, also, to infer from the field's lack of programmatic focus that the quality of monographic work done on the commons is inferior to that being done in other fields. One could argue that since so many scholars who come to the commons do so well, there is little point in assessing the state of the arts practiced there, and even less in prescribing agendas for future work. Yet as the term "commons" implies, there are issues of common interest to scholars who work there. To bring these issues into focus and to make suggestions about their resolution might remind us that the commons should not be parcelled out into small, private lots. Yet this privatization of the commons is now a real danger: some scholars have become so complacent and autonomous in their work that what was once the most synthetic of American history's subdisciplines threatens to become the least.

One cluster of issues has to do with "America." If there really is such a thing, it would be a shame to miss it. Yet the notion of America has become a matter of some controversy. Many generalizations made about it in the past are now felt to apply only to distinctive groups within American society. The revolt against holism in American studies is only one source of the controversy. There is also the spreading recognition that so very, very much of the intellectual life of the United States—especially of its learned elites—is defined by questions and traditions that transcend any national culture. Historiographical brows have sometimes furrowed concerning the "relation of American to European thought," an uninspired phrase that stops short of acknowledging that the intellectual history of the United States is in many crucial respects a province of the intellectual history of Europe, and is, as such, comparable to the intellectual histories of Great Britain, Germany, France, and other distinctive nations within what Richard Rorty calls "the conversation of the west."[11] The question of "America," then, has antithetical local and cosmopolitan dimensions: particularism within and universalism without have drawn upon the intellectual energies of Americans, and recognition of this fact has made the concept of "America" less central, analytically, than it once was.

The "locals" do not pose quite so striking a challenge to this concept as do the "cosmopolitans." Americanists generally do not doubt that groups of Americans defined regionally, ethnically, and religiously belong in American history. The efforts of southerners, Presbyterians, and blacks to think out and act upon the implications of their group identity in relation to American nationality provide the basis for standard scholarly fare among historians of the United States. The "cosmopolitans" are more likely to get out of American history altogether, and to become figures only in the specialized, international histories of biology, sociology, or philosophy. Perhaps this is as it should be, but if it will not do to assume that everything written in America expresses some mystical American spirit, neither will it do to assume that Americans participating in international discourse do so on terms that can be fully understood without assessing their simultaneous involvement in their national community.[12]

The problem of the "cosmopolitans" has sometimes been dealt with through a distinction between "American thought" and "thought in America." This distinction has most often been invoked with reference to philosophy, theology, and the natural sciences, where the nationality of ideas has been harder to specify and often irrelevant to understanding the ideas and their function in the lives of those who hold them.[13] It is one thing, according to this distinction, to talk about ideas and discursive practices that are peculiarly American, and another to talk about ideas and discursive practices that engage people who happen to be Americans; it is one thing to address an American intellectual tradition and another to address intellectual traditions present in America. This distinction cuts differently from period to period as well as from tradition to tradition. After American intellectuals came into comfortable leadership of the international circles of scholarship and science in the twentieth century, especially after World War One, they brought to their participation in those circles less of the cultural nationalist baggage carried by nineteenth-century predecessors preoccupied with their status as Americans in an essentially European world. The intellectual life of the colonial period, too, differs from the America-conscious epoch that stretches from Thomas Jefferson's Declaration of Independence to the late novels of Henry James, but colonialists have long been distinguished by the sophistication with which they treat the thinking of their European-American subjects.

Historians have had good reason to treat this distinction very gingerly. Many of the creative activities of American intellectuals have consisted of efforts to participate in the "conversation of the west" while at the same time acting upon or seeking to clarify the imperatives of American nationality.[14] Yet the distinction between "American thought" and "thought in America," if not taken too literally, offers an appropriately flexible orientation toward nonnationalistic American participation in international discourse. It invites, at the same time, a renewed, critical discussion of the problem of a unique, American intellectual tradition. This dual promise is best expressed in terms of two agendas that might well be posted on the commons, near enough to one another that scholars would be encouraged to keep both in mind.

One agenda would aim straight at the problem of "America," directing attention to whatever myths, languages, and arguments can be shown to serve at least some Americans *as Americans*. It would take as its most obvious datum the activities of public moralists: those who have taken it upon themselves to speak to, or on behalf of, what they have understood to be *the* American community. Prominent among these "public moralists" have been political controversialists, including politicians and office holders like James Madison and Abraham Lincoln as well as polemicists and commentators like Thomas Paine and Walter Lippmann. The role of public moralist has also been filled, of course, by clergymen, capitalists, novelists, jurists, social scientists, artists, labor leaders, and literary critics, but they, too, have made clear, in the process of performing this role, that their pronouncements on a host of cosmic and social issues were intended to enlighten a distinctly American public. This first agenda, then, would seek to develop a richer and more comprehensive account than we now have of the intellectual structure of American public life at given times, including the political languages within which people have formulated issues in that public life and have argued about its nature and destiny. We might well call it our Tocquevillian agenda.

As the adjective "Tocquevillian" implies, we already have an enormous professional literature addressed, more or less, to this first agenda. No doubt scholars now treat the singularity of American culture less casually than those who gave so bad a name to studies of the "American mind," but it is a purpose of the Tocquevillian agenda to harvest critically some of the results of this older scholarship, and to reformulate and pursue its concern with a distinctive, American intellectual tradition. This purpose might be defeated if use of the term "American" were restricted, in a fit of fastidiousness, to aspects of American life that involved every inhabitant. Just because some Americans resisted, or were excluded from, or never gained access to the kind of "selfhood" analyzed by Sacvan Bercovitch does not mean that Bercovitch is mistaken to call that selfhood "American." [15] Some Americans were "more American" than others in a specific and noninvidious sense: they were more extensively involved in, and dependent upon, a public culture created by men and women who were highly conscious of being Americans. We still have much to discover about how this culture was created, and about whose interests were advanced and hurt in the process of its creation.

If the first agenda would build upon the insight that there does exist an American national culture, the intellectual structure and demographic extent of which are matters for continuing inquiry, the second agenda would build upon the insight that America is, for some purposes, part of Europe. This second agenda would consist of major problems in the intellectual history of the Europe-centered West, and would presuppose that these problems transcend as well as draw upon the national histories of each of the major Western nations. These problems need not be expressed only in terms of "isms," but "modernism" is an especially useful example because it denotes a specifically Western phenomenon that is obviously a vital presence in the United States, yet is scarcely seen as a problem in American intellectual history. To be sure, we have studies of "modernist" endeavors on the part of some Americans in the arts and in literature, but these studies tend to be designed, executed, and read with reference only to the history of particular arts, and of modernism as such. By contrast, the problem of modernism is prominent on the agendas of students of the intellectual history of other Western nations.

The intellectual reality of America's involvement in Western thought has been obscured by a professional convention that contrasts the field of American intellectual history to the intellectual history of Europe, rather than to that of Great Britain, of France, or of Germany. This convention magnifies, universalizes, and renders more remote from America the intellectual history of the West that America actually shares with the various national cultures of Europe, whose students seem consistently able to maintain a more comfortable relationship with that larger history. Improvement will not come through patriotic and extravagant claims for America's impact on the intellectual history of the West; what is needed is simply a more widespread recognition that Americans sometimes *make and are made by* that history. An agenda designed to advance this recognition is not so easy to represent with any scholar's name, for none whose work can be seen in its terms have the stature of Tocqueville. In the absence of an exemplary student, we might well think of this second agenda as "Jamesian" in honor of both Henry and William James, two of this agenda's most exemplary *subjects.*

As the adjective "Jamesian" implies, aspects of American intellectual life relevant to this second agenda have not been altogether ignored. Yet most of the attention, as invocation of the James brothers might also suggest, has gone to American thinkers who won a large popular following within America while helping to make the intellectual history of the West. This is as it should be, but the second agenda can also encourage attention to thinkers and groups of thinkers less popular than the James brothers, less striking in their mark on modern history, and less decisively American in nationality. One might consider three movements of the middle decades of the twentieth century: logical positivism, the new criticism, and structural-functionalism. Each of these belongs to the history of a specialized discipline, but this fact need not result in their removal altogether from American history; each of them flourished, after all, more extensively in the United States than anywhere else. Any portrait of the intellectual life of educated Americans in, say, the year 1950, would be quite inadequate without attention to these three movements, just as studies of any of the three would be curiously restricted in scope if they ignored the national culture which turned out to be its most sustaining habitat.

Neither the Jamesian nor the Tocquevillian agenda, nor both together could bring the entirety of American intellectual life at any given historical moment into their scope, and one can trust that the diversity of the field of American intellectual history can survive any and all efforts at agenda-making. The point of this particular exercise is simply to call attention to important tasks that are not likely to be carried out at all unless done in the name of American intellectual history, and that could easily be pushed to the margins of the commons because of uncertainties attending now on the notion of "America."

If these uncertainties constitute one set of issues deserving our attention, a second set of such issues revolves around the notion of "language." "My language is the sum total of myself," observed one of the American thinkers most influential in the entire learned world of the West, Charles S. Peirce, in 1868. This aphorism has recently become a favorite epigraph for scholars in many disciplines seeking to come to grips with a transformation in philosophy of language described by Ian Hacking as "the switch from the primacy of private thought to that of public discourse." In the "Cartesian epoch," explains Hacking, "language had been a wonderful system of signs for conveying thoughts from one mind to another, but language was always secondary to ideas in the mind." Finally, in modern times, there "came at last the strange reversal; language became a necessarily public institution within which human selves are formed and by which people constitute the world they live in."[16] Historians have often taken for granted that "ideas" and "meanings" are the common coin of discourse carried out in the public realm of language.[17] Yet the term "ideas" has long-standing connotations of interiority; ideas are felt to be things "inside people's heads." The term "ideas" is not likely to fall out of use, but the term "language" is proving increasingly useful. Not only does it indicate more accurately the strata of human experience and striving in which the study of intellectual history is generally carried out; it promotes greater rigor in the design and execution of scholarly projects. When historians refer to the conviction that frameworks of meaning serve to enable and restrict social action, they increasingly do so in linguistic terms.

The current popularization of the insight that human society is ultimately constituted by language thus presents professional as well as intellectual opportunities. Why not translate as much political and social history as possible into the terms of language (and hence "intellectual history"), thereby transforming the commons into the seat of an empire of language extending as far as possible throughout the profession? Sensitivity to the imperial possibilities presented by twentieth-century views of language has been shown more by Europeanists than by Americanists. Although Michel Foucault prefers to call himself an "archaeologist" rather than "intellectual historian," many historians have had no trouble finding themselves in his program, nor noticing that program's omniverous absorption of the human past into a language-centered study. A recent manifesto by another Europeanist is worth quoting because it catches the intellectual opportunities presented by a more linguistically conscious history, and thereby clarifies the foundations for the potential imperial role of such history. Did the "masses" make the French Revolution, asks Keith Michael Baker?

> On the contrary, the power of their actions depended upon a set of symbolic representations and cultural meanings that constituted the significance of their behavior and gave it explosive force. [The masses] cannot be invoked as a political *deus ex machina* without considering further the structure of discourse defining the political arena in which they intervened.

Baker goes on to speculate about the possibility of "a multiplicity of overlapping and competing languages from which princes and parlementaries, reforming ministers and grain rioters, philosophes and jansenists, scientists and quacks (and many others) could each draw a voice," and to suggest that "the search for the ideological origins of the French Revolution will require us to understand how, within this multiplicity of discourses, a new political language was generated that cast many different kinds of behavior into a new symbolic order."[18]

Baker thus distances himself from the history-is-made-by-sweaty-armpits school, but his alternative need not become a new reductionism, according to which the gutsy masses are translated without remainder into the genteel terms of what Foucault would call a "discursive practice." The point is not to doubt Baker's ability to resist the temptation to linguistic imperialism, but to indicate how real it could become to scholars who grasp the intellectual potential of the study of the history of languages.

Perhaps we shall soon witness a linguistic imperialism comparable to other imperialisms of the recent academic past: the sociological imperialism that once proclaimed "social forces" to be more "real" than ideas, the logical imperialism that once declared meaningless all utterances not subject to the tests for truth and falsity ostensibly employed by physicists, and the quantitative imperialism that once envisioned reservations for aborigines who had not taken up multiple regression analysis. Among the potential volunteers for these new International Brigades, with battalions no doubt named for Saussure and Peirce, are scholars who think of themselves as "intellectual historians." These scholars have vivid memories of raids on the commons made by cadres from these older empires. An exasperated Pocock, for example, speaks for many when he growls about the "practice of referring to the extra-intellectual or extra-linguistic as 'reality,' and to the intellectual or linguistic equipment, at least by implication, as non-reality"; Pocock finds this practice "so rooted and widespread" that only students of ideas and language are faced with "constant reductionist pressure to abolish" their inquiry "and restate its findings in other men's terms." [19] How easy to understand the temptation to turn the tables when the opportunity is now presented by the changing fashions of the learned world! Yet as the captains and kings of the declining empires depart in keeping with the prophecy of Kipling, the would-be soldiers and administrators of the new empire of language would do well to inspect their own motives closely, and to be sure that intellectual promise rather than professional opportunism determines what is done to the commons and surrounding lands that might, conceivably, be annexed.

Whatever the destiny of the new empire of language now gaining ground in departments of philosophy, anthropology, and comparative literature, the study of American intellectual history will best prosper if it remains a commons, resistant in true "Republican" fashion to the ambitions of private developers and imperialists.

1. Morton White, *Social Thought in America: The Revolt Against Formalism*, 3rd ed. (New York: Oxford, 1976; originally published in 1949); Henry F. May, *The End of American Innocence* (New York: Knopf, 1959); Ralph Henry Gabriel, *The Course of American Democratic Thought* (New York: Ronald Press, 1940); Merle Curti, *The Growth of American Thought* (New York: Harper and Row, 1943); Stow Persons, *American Minds* (New York: Holt, Rinehart and Winston, 1958); Perry Miller, ed., *American Thought: Civil War to World War I* (New York: Holt, Rinehart and Winston, 1954).

2. William J. Bouwsma, "Intellectual History in the 1980s: From History of Ideas to History of Meaning," *Journal of Interdisciplinary History* 12 (1981): 280.

3. K. M. Minogue, "Method in Intellectual History: Quentin Skinner's Foundations," *Philosophy* 56 (1981): 542.

4. Bernard Bailyn, "The Challenge of Modern Historiography," *American Historical Review* 87 (1982): 22.

5. Bouwsma, "History of Meaning," pp. 283, 287-88.

6. Two helpful reassessments of Miller and his critics, each correcting many popular misconceptions, have just appeared: James Hoopes, "Art as History: Perry Miller's *New England Mind*," *American Quarterly* 34 (1982): 3-25; Francis T. Butts, "The Myth of Perry Miller," *American Historical Review* 87 (1982): 665-94.

7. Laurence Veysey, "Intellectual History and the New Social History," in *New Directions in American Intellectual History*, eds. John Higham and Paul K. Conkin (Baltimore: Johns Hopkins University Press, 1979), p. 9.

8. Gordon Wood, "Intellectual History and the Social Sciences," in Higham and Conkin, *New Directions*, pp. 32-33.

9. J. G. A. Pocock, *Politics, Language, and Time: Essays on Political Thought and History* (New York: Atheneum, 1971), esp. pp. 3–41; Quentin Skinner, "Some Problems in the Analysis of Political Thought and Action," *Political Theory* 2 (1974): 277–303. See also Pocock, "*The Machiavellian Moment* Revisited: A Study in History and Ideology," *Journal of Modern History* 53 (1981): 49–72, esp. pp. 52–53.

10. Veysey, "Intellectual History," esp. pp. 11, 13, 17. See also Veysey, "The New Social History' in the Context of American Historical Writing," *Reviews in American History* 7 (1979): 1–12. Although I disagree with much of what Veysey says in these two essays, they do articulate very effectively the whole range of complaints recently made about intellectual history, especially but not exclusively in the name of social history.

11. Richard Rorty, *Philosophy and the Mirror of Nature* (Princeton: Princeton University Press, 1980), p. 394. This book criticizes the epistemological preoccupations of modern philosophy and entreats the contemporary learned world to view its practices with the historical self-awareness that the study of intellectual history has traditionally sought to provide. For a more extensive discussion of this book, see my "The Voice of Intellectual History in the Conversation of Mankind: A Note on Rorty's *Philosophy and the Mirror of Nature*," *Newsletter of the Intellectual History Group* (Spring 1982): 23–28.

12. The extent to which even the beliefs that constitute scientific knowledge are to be explained with reference to such "external" conditions as the national and class interests of scientists is now a matter of animated controversy among students of the sociology, history, and philosophy of science. I allude to the controversy here because it has attracted very little notice among American historians, yet has generated some fairly rigorous methodological arguments about an enterprise basic to many projects in American intellectual history: the explanation of belief. See, for example, Larry Laudan, *Progress and Its Problems: Toward a Theory of Scientific Growth* (Berkeley: University of California Press, 1977), esp. the chapter on "The History of Ideas," pp. 171–195, and the extended exchange between Laudan and two critics: Barry Barnes, "Vicissitudes of Belief," *Social Studies of Science* 9 (1979): 247–63; Laudan, "The Pseudo-Science of Science," *Philosophy of Social Sciences* 11 (1981): 173–98; David Bloor, "The Strengths of the Strong Programme," *Philosophy of Social Sciences* 11 (1981): 199–213; and Laudan, "More on Bloor," *Philosophy of Social Sciences* 12 (1982): 71–74. Although the participants in this exchange are too stubborn to acknowledge common ground, and delight too much in scoring debater's points against one another, the exchange brings out the relevant methodological issues with a sharpness rarely found in the considerable body of literature devoted to the aims and methods of intellectual history generally.

13. See, for example, the very sensible essay by Norman S. Fiering, "Early American Philosophy vs. Philosophy in Early America," *Transactions of the Charles S. Peirce Society* 13 (1977): 216–37.

14. Two such episodes have been studied with admirable sensitivity by Henry F. May, *The Enlightenment in America* (New York: Oxford University Press, 1976), and Fred H. Matthews, *Quest for an American Sociology: Robert E. Park and the Chicago School* (Montreal: Queens and McGill Universities Press, 1977).

15. Sacvan Bercovitch, *The Puritan Origins of the American Self* (New Haven, Conn.: Yale University Press, 1975).

16. Ian Hacking, "Wittgenstein the Psychologist," *New York Review of Books* (April 1, 1982), p. 42.

17. This presumption and the prospects for its critical renewal are discussed in my "Historians and the Discourse of Intellectuals," in Higham and Conkin, *New Directions*, pp. 42–63.

18. Keith Michael Baker, "Enlightenment and Revolution in France: Old Problems, Renewed Approaches," *Journal of Modern History* 53 (1981): 303. See also Wood, "Social Sciences," p. 32.

19. Pocock, *Politics, Language, and Time*, p. 38.

DRIFT OR MASTERY? A CORPORATIST SYNTHESIS FOR AMERICAN DIPLOMATIC HISTORY

Thomas J. McCormick

The state of modern American diplomatic history somehow mirrors its subject matter: Camelot to crisis to conundrum—and then the ennui of the new "brown decade." What once imparted vitality and verve, excitement and expectancy to the field was the dynamic impact of left-revisionism. Its great virtue was to rescue historians from the sterile political science debate over realism versus idealism. The result was a new debate that was more honest and fervent, and conceptually more challenging and sophisticated. Revisionism, for friends and opponents alike, became the great intellectual multiplier. William Appleman Williams alone, in an incredible *tour de force,* not only stimulated and/or outraged, but probably made more careers than any historian since Charles A. Beard. Attacking or footnoting his basic thesis became a leading cottage industry.

That salubrious spread effect began to slow even before Jimmy Carter proclaimed our national malaise. The writing (or at least the publication) of revisionist-oriented diplomatic history fell from 25–30 percent of the whole in the early 1970s to 10–15 percent in the early 1980s.[1] Neoconservatives launched sharp and sometimes vituperative attacks that questioned not only the interpretations but the professionalism of some revisionists.[2] And a loose grouping, dubbed "post-revisionists," bounded into the breech to bridge the historiographical gap. Writing mainly on the early Cold War, they rejected revisionism as a package while still incorporating some of its parts: for example, the role of domestic economic variables or the nature and extent of the Soviet threat.[3]

Viewed superficially, it appears to be a vigorous, constructive dialectic. But the postrevisionist bridge is not a synthesis; it is a rope-bridge that will not support heavy intellectual traffic between revisionists and traditionalists. While interesting, postrevisionists remind one of what C. Wright Mills called "The NATO intellectuals," in whose work "arguments of a displeasing kind . . . are duly recognized, but they are neither connected with any other or related in a general way. Acknowledged in a scattered way, they are never put together. To do so is to risk being called, curiously enough, one-sided." Similarly, while postrevisionists may duly note materialist factors, they then

0048-7511/82/0104-0318 $01.00

hide them away in an undifferentiated and unconnected shopping list of variables. The operative premise is that multiplicity, rather than articulation, is equivalent to sophistication. Systematicism is not their strong suit.

It is that lack of systematic analysis which is the rub for the whole field. It is at the root of why our historiographical arguments have become tiresome and circular, why they produce neither a clear hegemonic winner nor any truly integrative synthesis. Revisionism, on the whole, has done a better job of footnoting *The Tragedy of American Diplomacy* than of refining and systematizing its conceptual framework. Traditionalism is less a system of analysis than a way of doing without one.[4] And postrevisionism largely does patch-jobs on traditionalist retreads. All three groups operate from different premises, seldom make them explicit, and even more rarely subject them to rigorous verification. They talk past each other rather than to each other. They share no intellectual framework where differences might be reduced to particulars for empirical investigation or value judgments for individual expression. If this is so, why is it so? Are there positive signs that hold hope for systematizing and elevating the inquiry of diplomatic historians, for creating a true rather than a pseudo-synthesis?

Aside from ideological differences (which will always be with us), the continuing and pervasive bias against social history (in a transnational context) seems the connecting point for the field's shortcomings.[5] Diplomatic historians seem unwilling, unable, or simply uncomfortable with placing or locating their subjects within the context of social structures (here and abroad), in identifying the sources of initiative (power) and the patterns of resistance and accommodation to those initiatives. In short, they seem ill-disposed to analyze the dynamic interactions of large aggregate groups and to discern patterns of behavior over relatively long periods of time. Instead, there is a continued bias toward intellectual history (beset with its own critical problems).[6] The result is a general preoccupation with isolated, discrete individuals or crisis-events, and a concomitant effort to use them as prisms for understanding larger changes. That bias is partly understandable. The nature of the sources employed and the decision-making process studied lends itself to "what one clerk said to another" history—and in some circumstances, crises do illuminate trends that might otherwise go unnoticed. But the penalties for overdoing that kind of history are nearly fatal for any effort to sophisticate the field.

Aside from the obvious problem of whether an individual or a group is representative, there is the far greater question: representative of what? There ought to be a methodological and conceptual imperative to place one's subject in this or that typology of similar individuals. But a bias favoring discrete individuals automatically narrows the number of gradations on the continuum. How many typologies can one create in that manner? Presumably no more than one to a customer; hence part of the reason for the field's predilection for dichotomies and pair-opposites of isolationists and internationalists, idealists and realists, Riga Axiom and Yalta Axiom proponents, or imperialists and antiimperialists. This Manichean simplification masks numerous clusters of groups along an ideal-type continuum.

A similar substitution of normative judgments for systematic analysis inheres in the field's continuing fixation with crisis-events: wars, peace treaties, conferences, confrontations, and sacrosanct doctrines. Overwhelmingly, the event is studied intensively but its placement in some larger context over time is often self-serving (exaggerating the event's importance) and arbitrary (intuited from the historian's *a priori* assumptions). Rare is the study that compares two or more points in the time continuum, or that encompasses both crisis and noncrisis situations over reasonably long periods of time.

Corollary to this crisis orientation is a Great Power fixation—a preoccupation with the major actors and grand alliances that fight hot- and cold-running wars. Simply, we overstudy core nations to the sharp neglect of periphery and semiperiphery regions: for example, Africa, India, the "ABC" nations, and Asian client-states like Korea, Taiwan, and Indonesia. Hence much of the Cold War literature is marred by a bipolar myopia about Soviet-American confrontation, and much of the work on European reconstruction is theoretically and empirically weak on the Third World role in that reconstruction. Indeed, perhaps most glaring is the indefensible neglect of the impact of the United States on hinterland regions. Peruse the field's leading textbooks and look hard for such word keys as modernization, dependency, diffusionism, development, or comparative advantage. Look and ye shall not find.[7] The reason inheres in the crisis-event bias. An event is a relatively fixed or short point in time. Impact—economic development or cultural change—is a slower, often uneven process over time. The former rarely sheds light on the latter.

Corollary also is a related overemphasis on the role of the State. The State, after all, does play peculiarly important functions in a crisis. If one's focus is the crisis-event, one's focus is also the State. But broaden the depth of field over time and one begins to appreciate the evermore important roles of nongovernmental actors: corporations, labor unions, missionaries, foundations, universities, professional associations, and the electronic media. Save for an interesting literature on peace groups, most such entities are sadly neglected. Moreover, even when they receive some attention, they tend to be "headquarters" histories that tell us more about America than its impact on others (a reflection perhaps of our provincial and nationalist bias). Even what we learn about ourselves is usually inadequate. Save for the excellent works on the 1920s (Hogan, Leffler, Parrini, Wilson), few offer a systematic conceptualization of how these private sector agents relate to State policy.[8]

But innovative things are happening. Some seem deadends, but others hold varying degrees of promise to bridge the ideological divide and to make the history of American foreign relations more systematic. Chiefly, they involve the refurbishing of the domestic political thesis, the introduction of bureaucratic studies, and some tentative forays into the realm of culture and ideology.

Writings on the domestic political thesis have been the most numerous.[9] This outpouring reflects an interesting reversal of early post-World War II historiography that stressed the primacy of externalized devils (Spain, Germany, the USSR). But this new emphasis (reminiscent of Thomas Bailey) on public opinion, electoral politics, and single-interest functional groups appears to hold little promise for systematizing the field. Almost all such studies rest on an implicit and highly debatable model of American pluralism—though rarely is the model explicated or alternative explanations acknowledged. They take little note of the literature on the decay and decline of twentieth-century pluralism or of supporting indicators to that effect: the decline in both voter participation and in party distinctions, the elitist nature of opinion that influences and the malleable nature of opinion that does not, or the increasing tendencies for hard decisions on foreign policy matters to be made outside parliamentary channels by the administrative apparatus and associated corporatists in business and labor. Instead, they embrace the American Dream—the view that decision-making is the end product of numerous private, voluntary, democratic groups competing with each other in a relatively coequal way in an open society. Perhaps true (certainly it is partially true—even a pluralistic residue is not insignificant). But if so, it must be demonstrated, not simply assumed and affirmed. The mystification of self-evident truths cannot substitute for systematic exploration.

Bureaucratic studies hold more promise, since they focus on a demonstrably important facet of modern, industrial life.[10] Moreover, while they also implicitly accept a pluralist model, they modify it by positing that their groups (State bureaucracies) are more equal (powerful) than other competing groups in the private sector. But once again, these scholarly versions of The Best and the Brightest assert their assumptions rather than demonstrate them. With rare exception (e.g., Werking), they do not attempt to place their bureaucratic subjects systematically within the larger framework of overall social structure or to substantiate who has initiative and who merely reacts. Indeed, with the exception of those few clearly influenced by C. Wright Mills, they hardly bother with a sociological, collective biography profile of their bureaucrats.[11] That, of course, relieves them of the responsibility of examining explanatory alternatives such as ruling class models that would define their subjects as the servants of power rather than its primary wielders. Moreover, even their internal treatment of State bureaucracies—with its stress on anarchy of territorial imperatives (a Hobbesian "war of all against all")—often tells us little of the character of internal stratification, the extent of centralization, the directional flow of information, or the sources of initiative. For example, it seems crucial to the plausibility of their State Elite model to demonstrate that primary initiatives come from professional careerists whose views are socialized by a lifetime of climbing a Jacob's ladder of G-rungs; not by "ins-and-outers" who shuttle back and forth between high positions in the State and parallel positions in the private corporate structure. How else can historians begin to get at the issue of whether one's social class or one's bureaucratic function determines one's behavior? In short, bureaucratic studies are intriguing, but their practitioners must become more systematic social historians if they are to be persuasive.

If the political thesis proponents stress one facet of process and bureaucratic studies emphasize one part of structure, the preliminary ventures into examinations of culture and ideology purport to be more holistic. Indeed, these enterprises are, in part, self-conscious efforts to bridge and integrate power and culture, business and ideology. Both Akira Iriye and Joan Hoff Wilson have performed a useful function as path-breaking scholars in calling attention to interrelationships often glossed over by others, and in implicitly posing the question of how and why cultural images and ideology change over time. Each has offered useful working definitions as a point of departure. Iriye has defined culture as the total network of "control mechanisms . . . governing the behavior" of society—subdividing that network into two components roughly analogous to Gramsci's concepts of civil and political society.[12] Wilson has implicitly defined ideology as the glue that ties together cultural images into a reasonably coherent system.[13]

At this juncture, however, they have approached their subjects at such an aggregate level of abstraction that they seem too vague, almost ahistorical, to have much analytical utility. Iriye, especially, comes perilously close to resurrecting the archaic notion of national character. This occasionally obtuse analysis again flows from insufficient social differentiation. Not all groups or classes in society necessarily share exactly the same cultural images and ideology, and with the same intensity. Even to the degree that they are sometimes homogenously shared as part of the process of national integration, that sharing may well be the result of some groups manipulating symbols and ideas to sustain their moral dominance and their legitimacy to rule—Gramsci's concept of ideological hegemony. Values and ideas—like knowledge—are not necessarily neutral. The capacity to wield them, and have others accept them, is an expression of power. So we are back once more to the strictures of social history: the necessity to identify the sources of power and initiative, the patterns of resistance, acceptance, or accommodation, and the dialectical feedback of those responses on the initiators.

What I have said thus far may seem cantankerous. I hope otherwise. Stripped to its essentials, all I suggest is that the field of diplomatic history suffers from two problems—a historiographical schism and a lack of analytical sophistication—and that there is only one solution applying to both. Whatever we do (and there are many mansions in this field), we must do systematically and we must be explicit about our systems. As Robert Wiebe wrote to me: "Welcome all comers . . . as long as they reckon with certain hard problems that lie at the core of any effective system for historical analysis. Who exercises power—how? why? Don't ask us to wade through a thousand pages on public opinion or pressure groups or diplomatic exchanges with Japan without framing the issues so that we see precisely where the objects of attention fit into a scheme of social analysis. Then we can respond fruitfully, meeting a system with a set of assumptions in a sensible exchange." [14] In that spirit, let me suggest that I perceive an emerging *corporatist* synthesis that offers a postpluralism mode of systematizing modern American society which is plausible and potentially of great value to scholars of American foreign relations.

Corporatism has not been a very popular concept since World War II, largely because of its pejorative association with fascism. But State corporatism represented only one variant, largely characteristic of prepluralist, authoritarian societies, where the State took the chief initiative, and where the resulting corporatist arrangements tended to be highly institutionalized and rigid. There is an increasing awareness that other variants of corporatism often evolve in pluralistic, democratic societies, and the resulting structures and arrangements do not wholly destroy pluralist ones; they simply subsume and coexist with them in varying degrees of tension and cooperation. In other words, there develops a mix of interest-group representation. Pluralism continues in the form of electoral politics and single-interest lobbying. But certain forms of power and initiative, especially national economic policy and foreign policy, are increasingly monopolized by large "syndicates" that represent very broad, societal functions rather than narrow, singular ones; for example, business (especially oligopoly capital), labor (especially organized unions), and farm (agrobusiness).

Such syndicates are very different from interest groups in a purely pluralist society. They are (in theory) interdependent and collaborating rather than autonomous and competing; endowed with de jure or de facto public authority rather than purely private; hierarchical and elitist rather than egalitarian; tied to the State, rather than separate from it, by an amalgam of informal-to-formal mechanisms and linkages; and cooperating, with each other and the State, to manage society's major affairs through self-regulation or public-private power-sharing.[15] In the historically specific case of the United States, Ellis Hawley and Michael Hogan use the term "associationalism" (a subtype of societal corporatism), which suggests that initiative comes more often from the private than the public sector; that public-private power-sharing arrangements are more informal and less institutionalized than in Europe or Latin America; that the role and power of labor is less developed than elsewhere (a very junior partner); and that pluralist processes and ideology remain more important than in other corporatist societies.[16]

This concept of an Americanized corporatism (a sort of corporate, pro-capitalist reformism) has evolved, rather unevenly, over a twenty-five year span. Moreover, it has been propelled by quite different, even antithetical sources. It began with the lineal descendants of Max Weber and Thorstein Veblen: organizational theorists like Adolph Berle, James Burnham, and Kenneth Boulding. It posited an organizational imperative ("organize or perish") in modern, industrial society that inevitably produced an evolution from organizations that were small-scale, informal and local/regional in scope to those that were large-scale, formal and national. Such organizations were characterized by bureaucracies staffed by technocratic and managerial experts, and were hierarchical in structure with an upward flow of information to a centralized decision-making top composed of a new declasse elite.

In the early 1960s, left-revisionists like William Appleman Williams (and later Kolko, Weinstein, and Radosh) amended and extended early organizational theory into a more full-blown and explicit system of corporatism.[17] Clearly influenced by studies of European and Latin American corporatism, they added two crucial components. First, they went beyond business corporations (the focus of organizational theory), and made a place for labor. Specifically, they described fledgling efforts to substitute class collaboration for class conflict via a corporatist ideology that stressed the community of interests, aims, and ideals between capital and labor: that is, the mutual stake in smoothing out the economic cycle at home and expanding the market for production abroad. Second, they posited an increasingly important role for the State: to arbitrate differences and coordinate the interests of capital and labor; to establish institutions (like the Federal Trade Commission) or create a legislative umbrella (like the Webb-Pomerene Act) that would sanction self-regulation and planning by the private sector; and to legitimize the process of concentration and rationalization and thus protect it against a hostile public opinion still steeped in nineteenth-century antimonopoly sentiment. This public-private power-sharing tended to be loose, informal, and ad hoc during peace and prosperity; more formal and institutionalized during war and depression.

Left-revisionist interest in corporatism declined, however, and largely evaporated in the early 1970s. The demise was fratricidal, involving criticism by radical labor historians that the emphasis on class collaboration denigrated workers' resistance to corporatist schemes and ideology, and that it implicitly raised the false notion that creeping corporatism could constitute a road to socialism through the socialization of institutions and decision-making. Non-Marxists (Chandler, Galambos, Wiebe, and Hays for example) were not deterred, however, and took up the cudgels in their wide-ranging discussions of "an emerging organizational synthesis," "the search for order," and the "new social history." [18] In particular, they made more concrete the symbiotic relationship between business and the State. Business needed the State to sanction rationalization, purchase goods and services with tax and borrowed dollars, to subsidize research and development, and invest in human capital (education). The State, in turn, needed business for its expertise, its specialized knowledge, and the legitimacy that adhered to devolving or sharing power with the private sector. Moreover, these authors created new insights into how that State-business symbiosis fit into the overall social structure of modern America. Hays's local-societal continuum, for example, made an implicit class analysis by stressing the procapitalist orientation of his cosmopolitan, system-making elite. So too did his emphasis on the importance of the struggle for the workplace—that is, the use of technology and knowledge (scientific management) and ideological hegemony (Americanization programs) to coerce or seduce workers into a trade-off of increased discipline and diminished autonomy for job security and material benefits.

Finally, and most recently, there has been a revival of left-revisionist interest generated chiefly by European and Latin American scholars who have surmised that the corporatist analysis they have used on their own subject areas may have analogous applicability for the United States. In the process, they have made two major contributions. First, they have argued that residual pluralism can and does remain important even in the midst of emerging corporatism. (Ellis Hawley and other non-Marxists make much the same point.) Specifically, they have noted that pluralist ideology, with its continued distrust of concentration and statism, limits the extent and scope of the State's role; that a democratically elected Congress remains essential to corporatism because of its appropriation powers to subsidize entitlement programs that are crucial to capital-labor collaboration; and that certain types of issues remain sensitive to pluralistic lobbying by environmentalists, consumer-advocates, and other special interest groups.

Second, they have interjected a dynamic quality into the class basis of corporatism by positing that the greater labor's capacity to resist high rates of
exploitation, the more likely business is to opt for class collaborative schemes
in order to deflect resistant labor away from "distributive" strategies that
might lead to a more socialized economy. Moreover, they directly confront
the question of why labor might be willing to accept nondistributive
approaches, or more accurately, "distribution in one class"; namely that they
are concretely rewarded for it. Partly those rewards are business support for
union centralization, industry-wide contracts, closed shops and dues check-
off; partly they are State support for "safety-net" programs, the legal recognition of unions' standing, and a moral commitment to full employment.[19] But
the heart of the reward system for labor collaboration is business and State
promotion of what Charles Maier calls "productionism": instead of
redividing the economic pie, enlarge the absolute whole while keeping the
relative shares the same.[20] And finally, they do speculate about what happens
when and if productionism fails—when the economic pie stagnates or contracts. In short, they treat corporatism as dynamic and class-specific rather
than schematic and abstract.

What all this suggests to me is that the necessary and, perhaps, sufficient
conditions for a corporatist synthesis have been obtained. Its intellectual
components are sophisticated and sufficiently in place to merit, perhaps,
being called a system of analysis. Its ecumenical base of support is quite
impressive: radicals and nonradicals, Americanists and non-Americanists,
historians and nonhistorians, and specialists in such divergent fields as
business, labor, and foreign policy—and on that last-named, Hogan, Leffler,
Maier, Parrini, Sklar, and Wilson have pointed the way to how corporatism
can help make sense out of the nation's foreign relations in this century.

The key to using corporatism in foreign policy studies is the simple proposition that people do not think one way about their national society and a
different way about the world society. Instead, they tend to project and inter-
nationalize conceptual frameworks first articulated at home. I suggest,
therefore, that what we call "Wilsonianism" or "multilateralism" or "interna-
tionalism" is, in fact, a system of globalized corporatism. There are two keys
to that assertion. (1) Both corporatism and Wilsonianism rest on the same
premise of productionism. The common enemy is wasteful competition (be it
between classes or nations) that aims at a distributive reallocation of wealth
and power. The shared alternative for both is the expansion and maximum
utilization of production: enlarge the economic pie rather than redivide it by
force. Just as productionism attempts to adjourn class war at home, so too it
attempts to adjourn national conflict abroad by forging a collaborative con-

sensus on the imperatives of growth. The interdependence of comparative advantage is to replace the dangerous and destabilizing competition of militarism, formal imperialism, and economic autarchy. (2) Both corporatism and Wilsonianism dictate some institutional arbitration and coordination between power-sharing entities. At home, the State apparatus performed that vital function. Abroad, the problem was far more difficult; neither the balance of power arrangements of the old order nor the world leagues of the new were very effectual. Only the emergence of American hegemony within the world-system temporarily solved the problem. The State apparatus of this society took on the dual function of promoting, protecting, and legitimizing productionism both globally and on the home front. While that involved a potential conflict of interests, both Western Europe and Japan felt compelled to trust the United States to balance its own internal interests against the needs of the system as a whole in the quarter-century after World War II.

The above macrolevel generalizations may have their utility as such, but that utility is limited unless they spawn mid-range generalizations that can be empirically tested. I offer the following examples of possible propositions for investigation and exploration. All flow from the basic equation that Wilsonianism = global corporatism.

1. *Given the internationalization of corporatism, one cannot understand American foreign policy in its hegemonic, postwar period outside the context of a world-systems analysis.* How else can one make sense out of American sacrifices of short-run economic advantages to alleviate the dollar gap and restore European and Japanese production, its ironic variation of a cosprosperity sphere that attempted to create a regional basis for the Japanese, thus inadvertently sowing the seeds for the Vietnam War, or the creation of a military umbrella to protect the free world-system in ways ultimately harmful to our domestic economy? These acts are understandable only when treated as hegemonic responsibilities (the burden of power) within a capitalist world-system.

2. *American imperialism is, in part, a social imperialism dictated by the class relationships within corporatism.* Corporatism rests upon a strategy of productionism—expanding production and the absolute economic pie. But since it also rests upon a bias against income redistribution, it can only dispose of its whole product, at acceptable levels of profit, by recourse to marketplace expansionism overseas. It is the antithesis of the zero-sum game: a supply-side interpretation that views imperialism as a major vehicle to finance labor's rewards for class collaboration within corporatism.

3. *Paradoxically, productionism abroad both rewards and alienates American labor, making the class collaboration of corporatism at least partly unstable.* Productionism requires the partial modernization of semiperiphery

areas if aggregate world demand is to absorb the whole product of the world-system. The result has been a shift from traditional, neomercantilist investments in primary commodity production to multinational investment in some forms of manufacturing. In a supply-side, trickle-down way, American labor is supposed to benefit ultimately from the process; and it is called upon to play its part in socializing Third World labor movements to the desirability of anticommunism and procapitalist collaboration. (The American Institute for Free Labor Development is a classic, corporatist example.) But in the short-haul, that process looks suspiciously to American labor like a global version of the "run-away" shop and, hence, tends to undermine class collaboration at home.

4. *The role of the State in domestic affairs tends to be replicated in its foreign policies.* The chief thrust of the "associative state," in America's version of societal corporatism, is to use its semiautonomous power to facilitate self-regulation and self-planning by the private sector. Howley calls it "privatism" in describing both the 1920s and the New Deal. Hogan, in his current work on the Marshall Plan, finds the same pattern repeated in foreign policy: State intervention is minimized and private initiative maximized. The vehicle employed is a patchwork of private and quasi-private groups: the President's Committee on Foreign Aid, the Committee for the Marshall Plan, the Public Advisory Board, Council on Foreign Relations study groups, or even ECA itself.[21]

5. *Elite leaders of corporatist syndicates are also the prime makers of American foreign policy.* Corporatism is essentially a collaborative arrangement between two senior partners, the State and oligopoly capital, and two junior partners, organized labor and the farm bloc. Each hierarchical syndicate produces its own elite: the National Security managers, multinational corporation heads, the executive committee of the AFL-CIO, the leaders of the American Farm Bureau. They often feel more in common with each other than they do with respective constituents. They are, at once, Hays's "cosmopolitans," Williams's "corporatists," Weinstein's "corporate liberals," and Mills's "power elite." But they are also Barnet's "national security managers," Minter and Shoup's "Imperial Brain Trust," and Domhoff's corporate rich "Who [make] American foreign policy." They both rationalize the system at home and expand the world-system abroad.

The foregoing are simply some suggested possibilities. There are, of course, others: for example, (a) the role of ideological hegemony and consensus-building—essential to a collaborative system—in persuading the CIO to purge its left-wing, abandon distributive policies, embrace productionism, and join the mainstream of bipartisan support for American foreign policy; (b) the nature and precise mechanisms of the linkages between American corporatist leaders and their overseas counterparts—be they trilateral partners in the core or compradores in the periphery; (c) the relationship between the economic cycle and America's modern wars: that is, what happens when productionism fails and the pie ceases to grow? I trust my point is sufficiently made.

Historical fields can change dramatically and rapidly. A decade and a half ago, American labor history was a boring wasteland. Today it is one of the most exciting areas of historical inquiry. Similarly, the study of American foreign relations need not remain mired in circular debates or in narrow empiricism. I think the emerging corporatist synthesis offers an ecumenical and sophisticated way out of our drift. But it is only one possible system of analysis, and time, in its own sweet way, will determine its level of acceptability. Even those who find corporatist synthesis inadequate are challenged to pose alternatives and make clear their line of reasoning. To re-quote Wiebe: "Welcome all comers just so long as they are systematic and explicit about their systems."

1. These percentage estimates were based on a survey of all books that dealt with American foreign relations historically and were reviewed between 1970 and 1980 in the *Journal of American History*, *Reviews in American History*, and the *American Historical Review*.

2. See, for example, Robert J. Maddox, *The New Left and the Origins of the Cold War* (Princeton, N.J.: Princeton University Press, 1974).

3. The best right-center variation of postrevisionism is probably John Gaddis, *The United States and the Origins of the Cold War, 1941–1947* (New York: Columbia University Press, 1972). Perhaps the best left-center one is Daniel Yergin, *The Shattered Peace* (Boston: Houghton Mifflin, 1977).

4. In the broad sense, I equate traditionalism with a mainstream liberal or pluralist interpretation. The so-called "realist" and "idealist" schools are merely subtypes of traditionalism. They differ in normative judgments rather than in interpretation.

5. Similar points were made in Thomas J. McCormick, "The State of American Diplomatic History," in *The State of American History*, ed. Herbert Bass (Chicago: Quadrangle, 1970). See also Charles Maier, "Marking Time: The Historiography of International Relations," in *The Past Before Us: Contemporary Historical Writing in the United States*, ed. Michael Kammen (Ithaca, N.Y.: Cornell University Press, 1980).

6. See Laurence Veysey, "The 'New' Social History in the Context of American Historical Writing," *Reviews in American History* 7, 1 (March 1979): 1–12.

7. Explored were the most recent editions of American diplomatic history textbooks by Thomas A. Bailey, Samuel F. Bemis, Wayne S. Cole, Alexander DeConde, Robert Ferrell, Lloyd Gardner (with LaFeber and McCormick), Thomas Patterson, and Julius Pratt.

8. Michael Hogan, *Informal Entente: The Private Structure of Cooperation in Anglo-American Economic Diplomacy* (Columbia: University of Missouri Press, 1977); Melvyn Leffler, *The Elusive Quest: America's Pursuit of European Stability and French Security* (Chapel Hill: University of North Carolina Press, 1978); Carl Parrini, *Heir to Empire* (Pittsburgh: University of Pittsburgh Press, 1969); Joan Hoff Wilson, *Ideology and Economics: U.S. Relations with the Soviet Union* (Columbia: University of Missouri Press, 1974).

9. See, for example, Robert Divine, *Since 1945: Politics and Diplomacy in Recent American History* (New York: New Viewpoints, 1976); Michael Leigh, *Mobilizing Consent: Public Opinion and American Foreign Policy* (Westport, Conn.: Greenwood Press, 1976); Ralph Levering, *American Opinion and the Russian Alliance* (Chapel Hill: University of North Carolina Press,

1976); Ernest May, *The Making of the Monroe Doctrine* (Cambridge, Mass.: Belknap Press, 1979); Lewis Purifoy, *Harry Truman's China Policy* (New York: New Viewpoints, 1976); Melvin Small, ed., *Public Opinion and Historians* (Detroit: Wayne State University Press, 1970).

10. See, for example, Graham Allison, *Essence of Decision: Exploring the Cuban Missile Crisis* (Boston: Little, Brown, 1971); I. M. Destler, *Presidents, Bureaucrats and Foreign Policy: Politics of Organizational Reform* (Princeton, N.J.: Princeton University Press, 1972); Iving Janis, *Victims of Groupthink: A Psychological Study of Foreign-policy Decisions and Fiascoes* (Boston: Houghton Mifflin, 1972); Howard Trivers, *Three Crises in American Foreign Affairs and a Continuing Revolution* (Carbondale: Southern Illinois University Press, 1972); Richard Werking, *The Master Architects: Building the United States Foreign Service, 1890-1913* (Lexington: University of Kentucky Press, 1977).

11. Richard Barnet's work is perhaps the best current example of Mills's ameliorating influence.

12. See especially Akira Iriye, "Culture and Power: International Relations as Intercultural Relations," *Diplomatic History* 3, 2 (1979): 115-28. His recent book, *Power and Culture: The Japanese-American War, 1941-1945* (Cambridge, Mass.: Harvard University Press, 1981) attempts to implement his ideas.

13. See the conclusion to Joan Hoff Wilson, *Ideology and Economics*.

14. Robert Wiebe to Thomas McCormick, personal correspondence, August 2, 1982.

15. Phillippe Schmitter, "Still the Century of Corporatism?" in *The New Corporatism*, ed. Frederick Pike (South Bend, Ind.: University of Notre Dame Press, 1974). Schmitter's piece is perhaps the best introductory essay to the concept of corporatism and includes an excellent bibliography.

16. Ellis Hawley, "The Discovery and Study of a 'Corporate Liberalism'," *Business History Review* 52, 3 (Fall 1978): 309-20; Michael Hogan, *Informal Entente*.

17. William A. Williams, *The Contours of American History* (Cleveland: World, 1961). See also Ronald Radosh, *American Labor and United States Foreign Policy* (New York: Random House, 1969); James Weinstein, *The Corporate Ideal in the Liberal State* (Boston: Beacon Press, 1968); Gabriel Kolko, *The Triumph of Conservatism* (New York: Free Press, 1964).

18. Alfred Chandler and Louis Galambos, "The Development of Large-Scale Economic Organizations in Modern America," *Journal of Economic History* 30, 1 (March 1970): 201-17; Robert Wiebe, *The Search for Order* (New York: Hill and Wang, 1967); Samuel Hays, *American Political History as Social Analysis* (Knoxville: University of Tennessee Press, 1980).

19. Perhaps the best discussion on labor and corporatism is Leo Panitch, "Trade Unions and the Capitalist State," *New Left Review* 125 (January 1980): 21-41.

20. Charles Maier, "Between Taylorism and Technocracy," *Journal of Contemporary History* 5, 2 (1970): 27-61; Maier, "The Politics of Productivity," *International Organization*, 31, 4 (1977): 607-33.

21. Professor Hogan has been good enough to share the first three chapters of his work-in-progress on the Marshall Plan origins.

NOTES ON CONTRIBUTORS

Numan V. Bartley, Department of History, University of Georgia, is the author of *The Creation of Modern Georgia* (University of Georgia Press, forthcoming).

Howard P. Chudacoff, Department of History, Brown University, is writing a series of essays on age and age consciousness in America, 1870–1930.

Eric Foner, Department of History, Columbia University, is the author of *Nothing But Freedom: The Aftermath of Emancipation* (Louisiana State University Press, forthcoming).

Estelle B. Freedman, Department of History, Stanford University, is the author of *Their Sisters' Keepers: Women's Prison Reform in America, 1830–1930* (1981).

David A. Hollinger, Department of History, University of Michigan, is the author of "William James and the Culture of Inquiry," *Michigan Quarterly Review* (1981).

Reginald Horsman, Department of History, University of Wisconsin-Milwaukee, is the author of *Race and Manifest Destiny: The Origins of American Racial Anglo-Saxonism* (1981).

Daniel Walker Howe, Department of History, University of California at Los Angeles, is the author of *The Political Culture of the American Whigs* (1980).

James Willard Hurst, Vilas Professor of Law, Emeritus, University of Wisconsin-Madison, is the author of *Law and Markets in United States History* (1982).

Michael Kammen, Department of History, Cornell University, is the editor of *The Past Before Us: Contemporary Historical Writing in the United States* (1980).

Stanley N. Katz, Department of History, Princeton University, is currently preparing a study of the impact of philanthropy on American social policy.

Peter Kolchin, Department of History, University of New Mexico, is the author of "In Defense of Servitude; American Proslavery and Russian Proserfdom Arguments, 1760–1860," *American Historical Review* (1980).

Stanley I. Kutler, Department of History, University of Wisconsin-Madison, is the author of *The American Inquisition: Justice and Injustice in the Cold War* (1982).

Elaine Tyler May, Department of American Studies, University of Minnesota, is the author of *Great Expectations: Marriage and Divorce in Post-Victorian America* (1980), and is currently researching the post-World War II American family.

Thomas J. McCormick, Department of History, University of Wisconsin-Madison, did much of the research for his anniversary contribution during an eight month stay as a Wilson Fellow at the Woodrow Wilson Center.

Ronald L. Numbers, Department of the History of Medicine, University of Wisconsin-Madison, is the editor of *Compulsory Health Insurance: The Continuing American Debate* (1982).

Nathan Reingold, Smithsonian Institution, is the editor of *Joseph Henry Papers.*

Daniel T. Rodgers, Department of History, Princeton University, is currently engaged in a study of political ideas in nineteenth-century Britain and America.

Mary P. Ryan, Department of History, University of California-Irvine, is the author of *Cradle of the Middle Class: The Family in Oneida County, New York, 1790–1865* (1981).

Jon C. Teaford, Department of History, Purdue University, is the author of *City and Suburb: The Political Fragmentation of Metropolitan America, 1850–1970* (1979).

Laurence Veysey, Board of Studies in History, University of California, Santa Cruz, is the author of "A Post-mortem on Daniel Bell's Post-industrialism," *American Quarterly* (1982).

Sean Wilentz, Department of History, Princeton University, is the author of the forthcoming *Chants Democratic: New York City and the Rise of the American Working Class, 1790–1850.*

Gavin Wright, Department of Economics, Stanford University, is the author of *The Political Economy of the Cotton South* (1978).

VOLUME 10

REVIEWS IN AMERICAN HISTORY

1982

Editor: *Stanley I. Kutler*, University of Wisconsin
Associate Editor: *Stanley N. Katz*, Princeton University
Assistant Editor: *Judith Kirkwood*

The Johns Hopkins University Press
Baltimore, Maryland 21218

Volume 10 • 1982

Library of Congress Catalog Number 72-13938
ISSN: 0048-7511

Grateful acknowledgment is made for assistance from the
Department of History of the University of Wisconsin-Madison.

REVIEWS IN AMERICAN HISTORY, its editors, editorial board and publisher disclaim responsibility and liability for statements, either of fact or of opinion, made by contributors.

Please direct all subscription inquiries and business communications to the publisher:

Journals Department
THE JOHNS HOPKINS UNIVERSITY PRESS
Whitehead Hall, 34th & Charles Sts.
Baltimore, Maryland 21218

Frequency of publication: quarterly—March, June, September, December.
Subscription price: Individuals—$16 per year
                       Institutions—$35 per year
                       Students—$14 per year
Address all *editorial* correspondence to:

Stanley I. Kutler, Editor
REVIEWS IN AMERICAN HISTORY
Department of History, University of Wisconsin
435 North Park Street, Madison, Wisconsin 53706

Second-class postage paid at Baltimore, Maryland and at additional mailing offices.

Printed at Everybodys Press, Hanover, Pa., U.S.A.

Postmaster please send address changes to: The Johns Hopkins University Press, Journals Division, Baltimore, Maryland 21218.

AUTHOR-TITLE-REVIEWER INDEX FOR
VOLUME 10 (1982)

No. 1 (March): 1–148
No. 2 (June): 149–296
No. 3 (September): 297–468
*No. 4 (December): 1–333

Abrams, Richard M., 454
Alexander, Charles C., 218
American City, The: From the Civil War to the New Deal, 205
American Foreign Relations: A Historiographical Review, 320
American Law of Slavery, 1810–1860, The: Considerations of Humanity and Interest, 358
American Medicine in Transition, 1840–1910, 94
America's Struggle Against Poverty, 1900–1980, 265
Anderson, Eric, 194
Anderson, Irvine H., 259
Anderson, Karen, 419
Aramco, the United States, and Saudi Arabia: A Study of the Dynamics of Foreign Oil Policy, 1933–1950, 259
Argersinger, Peter H., 391
As Equals and As Sisters: Feminism, the Labor Movement, and the Women's Trade Union League of New York, 109
At Home in America: Second Generation New York Jews, 346
Auschwitz and the Allies, 438
Axtell, James, 331

Bad Blood: The Tuskegee Syphilis Experiment, 229

Bartley, Numan V., 150*
Baseball: America's Diamond Mind, 1919–1941, 141
Bateman, Fred, 177
Bayley, Edwin R., 250
Beeman, Richard R., 163
Bender, Thomas, 255, 325
Beyond Suffrage: Women in the New Deal, 419
Billington, Ray Allen, 149
Bonomi, Patricia U., 335
Boyer, Paul, 448
Breen, T. H., 33
Brinkley, Alan, 265
Brodie, Fawn M., 269
Brody, David, 7
Brumberg, Joan Jacobs, 275
Buhle, Mari Jo, 384

Campbell, Ballard C., 78
Carter, Dan T., 408
Chudacoff, Howard P., 101*
City Trenches: Urban Politics and the Patterning of Class America, 325
Ciucci, Giorgio, 205
Clawson, Robert W., 454
Cochran, Thomas C., 177
Communism, Anticommunism, and the CIO, 245
Coogan, John W., 380
Coughtry, Jay, 168
Countryman, Edward, 335
Courts of Appeals in the Federal Judicial System: A Study of the Second, Fifth and District of Columbia Circuits, 123

Cradle of the Middle Class: The Family in Oneida County, New York, 1790-1865, 49

Creating the Entangling Alliance: The Origins of the North Atlantic Treaty Organization, 454

Crepeau, Richard C., 141

Dal Co, Francesco, 205
Dawidowicz, Lucy S., 438
Dawson, Nelson L., 234
DDT: Scientists, Citizens, and Public Policy, 129
De Pillis, Mario S., 65
Devine, Michael J., 99
Doenecke, Justus D., 72
Dunlap, Thomas R., 129
Dye, Nancy Schrom, 109

Edward Douglass White: Defender of the Conservative Faith, 105
Empire Can Wait: American Opposition to Hawaiian Annexation, 1893-1898, 374
End of Neutrality, The: The United States, Britain, and Maritime Rights, 1899-1915, 374
English America and the Restoration Monarchy of Charles II: Transatlantic Politics, Commerce, and Kinship, 24
Enigma of Felix Frankfurter, The, 241
Ettling, John, 229
European and the Indian, The: Essays in the Ethnohistory of Colonial North America, 331
Faithful Magistrates and Republican Lawyers: Creators of Virginia's Legal Culture, 1680-1810, 163
Faust, Drew Gilpin, 54
Fellman, Anita Clair, 369
Fellman, David, 120
Fellman, Michael, 369

Fiering, Norman, 28
Finkelman, Paul, 185, 358
Foner, Eric, 82*
Fredrickson, George M., 1
Freedman, Estelle B., 89, 196*
Friedman, Lawrence M., 402
Friendly, Fred W., 120
From Crisis to Crisis: American College Government, 1636-1819, 341
From Realignment to Reform: Political Change in New York State, 1893-1910, 391
Frontiers of Change: Early Industrialism in America, 177

Gelfand, Lawrence E., 99
Germ of Laziness, The: Rockefeller Philanthropy and Public Health in the New South, 229
George Washington Carver: Scientist and Symbol, 408
Gilbert, Martin, 438
Glad, Betty, 241
Goetzmann, William H., 149
Gould, Lewis L., 72
Graebner, William, 17
Gratton, Brian, 17
Greenberg, Kenneth S., 353
Greenwald, Maurine Weiner, 109
Griffin, Clifford S., 269
Grob, Gerald N., 89
Grossberg, Michael, 84

Haines, Gerald K., 320
Hall, Kermit L., 123
Haller, John S., Jr., 94
Hamilton, Virginia Van der Veer, 105
Hansen, Klaus J., 65
Hardeman, Nicholas P., 182
Harris, Carl V., 78
Harris, Howell John, 413
Hawkins, Hugh, 341

Herbst, Jurgen, 341

Here the County Lies: Nationalism and the Arts in Twentieth-Century America, 218

Herken, Gregg, 448

Hermann, Janet Sharp, 60

Henretta, James A., 158

Higginbotham, Don, 44

Highsaw, Robert B., 105

Hirsch, H. N., 241

History of Retirement, A: The Meaning and Function of an American Institution, 1885-1978, 17

Holbo, Paul S., 347

Hollander, Paul, 424

Hollinger, David A., 306*

Holocaust and the Historians, The, 438

Horsman, Reginald, 353, 234*

Howard, J. Woodford, Jr., 123

Howe, Daniel Walker, 28*

Hurst, Willard, 292*

Imperfect Diamond, The: The Story of Baseball's Reserve System and the Men Who Fought to Change It, 141

Imperfect Union, An: Slavery, Federalism, and Comity, 185

In Defiance of the Law: The Standing-Army Controversy, the Two Constitutions, and the Coming of the American Revolution, 38

Innes, Stephen, 33

Ireland, Timothy P., 454

Jacksonian Jew: The Two Worlds of Mordecai Noah, 346

James M. Landis: Dean of the Regulators, 234

James, Sydney V., 168

Joe McCarthy and the Press, 250

John W. Foster: Politics and Diplomacy in the Imperial Era, 1873-1917, 99

Jones, James H., 229

Kammen, Michael, 1*

Kaplan, Lawrence S., 454

Katznelson, Ira, 325

Kessler-Harris, Alice, 419

Kolchin, Peter, 173, 64*

Koppes, Clayton R., 259

Korman, Gerd, 438

Kraditor, Aileen S., 7

Krueger, Thomas A., 115

Kupperman, Karen Ordahl, 331

Land of Savagery, Land of Promise: The European Image of the American Frontier in the Nineteenth Century, 149

Lane, Roger, 402

Law and Urban Growth: Civil Litigation in the Boston Trial Courts, 1880-1900, 84

Leavitt, Judith Walzer, 194

Leopold, Richard W., 320

Levenstein, Harvey A., 245

Light-Horse Harry Lee and the Legacy of the American Revolution, 44

Lindsey, David, 72

Louis D. Brandeis, Felix Frankfurter, and the New Deal, 234

Lowenfish, Lee, 141

Lupien, Tony, 141

Making Sense of Self: Medical Advice Literature in Late Nineteenth-Century America, 369

Manieri-Elia, Mario, 205

Mary Boykin Chesnut: A Biography, 54

Mary Chesnut's Civil War, 54

Mathews, Jane De Hart, 218

May, Elaine Tyler, 216*

McCarthy and McCarthyism in Wisconsin, 250
McCormick, Richard L., 391
McCormick, Thomas J., 318*
McCullough, David, 396
McMurry, Linda O., 408
Miller, Zane L., 255
Minnesota Rag: The Dramatic Story of the Landmark Supreme Court Case that Gave New Meaning to Freedom of the Press, 120
Moore, Deborah Dash, 346
Monkkonen, Eric H., 212
Moral Philosophy at Seventeenth-Century Harvard: A Discipline in Transition, 28
Morantz, Regina Markell, 369
Mormonism and the American Experience, 65
Mornings on Horseback, 396
Morris, Robert C., 364
Muhlenfeld, Elisabeth, 54
"Myne Owne Ground": Race and Freedom on Virginia's Eastern Shore, 1640-1676, 33

Nash, Gary B., 33
NATO After Thirty Years, 454
Neu, Charles E., 223
Neusner, Jacob, 135
New Metropolis, The: New York City, 1840-1857, 201
Nicholas, H. G., 431
Notorious Triangle, The: Rhode Island and the African Slave Trade, 1700-1807, 168
Nugent, Walter, 158
Numbers, Ronald L., 245*

O'Brien, Michael, 250
Osborne, Thomas J., 374

Palmer, Colin A., 229
Patterson, James T., 265

Patti, Archimedes L. A., 454
People in Revolution, A: The American Revolution and Political Society in New York, 1760-1790, 335
Percival, Robert V., 402
Perkins, John H., 129
Pessen, Edward, 49
Police in Urban America, 1860-1920, 212
Political Pilgrims: Travels of Western Intellectuals to the Soviet Union, China, and Cuba, 1928-1978, 424
Presidencies of James A. Garfield and Chester A. Arthur, The, 72
Presidency of William McKinley, The, 72
Pursuit of a Dream, The, 60

Rabinowitz, Howard N., 194
Race and Manifest Destiny: The Origins of American Racial Anglo-Saxonism, 353
Race and Politics in North Carolina, 1872-1901: The Black Second, 194
Radical Persuasion, The, 1890-1917: Aspects of the Intellectual History and the Historiography of Three American Radical Organizations, 7
Rappaport, Armin, 380
Rawley, James A., 173
Reading, 'Riting and Reconstruction: The Education of Freedmen in the South, 1861-1870, 364
Reid, John Phillip, 38
Reingold, Nathan, 264*
Representative Democracy: Public Policy and Midwestern Legislatures in the Late Nineteenth Century, 78
Richard Nixon: The Shaping of His Character, 269
Riess, Steven A., 141

Right to Manage, The: Industrial Relations Policies of American Business in the 1940s, 413

Rischin, Moses, 346

Ritchie, Donald A., 234

Ritchie, Robert C., 24

Roberts, Randy, 141

Rock in a Weary Land, A: The African Methodist Episcopal Church During the Civil War and Reconstruction, 364

Rodgers, Daniel T., 113*

Roeber, A. G., 163

Roots of Justice, The: Crime and Punishment in Alameda County, California, 1870–1910, 402

Rosenstone, Robert A., 297

Rotberg, Robert I., 1

Rothman, David J., 311

Royster, Charles, 44

Russia and the United States: U.S.-Soviet Relations from the Soviet Point of View, 12

Ryan, Mary P., 49, 181*

Sarna, Jonathon D., 346

Schwarz, Jordan A., 115

Shucks, Shocks and Hominy Blocks: Corn as a Way of Life in Pioneer America, 182

Silverman, Jason H., 60

Silverman, Robert A., 84

Sivachev, Nikolai V., 12

Soifer, Aviam, 185

Sosin, J. M., 24, 38

Spann, Edward K., 201

Speculator, The: Bernard M. Baruch in Washington, 1917–1965, 115

Spence, Clark C., 182

Stranger at Home: "The Holocaust," Zionism, and American Judaism, 135

Structures of American Social History, 158

Suburb: Neighborhood and Community in Forest Park, Ohio, 1935–1976, 255

Tafuri, Manfredo, 205

Taubman, William, 12

Teaford, Jon C., 201, 133*

Their Sisters' Keepers: Women's Prison Reform in America, 1830–1930, 89

Tomes, Nancy, 275

Tomlins, Christopher L., 413

Touching Base: Professional Baseball and American Culture in the Progressive Era, 141

Transatlantic Slave Trade, The: A History, 173

Trask, David F., 99

Tushnet, Mark, 358

Twombly, Robert C., 205

Urofsky, Melvin I., 135

Veysey, Laurence, 281*

Villa, Brian L., 431

Walker, Clarence E., 364

Walker, Samuel, 212

Walter, J. Samuel, 320

Wandersee, Winifred D., 419

War with Spain in 1898, The, 99

Ware, Susan, 419

Wartime Women: Sex Roles, Family Relations, and the Status of Women During World War II, 419

Washington Despatches, 1941–1945: Weekly Political Reports from the British Embassy, 431

Weinstein, Edwin A., 223

White Supremacy: A Comparative Study in American and South African History, 1

Whitfield, Stephen J., 424

Why Viet Nam? Prelude to America's Albatross, 454

Wigdor, David, 234

Wilentz, Sean, 45*
Wilson, John F., 28
Withey, Lynne, 109
Winning Weapon, The: The Atomic Bomb in the Cold War, 1945–1950, 448
Women and American Socialism, 1870–1920, 384
Women, War, and Work: The Impact of World War I on Women Workers in the United States, 109
Women's Work and Family Values:

1920–1940, 419
Woodrow Wilson: A Medical and Psychological Biography, 223
Woodward, C. Vann, 54
Wreszin, Michael, 250
Wright, Gavin, 164*
Wyatt-Brown, Bertram, 396

Zaretsky, Eli, 384
Zakovlev, Nikola N., 12
Zieger, Robert H., 245

history

The Letters of Ellen Tucker Emerson

edited by Edith E. W. Gregg, foreword by Gay Wilson Allen. "Ralph Waldo Emerson's elder daughter wrote letters prolifically and engagingly. This massive collection of them, edited by her grandniece, constitutes an important addition to our knowledge of 19th-century American life, packed as it is with social and domestic detail as well as intimate glimpses of an eminent family and their many distinguished friends. . . . she was curious, lively, articulate, and warmhearted, and her letters should appeal to the general reader as well as to the social historian."—*Publishers Weekly.* Two volumes, boxed, illustrated, $75

Kent State/May 4
Echoes Through a Decade

edited by Scott L. Bills. Essays and interviews reveal how students, faculty, administrators, townspeople, lawyers grappled with the emotional, legal, political, and educational problems resulting from the Kent State shootings. A valuable and necessary postscript to the climactic event of the Protest Years. "A very real source for understanding and contemplation of what this event meant at the time and especially for the readjustments that have come in our American society and will continue to come as a result of that period."—*William W. Scranton.* Illustrated, $16.50

War and American Thought
From the Revolution to the Monroe Doctrine

by Reginald C. Stuart. A revealing examination of the Founding Fathers' views of war as an instrument of policy and in its conduct. How these basically restrained views changed with the growth of nationalism in the early years of the new republic is reflected in the subsequent history of the nation. $19.50

The Kent State University Press
Kent, Ohio 44242

U.S. POSTAL SERVICE
STATEMENT OF OWNERSHIP, MANAGEMENT AND CIRCULATION
(Required by 39 U.S.C. 3685)

1. TITLE OF PUBLICATION	A. PUBLICATION NO.	2. DATE OF FILING
Reviews in American History	0 9 4 8 7 5 1 1	October 1, 1982

3. FREQUENCY OF ISSUE	A. NO. OF ISSUES PUBLISHED ANNUALLY	B. ANNUAL SUBSCRIPTION PRICE
Quarterly	4	$30.00

4. COMPLETE MAILING ADDRESS OF KNOWN OFFICE OF PUBLICATION (Street, City, County, State and ZIP Code) (Not printers)

The Johns Hopkins University Press, Baltimore, Maryland 21218

5. COMPLETE MAILING ADDRESS OF THE HEADQUARTERS OR GENERAL BUSINESS OFFICES OF THE PUBLISHERS (Not printers)

The Johns Hopkins University Press, Baltimore, Maryland 21218

6. FULL NAMES AND COMPLETE MAILING ADDRESS OF PUBLISHER, EDITOR, AND MANAGING EDITOR (This item MUST NOT be blank)

PUBLISHER (Name and Complete Mailing Address)
Dr. Stanley I. Kutler
435 N. Park Street, University of Wisconsin, Madison, Wisconsin 53706

EDITOR (Name and Complete Mailing Address)
None

MANAGING EDITOR (Name and Complete Mailing Address)
None

7. OWNER (If owned by a corporation, its name and address must be stated and also immediately thereunder the names and addresses of stockholders owning or holding 1 percent or more of total amount of stock. If not owned by a corporation, the names and addresses of the individual owners must be given. If owned by a partnership or other unincorporated firm, its name and address, as well as that of each individual must be given. If the publication is published by a nonprofit organization, its name and address must be stated.) (Item must be completed)

FULL NAME	COMPLETE MAILING ADDRESS
The Johns Hopkins University	Baltimore, Maryland 21218

8. KNOWN BONDHOLDERS, MORTGAGEES, AND OTHER SECURITY HOLDERS OWNING OR HOLDING 1 PERCENT OR MORE OF TOTAL AMOUNT OF BONDS, MORTGAGES OR OTHER SECURITIES (If there are none, so state)

FULL NAME	COMPLETE MAILING ADDRESS
None	

9. FOR COMPLETION BY NONPROFIT ORGANIZATIONS AUTHORIZED TO MAIL AT SPECIAL RATES (Section 411.3, DMM only)
The purpose, function, and nonprofit status of this organization and the exempt status for Federal income tax purposes (Check one)

(1) ☒ HAS NOT CHANGED DURING PRECEDING 12 MONTHS	(2) ☐ HAS CHANGED DURING PRECEDING 12 MONTHS	(If changed, publisher must submit explanation of change with this statement.)

10.	EXTENT AND NATURE OF CIRCULATION	AVERAGE NO. COPIES EACH ISSUE DURING PRECEDING 12 MONTHS	ACTUAL NO. COPIES OF SINGLE ISSUE PUBLISHED NEAREST TO FILING DATE
A.	TOTAL NO. COPIES (Net Press Run)	2628	2631
B.	PAID CIRCULATION 1. SALES THROUGH DEALERS AND CARRIERS, STREET VENDORS AND COUNTER SALES	None	None
	2. MAIL SUBSCRIPTION	2091	2255
C.	TOTAL PAID CIRCULATION (Sum of 10B1 and 10B2)	2091	2255
D.	FREE DISTRIBUTION BY MAIL, CARRIER OR OTHER MEANS SAMPLES, COMPLIMENTARY, AND OTHER FREE COPIES	30	30
E.	TOTAL DISTRIBUTION (Sum of C and D)	2121	2285
F.	COPIES NOT DISTRIBUTED 1. OFFICE USE, LEFT OVER, UNACCOUNTED, SPOILED AFTER PRINTING	507	346
	2. RETURN FROM NEWS AGENTS	None	None
G.	TOTAL (Sum of E, F1 and 2 - should equal net press run shown in A)	2628	2631

11. I certify that the statements made by me above are correct and complete	SIGNATURE AND TITLE OF EDITOR, PUBLISHER, BUSINESS MANAGER, OR OWNER *Marie R. Hansen*

PS Form 3526 July 1981 (See instruction on reverse) (Page 1)

From Italy to San Francisco
The Immigrant Experience

 Dino Cinel. This study of a 2,000-family sample of Italians who immigrated to San Francisco from the 1850's to the 1930's takes in three generations—the immigrants themselves, their parents in nine selected communities in Italy, and their children born in San Francisco. Regional differences profoundly affected the immigrants' adaptation to American life, yet a common pattern is discernible: a slow transition up the scale from *campanilismo* (identification with one's home town), first to regional loyalty, then to Italian nationalism, and finally to assimilation. Woven throughout the account are the lives of individual Italians, from the prominent banker A.P. Giannini to obscure fishermen and peddlers, who have contributed to the colorful history of San Francisco. Illustrated. $25.00

After the Gold Rush
Society in Grass Valley and Nevada City, California, 1849–1870

 Ralph Mann. This history follows the rise of society in California's two largest and richest gold-mining towns from their chaotic founding as Gold Rush camps to the industrialization of their mines. Situated only 4 miles apart, Grass Valley and Nevada City had different kinds of gold deposits and different mining operations that attracted populations vastly different in race and class. The author analyzes this changing and conflicting ethnic pattern (Yankee merchants, Irish and Cornish miners, black and Chinese laborers), traces the emergence of the middle class and the development of traditional family structures, and considers the economic and social character of each town in comparison with other contemporary American frontier settlements. $25.00

Order from your bookstore, please

Stanford University Press

JOURNAL OF AMERICAN ETHNIC HISTORY

A Publication of the Immigration History Society

The *Journal of American Ethnic History* focuses on the immigrant and ethnic history of the North American people. No present journal of ethnicity takes as its special field the ethnic complexity of North America or concentrates on its history. This *Journal* does both with the purpose of serving as an outlet for scholarly articles on such topics as the process of migration, adjustment and assimilation, group relations, mobility, politics, culture, and group identity; setting intellectual standards; and offering needed direction and encouragement to teaching and research in the field. The *Journal of American Ethnic History* also provides a forum for scholarly discussion and interaction between specialists of various ethnic groups, methodologies, and disciplines.

Volume I, Number 1 includes:

"Integrating America: The Problem of Assimilation in the Nineteenth Century" —John Higham

"Creating Crevecoeur's 'New Man': He Had a Dream"—Moses Rischin

"'Beyond the Melting Pot' Twenty Years After"—Nathan Glazer

"Staying Together: Chain Migration and Patterns of Slovak Settlement in Pittsburgh Prior to World War I"—June Alexander

A Review entitled "Legends of Chinese America."

Book reviews by John Bodnar, Carlton Qualey, Francesco Cordasco, Mary Young, David Reimers, David Gerber, William Toll and others dealing with the Black, Native American, Mexican, European, Puerto Rican, and Asian immigrant and ethnic experience.

Editor: Ronald H. Bayor, Georgia Institute of Technology.
Published semiannually.

Subscription rates: Individuals $12/1 yr., $32/3 yr.; Institutions $27/1 yr., $76/3 yr.; Foreign Surface Mail, add $2; Foreign Air Mail, add $4.

Please address orders and inquiries to:
Journal of American Ethnic History
Department 2000
Transaction Periodicals Consortium
Rutgers-The State University
New Brunswick, New Jersey 08903